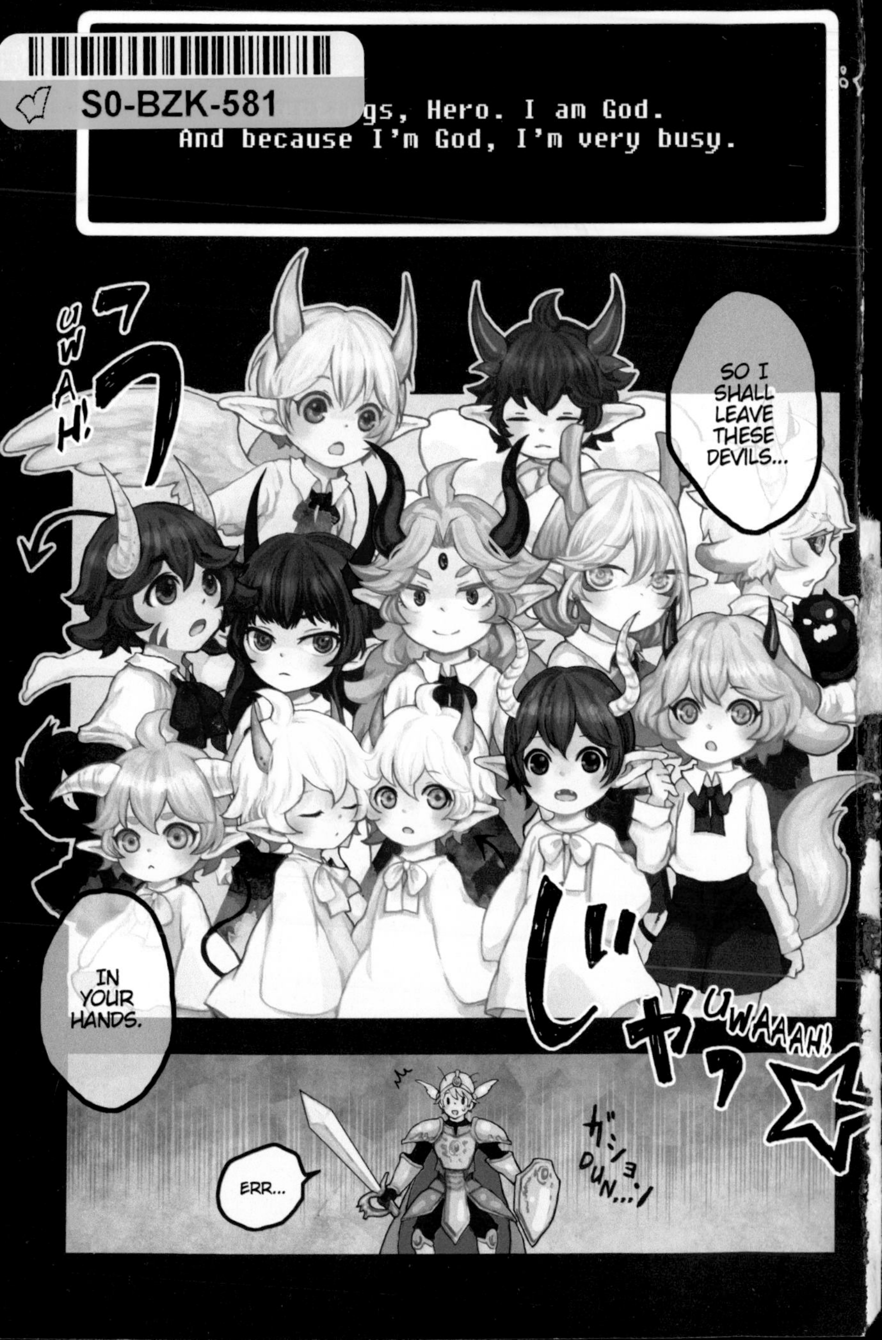
gs, Hero. I am God.
And because I'm God, I'm very busy.
SO I SHALL LEAVE THESE DEVILS...
UWAH!
IN YOUR HANDS.
じゃっ☆
UWAAAAH!
ガション
DUN...!
ERR...

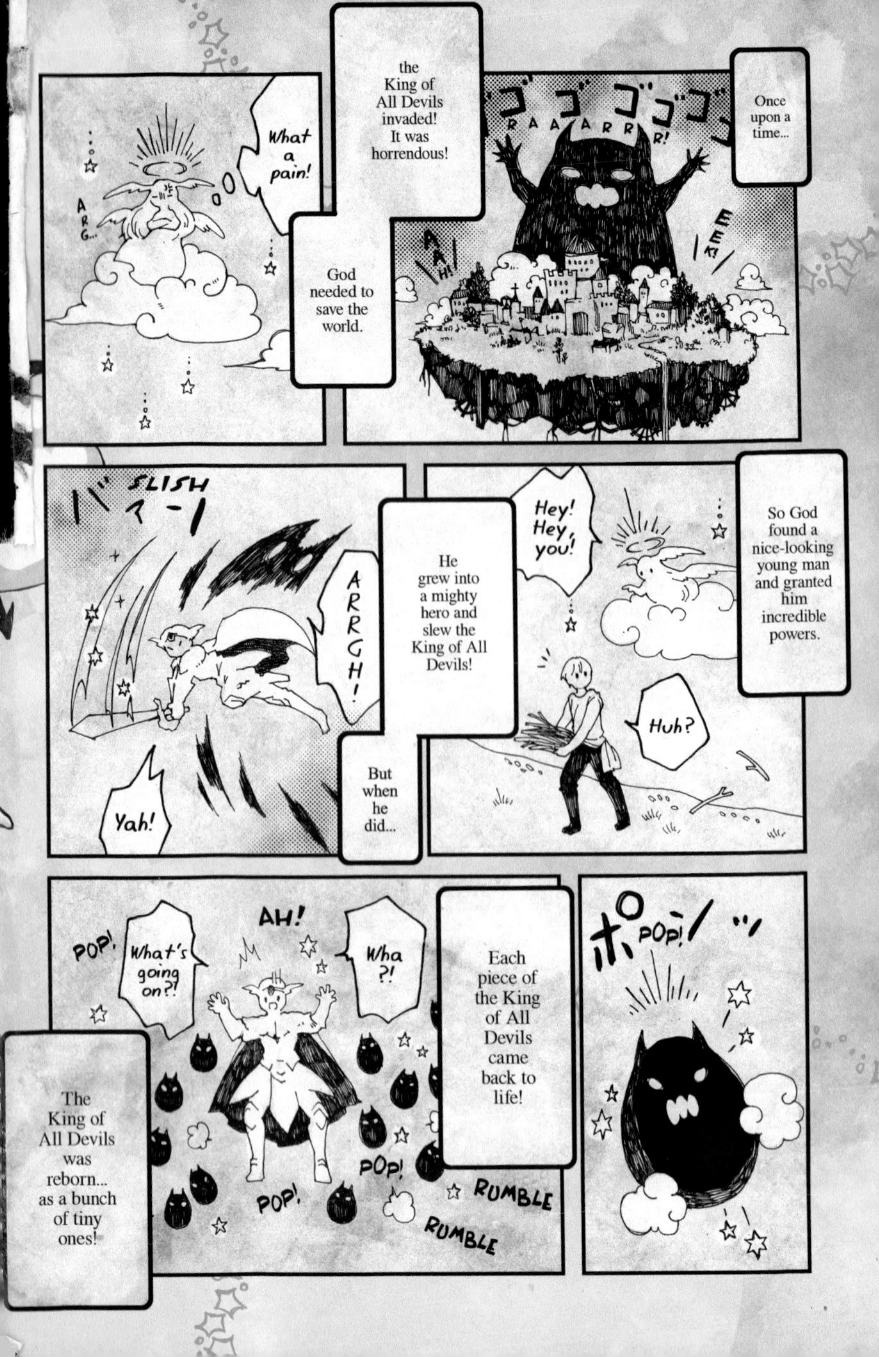
Once upon a time...
RAAARRR!
EEE!
AAH!
the King of All Devils invaded! It was horrendous!
God needed to save the world.
What a pain!
ARG...
So God found a nice-looking young man and granted him incredible powers.
Hey! Hey, you!
Huh?
He grew into a mighty hero and slew the King of All Devils!
SLISH
ARRGH!
Yah!
But when he did...
POP!
Each piece of the King of All Devils came back to life!
Wha?!
AH!
What's going on?!
POP!
POP!
POP!
RUMBLE
RUMBLE
The King of All Devils was reborn... as a bunch of tiny ones!

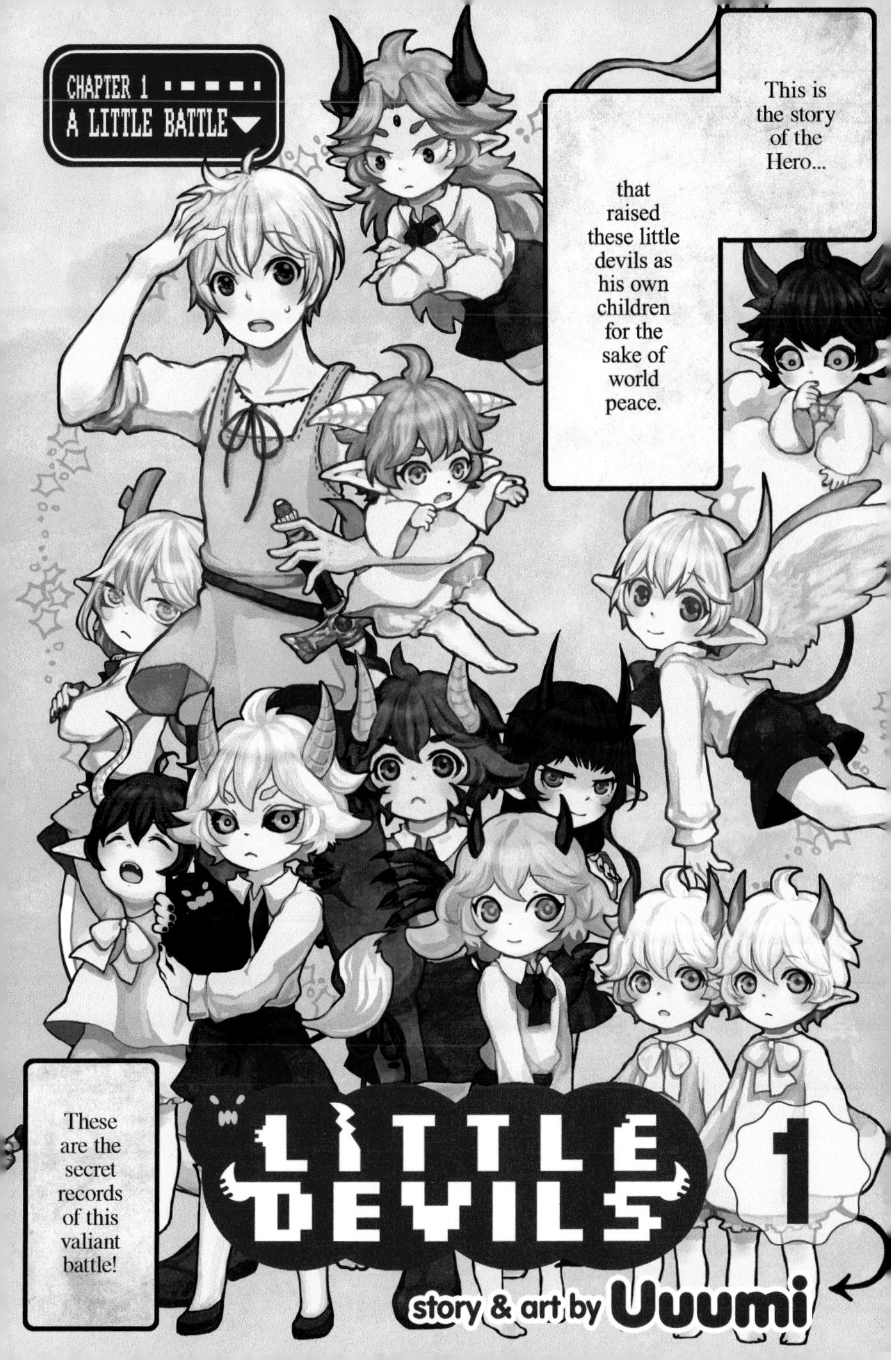
This is the story of the Hero...
that raised these little devils as his own children for the sake of world peace.
CHAPTER 1
A LITTLE BATTLE
LITTLE DEVILS
1
These are the secret records of this valiant battle!
story & art by Uuumi

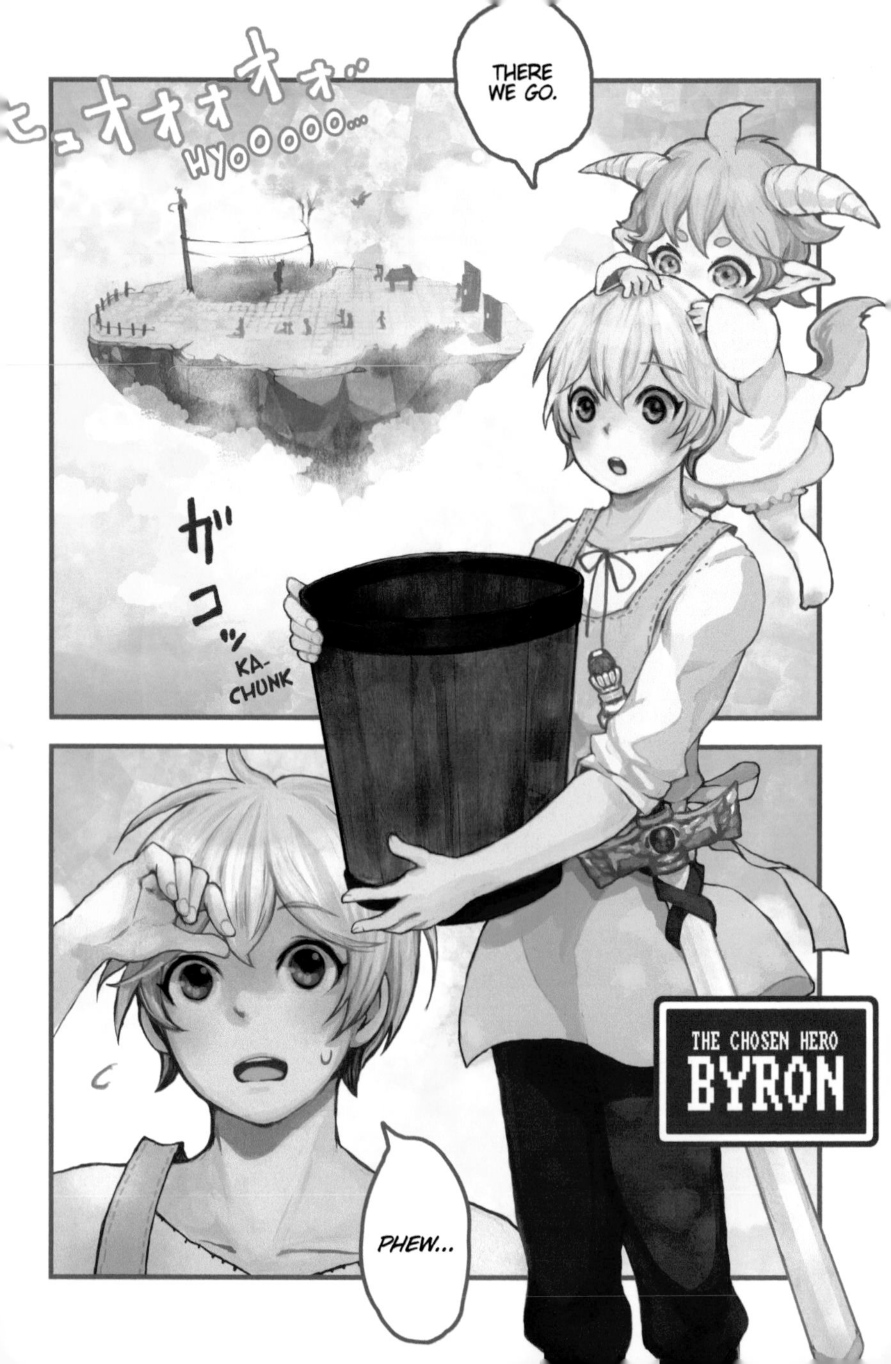
THERE WE GO.
ヒュオオオオォ
HYOOOOO...
ガコッ
KA-CHUNK
THE CHOSEN HERO
BYRON
PHEW...

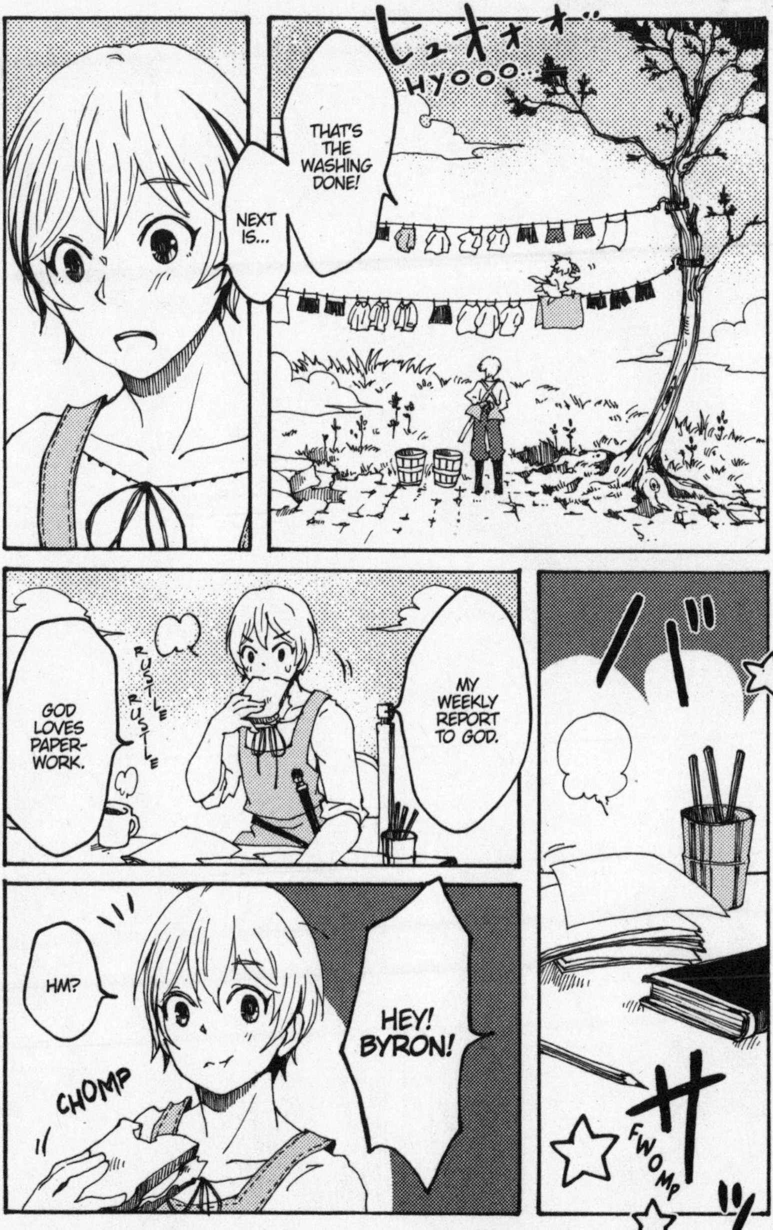
HYOOO..
THAT'S THE WASHING DONE!
NEXT IS...
FWOMP
MY WEEKLY REPORT TO GOD.
RUSTLE RUSTLE
GOD LOVES PAPER-WORK.
HEY! BYRON!
HM?
CHOMP

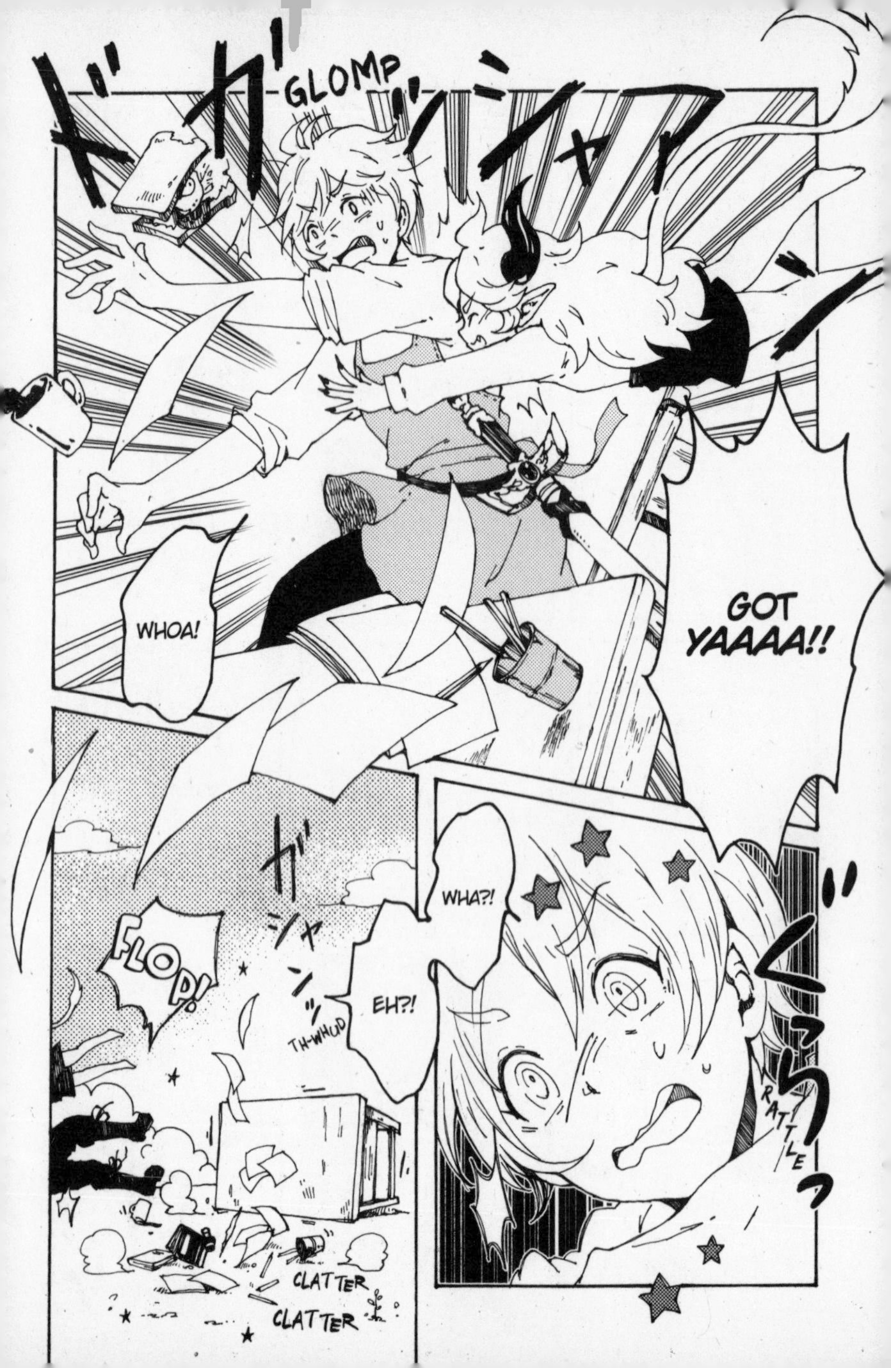
ドガシャア
GLOMP
GOT YAAAA!!
WHOA!
ぐらっ
RATTLE
WHA?!
EH?!
ガシャ
TH-WHUD
FLOP!
CLATTER
CLATTER

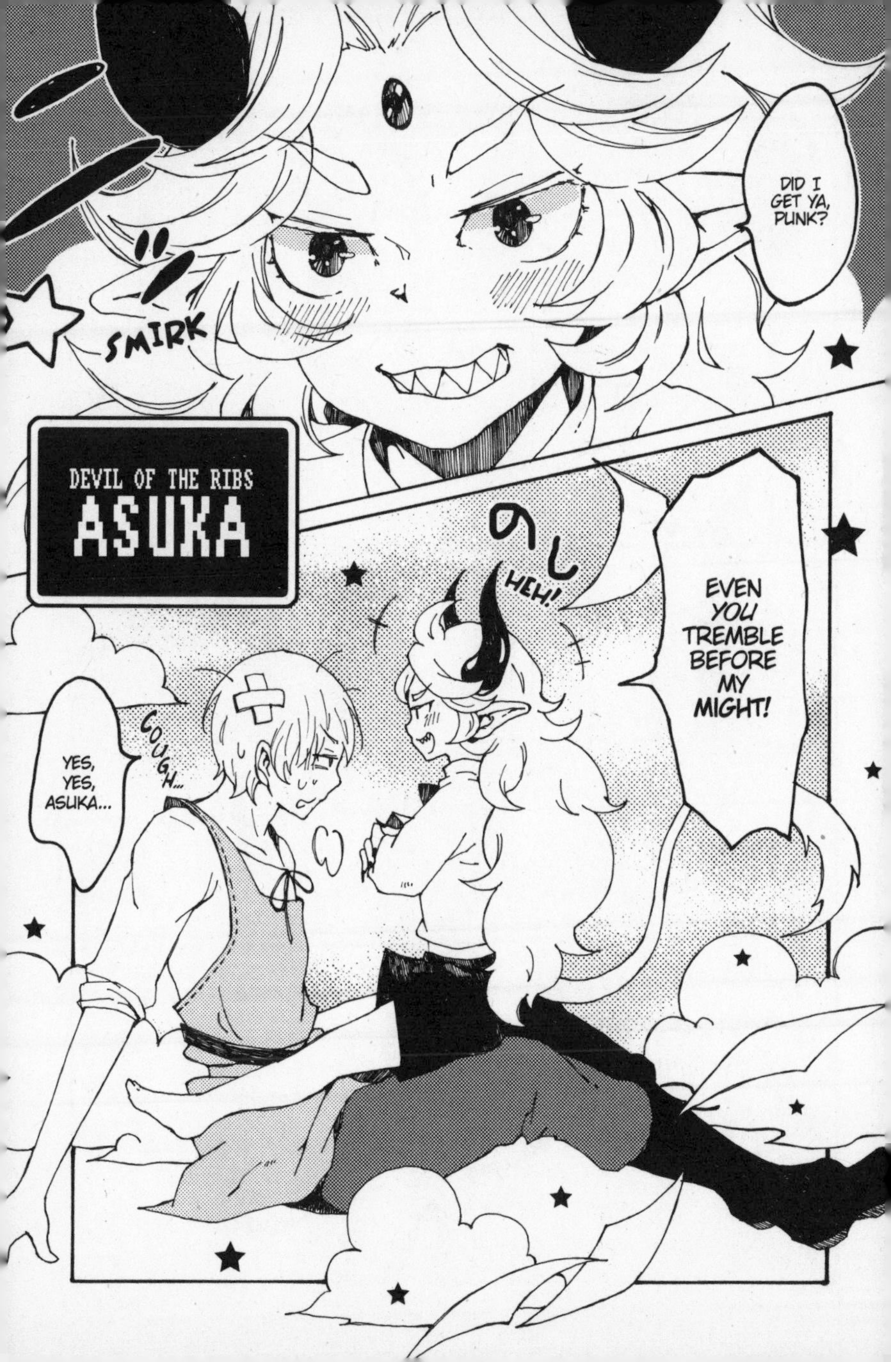
DID I GET YA, PUNK?
SMIRK
DEVIL OF THE RIBS
ASUKA
のし
HEH!
EVEN YOU TREMBLE BEFORE MY MIGHT!
COUGH...
YES, YES, ASUKA...

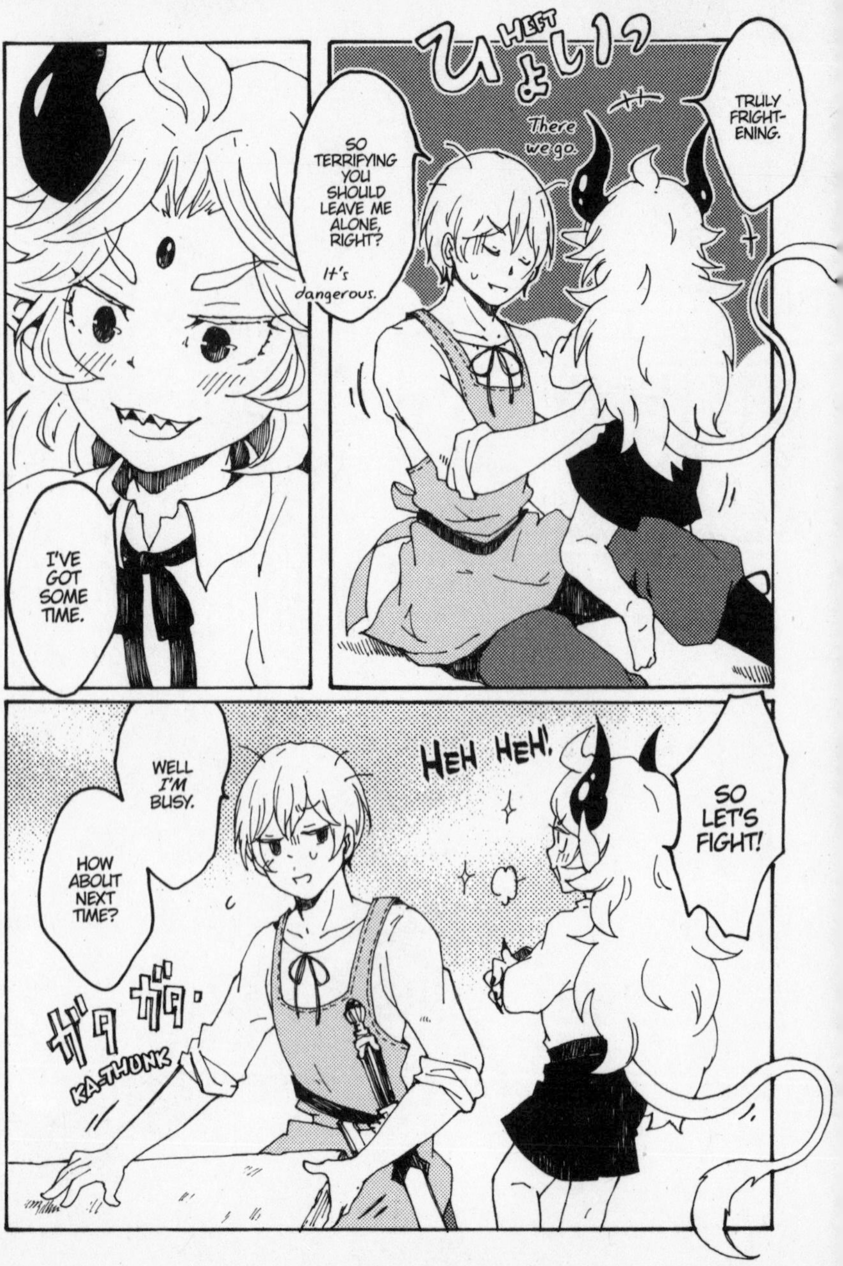
TRULY FRIGHT-ENING.
ひょいっ
HEFT
There we go.
SO TERRIFYING YOU SHOULD LEAVE ME ALONE, RIGHT?
It's dangerous.
I'VE GOT SOME TIME.
SO LET'S FIGHT!
HEH HEH!
WELL I'M BUSY.
HOW ABOUT NEXT TIME?
ガタガタ
KA-THUNK

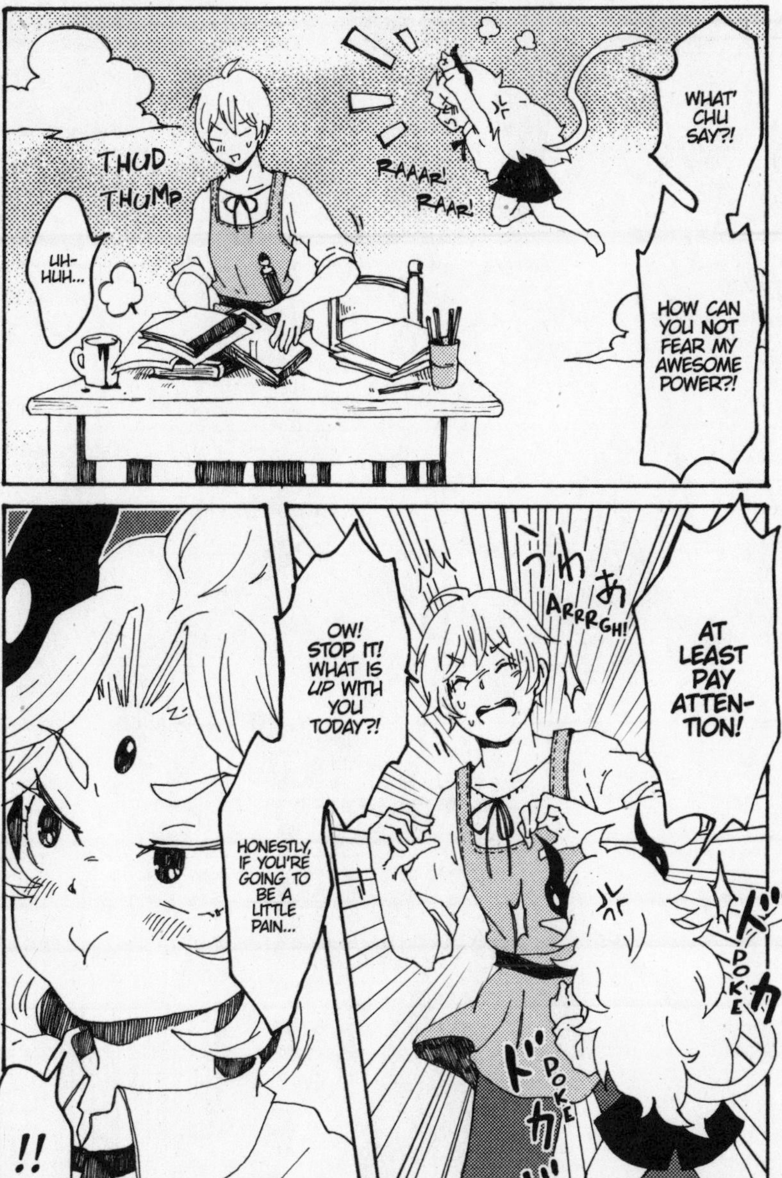
WHAT'CHU SAY?!
HOW CAN YOU NOT FEAR MY AWESOME POWER?!
RAAAR! RAAR!
THUD THUMP
UH-HUH...
AT LEAST PAY ATTEN-TION!
うわあ ARRRGH!
OW! STOP IT! WHAT IS UP WITH YOU TODAY?!
ドカ POKE
ドカ POKE
ドカ POKE
HONESTLY, IF YOU'RE GOING TO BE A LITTLE PAIN...
!!

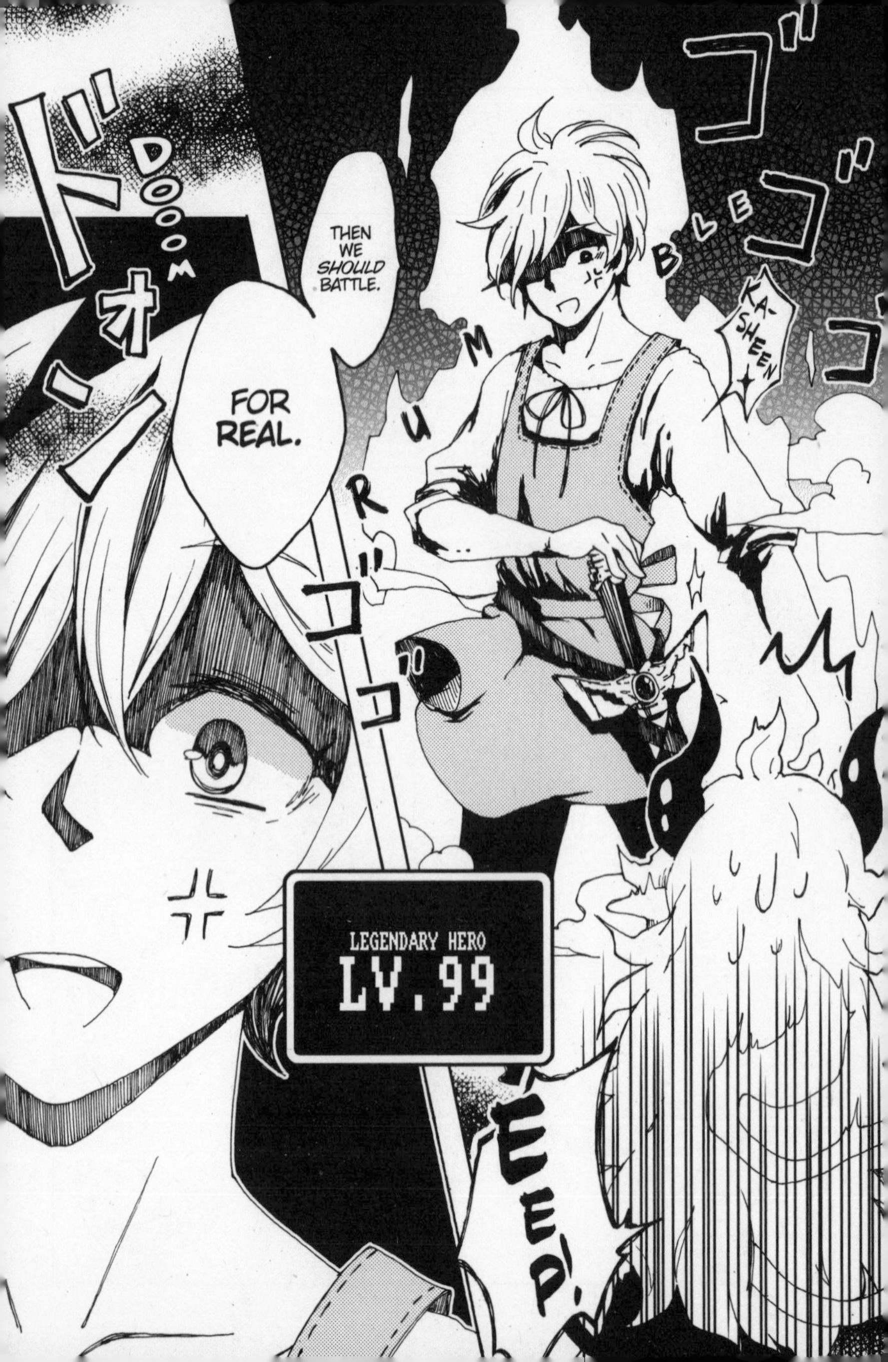
ゴゴゴ
RUMBLE
KA-SHEEN
THEN WE SHOULD BATTLE.
FOR REAL.
ドォーン
DOOOOM
ゴゴ
LEGENDARY HERO
LV.99
EEEP!

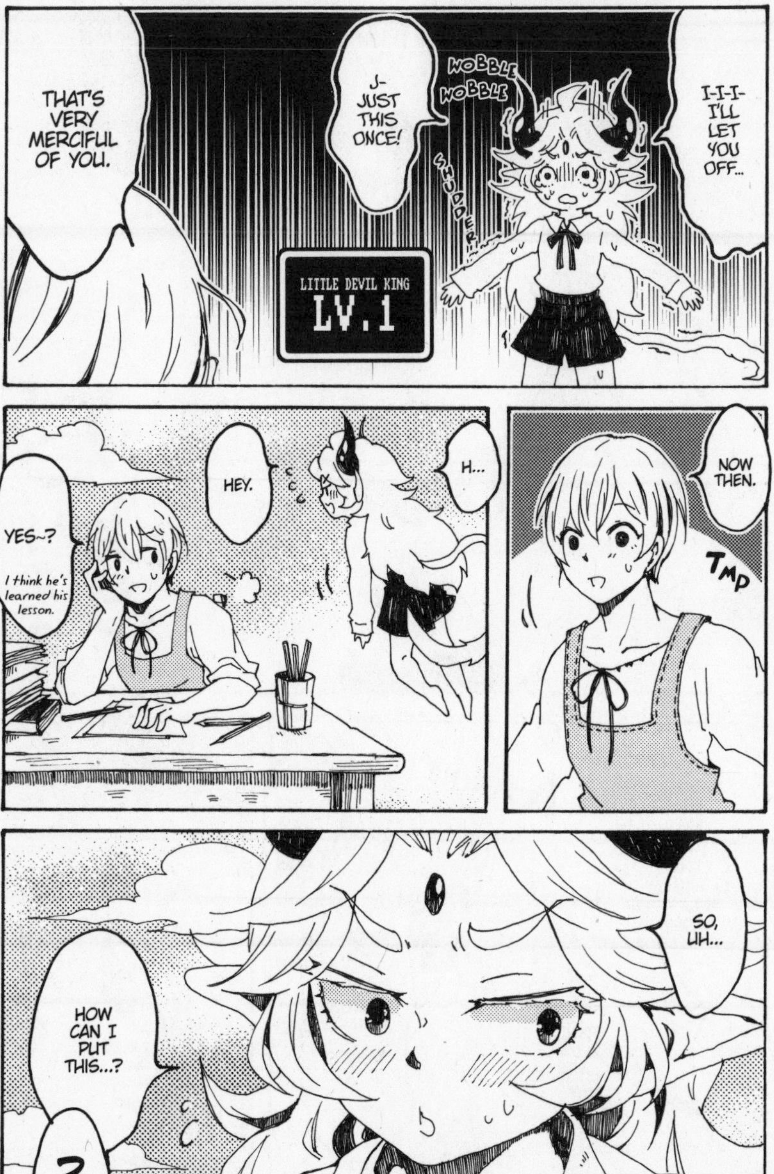
I-I-I-I'LL LET YOU OFF...
WOBBLE WOBBLE
SHUDDER
J- JUST THIS ONCE!
LITTLE DEVIL KING
LV.1
THAT'S VERY MERCIFUL OF YOU.
NOW THEN.
TMP
H...
HEY.
YES~?
I think he's learned his lesson.
SO, UH...
HOW CAN I PUT THIS...?
?

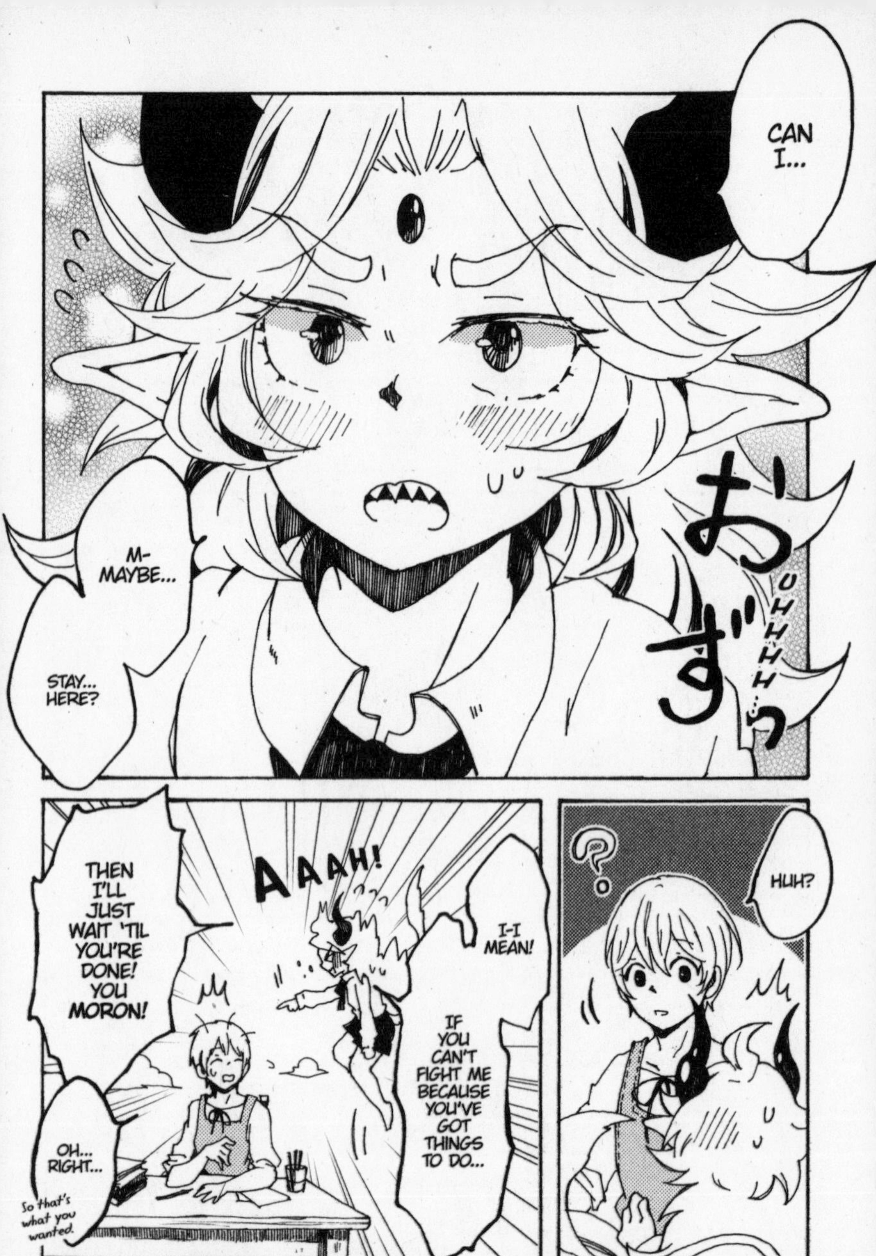
CAN I...
おずっ
UHHHH...
M-MAYBE...
STAY... HERE?
HUH?
I-I MEAN!
IF YOU CAN'T FIGHT ME BECAUSE YOU'VE GOT THINGS TO DO...
AAAH!
THEN I'LL JUST WAIT 'TIL YOU'RE DONE! YOU MORON!
OH... RIGHT...
So that's what you wanted.

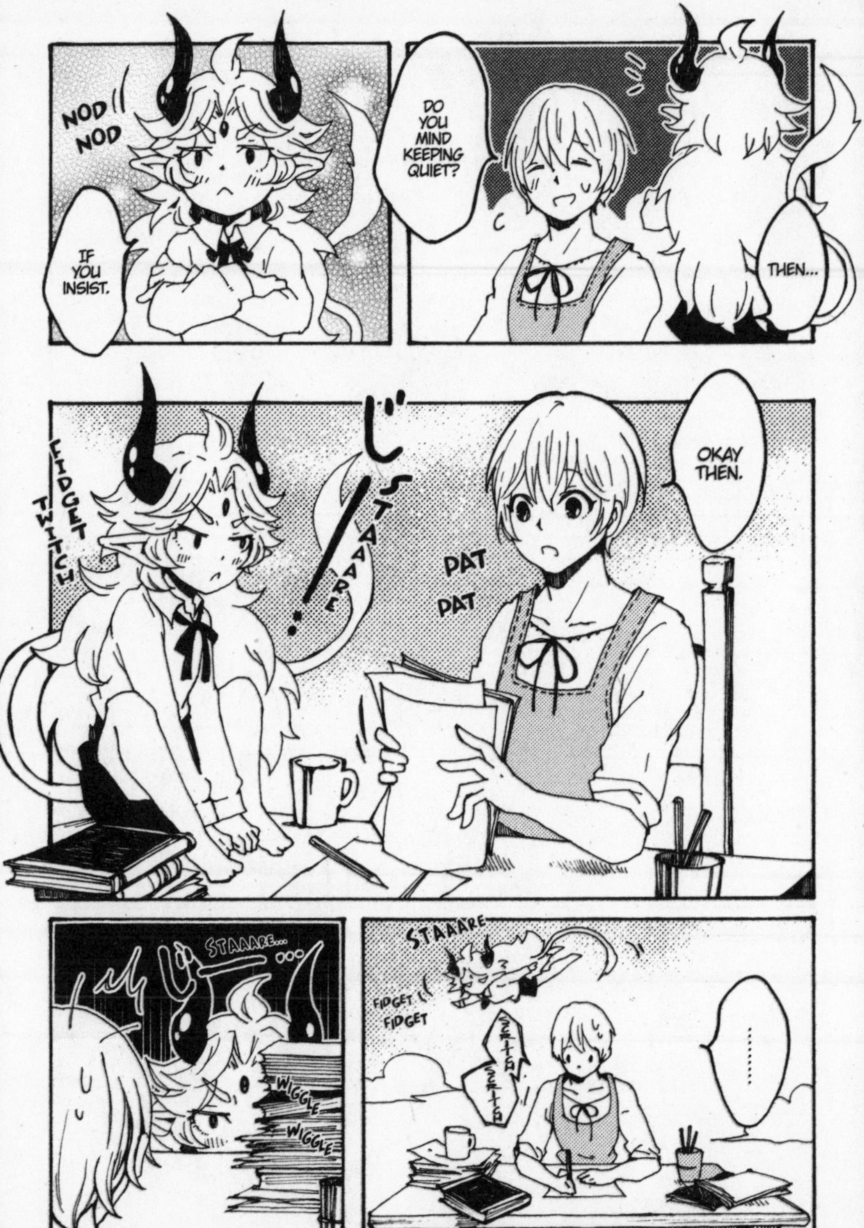
THEN...
DO YOU MIND KEEPING QUIET?
NOD NOD
IF YOU INSIST.
OKAY THEN.
PAT PAT
じー
STAAARE
FIDGET TWITCH
......
STAAARE
FIDGET FIDGET
SCRITCH SCRITCH
STAAARE...
じー
WIGGLE WIGGLE

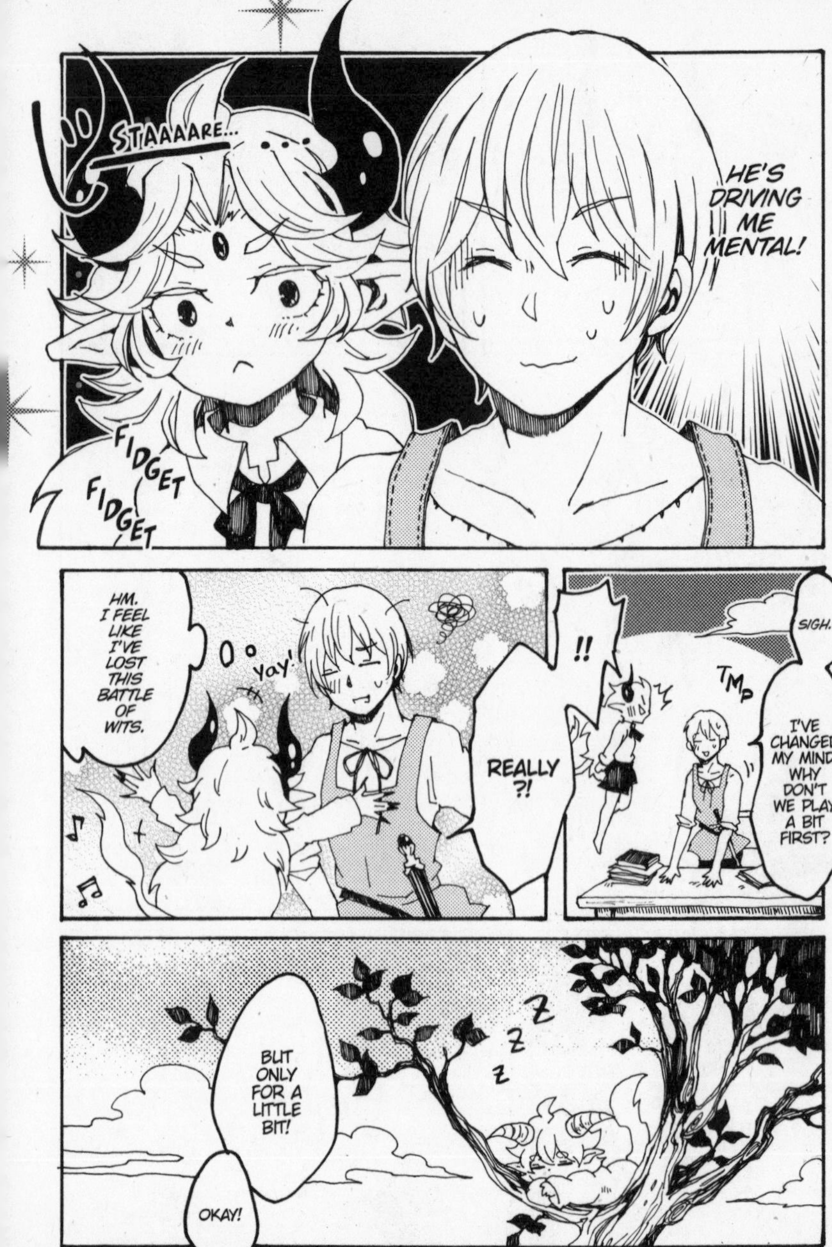
HE'S DRIVING ME MENTAL!
STAAAARE...
FIDGET FIDGET
SIGH...
TMP
I'VE CHANGED MY MIND, WHY DON'T WE PLAY A BIT FIRST?
!!
REALLY ?!
HM. I FEEL LIKE I'VE LOST THIS BATTLE OF WITS.
Yay!
Z Z Z
BUT ONLY FOR A LITTLE BIT!
OKAY!

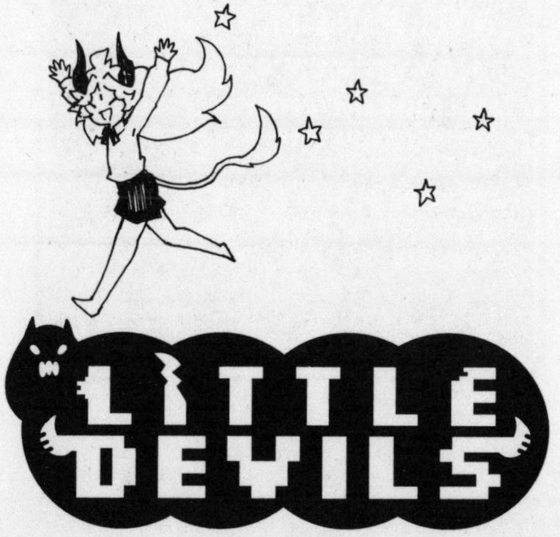

LITTLE DEVILS

DEVIL OF THE RIBS - ASUKA ▼

The hellion oldest brother.
Stronger and tougher than anyone else
and proud of it.
Exhausting to be around as he runs
rampant around the place, but has his
moments of brotherly love.
Sometimes he's quick to anger and
flashes his claws.

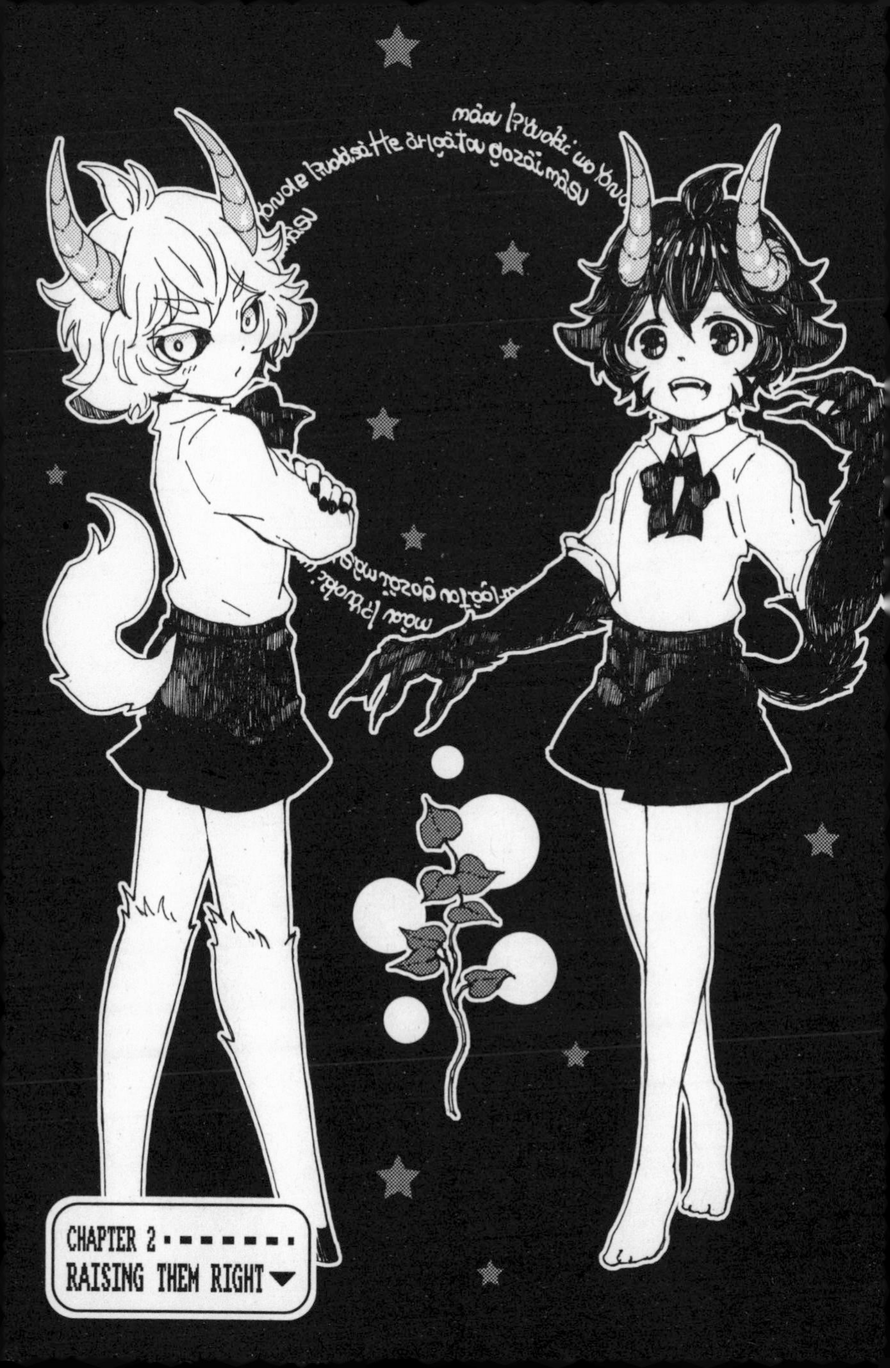
CHAPTER 2
RAISING THEM RIGHT

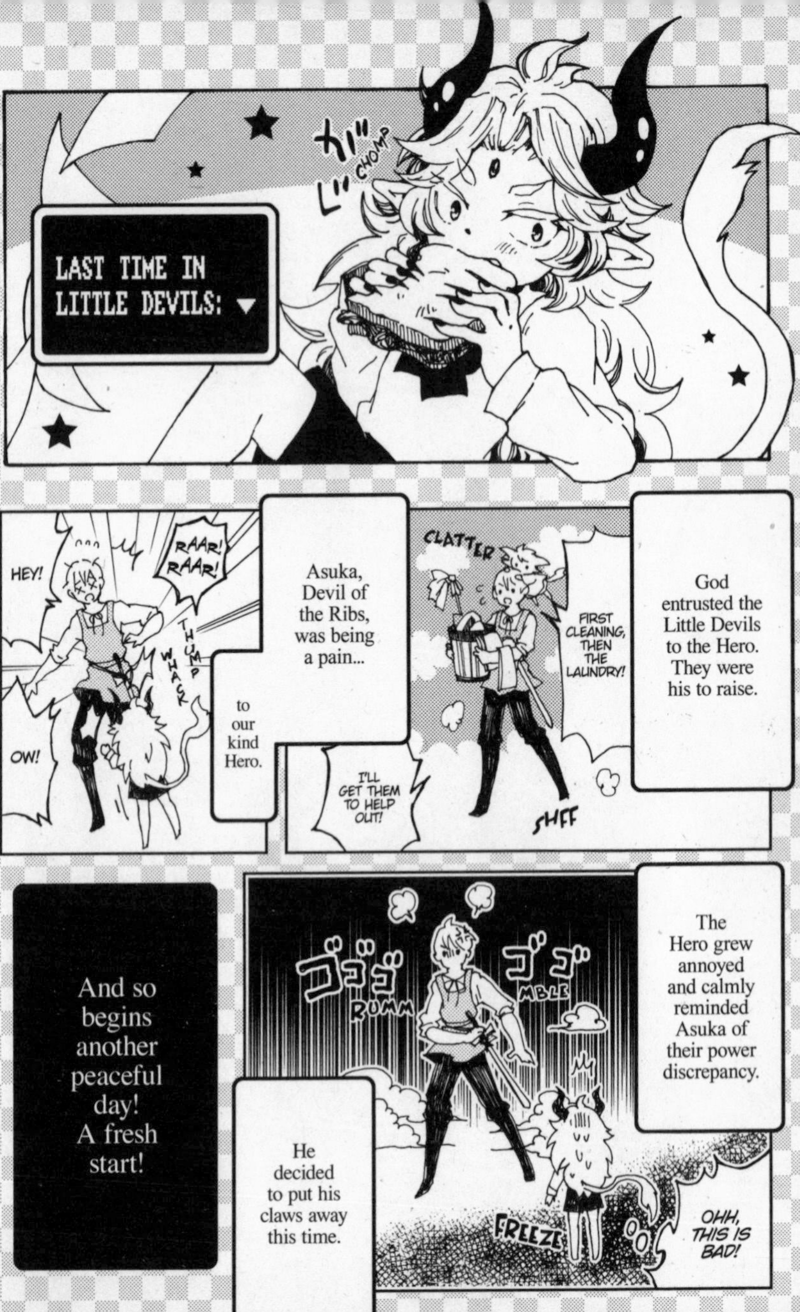
LAST TIME IN LITTLE DEVILS:
CHOMP
God entrusted the Little Devils to the Hero. They were his to raise.
CLATTER
FIRST CLEANING, THEN THE LAUNDRY!
I'LL GET THEM TO HELP OUT!
SHFF
Asuka, Devil of the Ribs, was being a pain...
to our kind Hero.
RAAR! RAAR!
HEY!
THUMP
WHACK
OW!
The Hero grew annoyed and calmly reminded Asuka of their power discrepancy.
RUMM
MBLE
He decided to put his claws away this time.
FREEZE
OHH, THIS IS BAD!
And so begins another peaceful day! A fresh start!

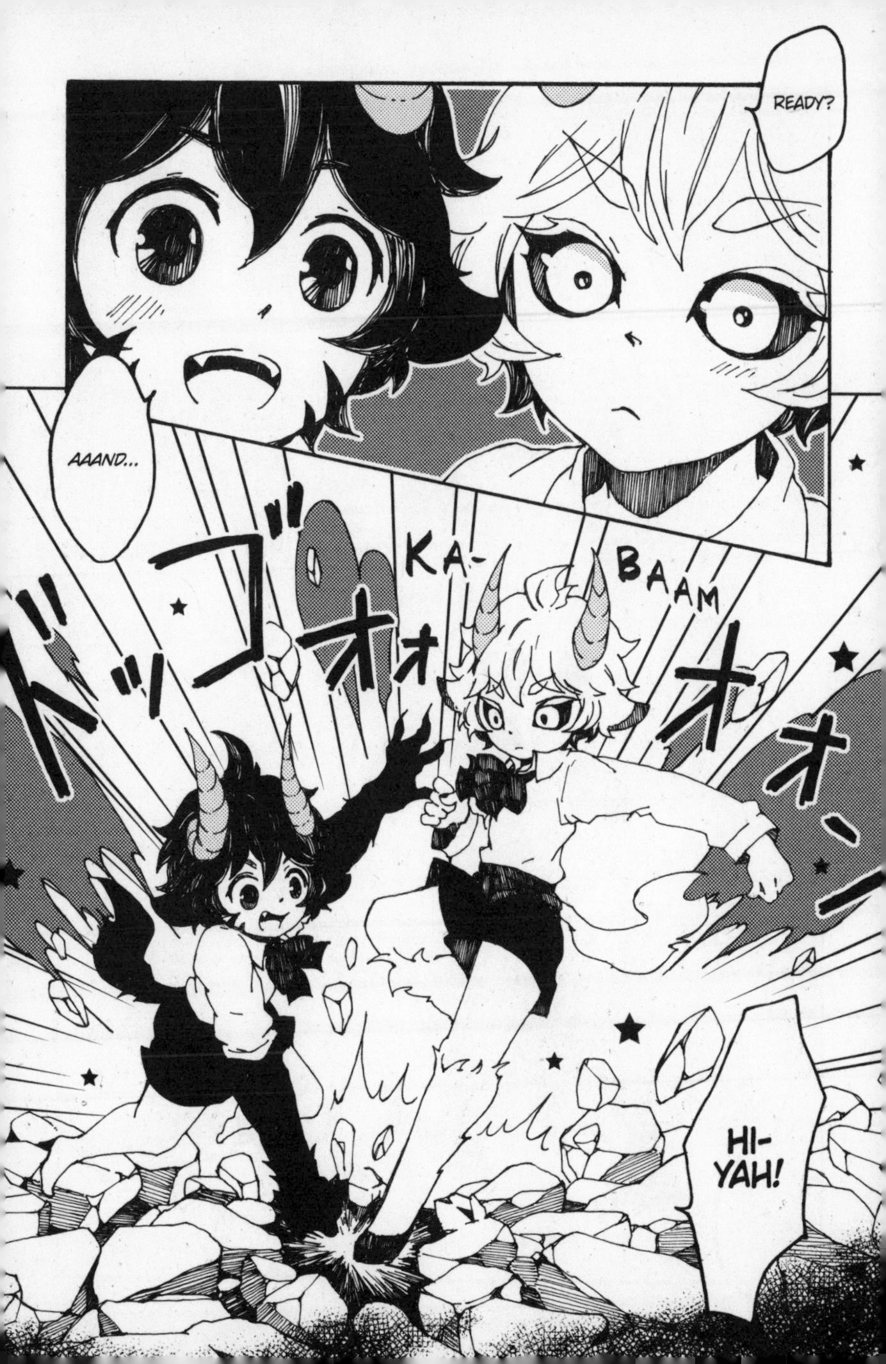

READY?
AAAND...
KA-BAAM
HI-YAH!

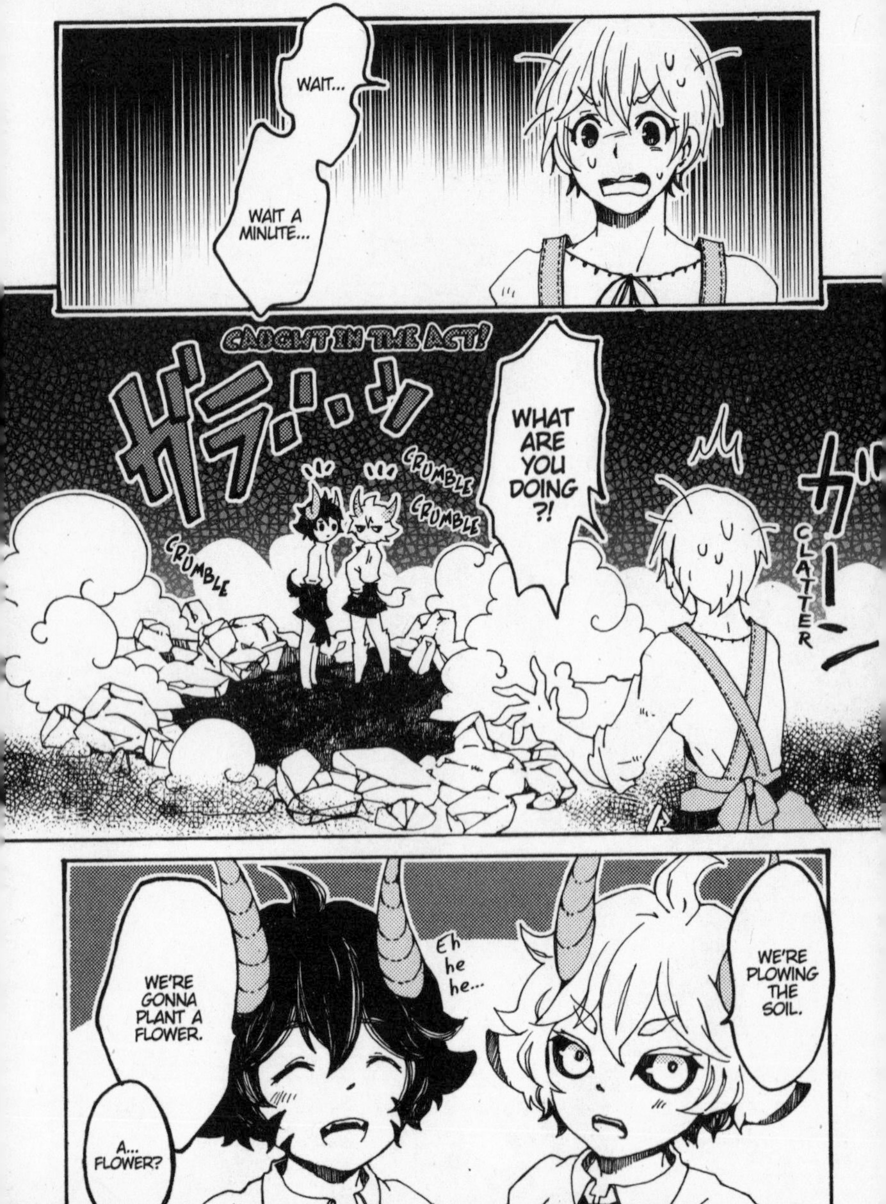
WAIT...
WAIT A MINUTE...
CLATTER
WHAT ARE YOU DOING?!
CRUMBLE CRUMBLE
CAUGHT IN THE ACT!
CRUMBLE
WE'RE PLOWING THE SOIL.
Eh he he...
WE'RE GONNA PLANT A FLOWER.
A... FLOWER?

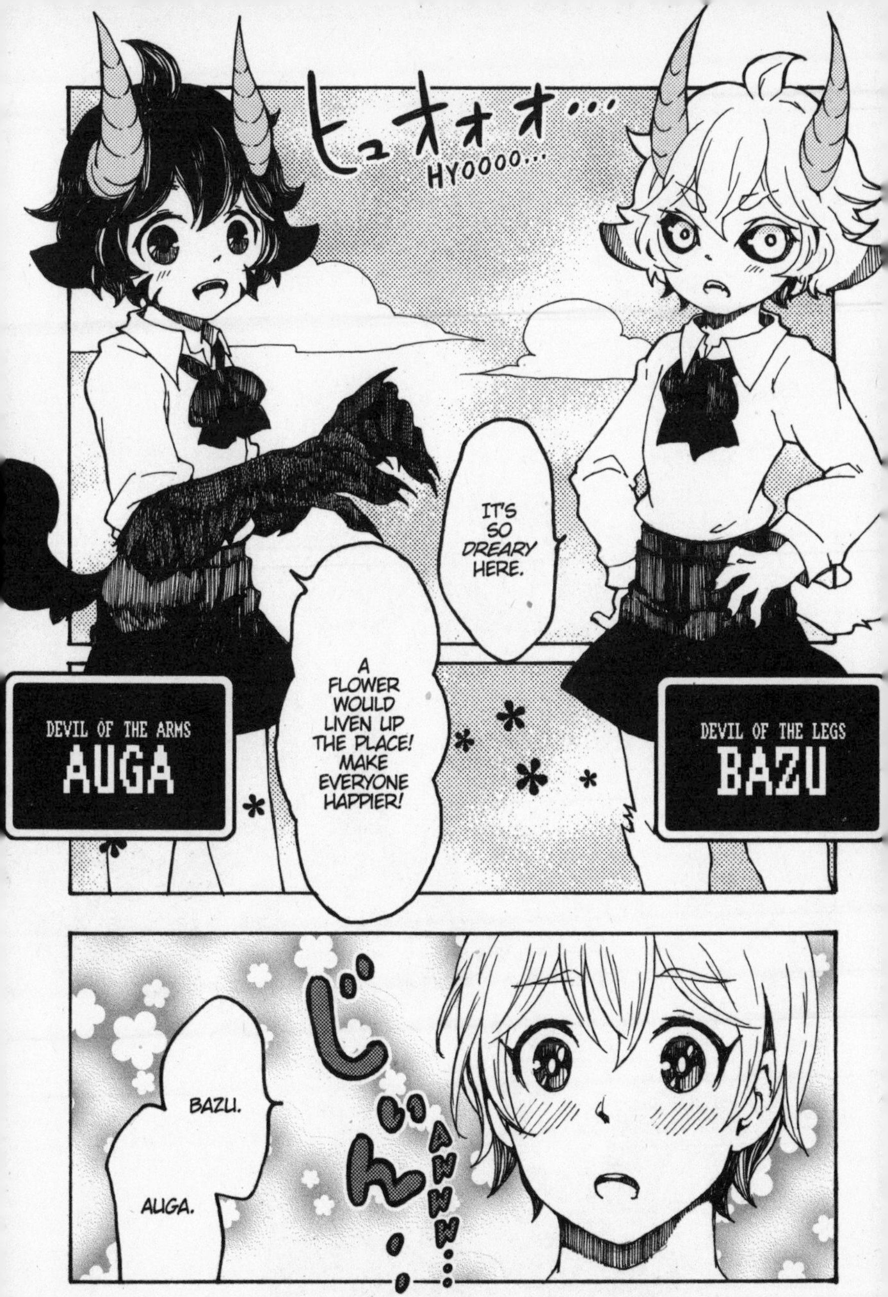

ヒュオォオ…
HYOOOO...
IT'S SO DREARY HERE.
A FLOWER WOULD LIVEN UP THE PLACE! MAKE EVERYONE HAPPIER!
DEVIL OF THE LEGS BAZU
DEVIL OF THE ARMS AUGA
じいいん
AWWW...
BAZU.
AUGA.

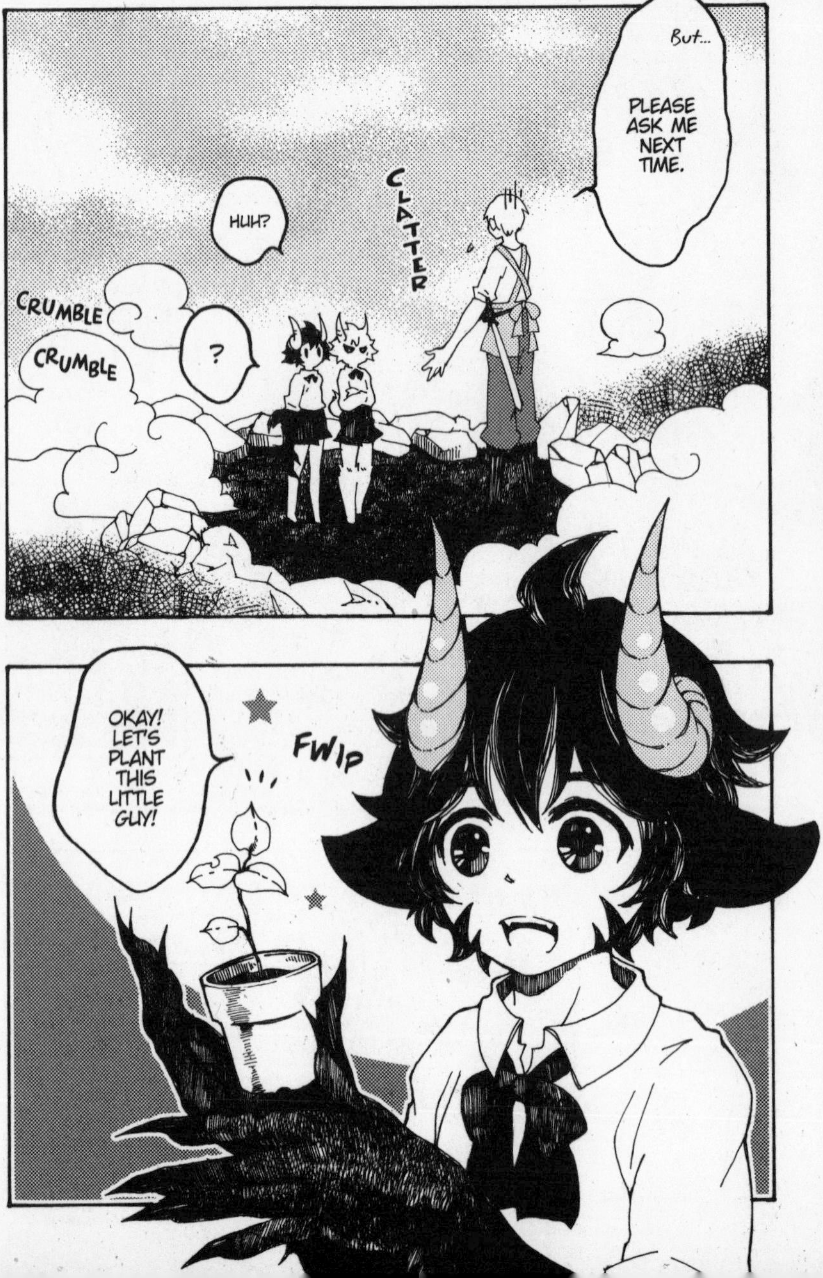
But...
PLEASE ASK ME NEXT TIME.
CLATTER
HUH?
?
CRUMBLE
CRUMBLE
FWIP
OKAY! LET'S PLANT THIS LITTLE GUY!

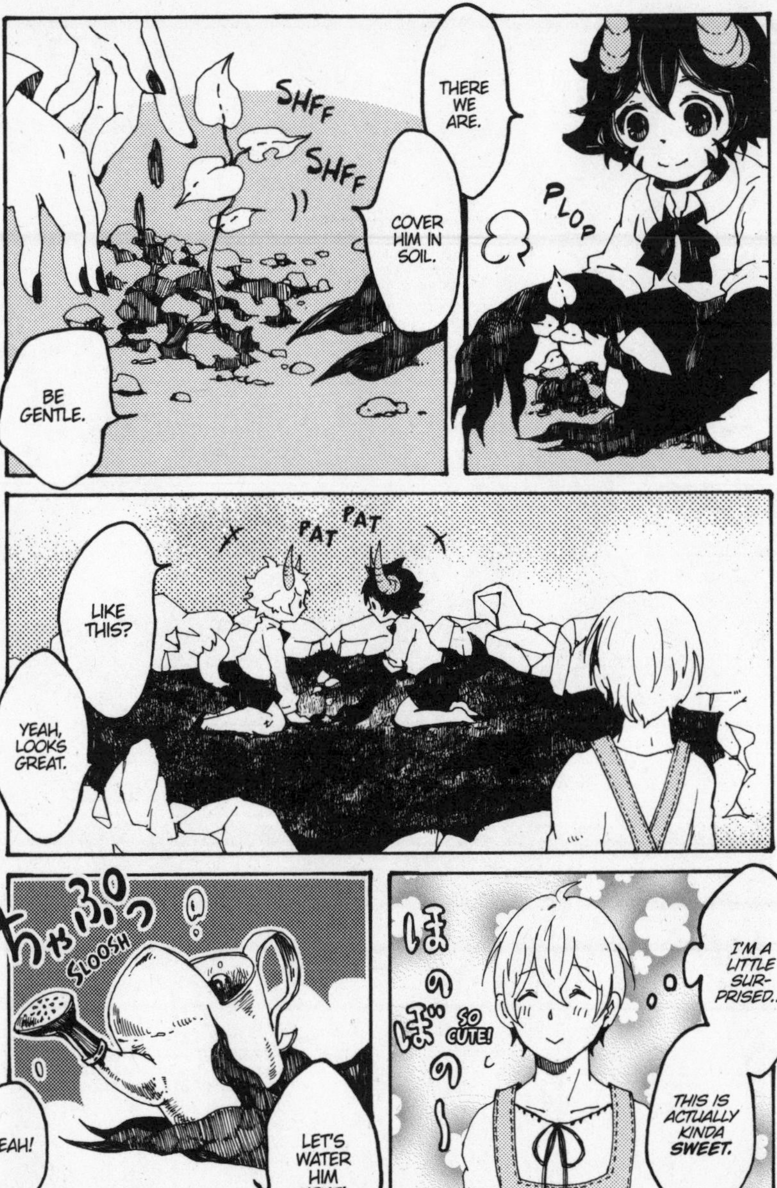
THERE WE ARE.
PLOP
SHFF
SHFF
COVER HIM IN SOIL.
BE GENTLE.
PAT
PAT
LIKE THIS?
YEAH, LOOKS GREAT.
I'M A LITTLE SUR-PRISED...
ほのぼの～
SO CUTE!
THIS IS ACTUALLY KINDA **SWEET.**
ちゃぷっ
SLOOSH
LET'S WATER HIM NEXT!
YEAH!

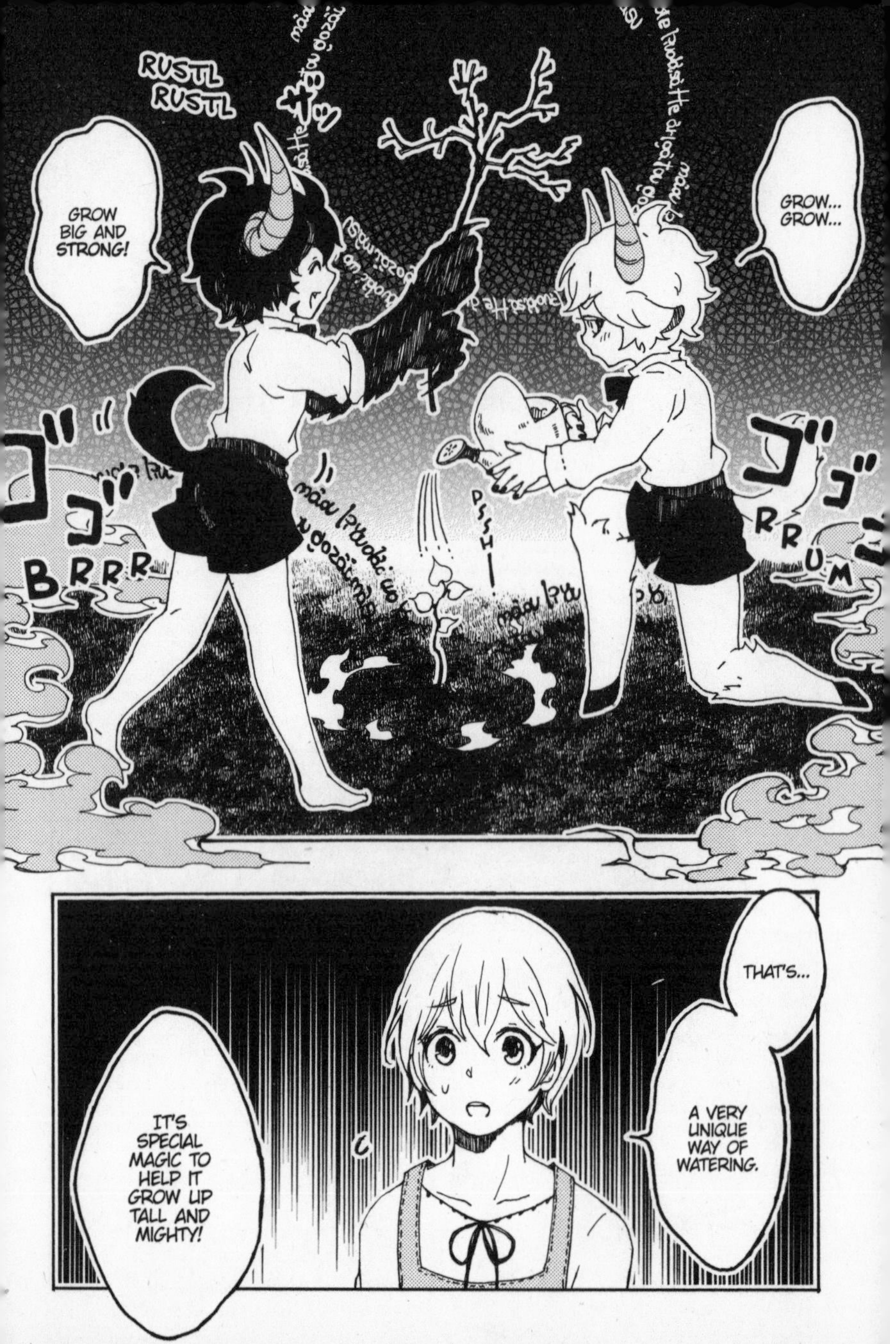
GROW... GROW...
RRUM
GROW BIG AND STRONG!
RUSTL RUSTL
PSSH
BRRR
THAT'S...
A VERY UNIQUE WAY OF WATERING.
IT'S SPECIAL MAGIC TO HELP IT GROW UP TALL AND MIGHTY!

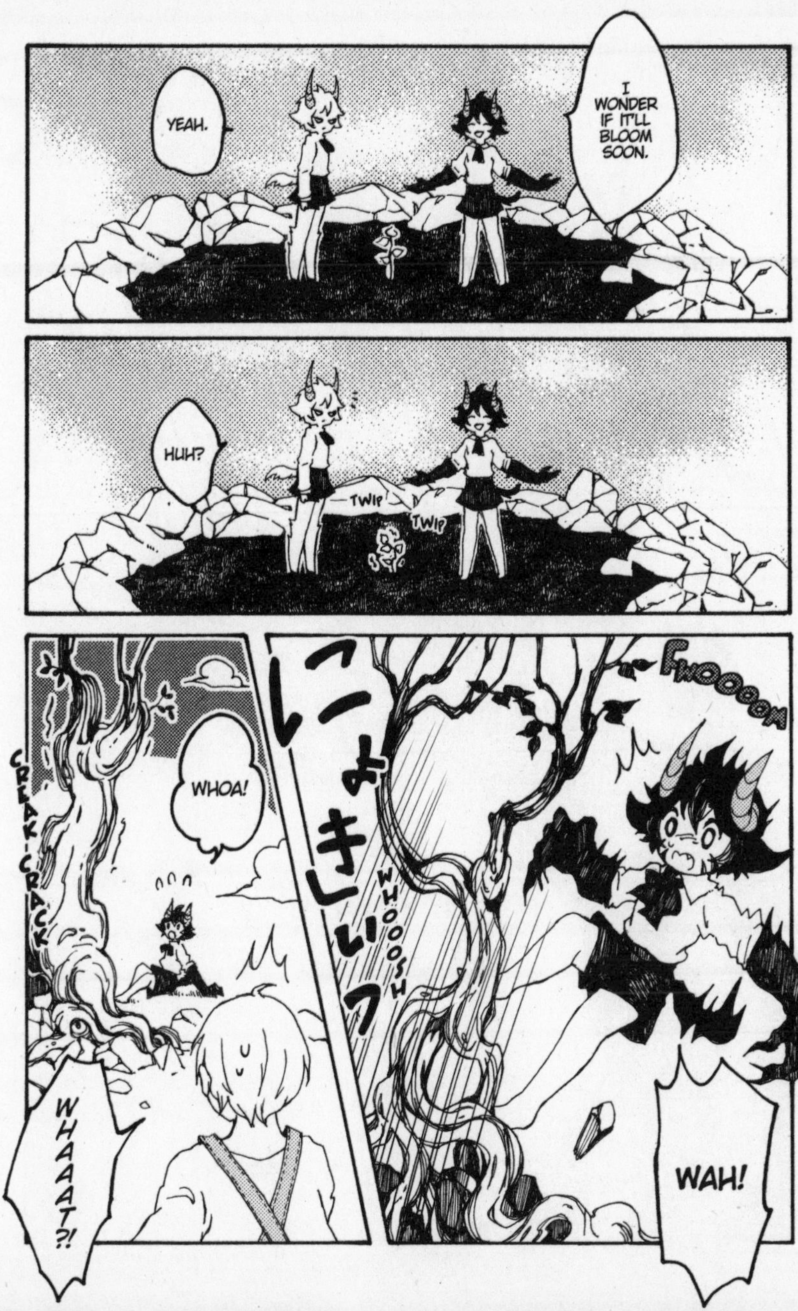
I WONDER IF IT'LL BLOOM SOON.
YEAH.
HUH?
TWIP
TWIP
FWOOOOM
WAH!
WHOOOSH
WHOA!
CREAK-CRACK
WHAAAT?!

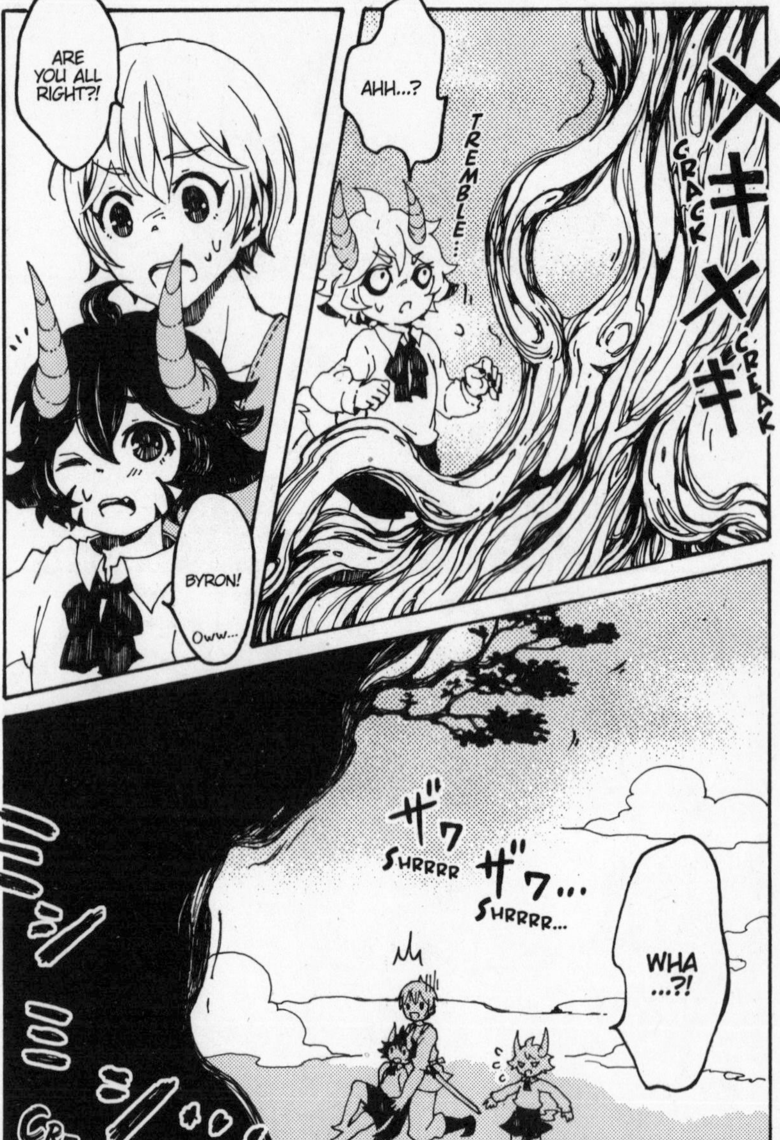
AHH...?
TREMBLE...
CRACK
CREAK
ARE YOU ALL RIGHT?!
BYRON!
Oww...
ザワ
SHRRRR
ザワ...
SHRRRR...
WHA ...?!
CREAK...

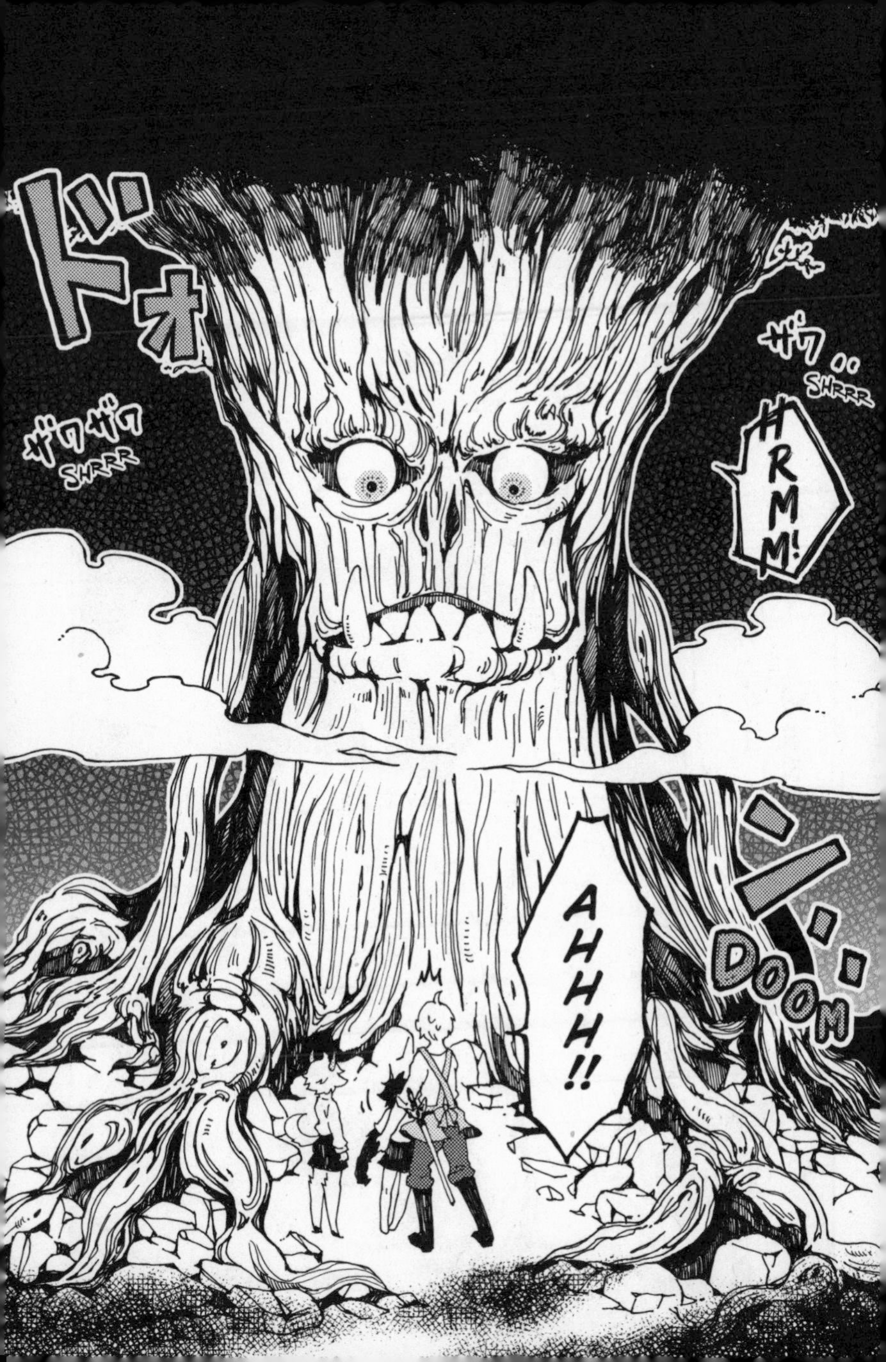

ザワ..
SHRRR
HRMM!
ドオ
ザワザワ
SHRRR
AHHH!!
ン..
DOOM

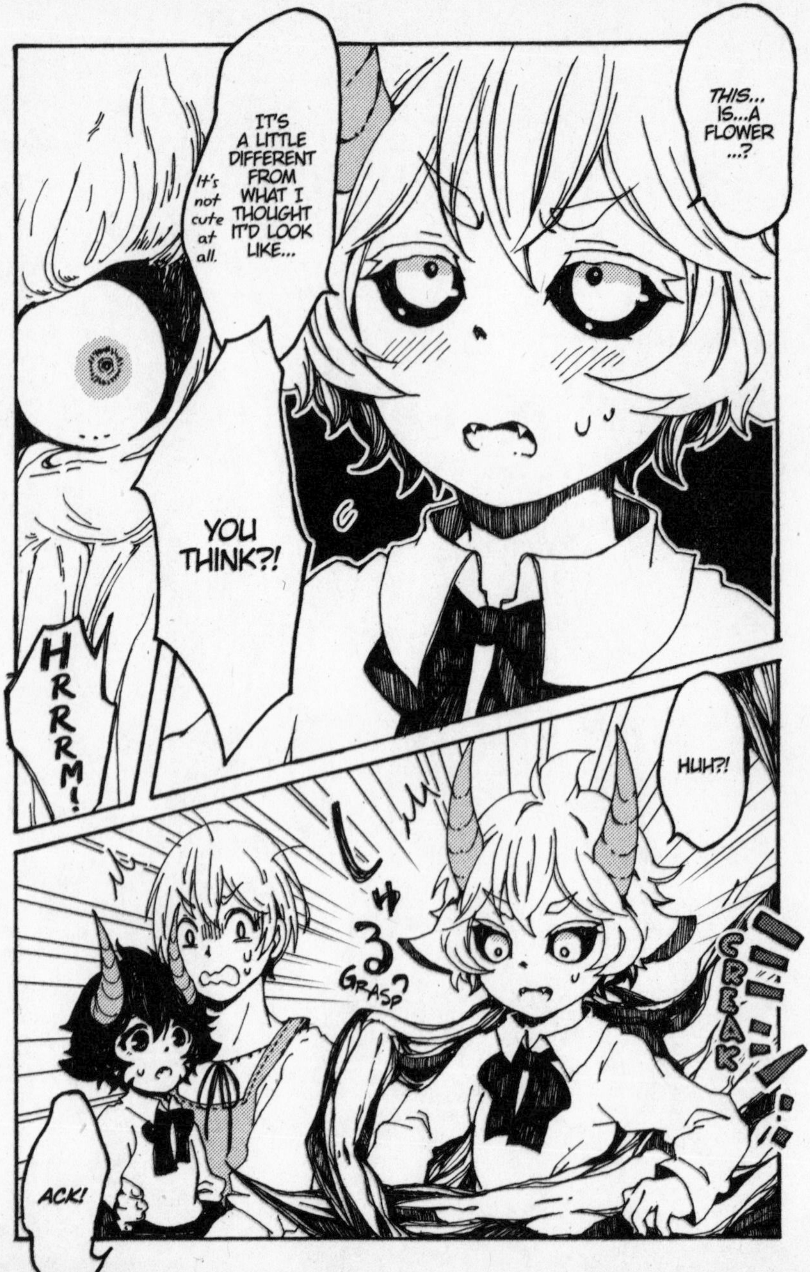
THIS... IS...A FLOWER ...?
IT'S A LITTLE DIFFERENT FROM WHAT I THOUGHT IT'D LOOK LIKE...
It's not cute at all.
YOU THINK?!
HRRRM!
HUH?!
CREAK
しゅる
GRASP
ACK!

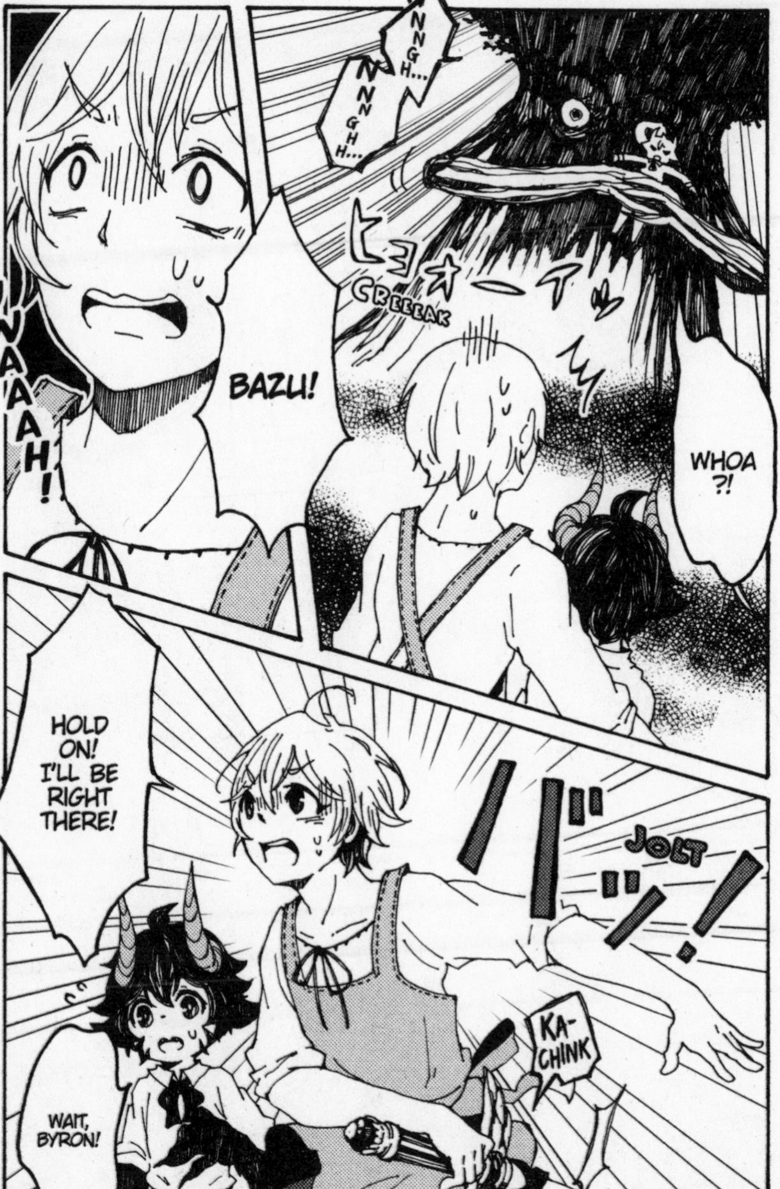
NNNGH...
NNNGH...
CREEEAK
WHOA?!
BAZU!
UWAAAAH!
JOLT
KA-CHINK
HOLD ON! I'LL BE RIGHT THERE!
WAIT, BYRON!

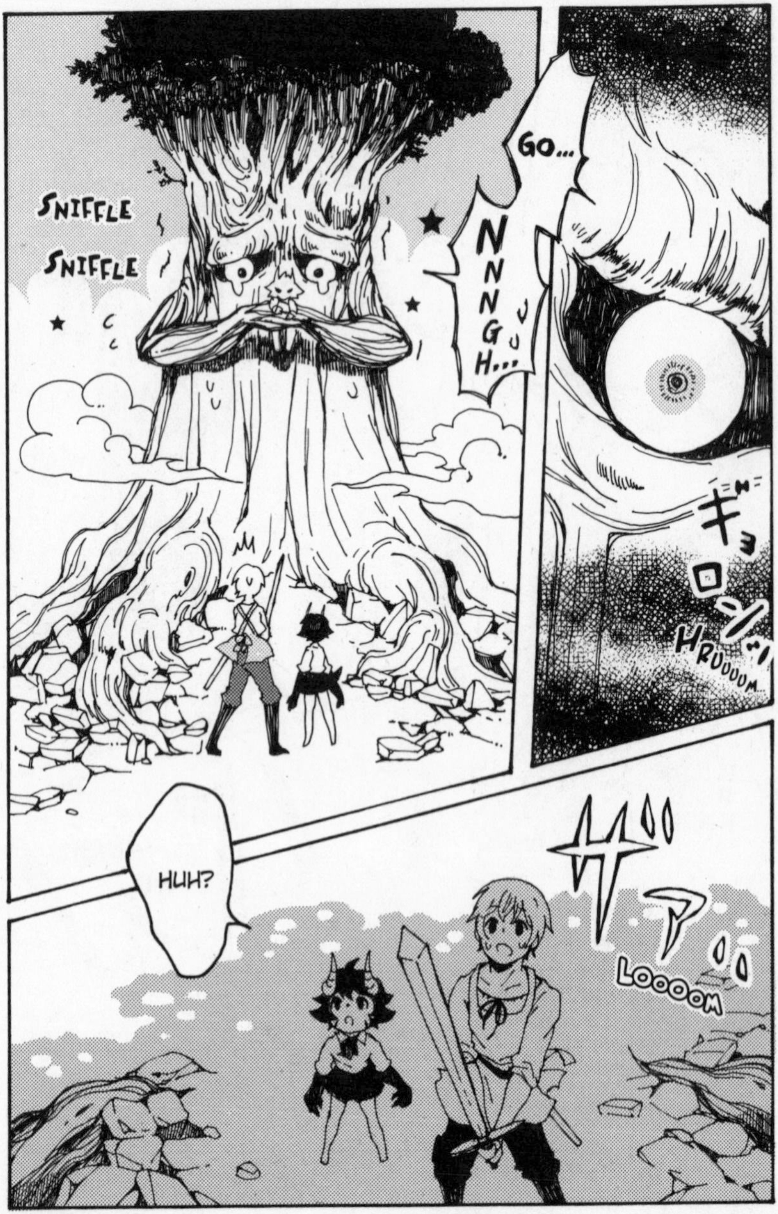
GO...
NNNGH...
ギョロッ
HRUUUUUM...
SNIFFLE
SNIFFLE
HUH?
ザァ
LOOOOM

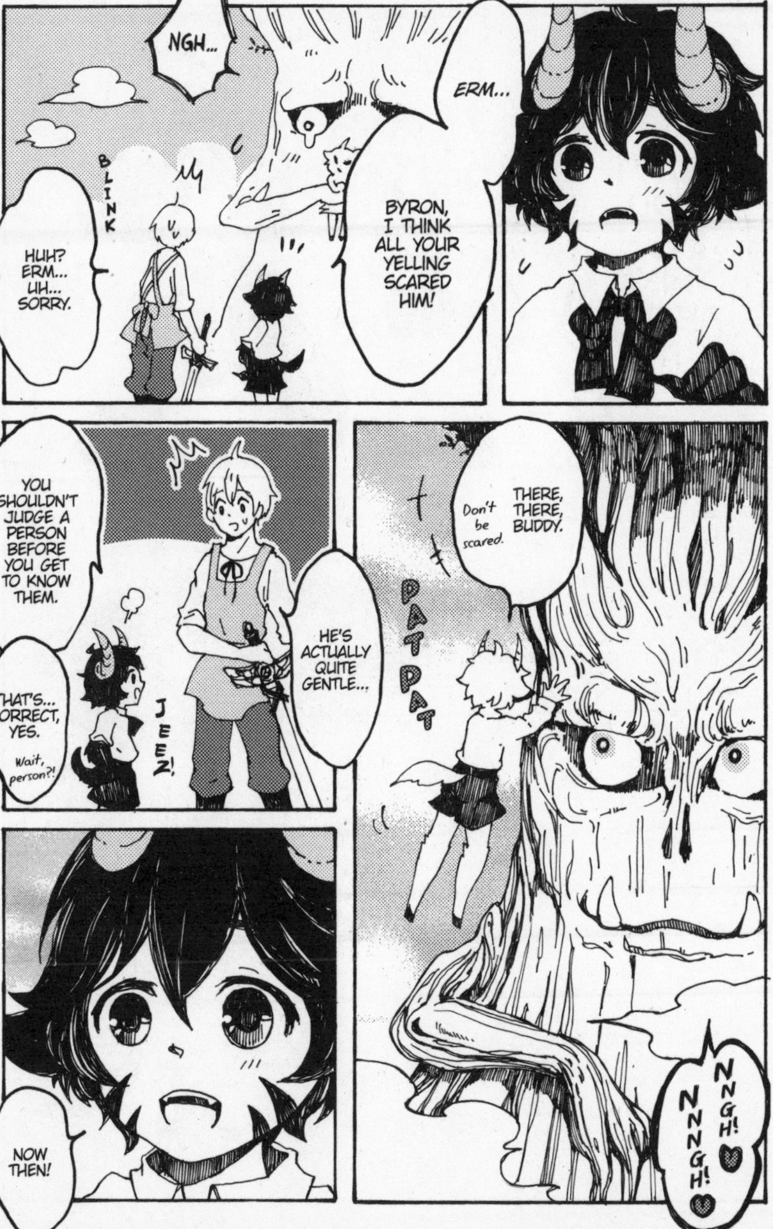
ERM...
BYRON, I THINK ALL YOUR YELLING SCARED HIM!
NGH...
BLINK
HUH? ERM... UH... SORRY.
THERE, THERE, BUDDY.
Don't be scared.
PAT PAT
NNGH!
NNNGH!
HE'S ACTUALLY QUITE GENTLE...
YOU SHOULDN'T JUDGE A PERSON BEFORE YOU GET TO KNOW THEM.
JEEZ!
THAT'S... CORRECT, YES.
Wait, person?!
TSK TSK!
NOW THEN!

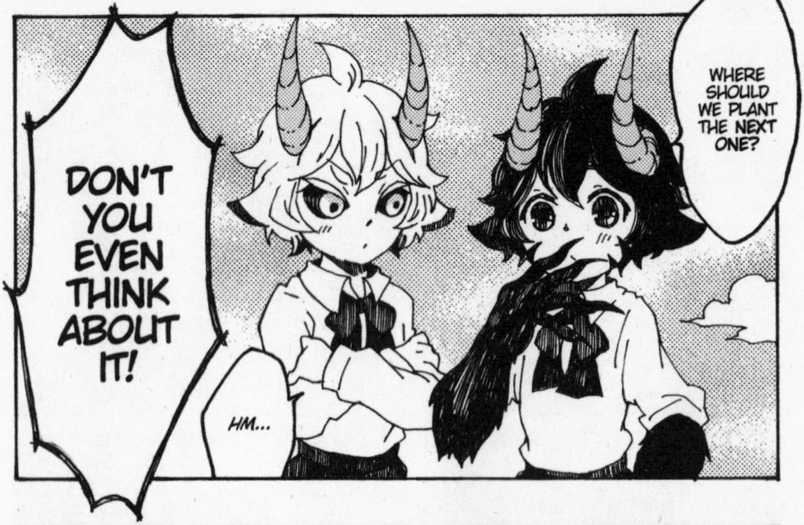
WHERE SHOULD WE PLANT THE NEXT ONE?
HM...
DON'T YOU EVEN THINK ABOUT IT!

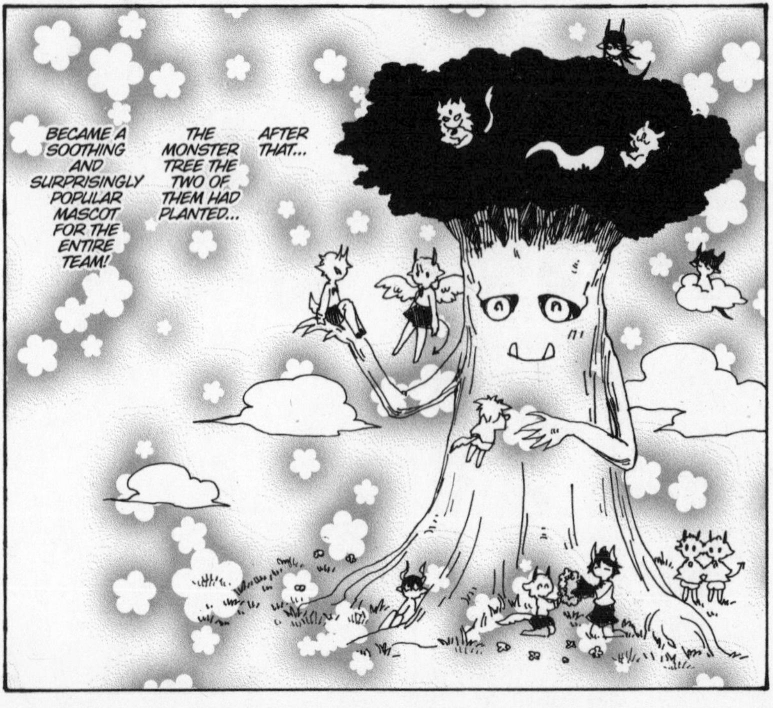
AFTER THAT...
THE MONSTER TREE THE TWO OF THEM HAD PLANTED...
BECAME A SOOTHING AND SURPRISINGLY POPULAR MASCOT FOR THE ENTIRE TEAM!

LITTLE DEVILS

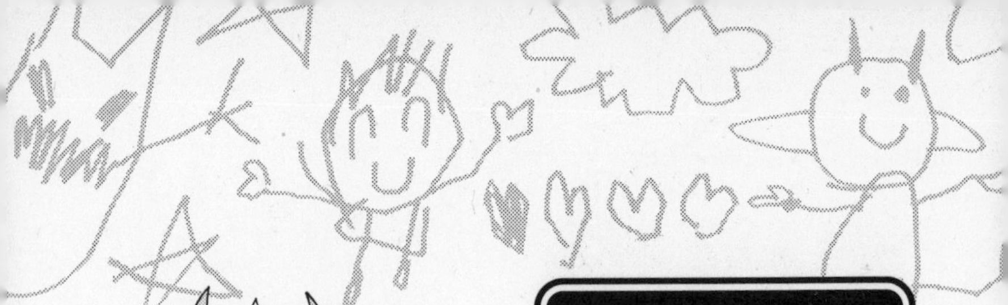

EVIL OF THE ARMS - AUGA ▼

The fourth eldest devil and definitely the most chilled out.
The strongest of all the siblings despite his soft touch.
Keeps an open mind.
Loves flowers.

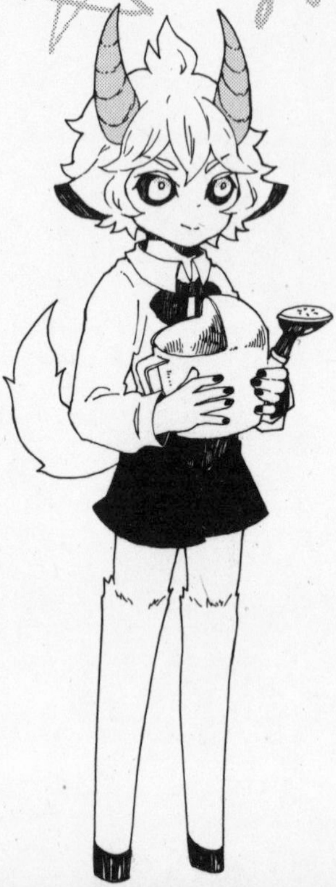

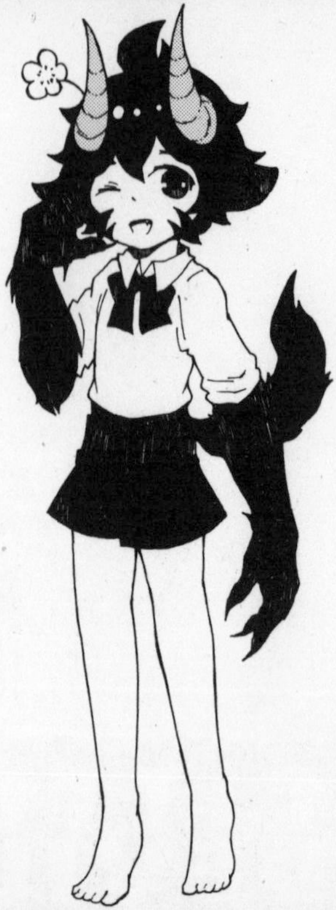

DEVIL OF THE LEGS - BAZU ▼

The second eldest devil who does things at his own pace.
A gentle soul but has a quietly reassuring presence.
Loves to take care of others and is even pretty good at doing it.

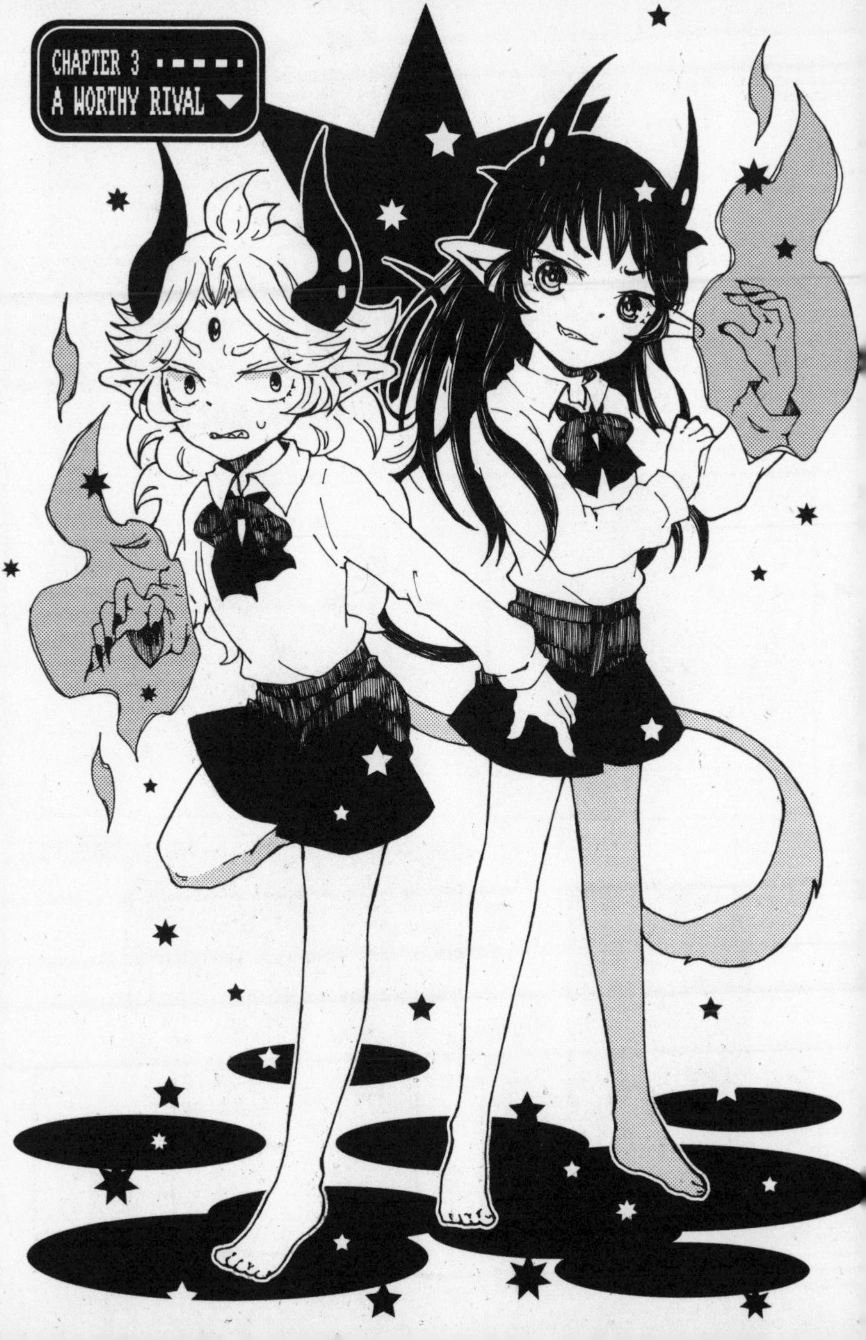
CHAPTER 3
A WORTHY RIVAL

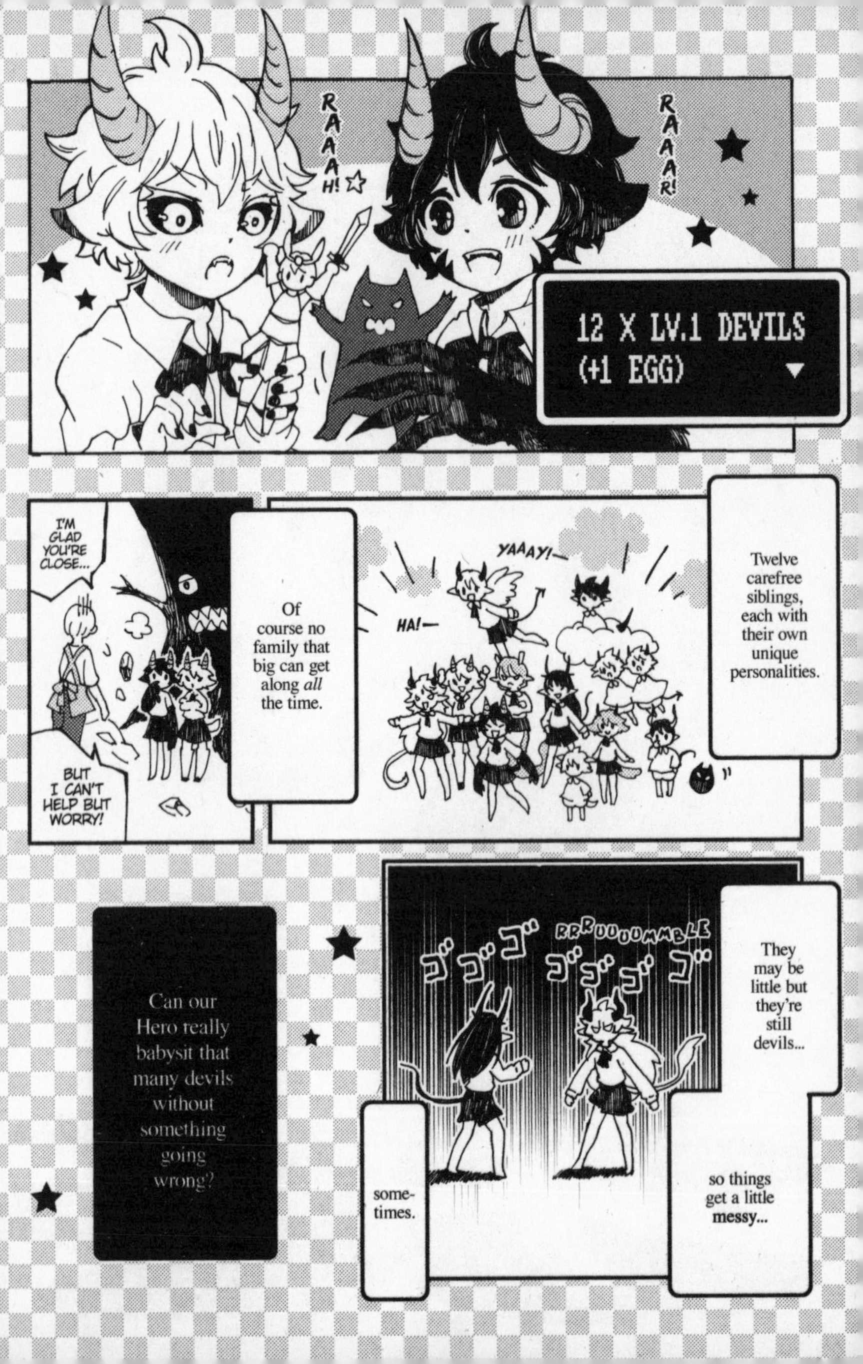
RAAAR!
RAAAH!
12 X LV.1 DEVILS
(+1 EGG)
Twelve carefree siblings, each with their own unique personalities.
YAAAY!—
HA!—
Of course no family that big can get along *all* the time.
I'M GLAD YOU'RE CLOSE...
BUT I CAN'T HELP BUT WORRY!
They may be little but they're still devils...
RRRUUUUMMBLE
ゴゴゴゴ
ゴゴゴ
so things get a little **messy**...
some-times.
Can our Hero really babysit that many devils without something going wrong?

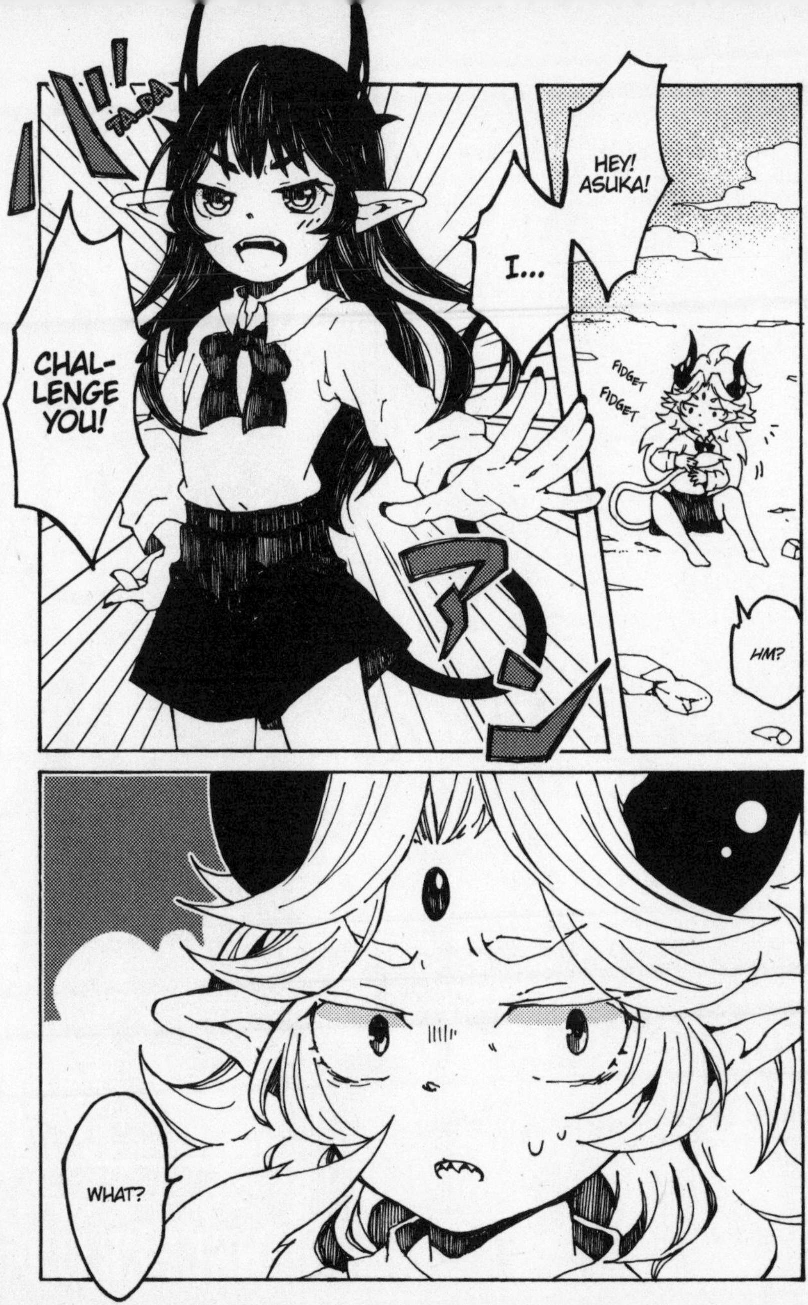
HEY! ASUKA!
I...
FIDGET
FIDGET
HM?
TA-DA
CHAL-LENGE YOU!
WHAT?

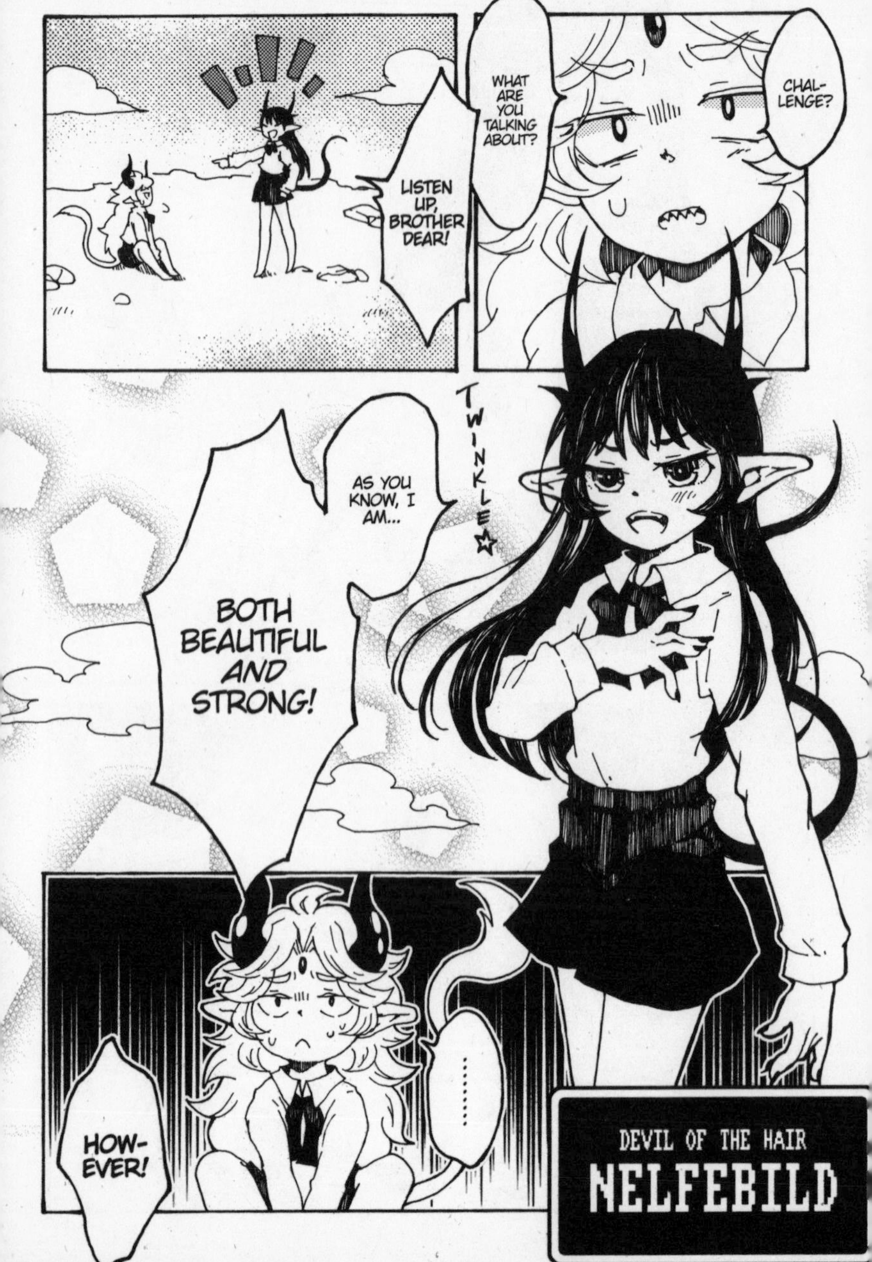
CHAL-LENGE?
WHAT ARE YOU TALKING ABOUT?
LISTEN UP, BROTHER DEAR!
TWINKLE☆
AS YOU KNOW, I AM...
BOTH BEAUTIFUL AND STRONG!
DEVIL OF THE HAIR
NELFEBILD
......
HOW-EVER!

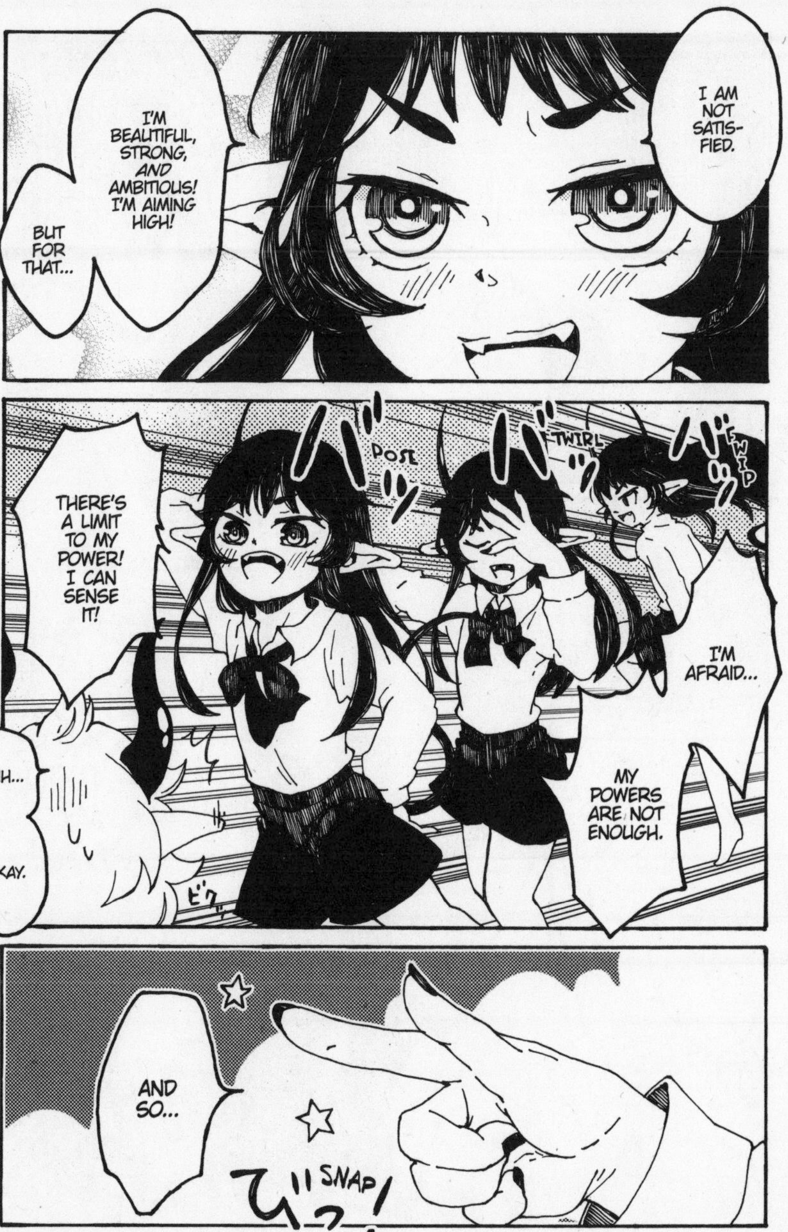
I AM NOT SATISFIED.
I'M BEAUTIFUL, STRONG, AND AMBITIOUS! I'M AIMING HIGH!
BUT FOR THAT...
FWIP
TWIRL
POSE
THERE'S A LIMIT TO MY POWER! I CAN SENSE IT!
I'M AFRAID...
MY POWERS ARE NOT ENOUGH.
UH...
OKAY.
AND SO...
SNAP!

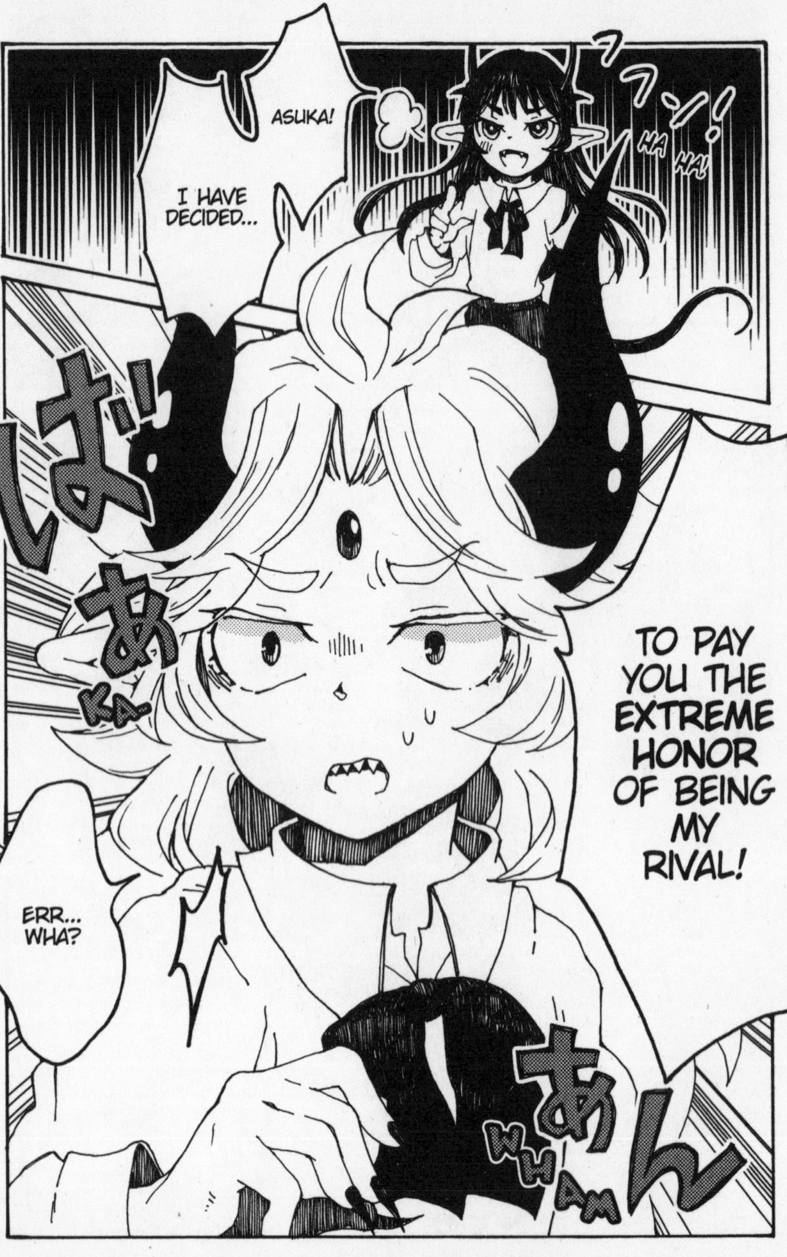
フフーン!
HA HA!
ASUKA!
I HAVE DECIDED...
TO PAY YOU THE EXTREME HONOR OF BEING MY RIVAL!
KA-
ERR... WHA?
あん
WHAM

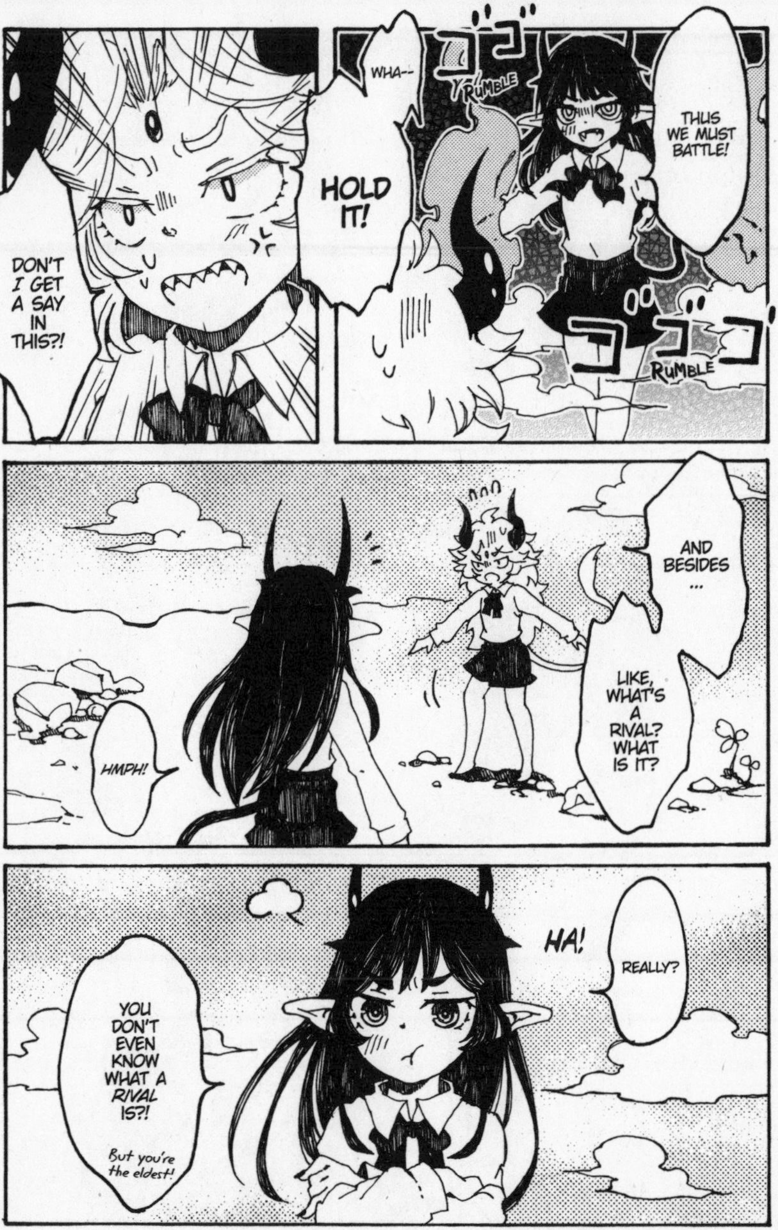
THUS WE MUST BATTLE!
ゴゴ
RUMBLE
ゴゴゴ
RUMBLE
WHA--
HOLD IT!
DON'T I GET A SAY IN THIS?!
AND BESIDES ...
LIKE, WHAT'S A RIVAL? WHAT IS IT?
HMPH!
HA!
REALLY?
YOU DON'T EVEN KNOW WHAT A RIVAL IS?!
But you're the eldest!

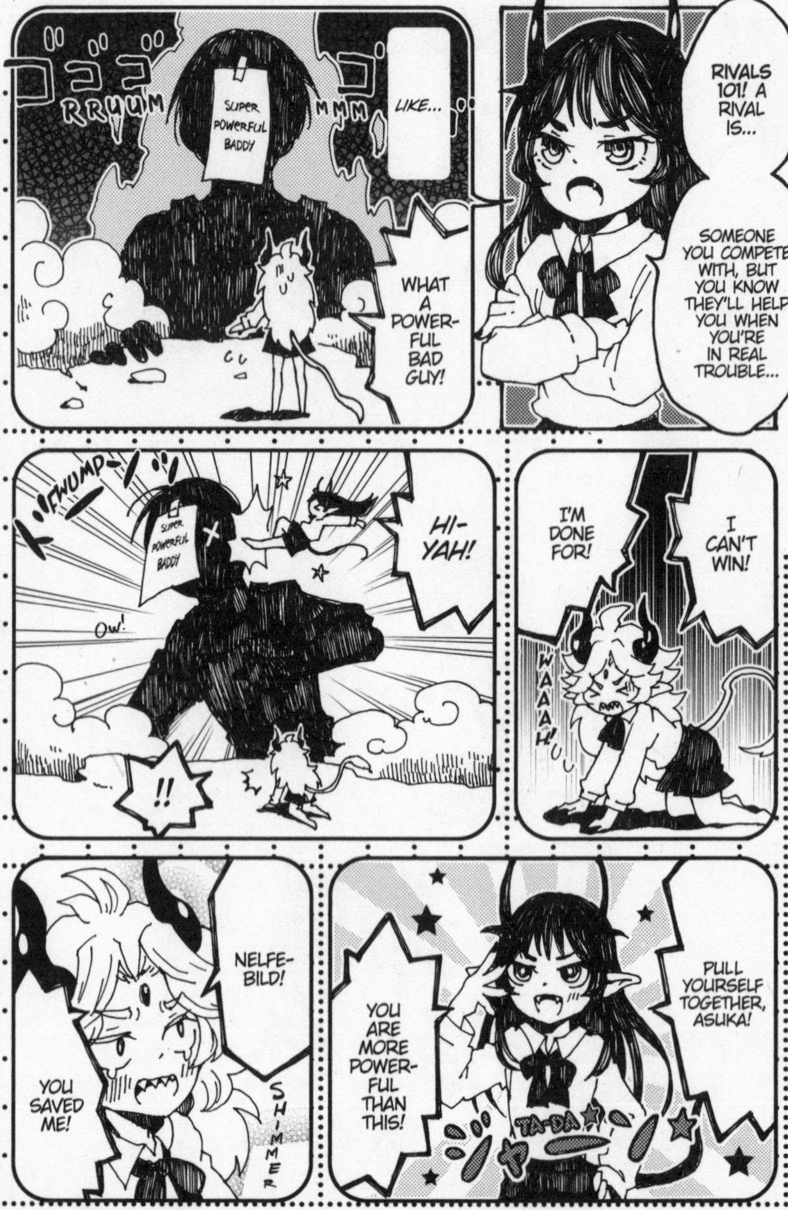
RIVALS 101! A RIVAL IS...
SOMEONE YOU COMPETE WITH, BUT YOU KNOW THEY'LL HELP YOU WHEN YOU'RE IN REAL TROUBLE...
LIKE...
ゴゴゴ RRUUM
ゴ MMM
SUPER POWERFUL BADDY
WHAT A POWERFUL BAD GUY!
I CAN'T WIN!
I'M DONE FOR!
WAAAAH!
HI-YAH!
FWUMP
SUPER POWERFUL BADDY
OW!
!!
PULL YOURSELF TOGETHER, ASUKA!
YOU ARE MORE POWERFUL THAN THIS!
TA-DA
NELFEBILD!
SHIMMER
YOU SAVED ME!

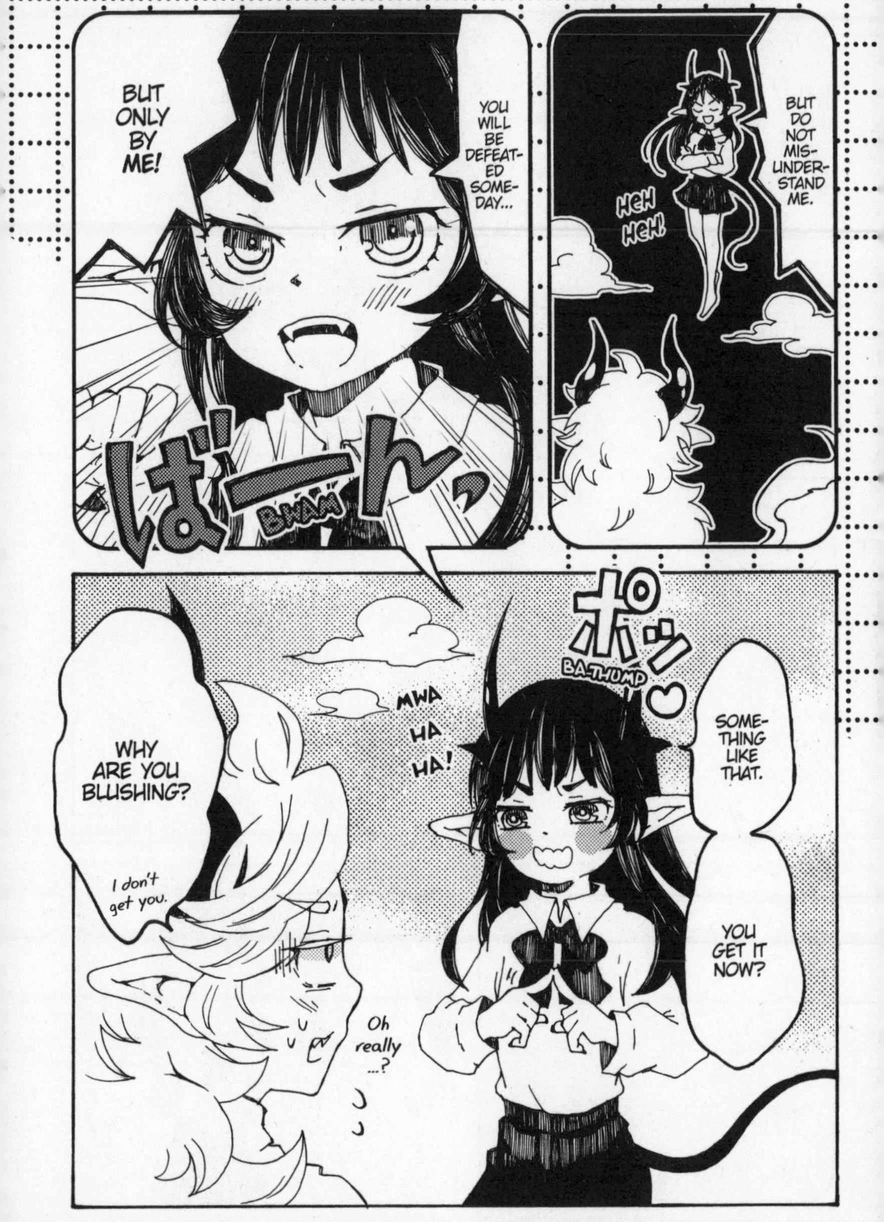
BUT DO NOT MIS-UNDERSTAND ME.
HEH HEH!
YOU WILL BE DEFEAT-ED SOME-DAY...
BUT ONLY BY ME!
ばーん
BWAM
ポッ
BA-THUMP
SOME-THING LIKE THAT.
YOU GET IT NOW?
MWA HA HA!
WHY ARE YOU BLUSHING?
I don't get you.
Oh really ...?

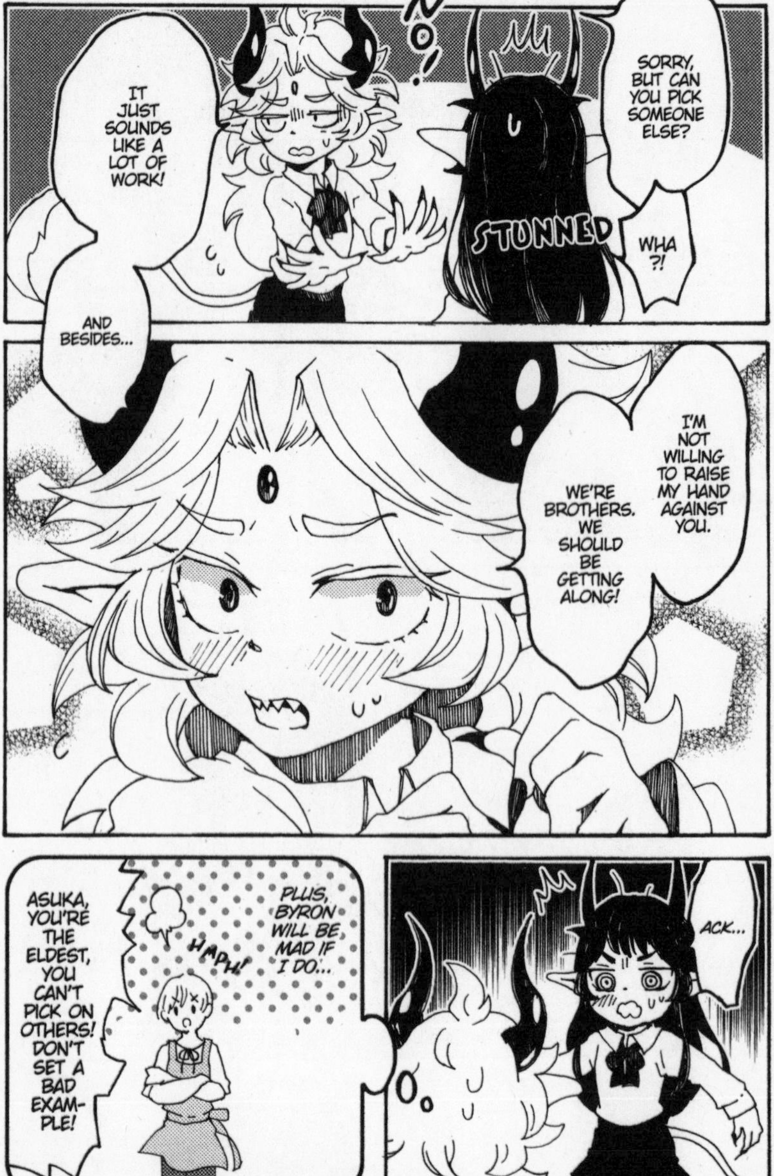
SORRY, BUT CAN YOU PICK SOMEONE ELSE?
NO!
IT JUST SOUNDS LIKE A LOT OF WORK!
WHA ?!
STUNNED
AND BESIDES...
I'M NOT WILLING TO RAISE MY HAND AGAINST YOU.
WE'RE BROTHERS. WE SHOULD BE GETTING ALONG!
ACK...
PLUS, BYRON WILL BE MAD IF I DO...
HMPH!
ASUKA, YOU'RE THE ELDEST, YOU CAN'T PICK ON OTHERS! DON'T SET A BAD EXAMPLE!

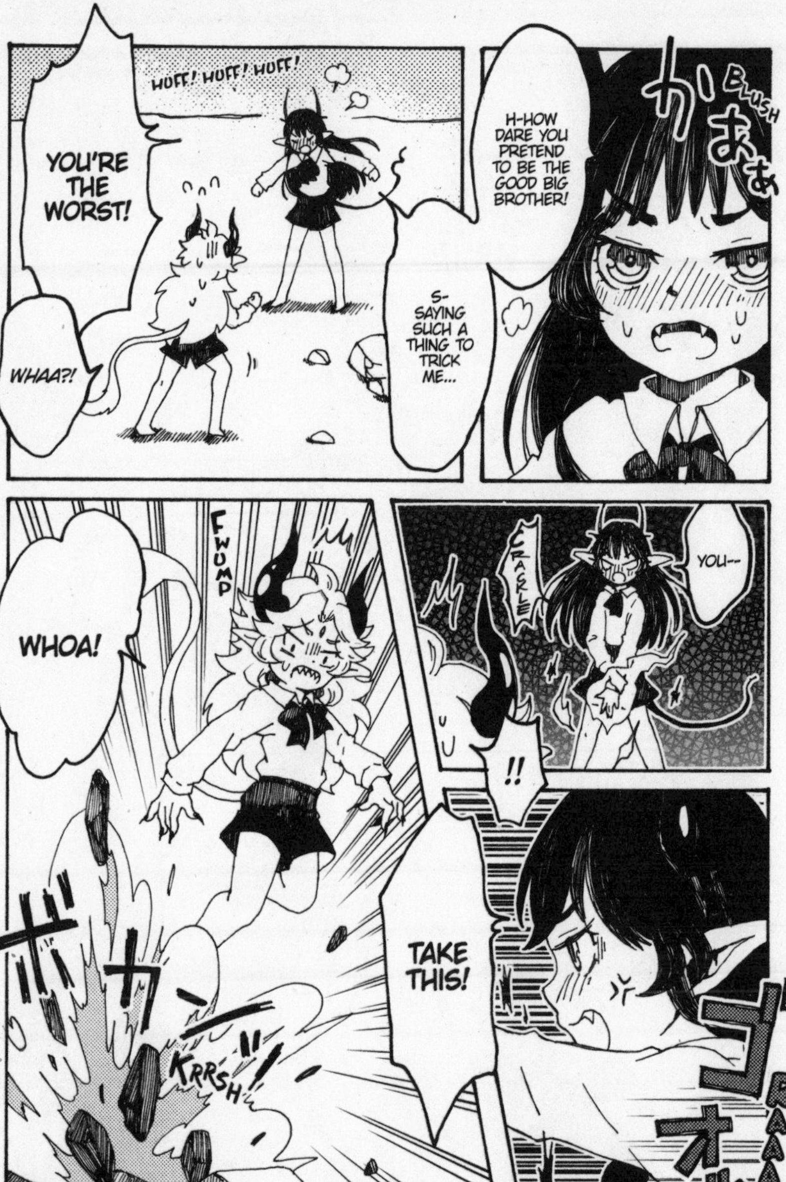

かぁぁ
BLUSH
H-HOW DARE YOU PRETEND TO BE THE GOOD BIG BROTHER!
S-SAYING SUCH A THING TO TRICK ME...
HUFF! HUFF! HUFF!
YOU'RE THE WORST!
WHAA?!
YOU--
CRACKLE
!!
TAKE THIS!
ゴォッ
RAAAR
FWUMP
WHOA!
KRRSH

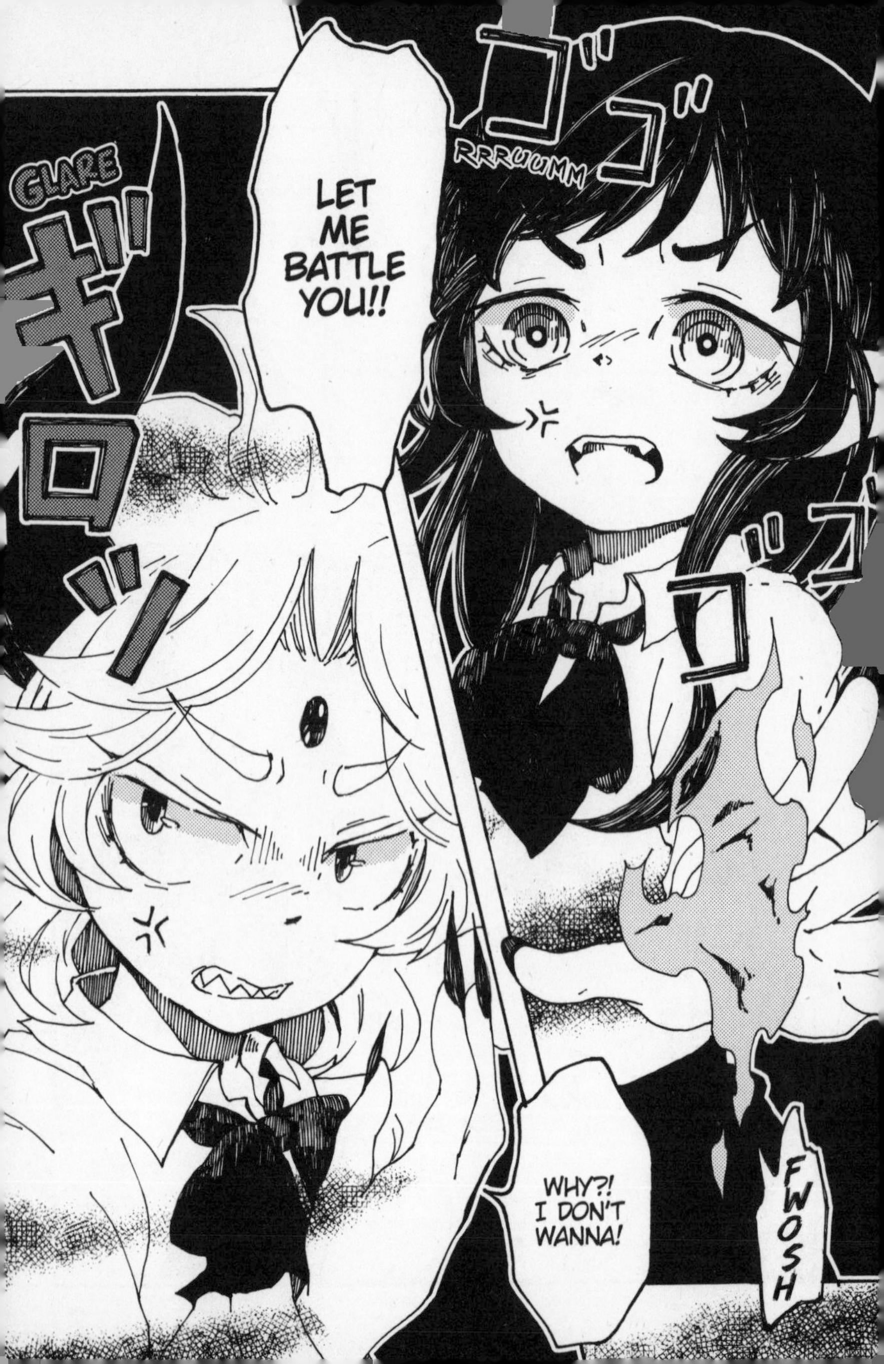
ゴゴ
RRRUUMM
LET ME BATTLE YOU!!
GLARE
ギロッ
WHY?! I DON'T WANNA!
ゴゴ
FWOSH

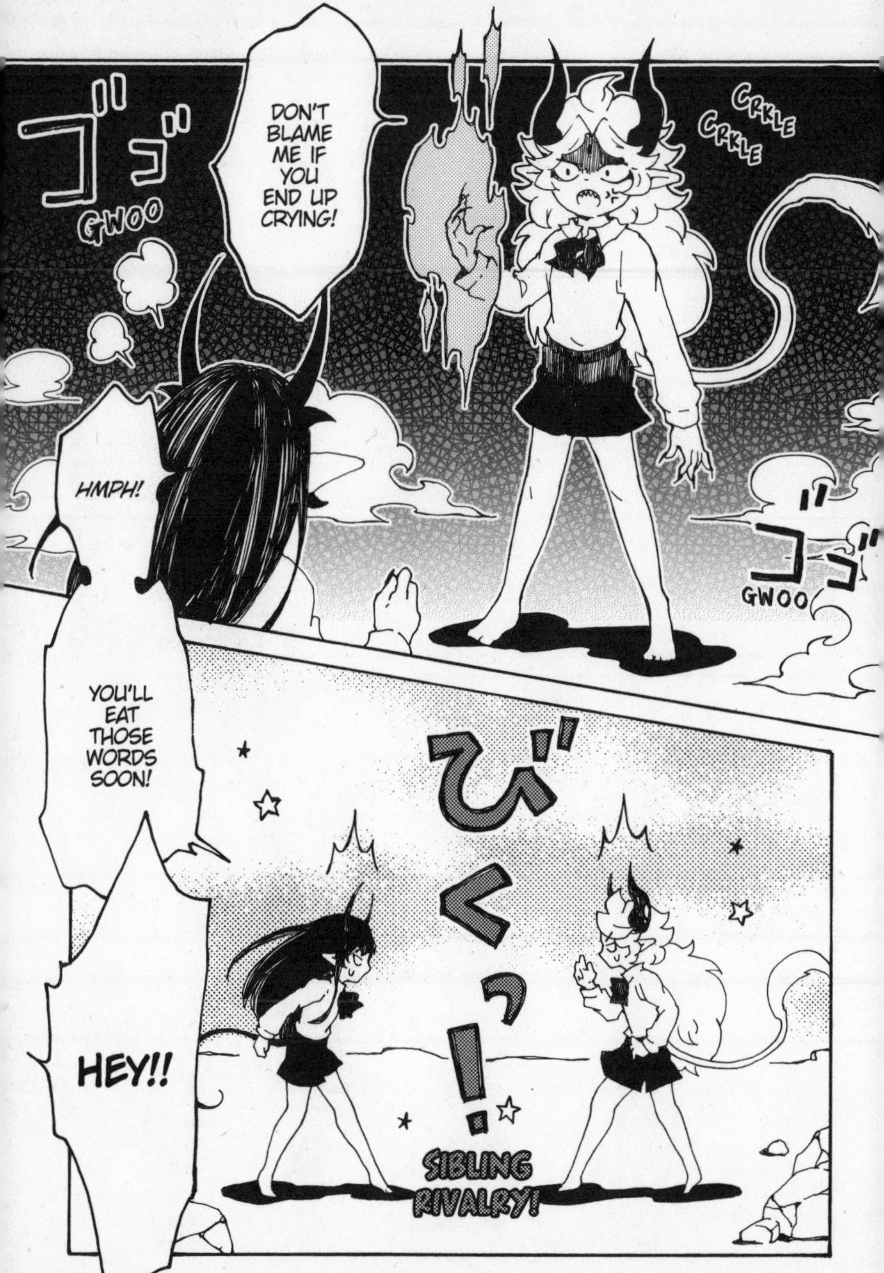
CRKLE CRKLE
ゴゴ GWOO
DON'T BLAME ME IF YOU END UP CRYING!
ゴゴ GWOO
HMPH!
YOU'LL EAT THOSE WORDS SOON!
びくっ!
SIBLING RIVALRY!
HEY!!

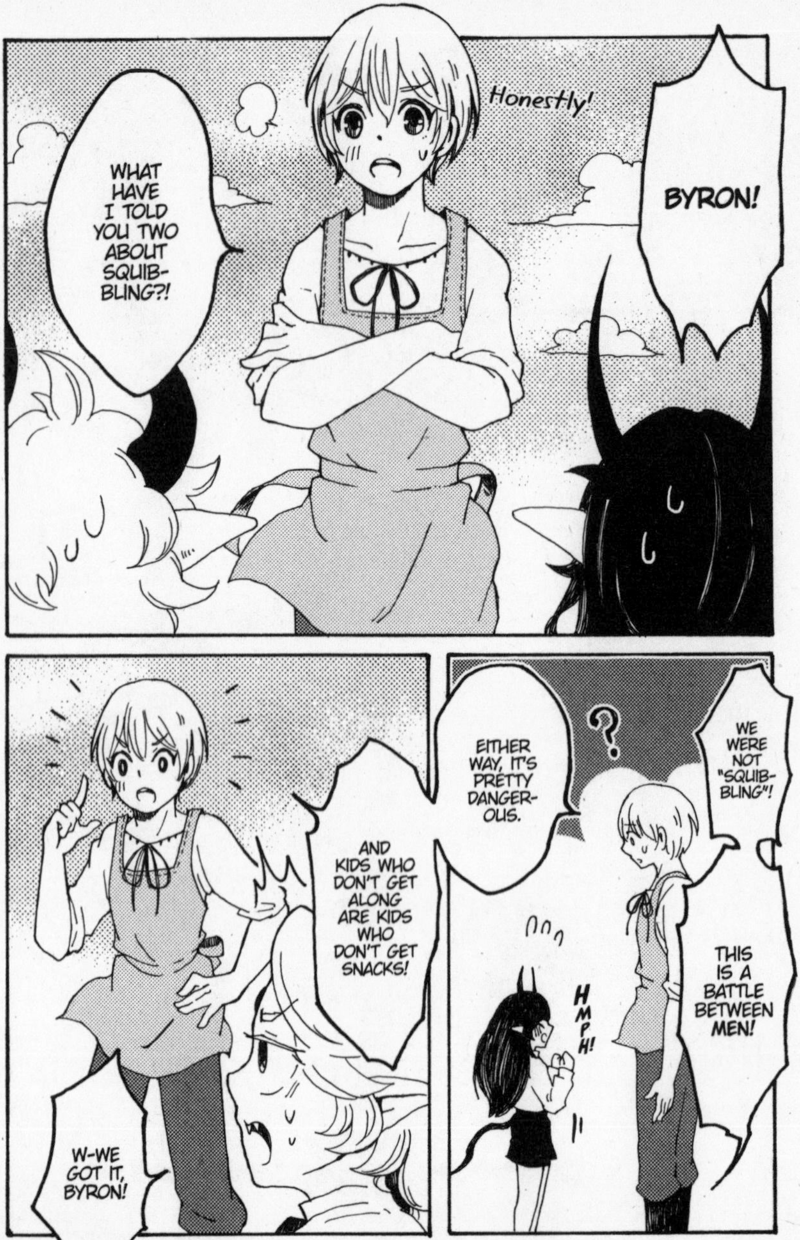
BYRON!
Honestly!
WHAT HAVE I TOLD YOU TWO ABOUT SQUIBBLING?!
WE WERE NOT "SQUIBBLING"!
?
THIS IS A BATTLE BETWEEN MEN!
HMPH!
EITHER WAY, IT'S PRETTY DANGEROUS.
AND KIDS WHO DON'T GET ALONG ARE KIDS WHO DON'T GET SNACKS!
W-WE GOT IT, BYRON!

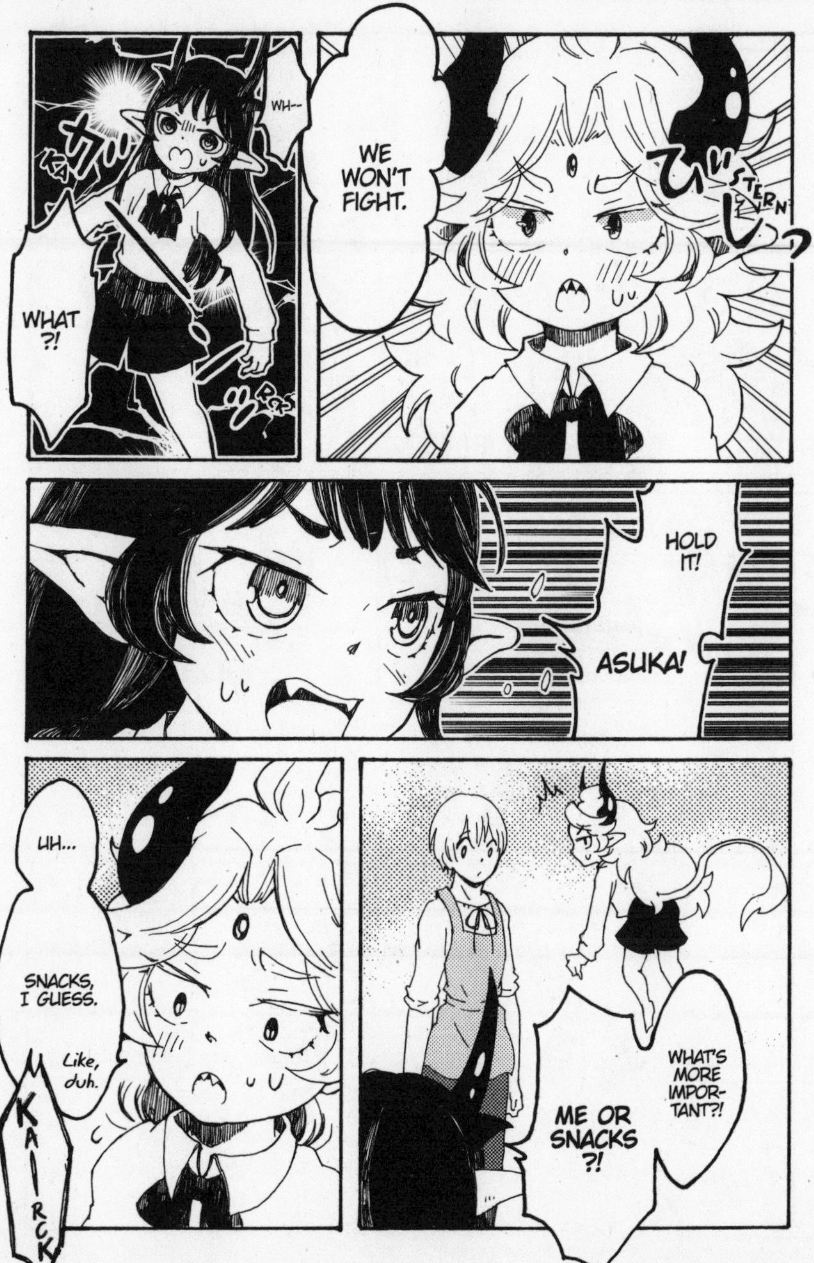
WE WON'T FIGHT.
STERN
WH--
KA
WHAT?!
HOLD IT!
ASUKA!
WHAT'S MORE IMPORTANT?!
ME OR SNACKS?!
...
UH...
SNACKS, I GUESS.
Like, duh.
KAIRCK

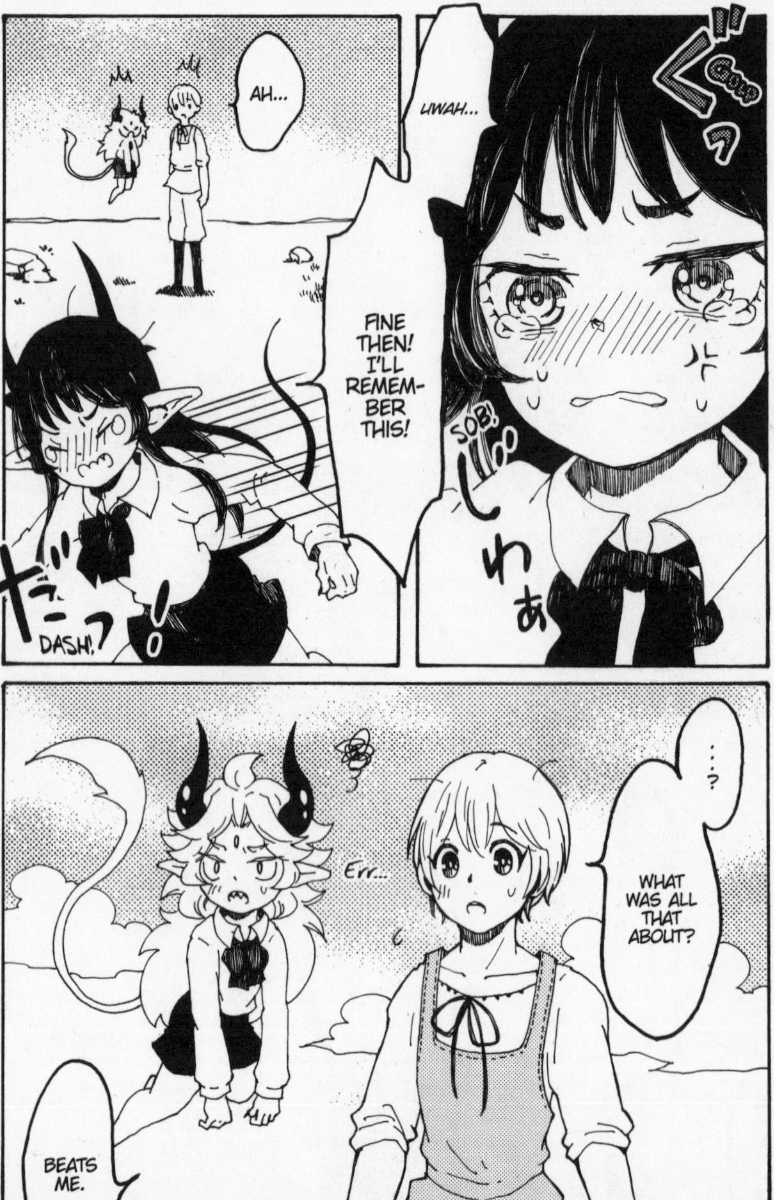
ぐっ
GULP
UWAH...
FINE THEN! I'LL REMEMBER THIS!
SOB!
じわぁ
AH...
ダーッ
DASH!
...?
WHAT WAS ALL THAT ABOUT?
Err...
BEATS ME.

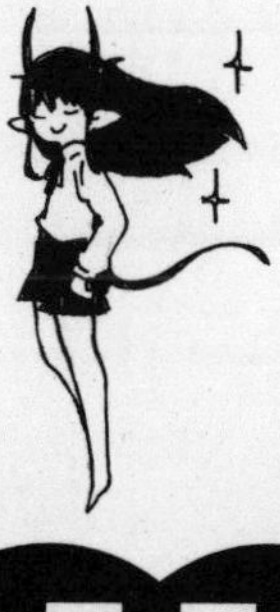

LITTLE DEVILS

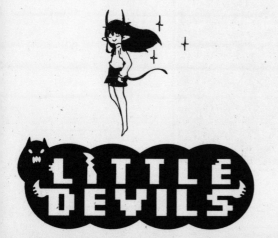

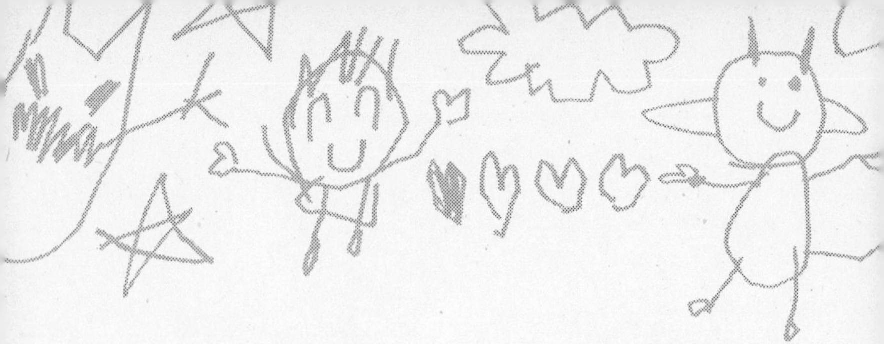

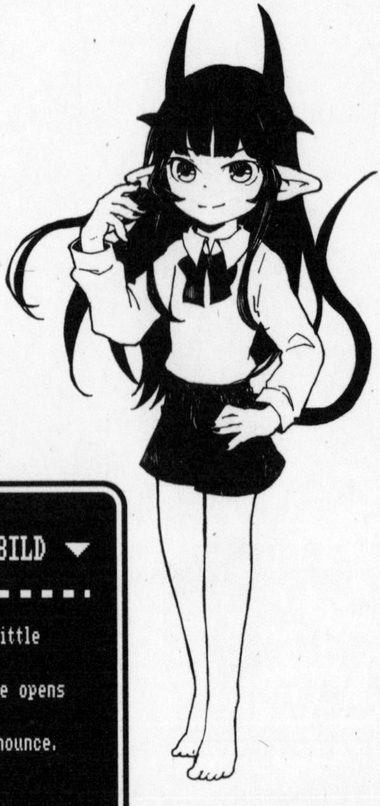

DEVIL OF THE HAIR - NELFEBILD ▼

The sixth--and most narcissistic--little devil.
Cute when silent but beware when he opens his mouth.
His name is long and tough to pronounce.
Everyone calls him "Nelfe."

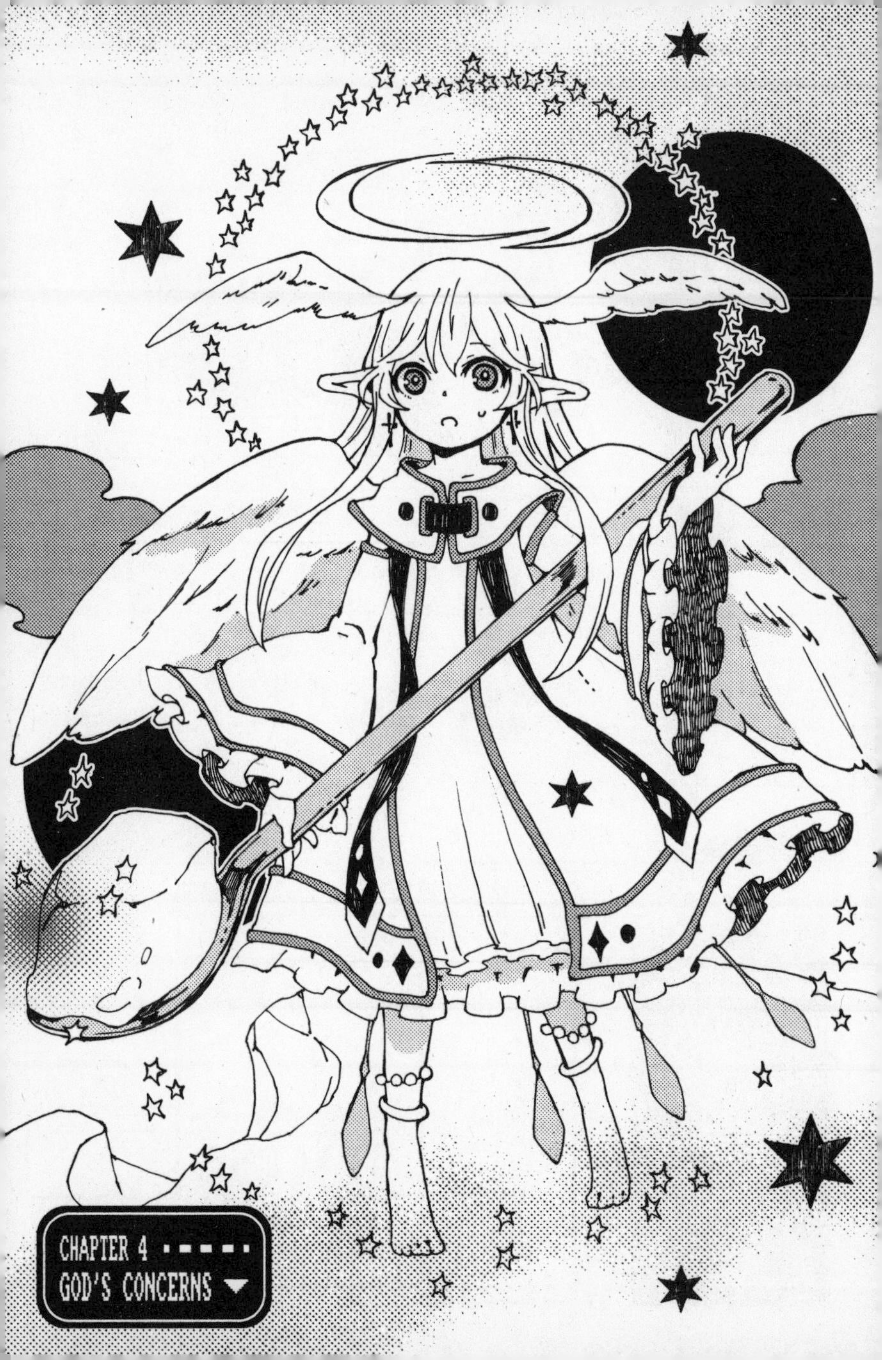
CHAPTER 4
GOD'S CONCERNS

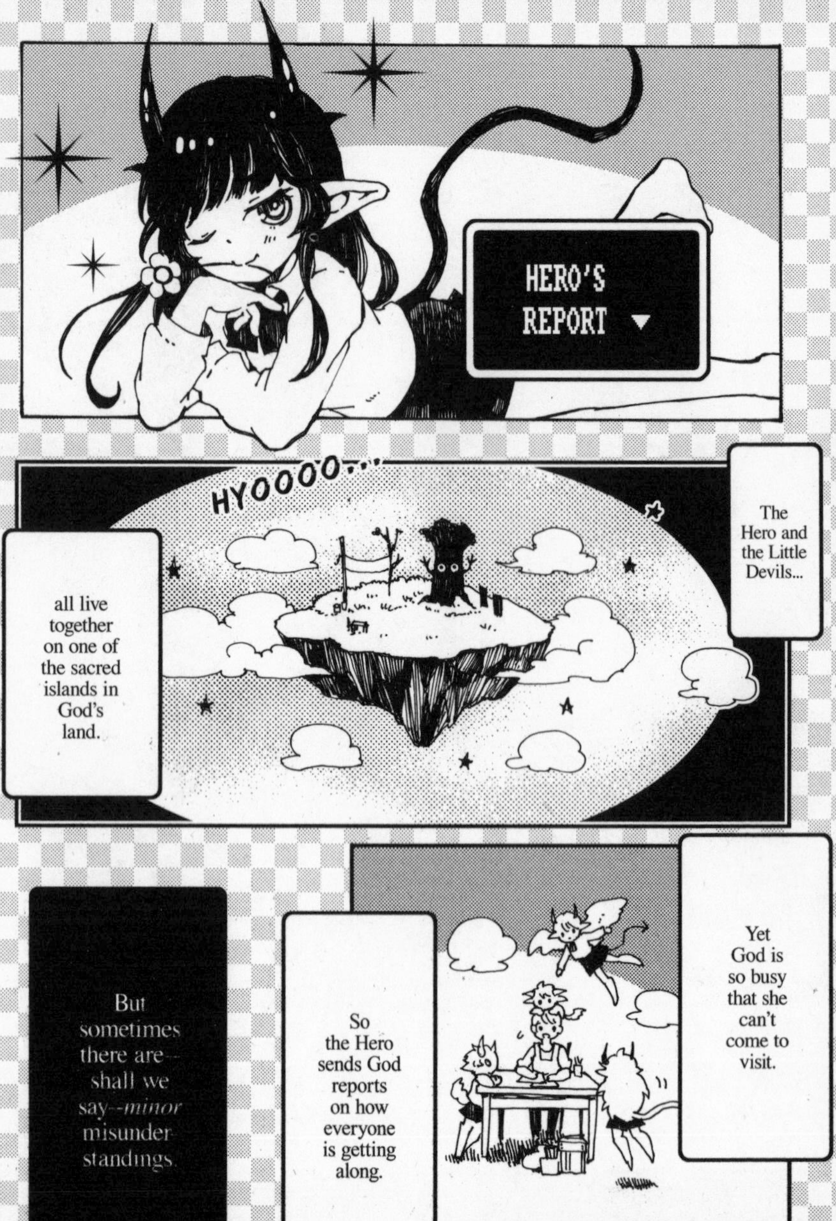
HERO'S REPORT ▼
The Hero and the Little Devils...
HYOOOO...
all live together on one of the sacred islands in God's land.
Yet God is so busy that she can't come to visit.
So the Hero sends God reports on how everyone is getting along.
But sometimes there are--shall we say--*minor* misunderstandings.

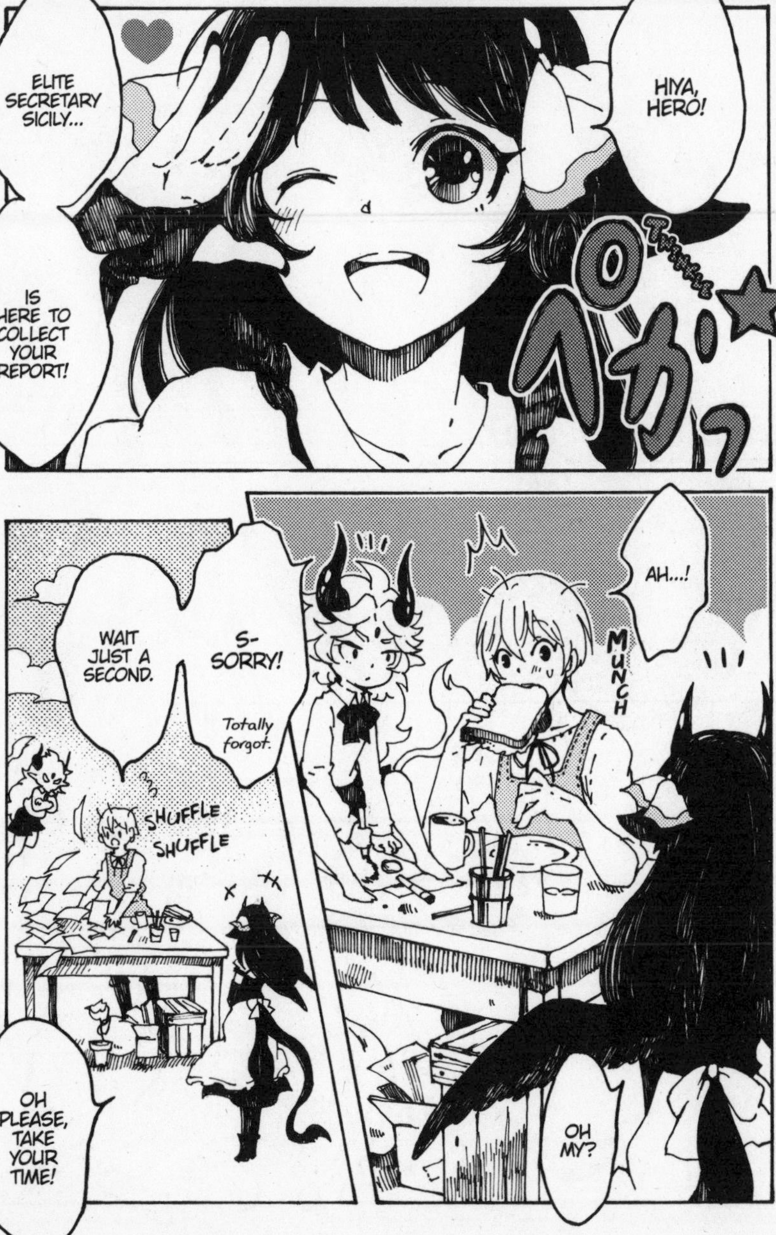
HIYA, HERO!
ELITE SECRETARY SICILY...
IS HERE TO COLLECT YOUR REPORT!
TWINKLE
ぺかっ☆
AH...!
MUNCH
OH MY?
S-SORRY!
Totally forgot.
WAIT JUST A SECOND.
SHUFFLE SHUFFLE
OH PLEASE, TAKE YOUR TIME!

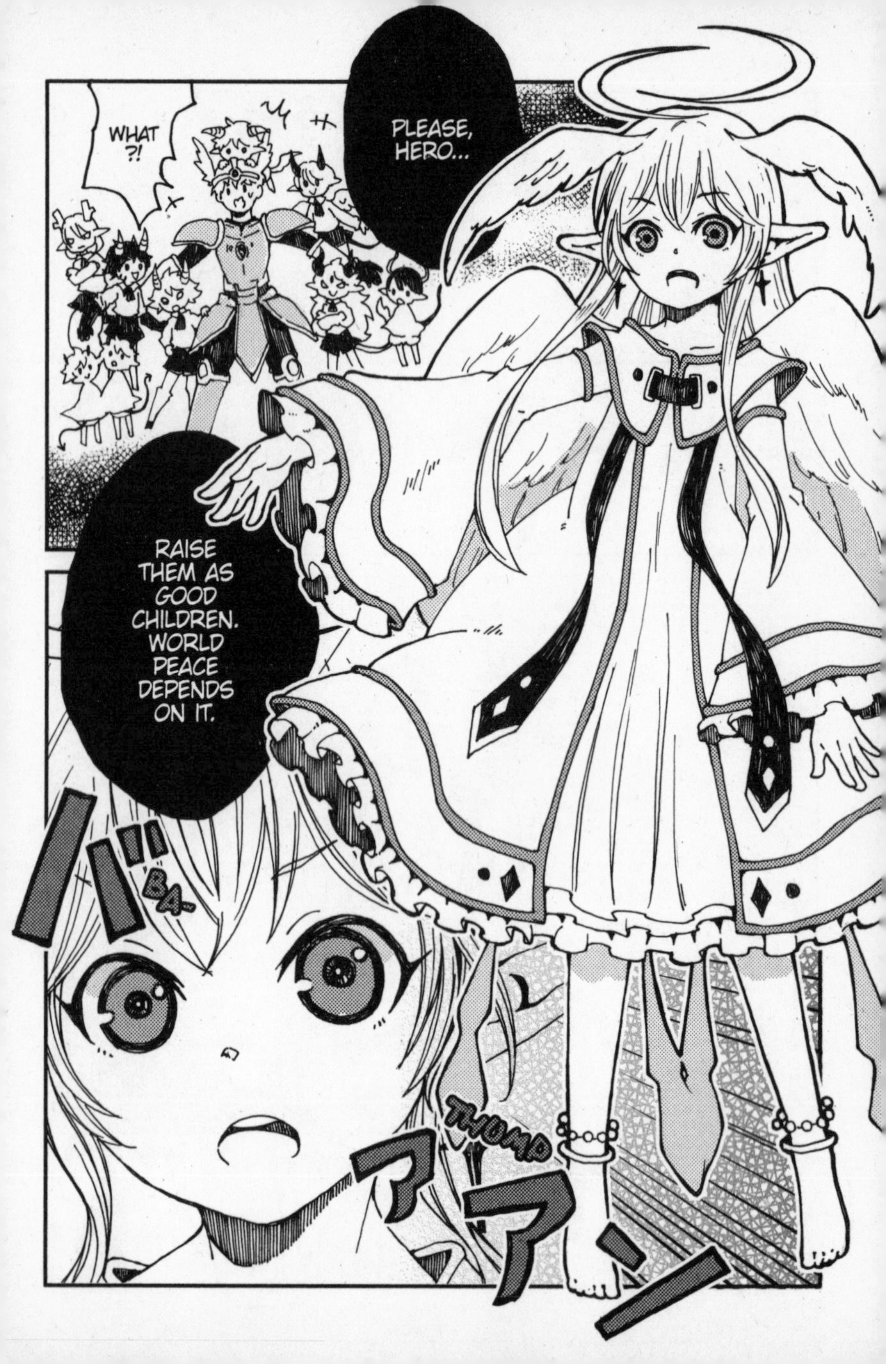
PLEASE, HERO...
WHAT ?!
RAISE THEM AS GOOD CHILDREN. WORLD PEACE DEPENDS ON IT.
BA-
THUMP

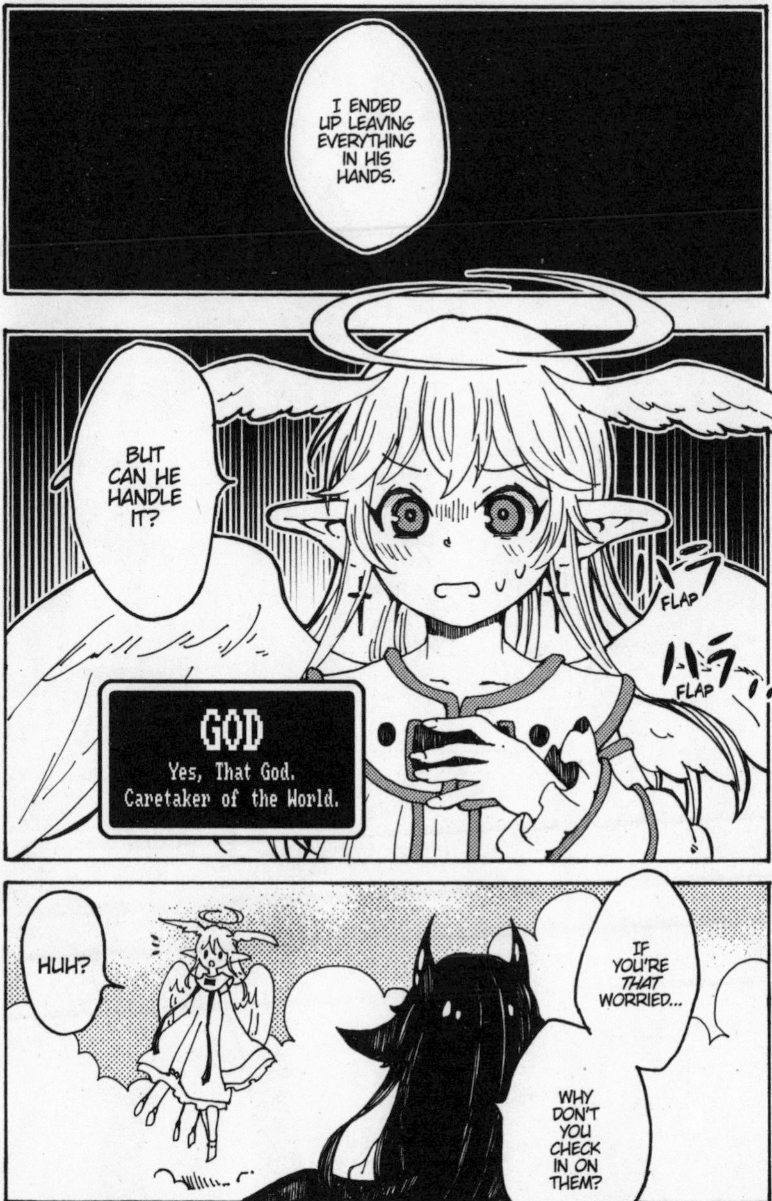
I ENDED UP LEAVING EVERYTHING IN HIS HANDS.
BUT CAN HE HANDLE IT?
ハラ FLAP
ハラ FLAP
GOD
Yes, That God.
Caretaker of the World.
IF YOU'RE *THAT* WORRIED...
WHY DON'T YOU CHECK IN ON THEM?
HUH?

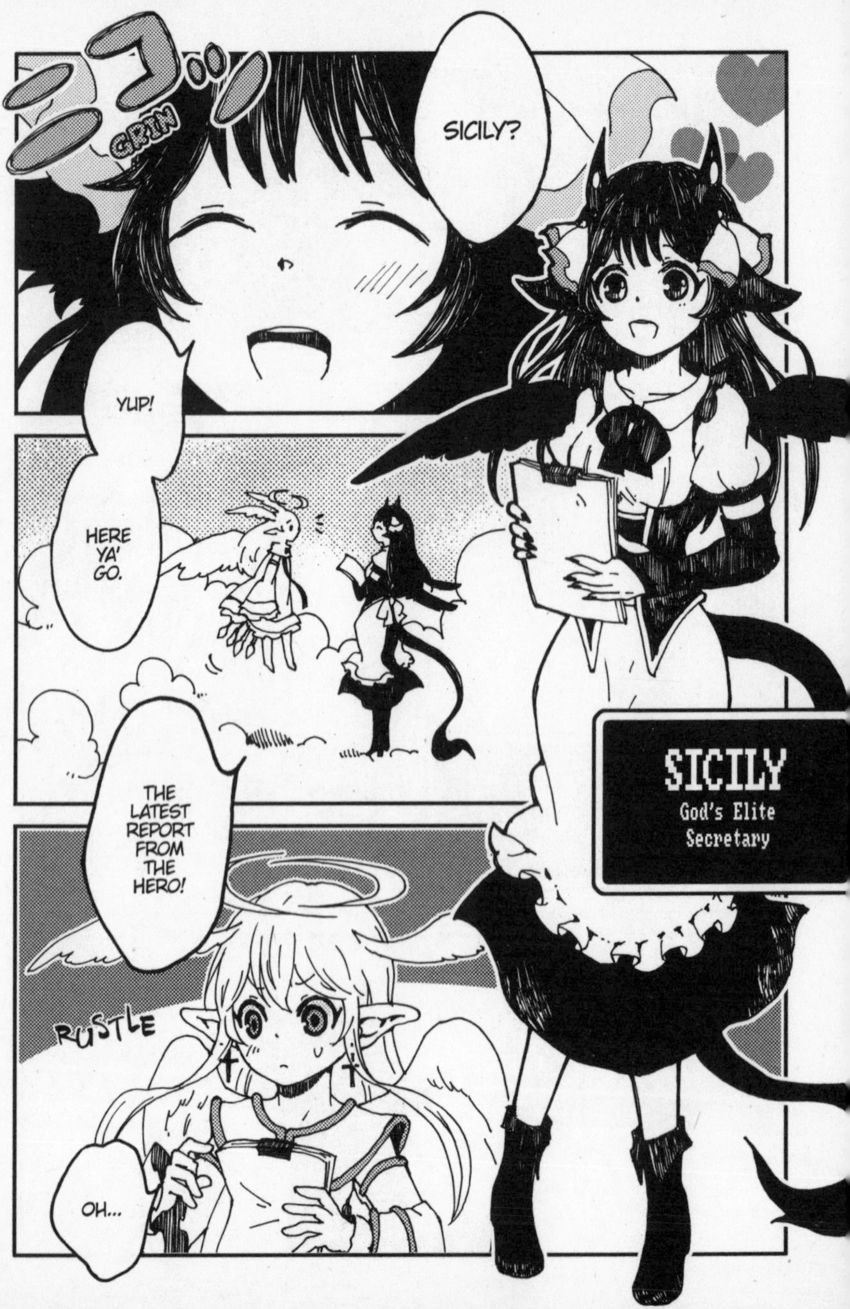
SICILY?
GRIN
YUP!
SICILY
God's Elite Secretary
HERE YA' GO.
THE LATEST REPORT FROM THE HERO!
RUSTLE
OH...

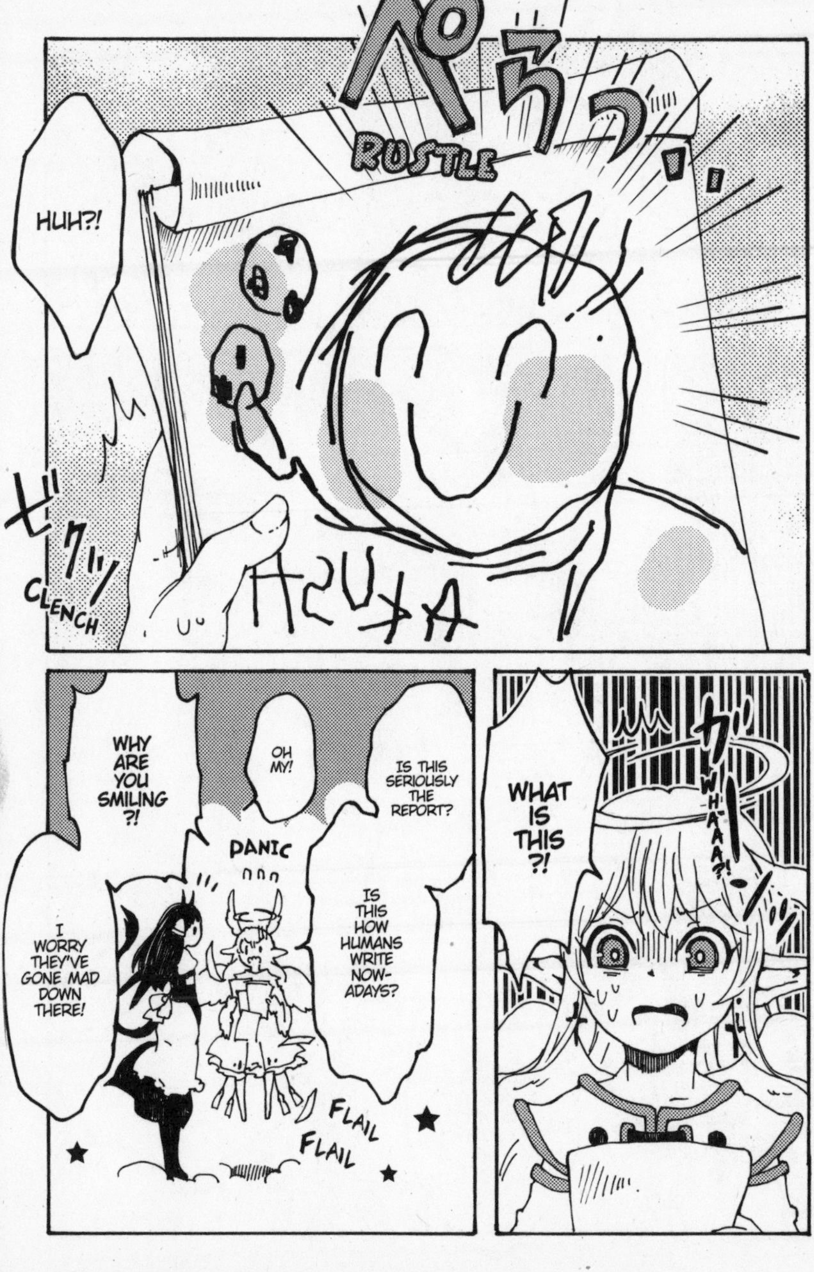
ぺろっ
RUSTLE
HUH?!
ビクッ
CLENCH
ガッ
WHAAAA?!
WHAT IS THIS ?!
IS THIS SERIOUSLY THE REPORT?
OH MY!
IS THIS HOW HUMANS WRITE NOW-ADAYS?
WHY ARE YOU SMILING ?!
PANIC
I WORRY THEY'VE GONE MAD DOWN THERE!
FLAIL
FLAIL

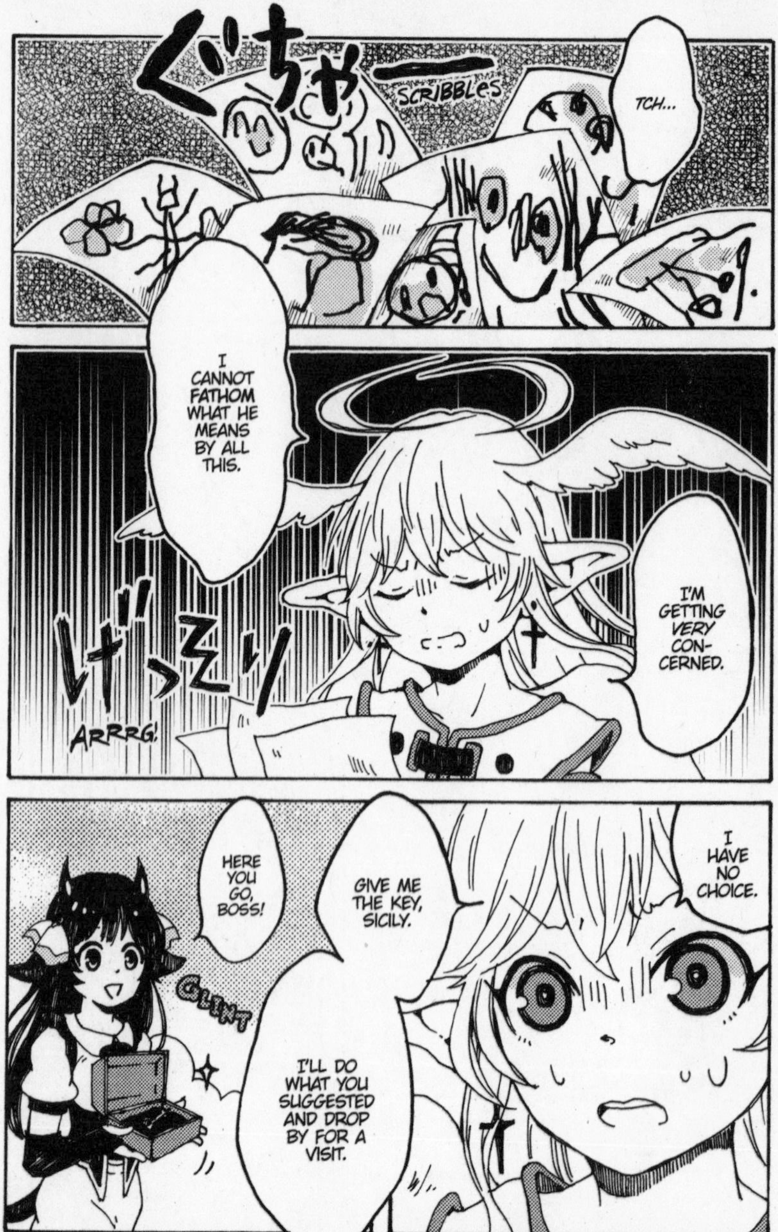
TCH...
ぐちゃー
SCRIBBLES
I CANNOT FATHOM WHAT HE MEANS BY ALL THIS.
I'M GETTING VERY CON-CERNED.
げっそり
ARRRG!
I HAVE NO CHOICE.
GIVE ME THE KEY, SICILY.
I'LL DO WHAT YOU SUGGESTED AND DROP BY FOR A VISIT.
HERE YOU GO, BOSS!
GLINT

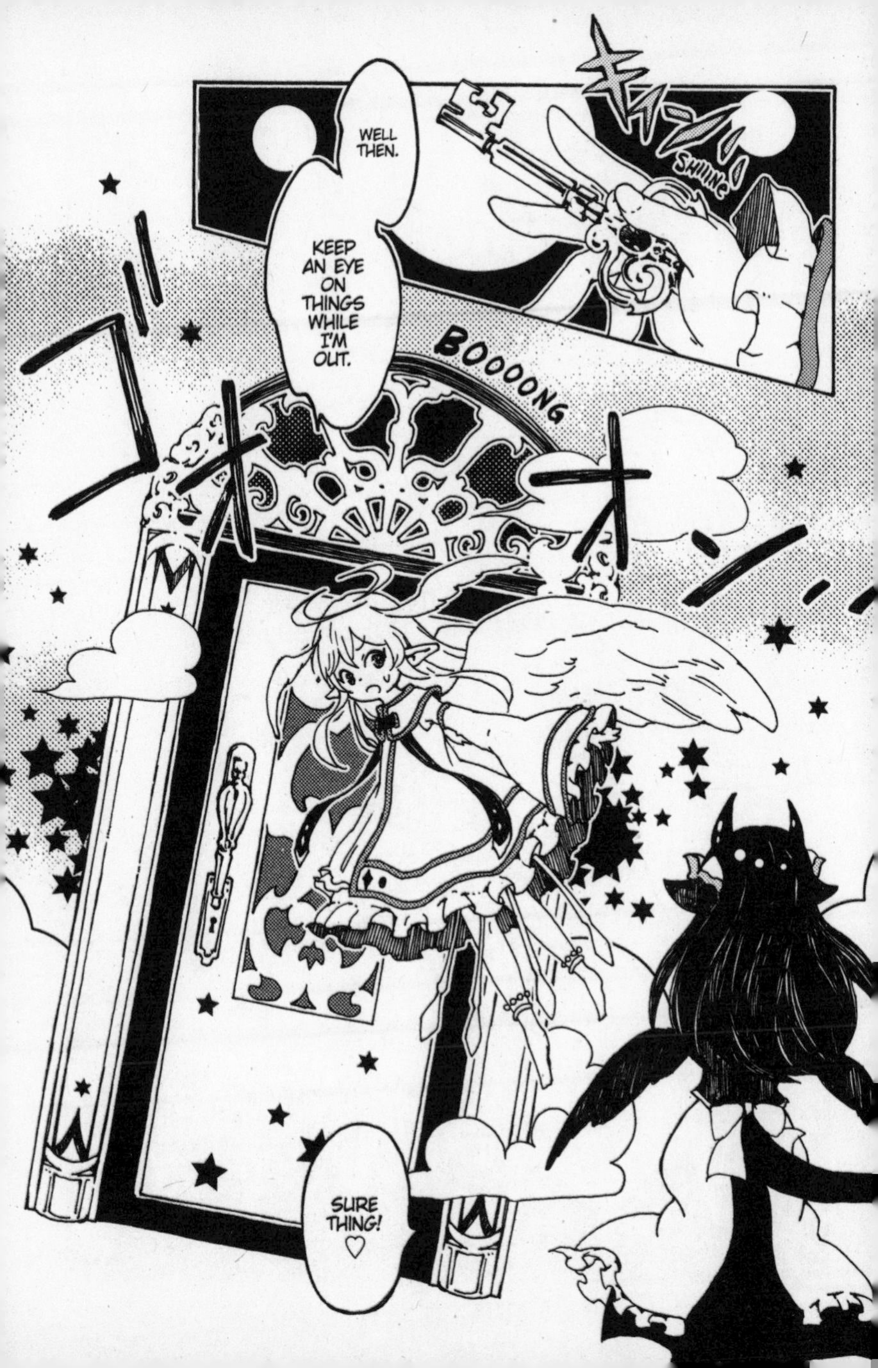
SHIIING
WELL THEN.
KEEP AN EYE ON THINGS WHILE I'M OUT.
BOOOOONG
SURE THING! ♡

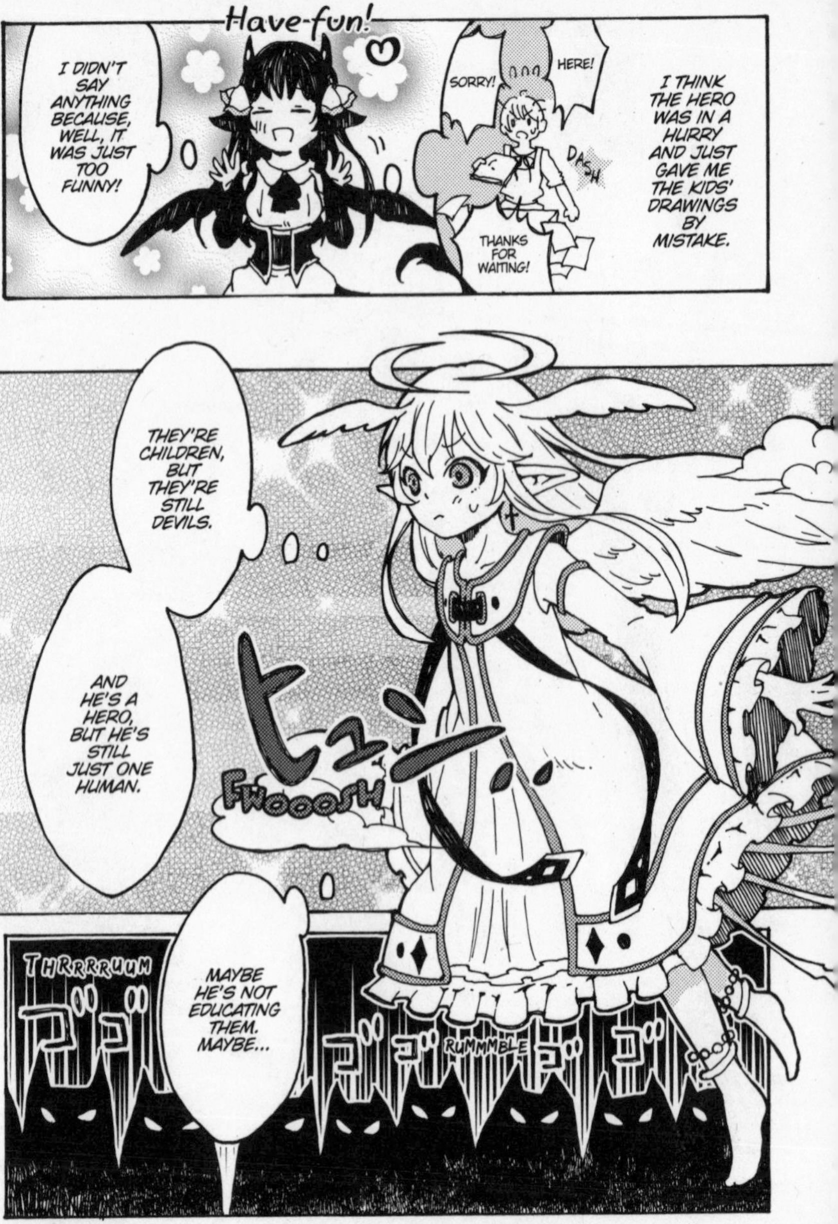

I THINK THE HERO WAS IN A HURRY AND JUST GAVE ME THE KIDS' DRAWINGS BY MISTAKE.
HERE!
SORRY!
DASH
THANKS FOR WAITING!
Have-fun!
I DIDN'T SAY ANYTHING BECAUSE, WELL, IT WAS JUST TOO FUNNY!
FWOOOSH
THEY'RE CHILDREN, BUT THEY'RE STILL DEVILS.
AND HE'S A HERO, BUT HE'S STILL JUST ONE HUMAN.
RUMMMBLE
MAYBE HE'S NOT EDUCATING THEM. MAYBE...
THRRRRUUM

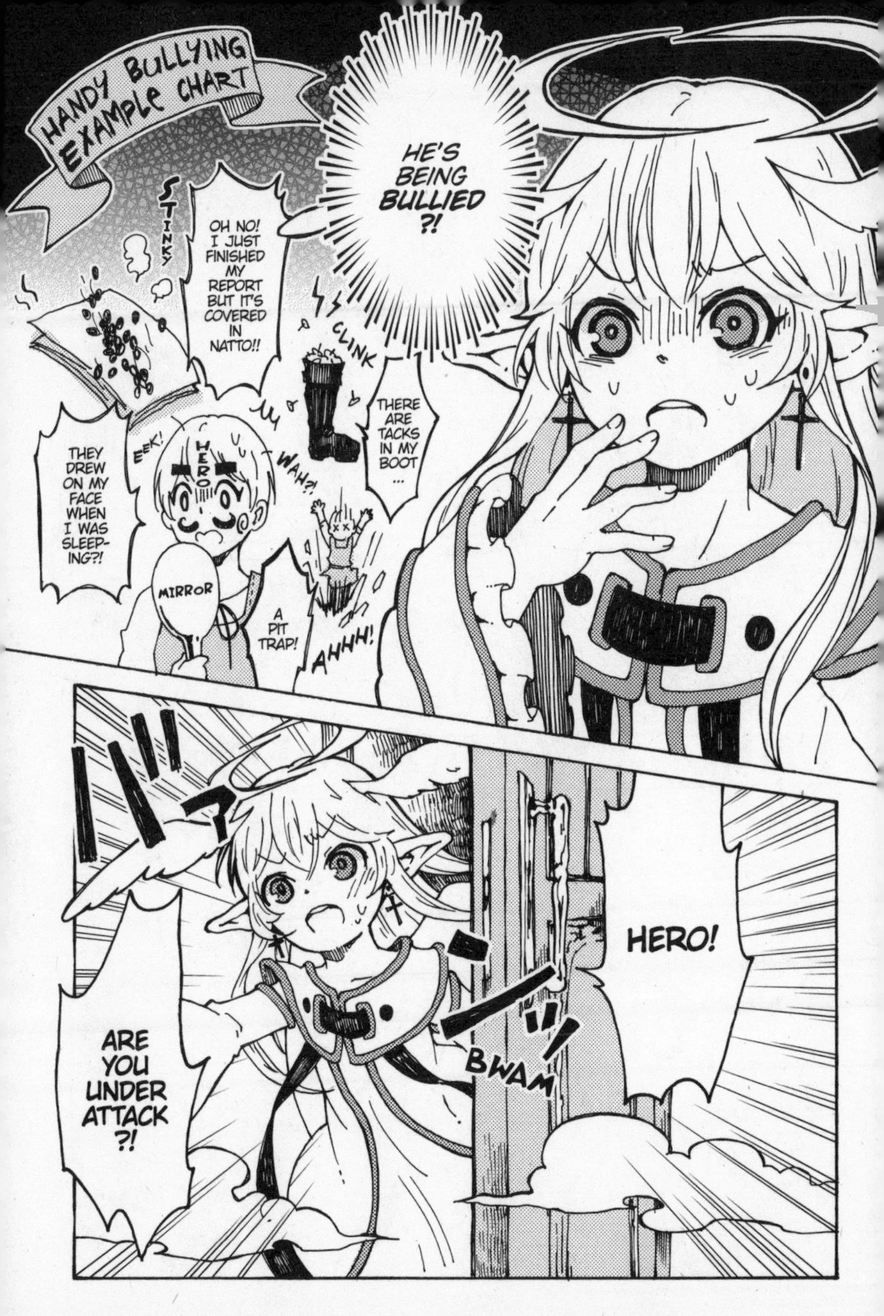
HE'S BEING BULLIED?!
HANDY BULLYING EXAMPLE CHART
OH NO! I JUST FINISHED MY REPORT BUT IT'S COVERED IN NATTO!!
STINKY
CLINK
THERE ARE TACKS IN MY BOOT...
EEK!
HERO
WAH?!
THEY DREW ON MY FACE WHEN I WAS SLEEPING?!
MIRROR
A PIT TRAP!
AHHH!
HERO!
BWAM
ARE YOU UNDER ATTACK?!

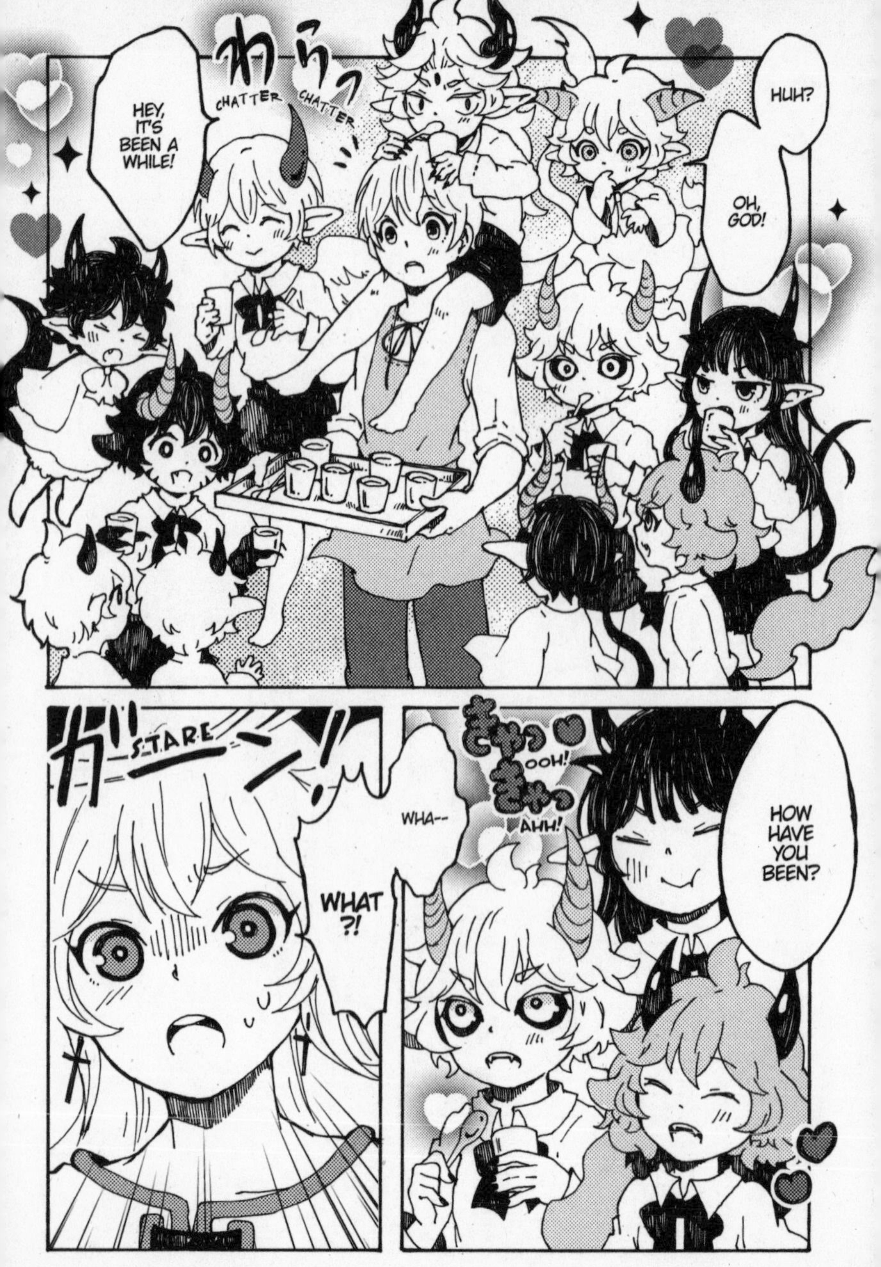
HUH?
OH, GOD!
わらっ CHATTER CHATTER
HEY, IT'S BEEN A WHILE!
HOW HAVE YOU BEEN?
きゃっ OOH!
きゃっ AHH!
WHA--
WHAT?!
ガッ STARE

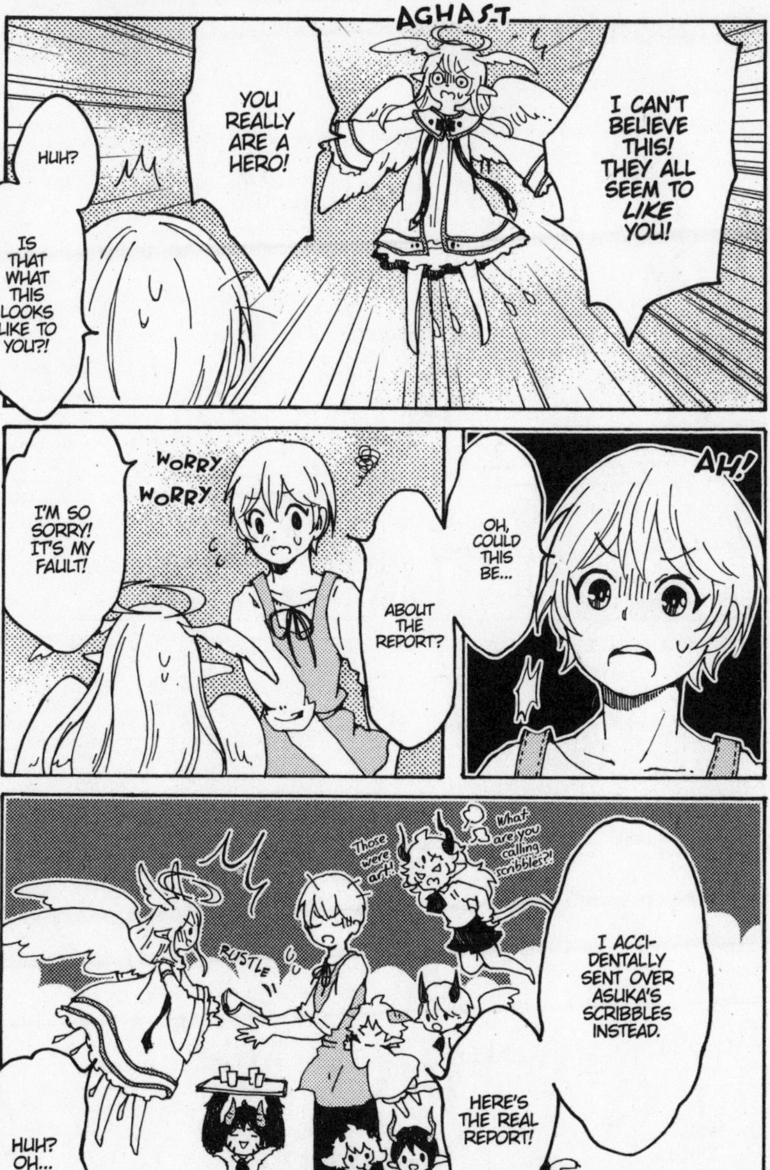
AGHAST
I CAN'T BELIEVE THIS! THEY ALL SEEM TO LIKE YOU!
YOU REALLY ARE A HERO!
HUH?
IS THAT WHAT THIS LOOKS LIKE TO YOU?!
AH!
OH, COULD THIS BE...
ABOUT THE REPORT?
WORRY WORRY
I'M SO SORRY! IT'S MY FAULT!
What are you calling scribbles?!
Those were art!
I ACCI-DENTALLY SENT OVER ASUKA'S SCRIBBLES INSTEAD.
HERE'S THE REAL REPORT!
RUSTLE
HUH? OH...

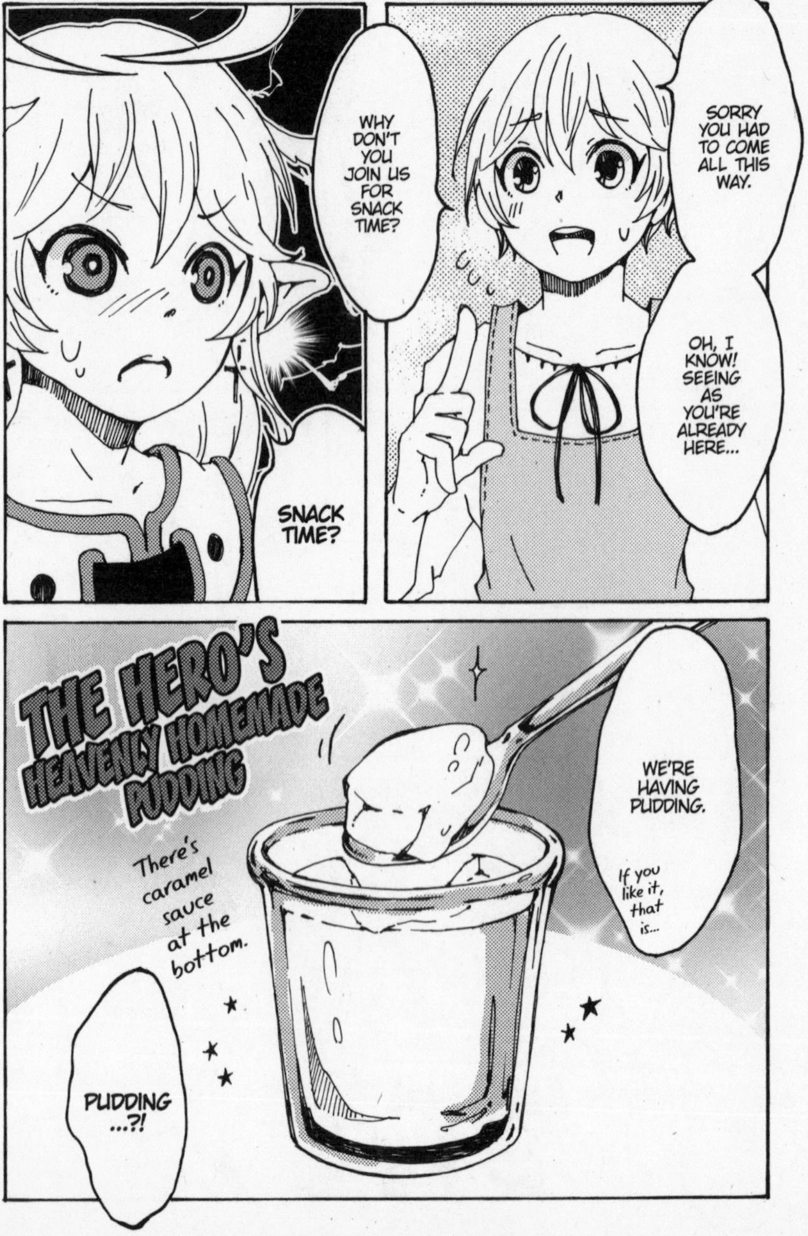
SORRY YOU HAD TO COME ALL THIS WAY.
OH, I KNOW! SEEING AS YOU'RE ALREADY HERE...
WHY DON'T YOU JOIN US FOR SNACK TIME?
SNACK TIME?
WE'RE HAVING PUDDING.
If you like it, that is...
THE HERO'S HEAVENLY HOMEMADE PUDDING
There's caramel sauce at the bottom.
PUDDING ...?!

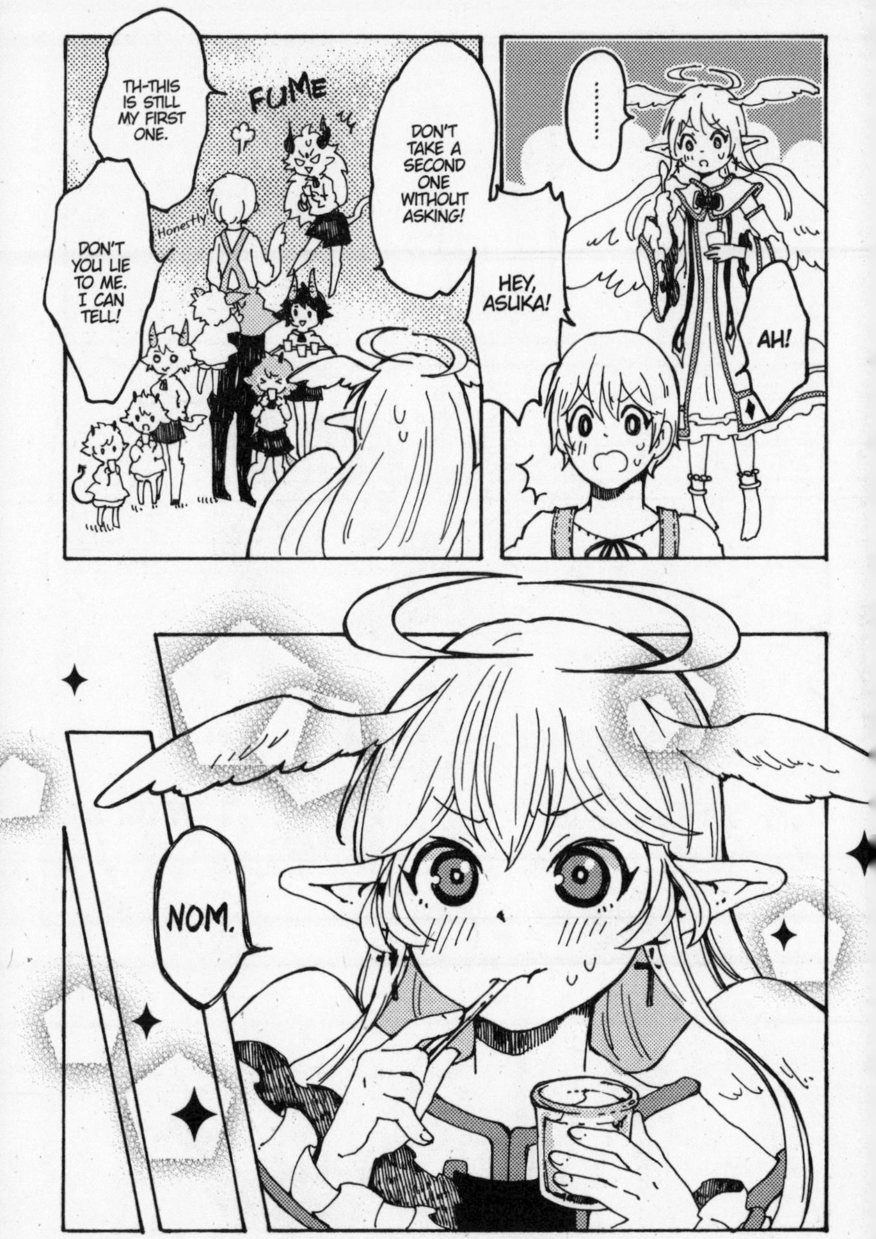
......
HEY, ASUKA!
AH!
DON'T TAKE A SECOND ONE WITHOUT ASKING!
TH-THIS IS STILL MY FIRST ONE.
FUME
Honestly
DON'T YOU LIE TO ME. I CAN TELL!
NOM.

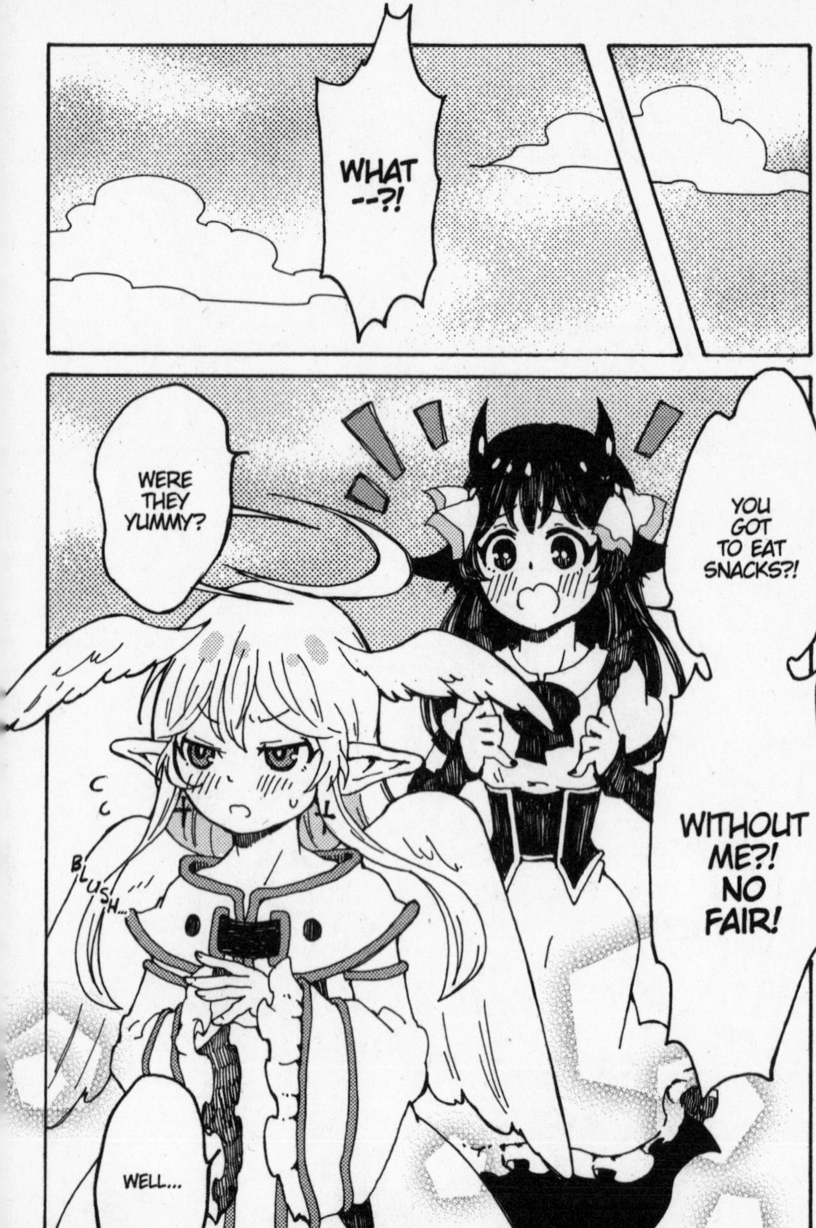
WHAT --?!
YOU GOT TO EAT SNACKS?!
WITHOUT ME?! NO FAIR!
WERE THEY YUMMY?
BLUSH...
WELL...
Yeah.

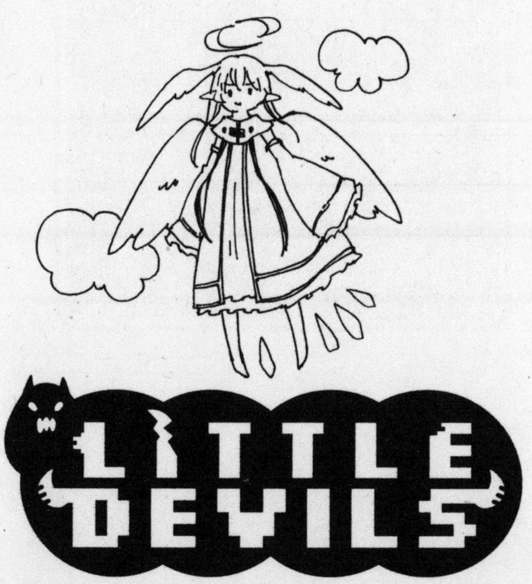

LITTLE DEVILS

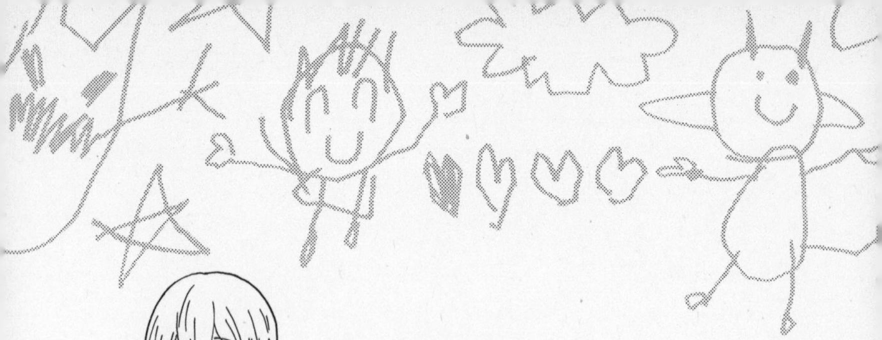

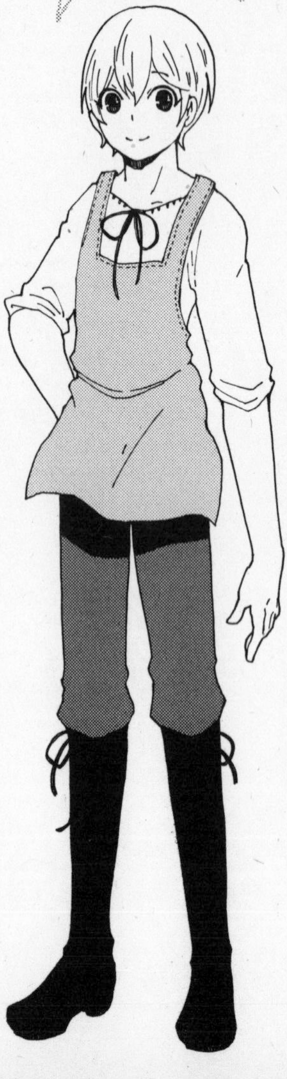

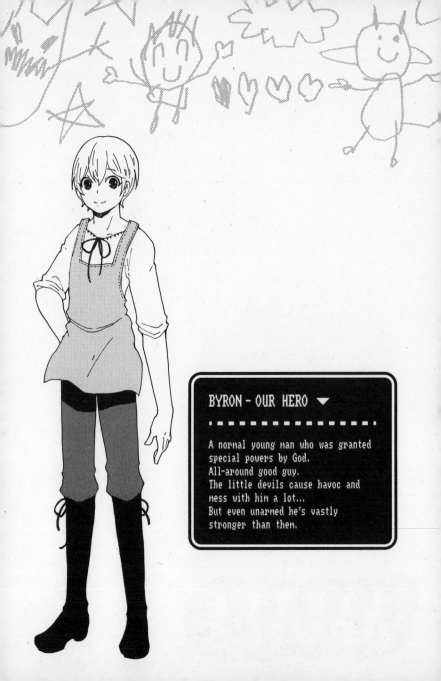

BYRON - OUR HERO ▼

A normal young man who was granted special powers by God.
All-around good guy.
The little devils cause havoc and mess with him a lot...
But even unarmed he's vastly stronger than them.

CHAPTER 5
GREEDY BOOKWORM

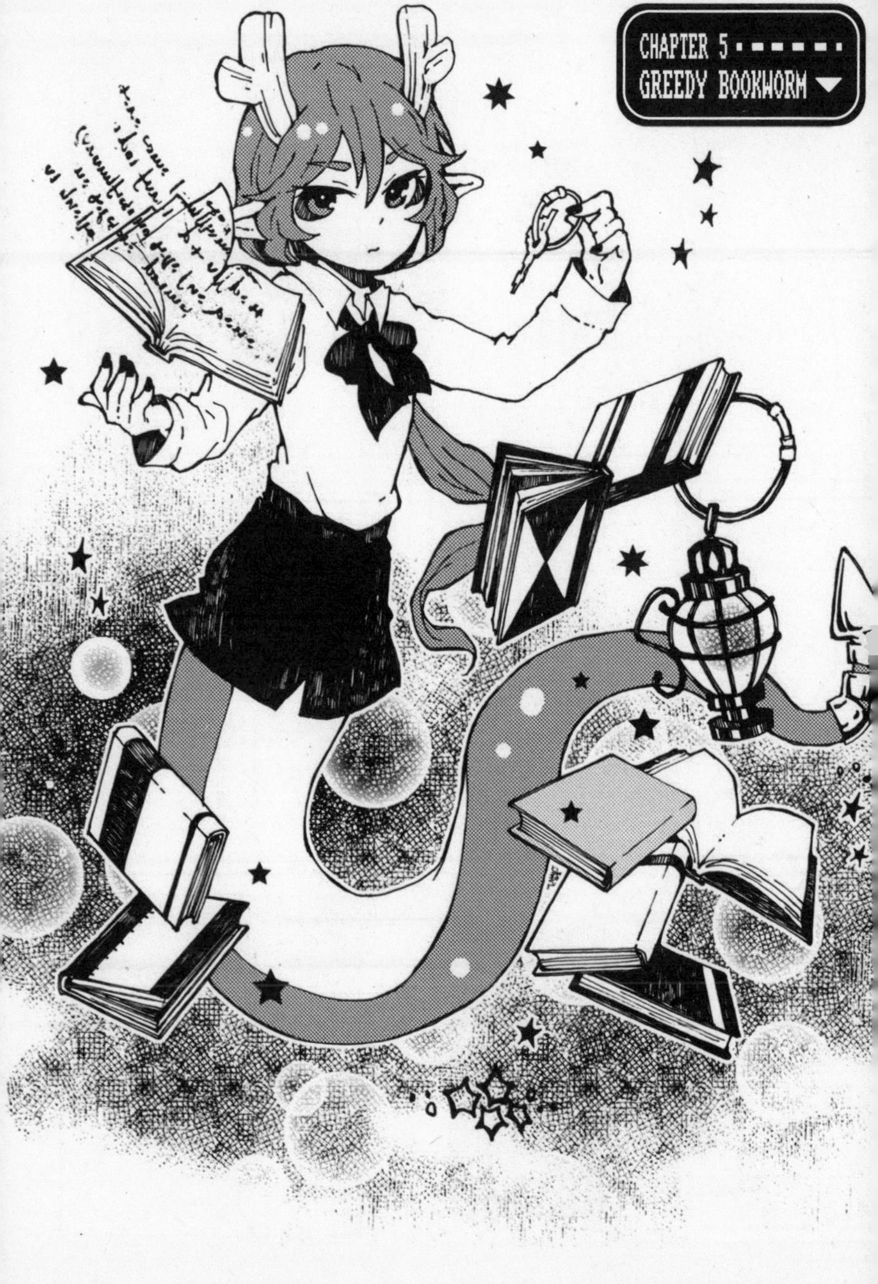

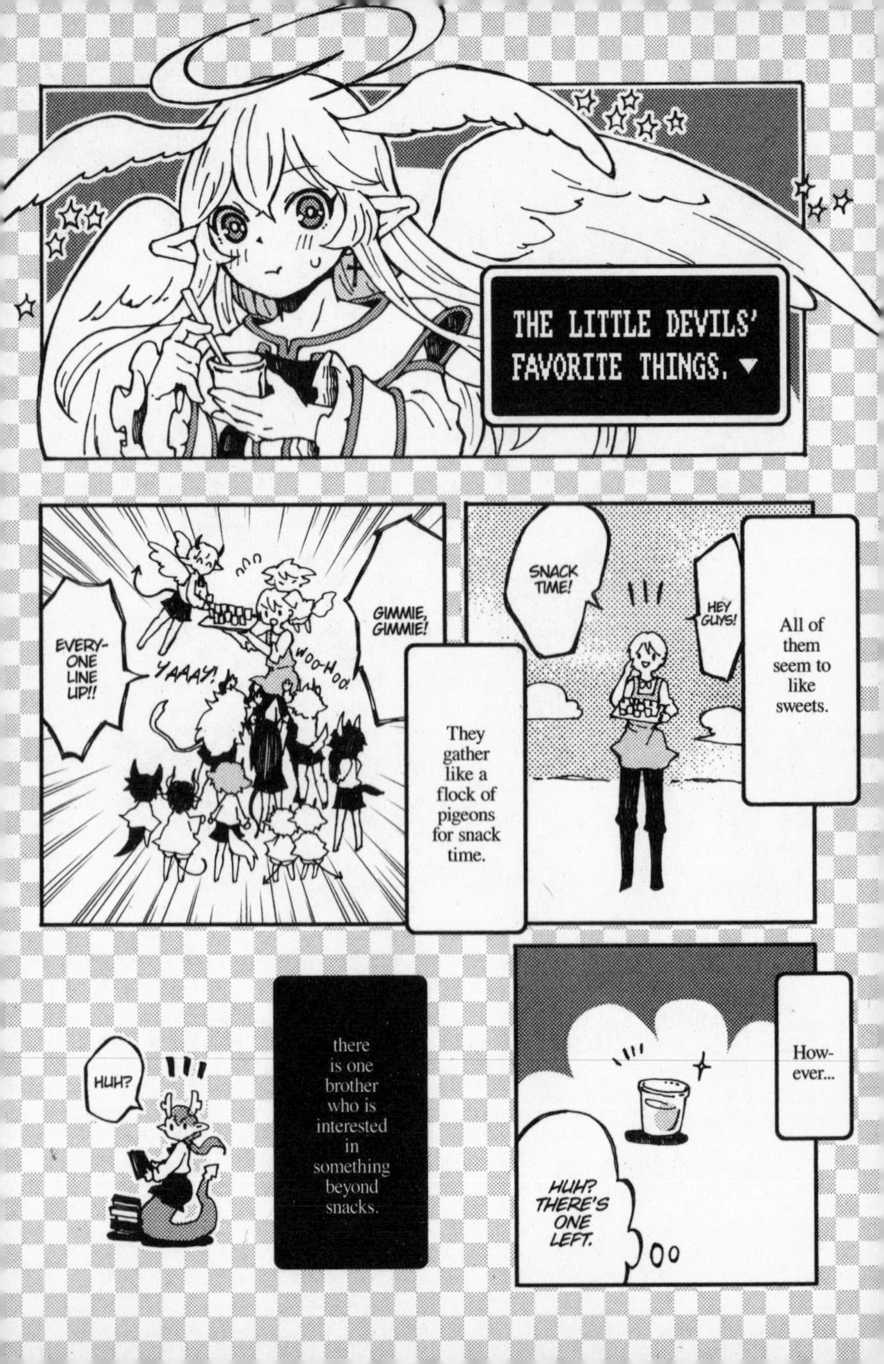
THE LITTLE DEVILS' FAVORITE THINGS.
All of them seem to like sweets.
HEY GUYS!
SNACK TIME!
They gather like a flock of pigeons for snack time.
GIMMIE, GIMMIE!
WOO-HOO!
YAAAY!
EVERY-ONE LINE UP!!
How-ever...
HUH? THERE'S ONE LEFT.
there is one brother who is interested in something beyond snacks.
HUH?

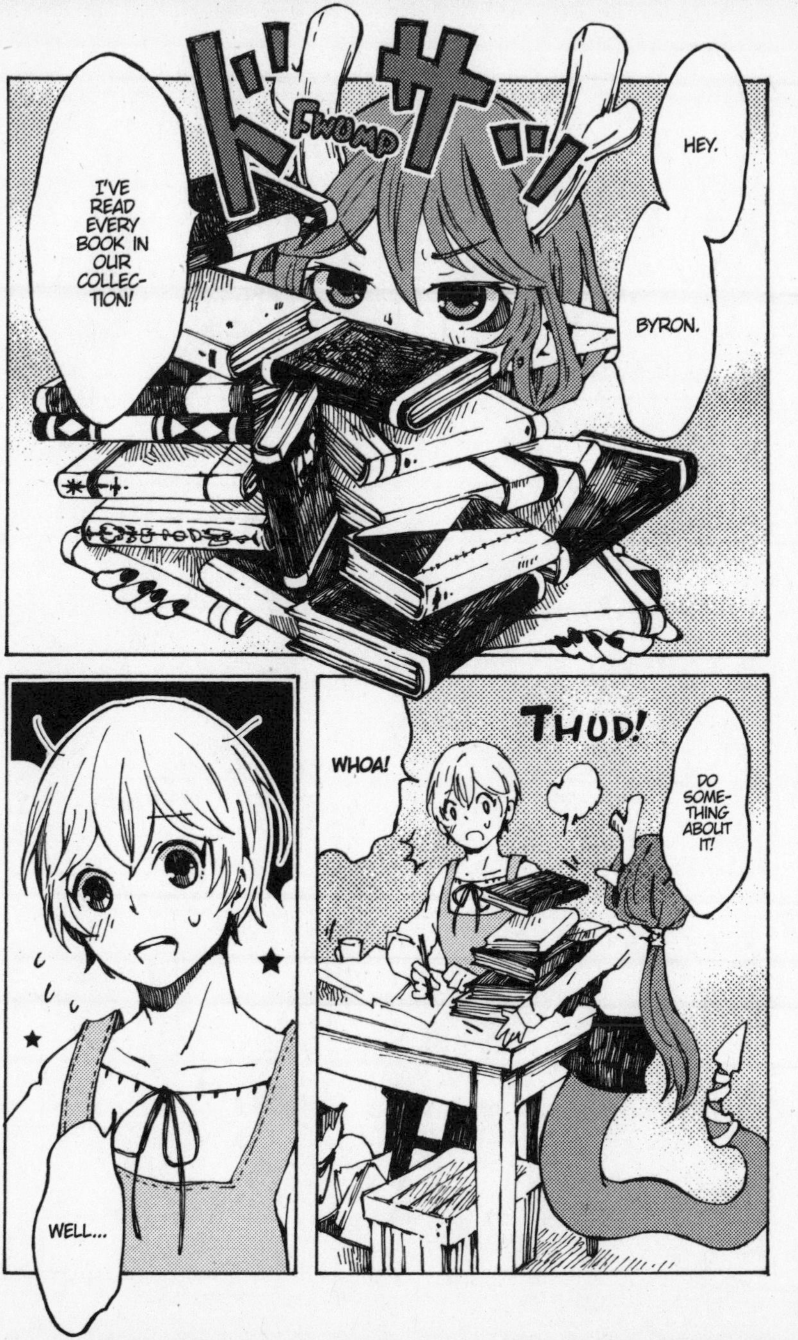
HEY.
BYRON.
ドサッ
FWOMP
I'VE READ EVERY BOOK IN OUR COLLECTION!
DO SOMETHING ABOUT IT!
THUD!
WHOA!
WELL...

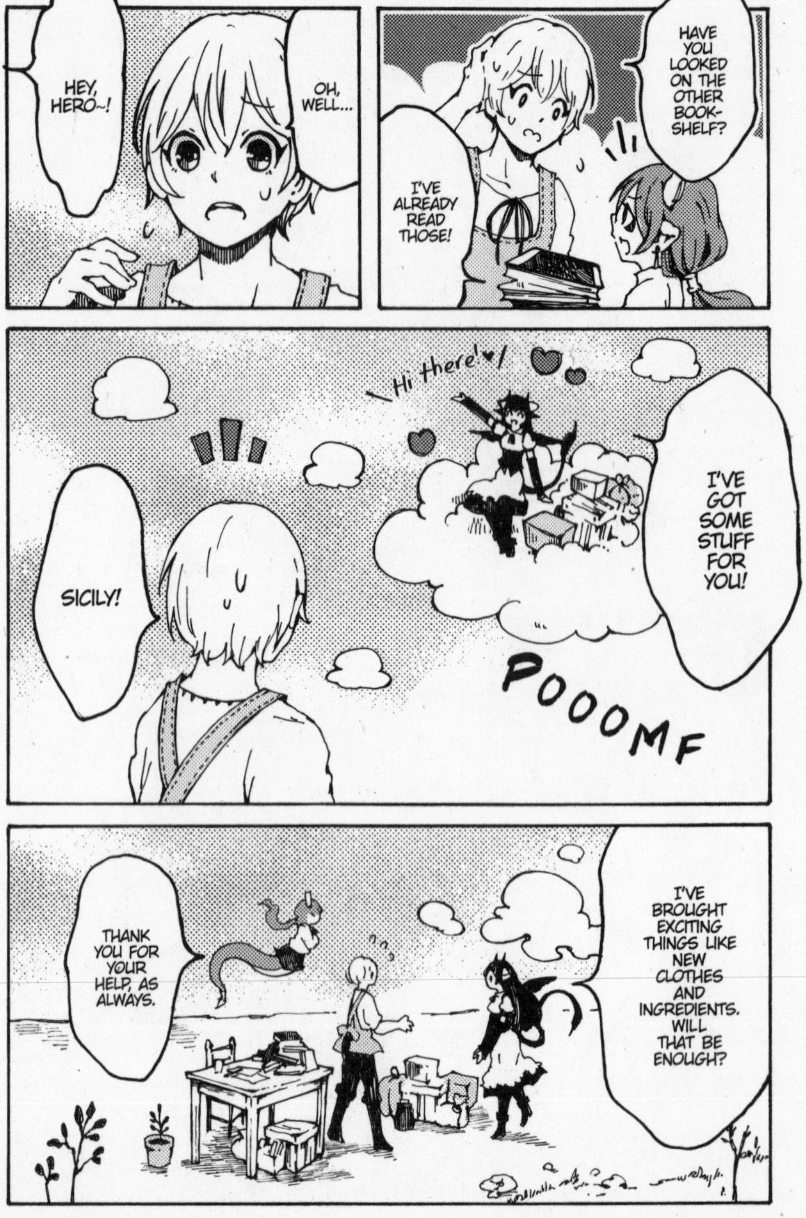
HAVE YOU LOOKED ON THE OTHER BOOK-SHELF?
I'VE ALREADY READ THOSE!
OH, WELL...
HEY, HERO~!
I'VE GOT SOME STUFF FOR YOU!
Hi there!♥
SICILY!
POOOMF
I'VE BROUGHT EXCITING THINGS LIKE NEW CLOTHES AND INGREDIENTS. WILL THAT BE ENOUGH?
THANK YOU FOR YOUR HELP, AS ALWAYS.

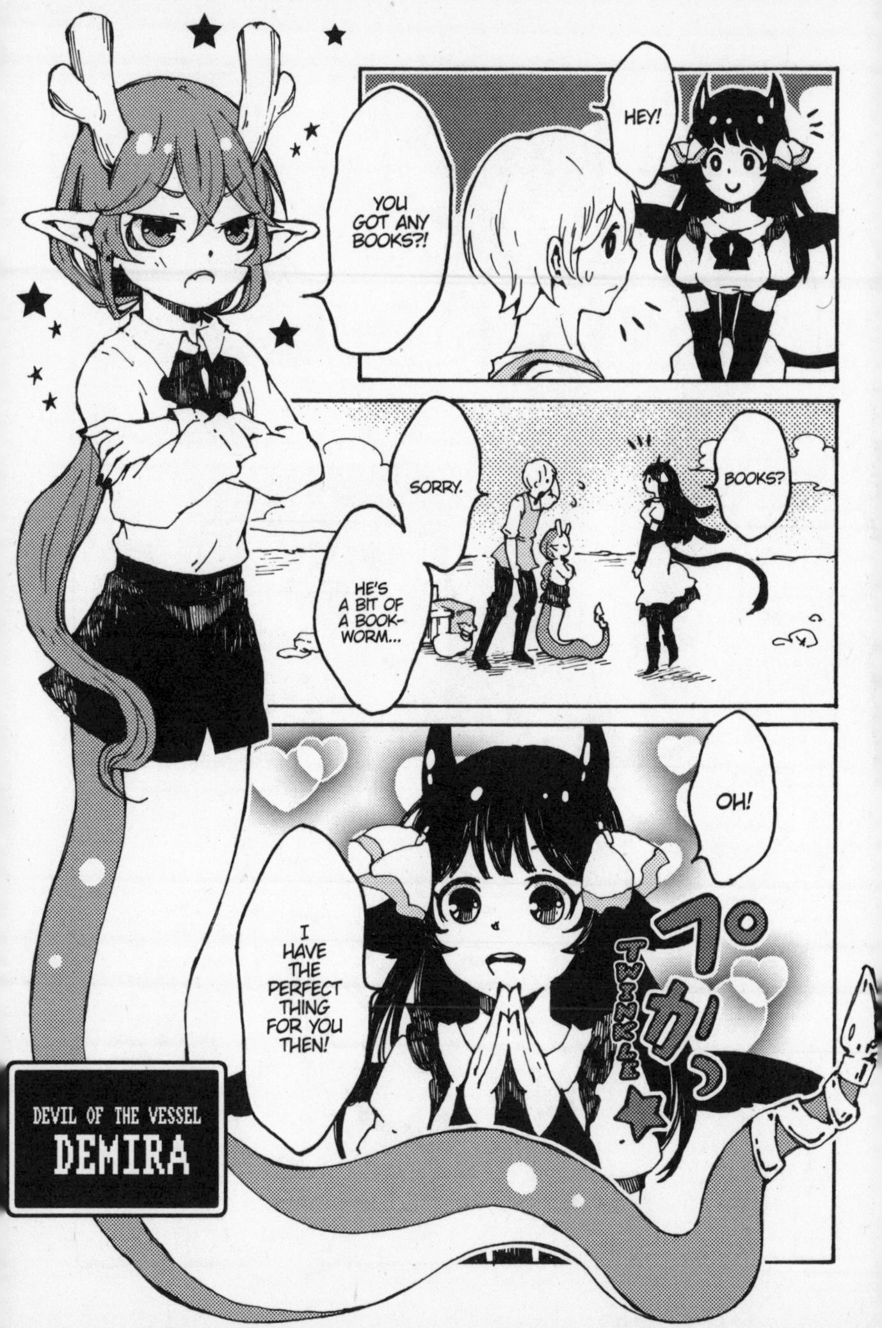
HEY!
YOU GOT ANY BOOKS?!
BOOKS?
SORRY.
HE'S A BIT OF A BOOK-WORM...
OH!
ぺかっ
TWINKLE
I HAVE THE PERFECT THING FOR YOU THEN!
DEVIL OF THE VESSEL
DEMIRA

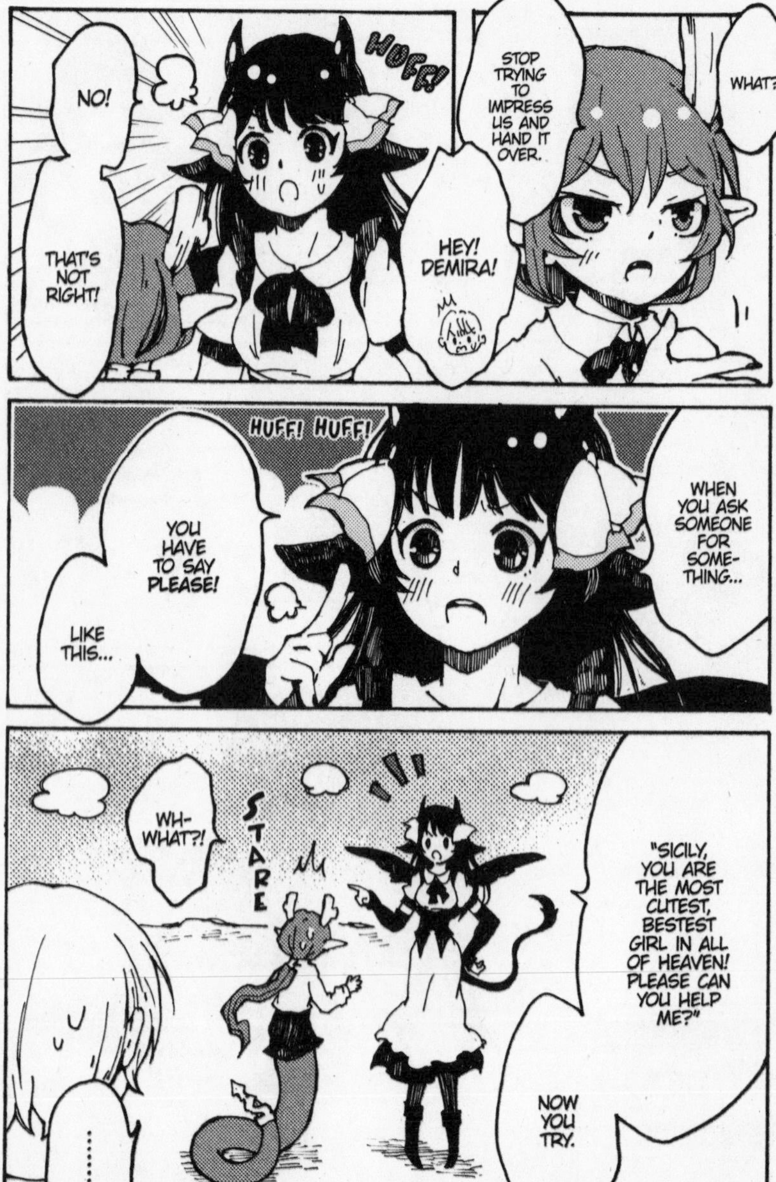
WHAT?
STOP TRYING TO IMPRESS US AND HAND IT OVER.
HEY! DEMIRA!
HUFF!
NO!
THAT'S NOT RIGHT!
WHEN YOU ASK SOMEONE FOR SOME-THING...
HUFF! HUFF!
YOU HAVE TO SAY PLEASE!
LIKE THIS...
"SICILY, YOU ARE THE MOST CUTEST, BESTEST GIRL IN ALL OF HEAVEN! PLEASE CAN YOU HELP ME?"
NOW YOU TRY.
!!
STARE
WH-WHAT?!
....

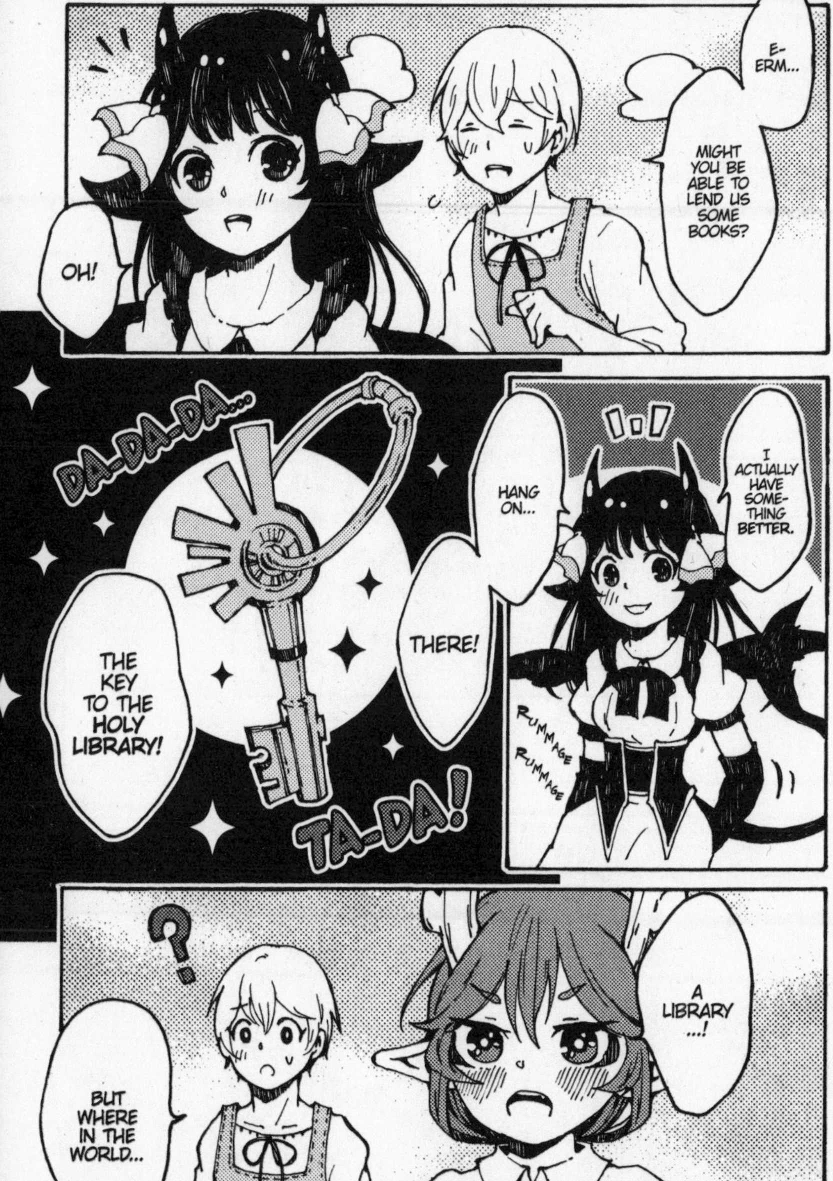
E-ERM...
MIGHT YOU BE ABLE TO LEND US SOME BOOKS?
OH!
I ACTUALLY HAVE SOME-THING BETTER.
HANG ON...
RUMMAGE RUMMAGE
THERE!
DA-DA-DA...
THE KEY TO THE HOLY LIBRARY!
TA-DA!
A LIBRARY ...!
BUT WHERE IN THE WORLD...

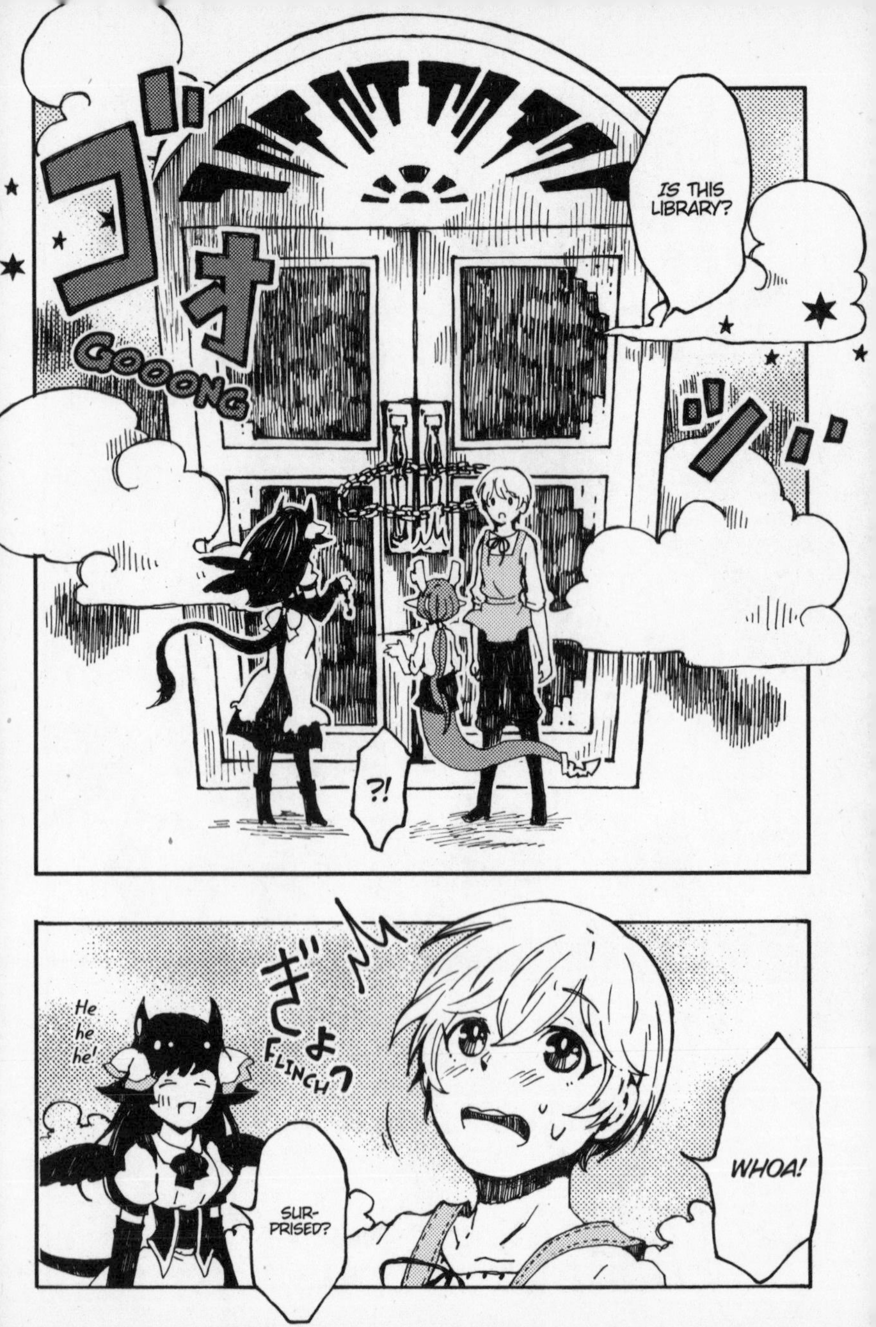
IS THIS LIBRARY?
GOOOONG
?!
WHOA!
ぎょっ
FLINCH
SUR-PRISED?
He he he!

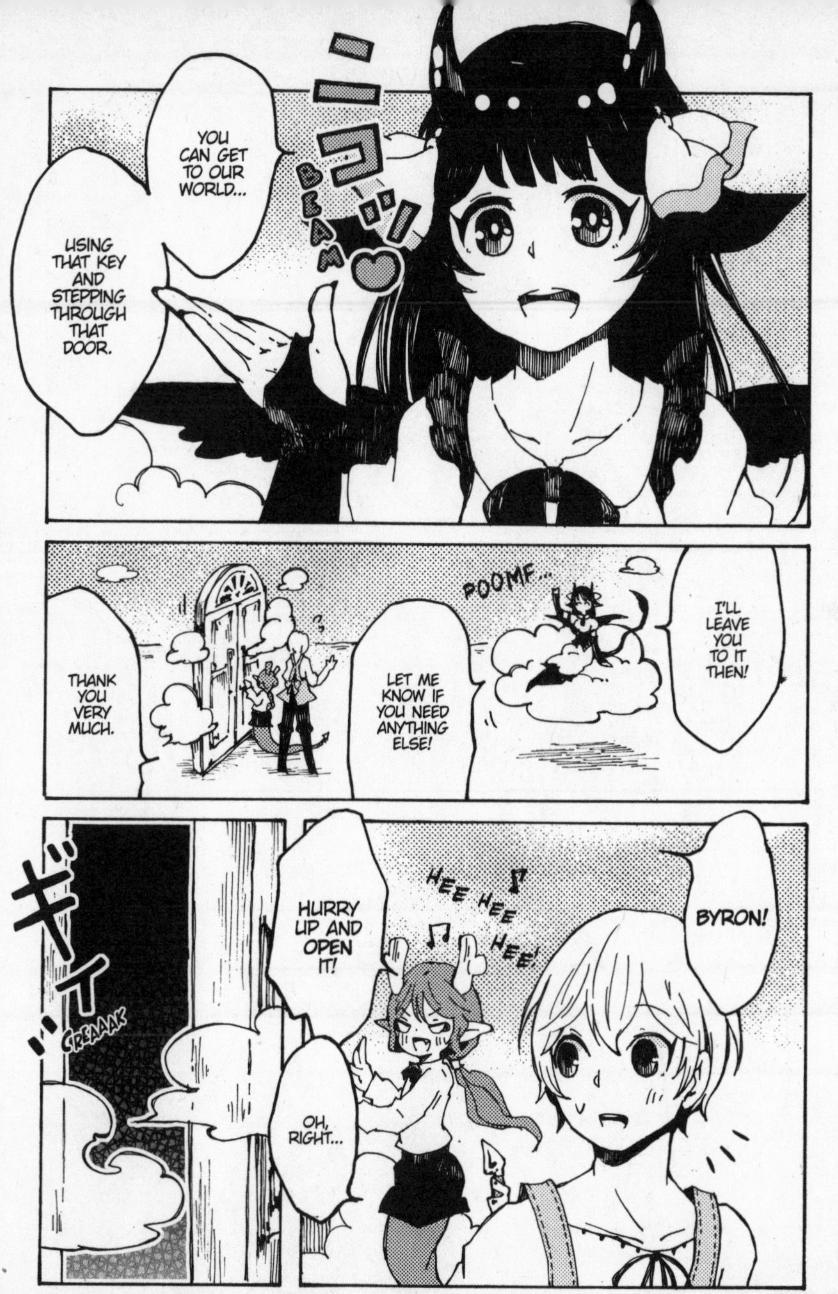
YOU CAN GET TO OUR WORLD...
USING THAT KEY AND STEPPING THROUGH THAT DOOR.
BEAM
I'LL LEAVE YOU TO IT THEN!
POOMF...
LET ME KNOW IF YOU NEED ANYTHING ELSE!
THANK YOU VERY MUCH.
BYRON!
HEE HEE HEE!
HURRY UP AND OPEN IT!
OH, RIGHT...
CREAAAK

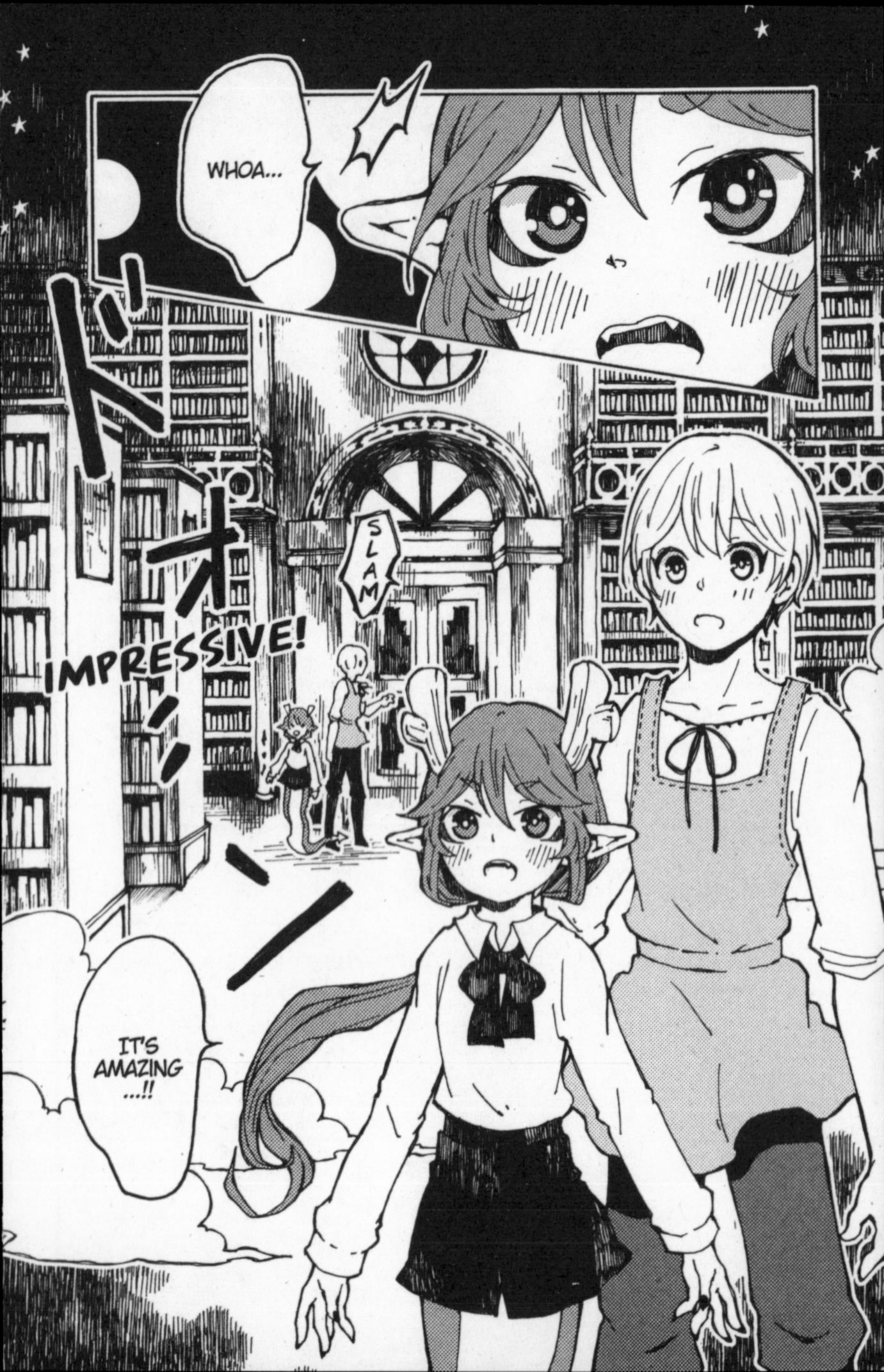
WHOA...
SLAM
IMPRESSIVE!
IT'S AMAZING ...!!

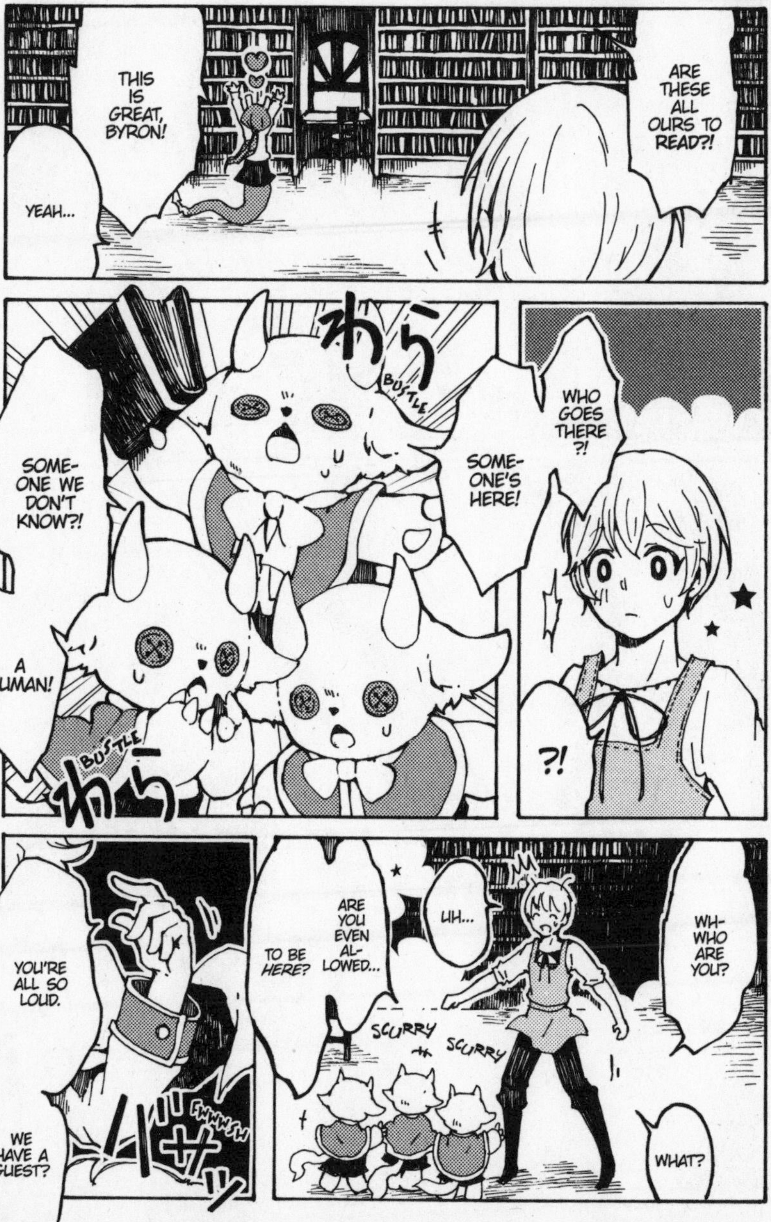
ARE THESE ALL OURS TO READ?!
THIS IS GREAT, BYRON!
YEAH...
WHO GOES THERE?!
?!
SOME-ONE'S HERE!
わら
BUSTLE
SOME-ONE WE DON'T KNOW?!
A HUMAN!
BUSTLE
わら
WH-WHO ARE YOU?
UH...
ARE YOU EVEN AL-LOWED...
TO BE HERE?
SCURRY
SCURRY
WHAT?
YOU'RE ALL SO LOUD.
WE HAVE A GUEST?

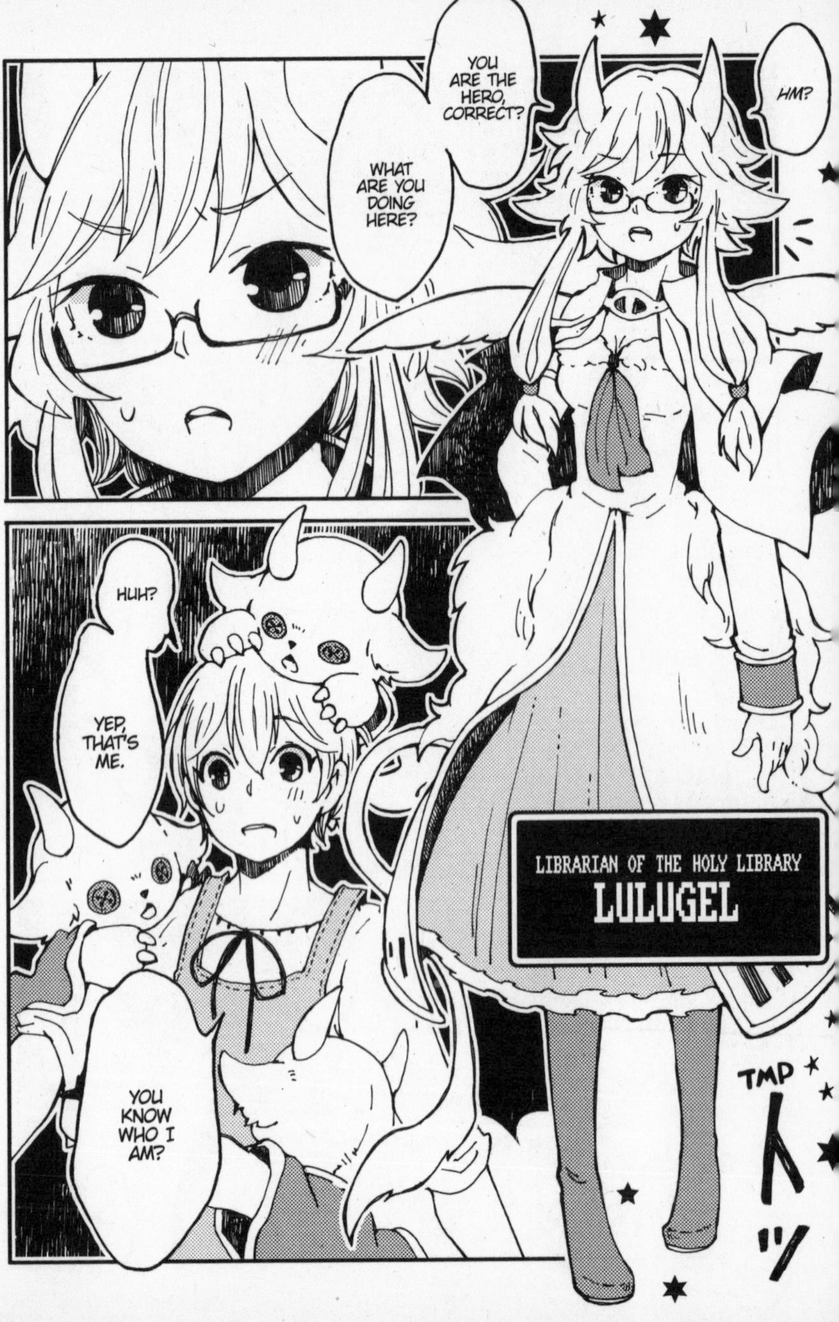
HM?
LIBRARIAN OF THE HOLY LIBRARY
LULUGEL
TMP
YOU ARE THE HERO, CORRECT?
WHAT ARE YOU DOING HERE?
HUH?
YEP, THAT'S ME.
YOU KNOW WHO I AM?

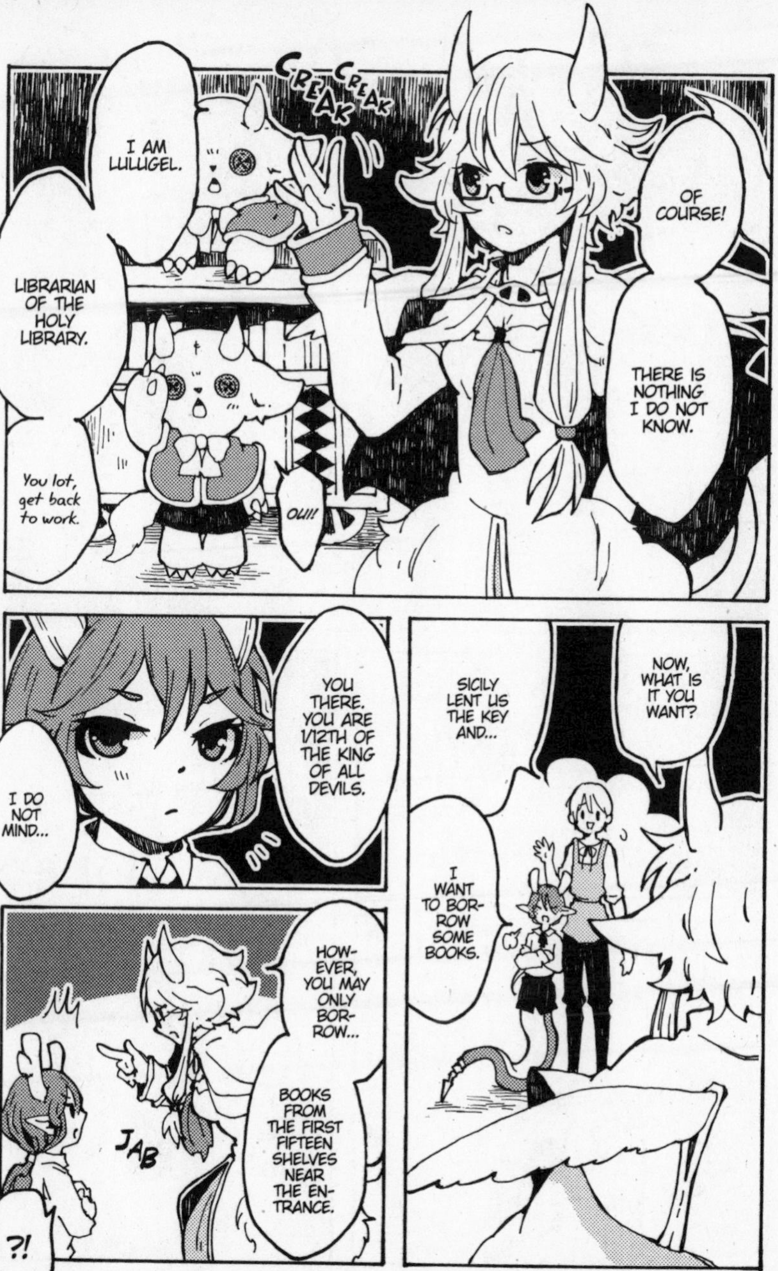
OF COURSE!
THERE IS NOTHING I DO NOT KNOW.
CREAK CREAK
I AM LULUGEL.
LIBRARIAN OF THE HOLY LIBRARY.
OUI!!
You lot, get back to work.
NOW, WHAT IS IT YOU WANT?
SICILY LENT US THE KEY AND...
I WANT TO BOR-ROW SOME BOOKS.
YOU THERE. YOU ARE 1/12TH OF THE KING OF ALL DEVILS.
I DO NOT MIND...
HOW-EVER, YOU MAY ONLY BOR-ROW...
BOOKS FROM THE FIRST FIFTEEN SHELVES NEAR THE EN-TRANCE.
JAB
?!

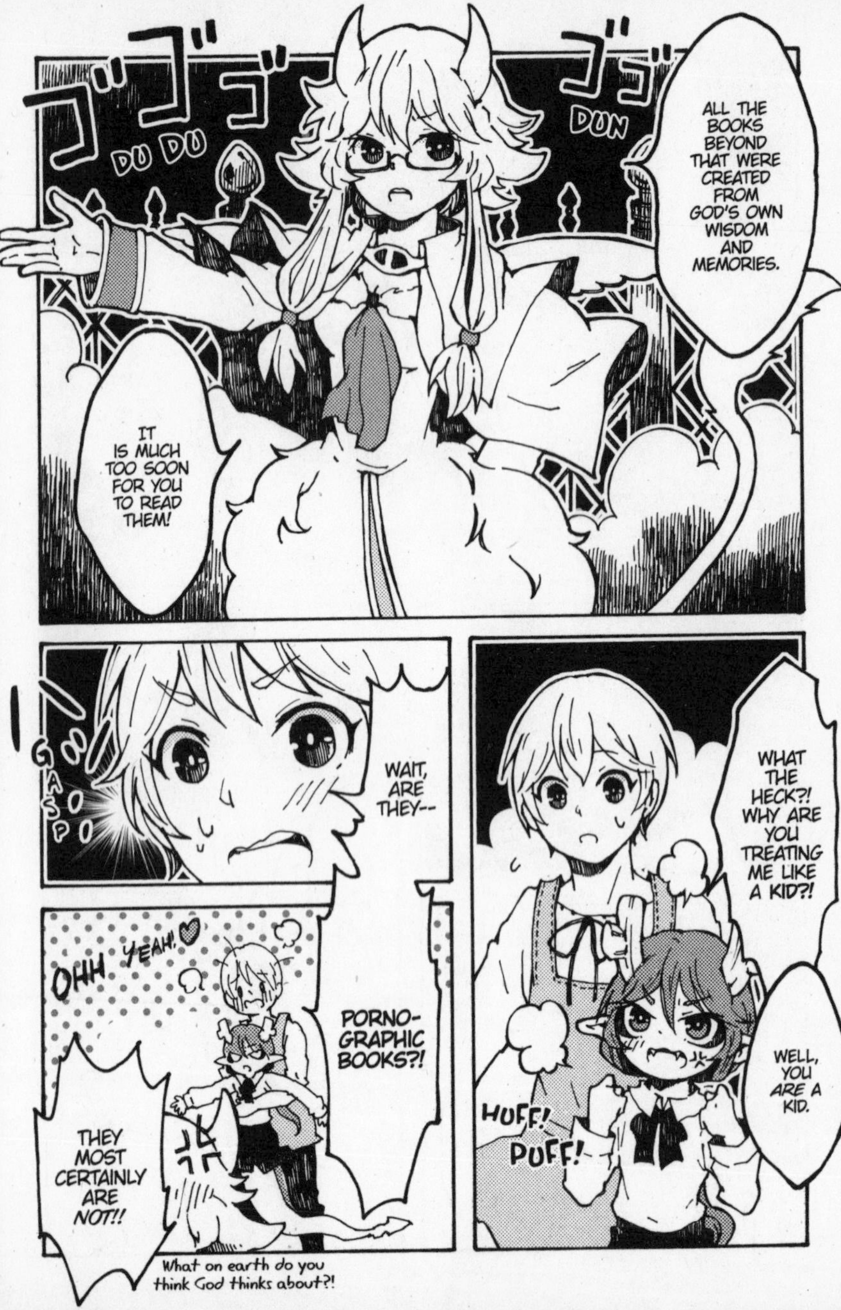
ゴゴ
DUN
ALL THE BOOKS BEYOND THAT WERE CREATED FROM GOD'S OWN WISDOM AND MEMORIES.
ゴゴゴ
DU DU
IT IS MUCH TOO SOON FOR YOU TO READ THEM!
WHAT THE HECK?! WHY ARE YOU TREATING ME LIKE A KID?!
WELL, YOU *ARE* A KID.
HUFF! PUFF!
WAIT, ARE THEY--
GASP
PORNO-GRAPHIC BOOKS?!
OHH YEAH!♥
THEY MOST CERTAINLY ARE *NOT*!!
What on earth do you think God thinks about?!

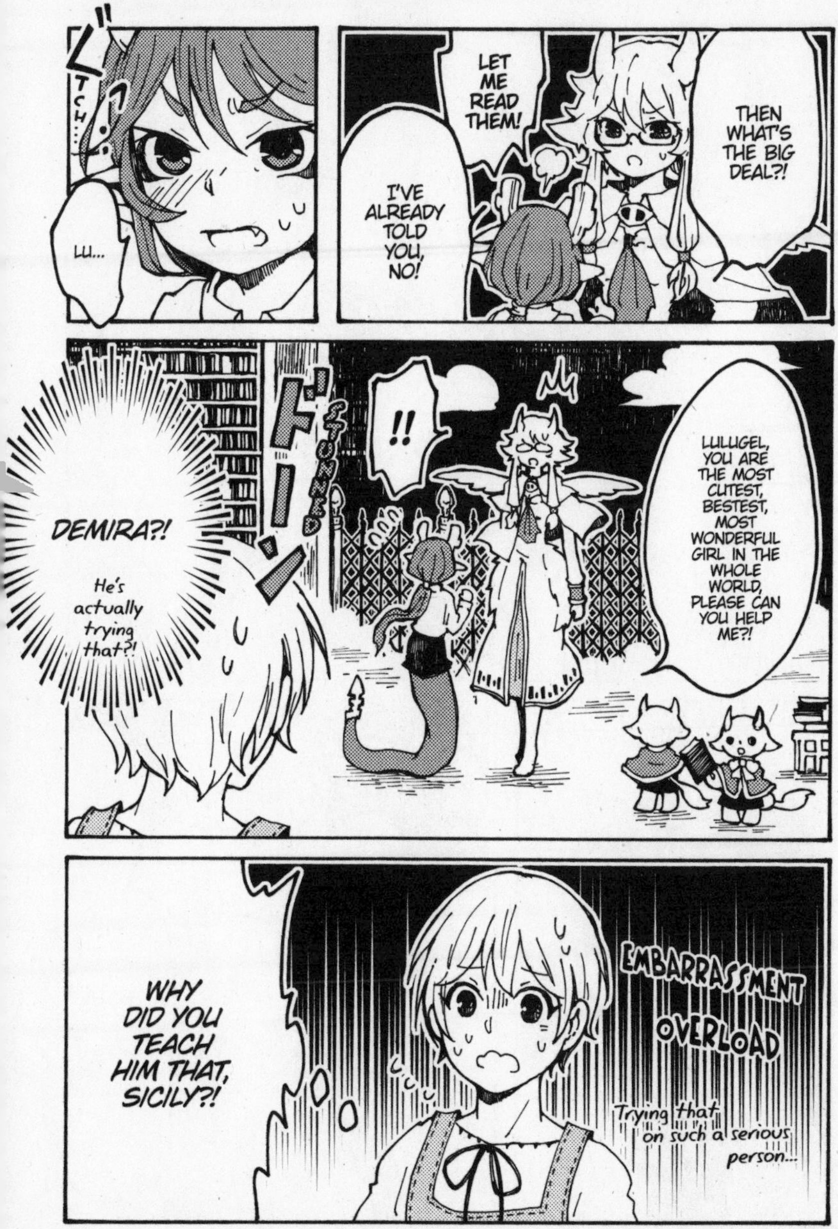
THEN WHAT'S THE BIG DEAL?!
LET ME READ THEM!
I'VE ALREADY TOLD YOU, NO!
TCH...
LU...
LULUGEL, YOU ARE THE MOST CUTEST, BESTEST, MOST WONDERFUL GIRL IN THE WHOLE WORLD, PLEASE CAN YOU HELP ME?!
!!
ドー!
STUNNED
DEMIRA?!
He's actually trying that?!
EMBARRASSMENT OVERLOAD
Trying that on such a serious person...
WHY DID YOU TEACH HIM THAT, SICILY?!

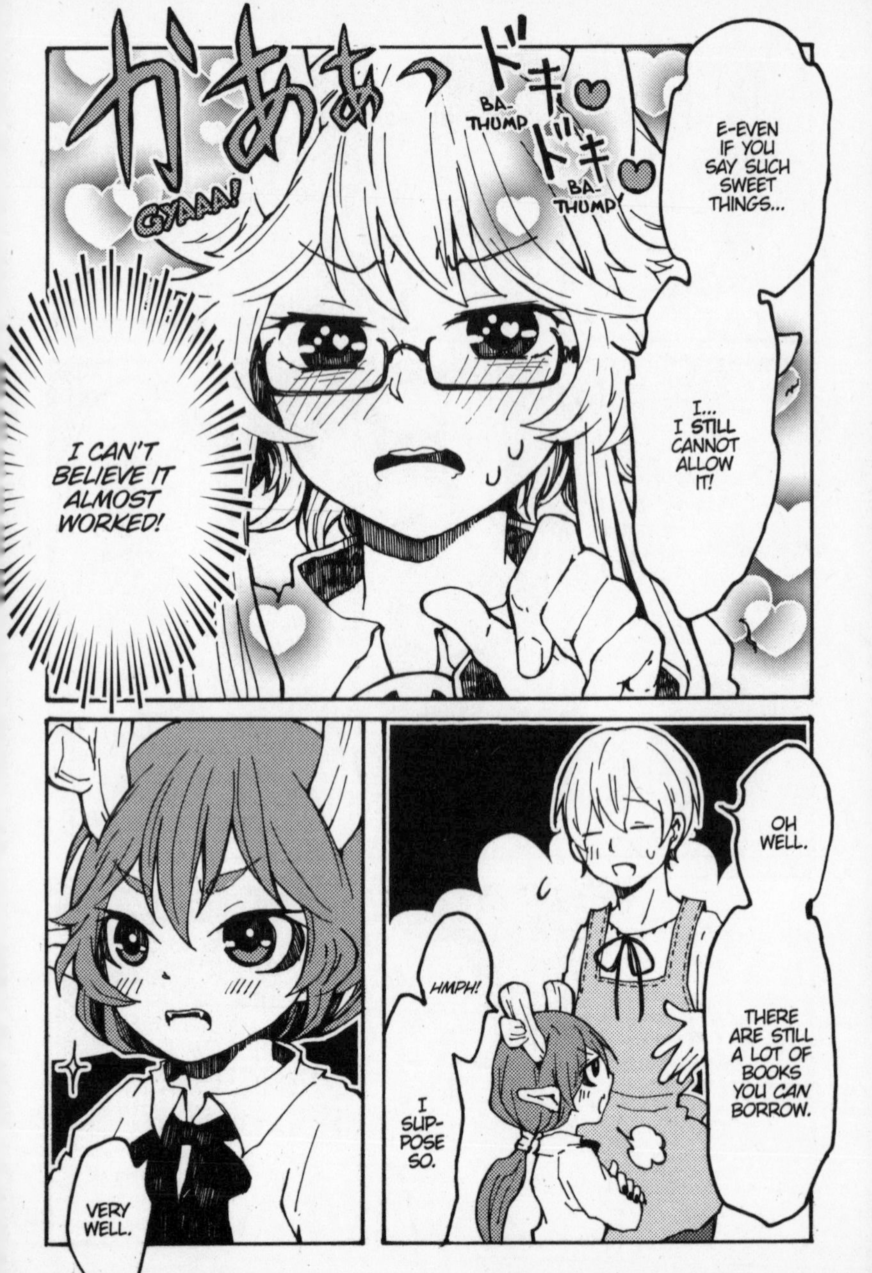
E-EVEN IF YOU SAY SUCH SWEET THINGS...
I... I STILL CANNOT ALLOW IT!
ドキ
BA-THUMP
ドキ
BA-THUMP
かあぁっ
GYAAA!
I CAN'T BELIEVE IT ALMOST WORKED!
OH WELL.
THERE ARE STILL A LOT OF BOOKS YOU CAN BORROW.
HMPH!
I SUP-POSE SO.
VERY WELL.

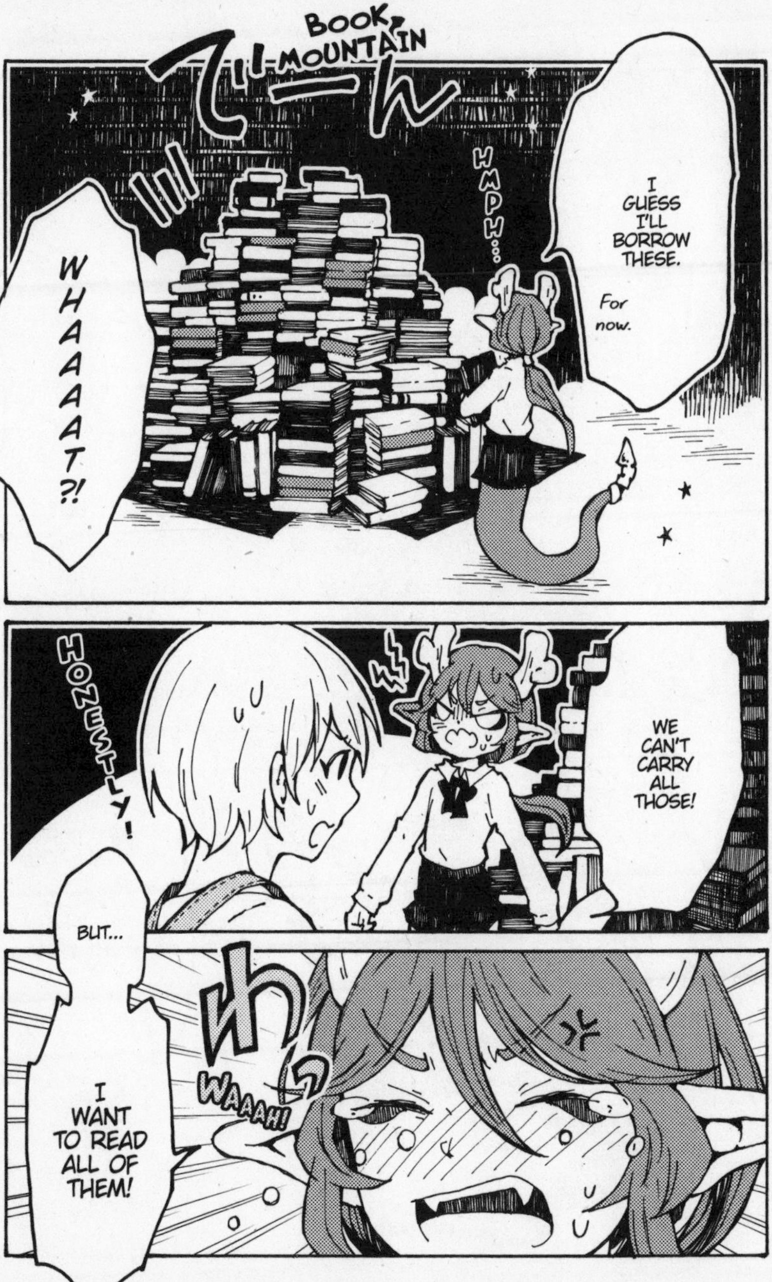
BOOK MOUNTAIN
てーん
I GUESS I'LL BORROW THESE.
For now.
HMPH...
WHAAAAAT?!
WE CAN'T CARRY ALL THOSE!
HONESTLY!
BUT...
I WANT TO READ ALL OF THEM!
わっ
WAAAH!

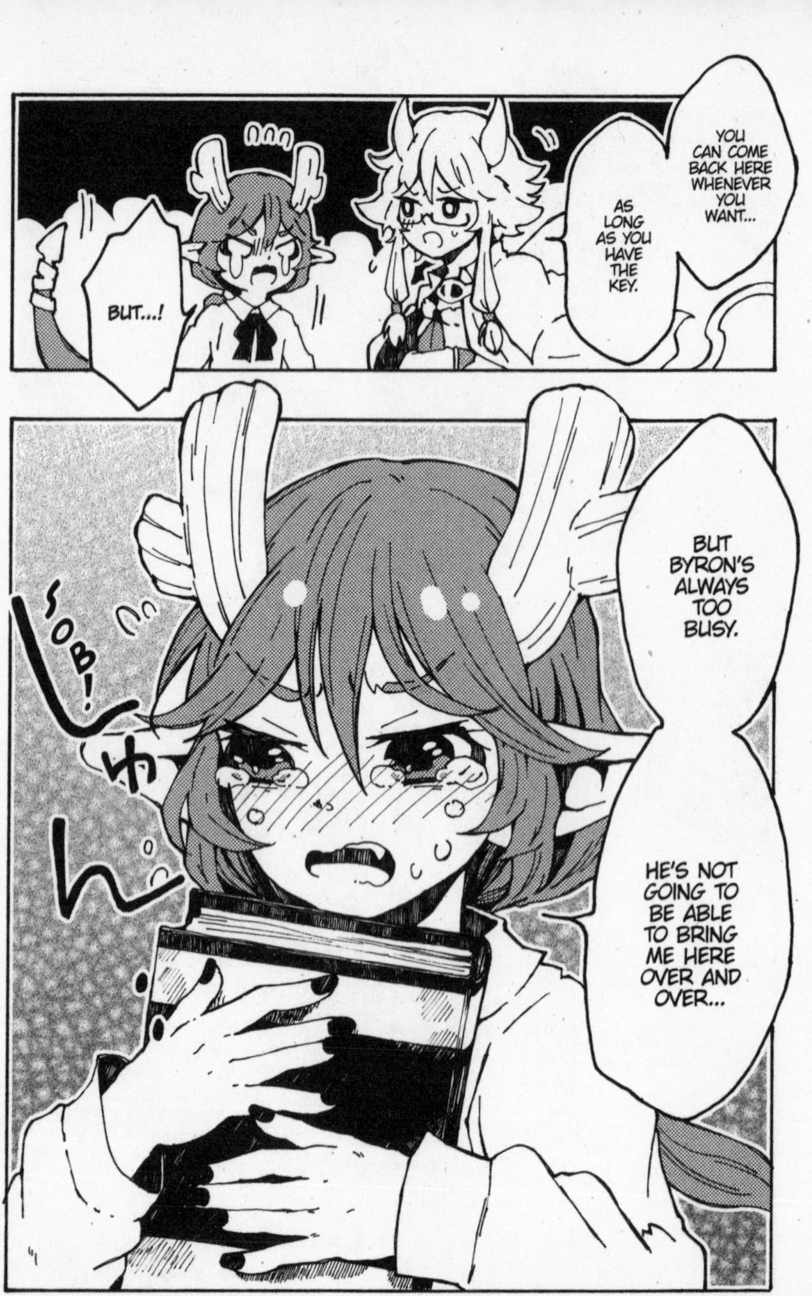
YOU CAN COME BACK HERE WHENEVER YOU WANT...
AS LONG AS YOU HAVE THE KEY.
BUT...!
BUT BYRON'S ALWAYS TOO BUSY.
HE'S NOT GOING TO BE ABLE TO BRING ME HERE OVER AND OVER...
SOB!
しゅん

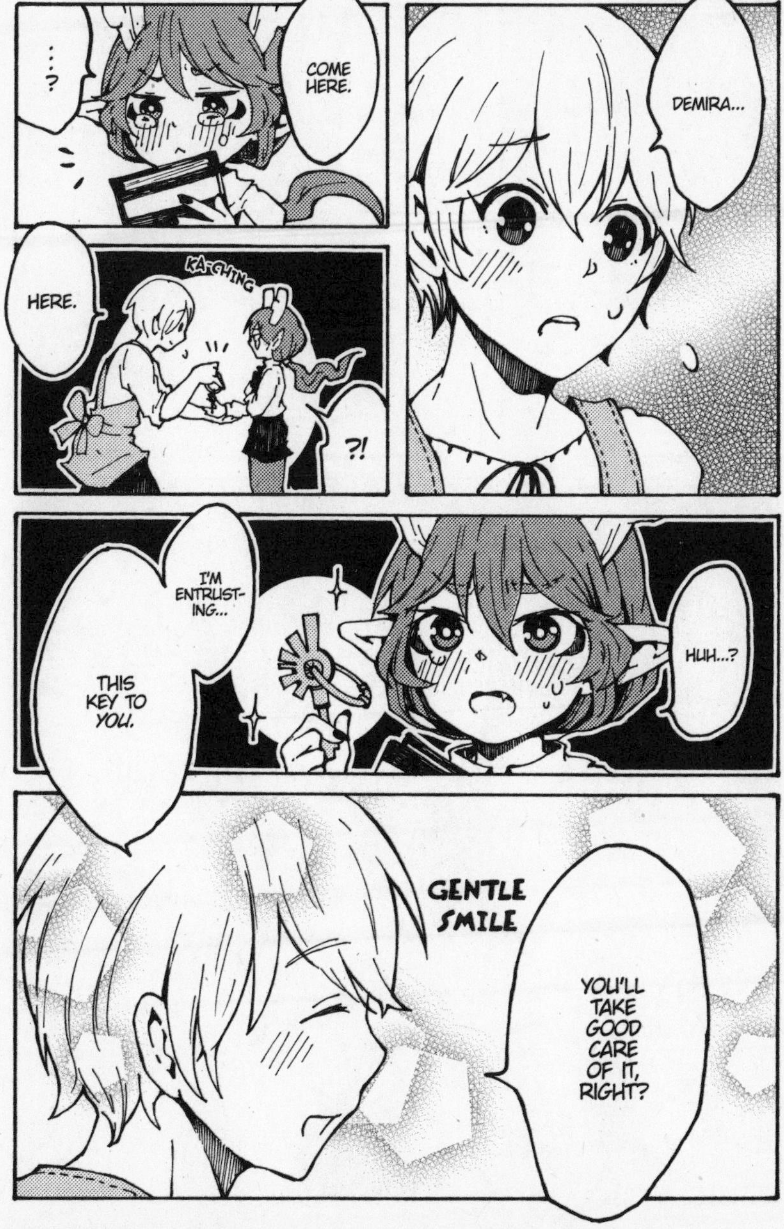
DEMIRA...
COME HERE.
...?
HERE.
KA-CHING
?!
HUH...?
I'M ENTRUST-ING...
THIS KEY TO YOU.
GENTLE SMILE
YOU'LL TAKE GOOD CARE OF IT, RIGHT?

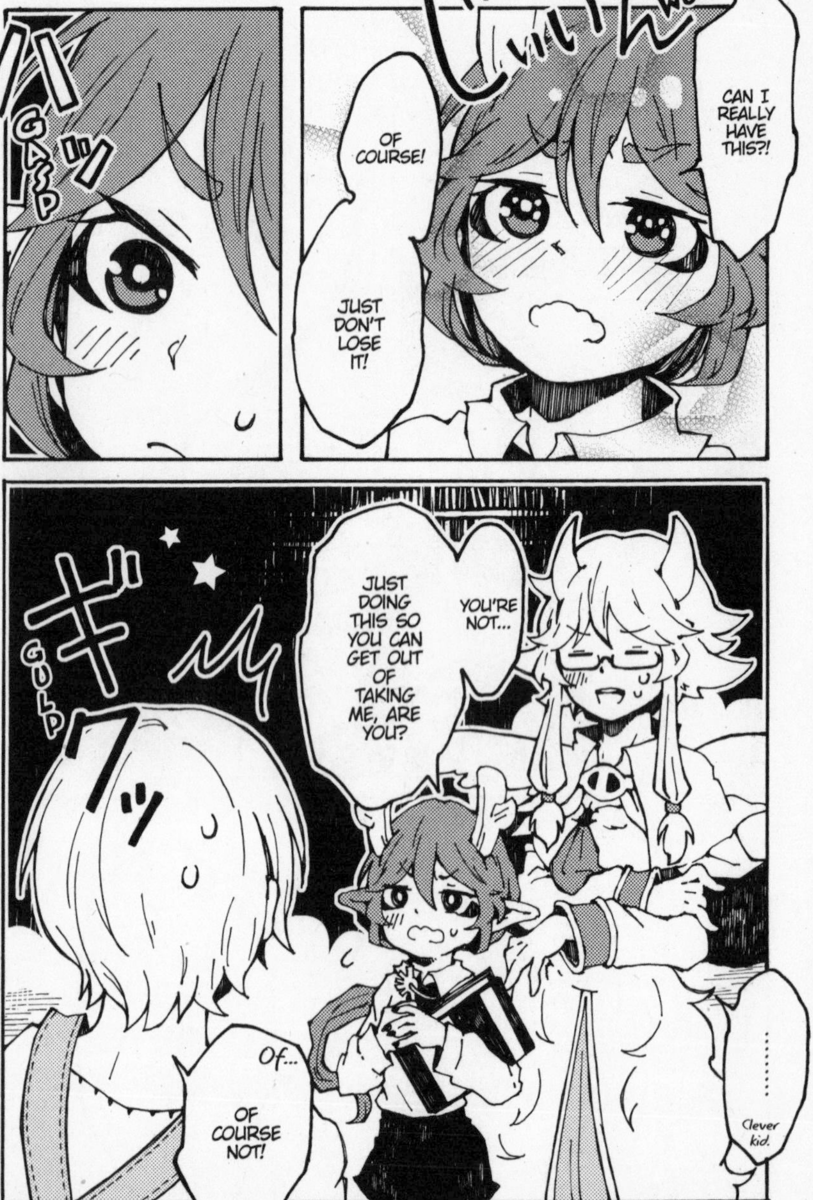
CAN I REALLY HAVE THIS?!
じぃぃん
wow...
OF COURSE!
JUST DON'T LOSE IT!
ハッ
GASP
YOU'RE NOT...
JUST DOING THIS SO YOU CAN GET OUT OF TAKING ME, ARE YOU?
ギクッ
GULP
......
Clever kid.
Of...
OF COURSE NOT!

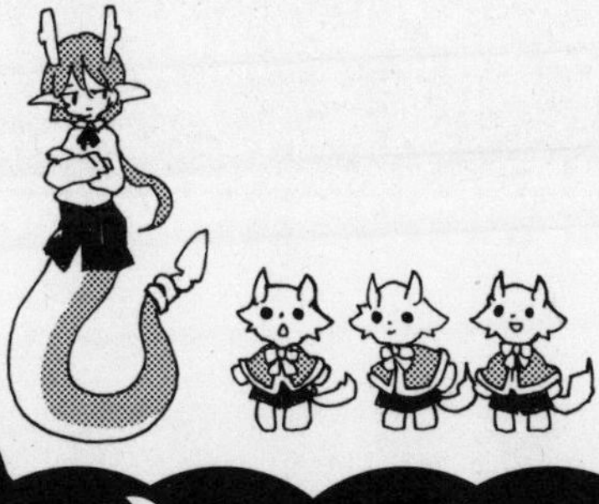

LITTLE DEVILS

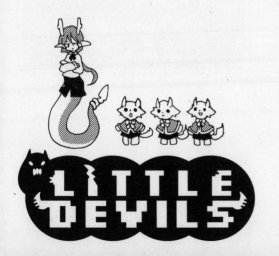

DEVIL OF THE VESSEL-DEMIRA ▼

....

The cool-tempered fifth eldest devil.
Bookworm.
Slithers on his tail.
People sometimes step on his tail so
Kaiser made a special armored tip for
it.

CHAPTER 6
A RECIPE TO CHARM

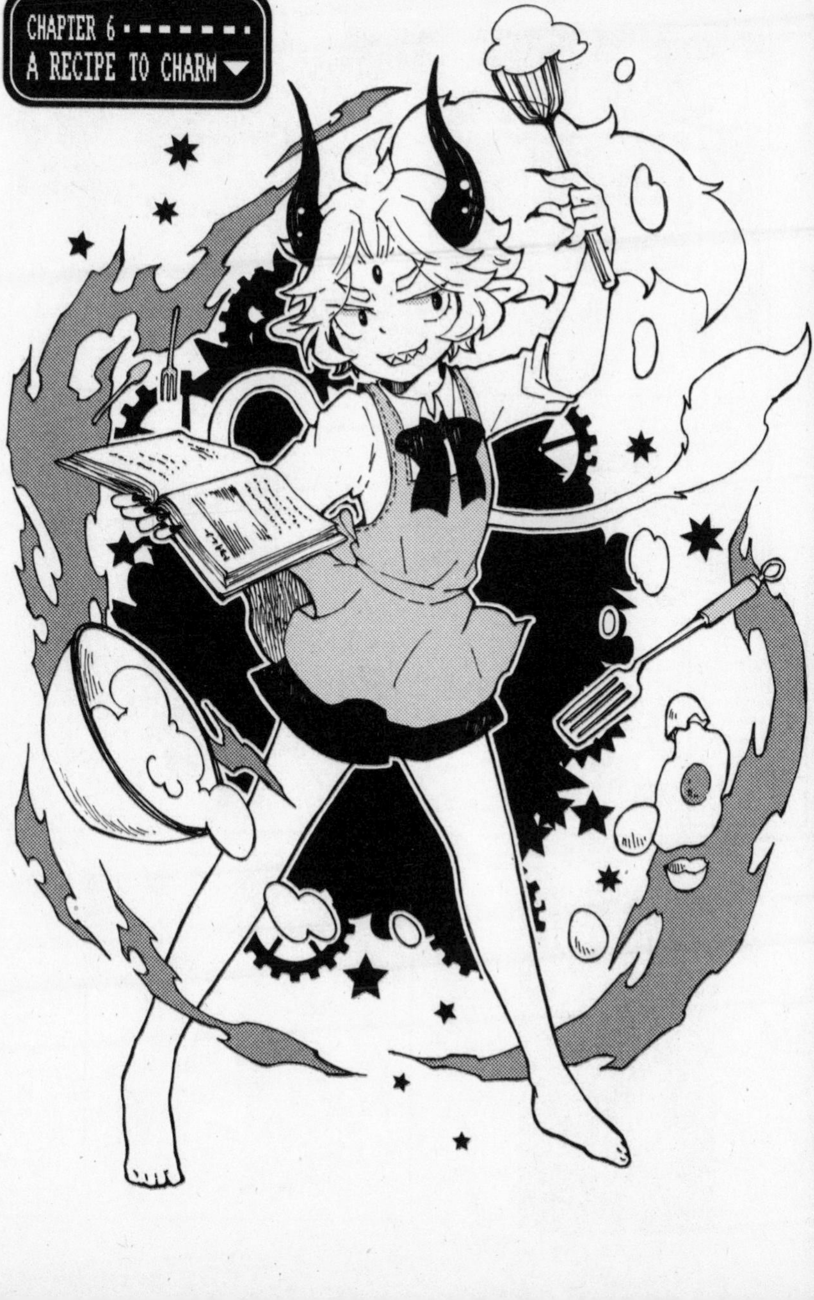

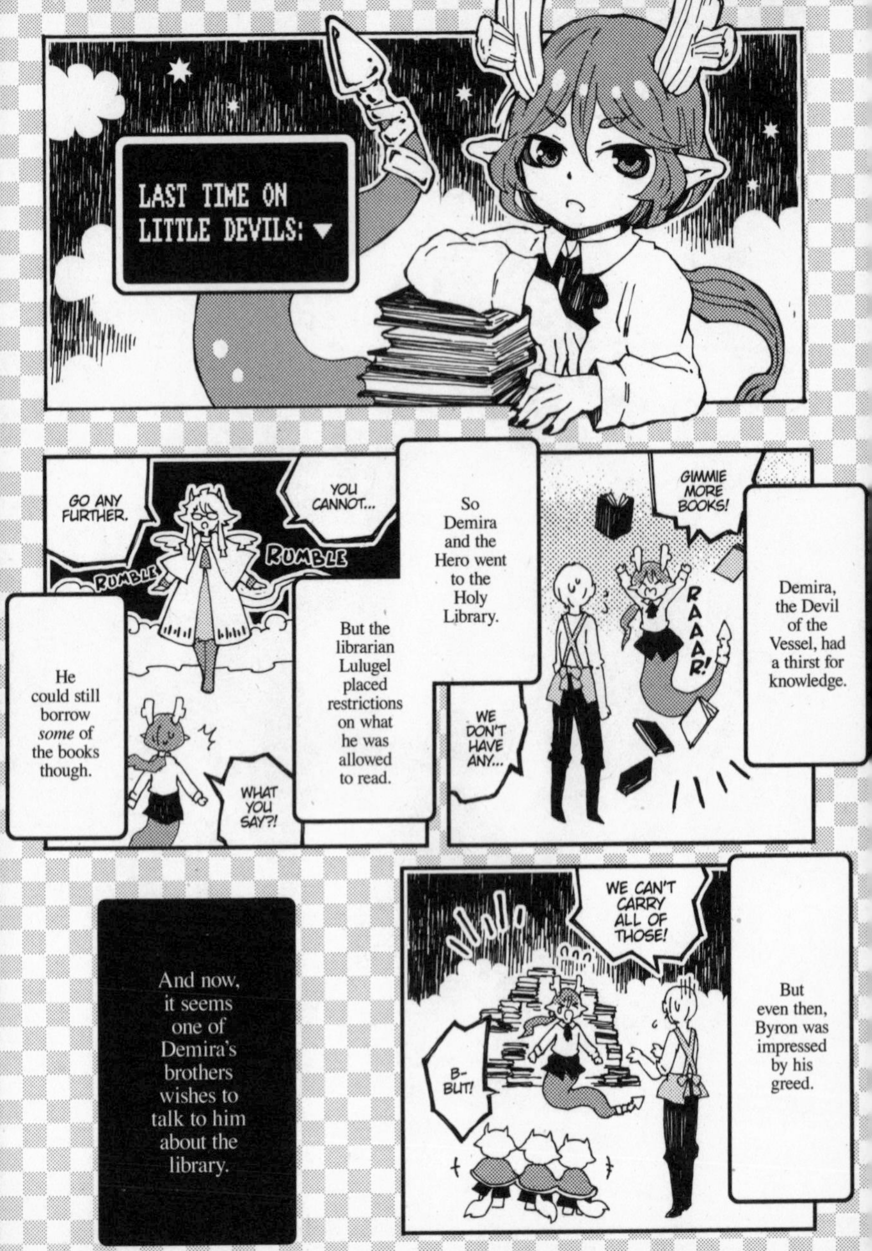
LAST TIME ON LITTLE DEVILS: ▼
Demira, the Devil of the Vessel, had a thirst for knowledge.
GIMMIE MORE BOOKS!
RAAAR!
WE DON'T HAVE ANY...
So Demira and the Hero went to the Holy Library.
YOU CANNOT...
GO ANY FURTHER.
RUMBLE
RUMBLE
But the librarian Lulugel placed restrictions on what he was allowed to read.
He could still borrow *some* of the books though.
WHAT YOU SAY?!
But even then, Byron was impressed by his greed.
WE CAN'T CARRY ALL OF THOSE!
B-BUT!
And now, it seems one of Demira's brothers wishes to talk to him about the library.

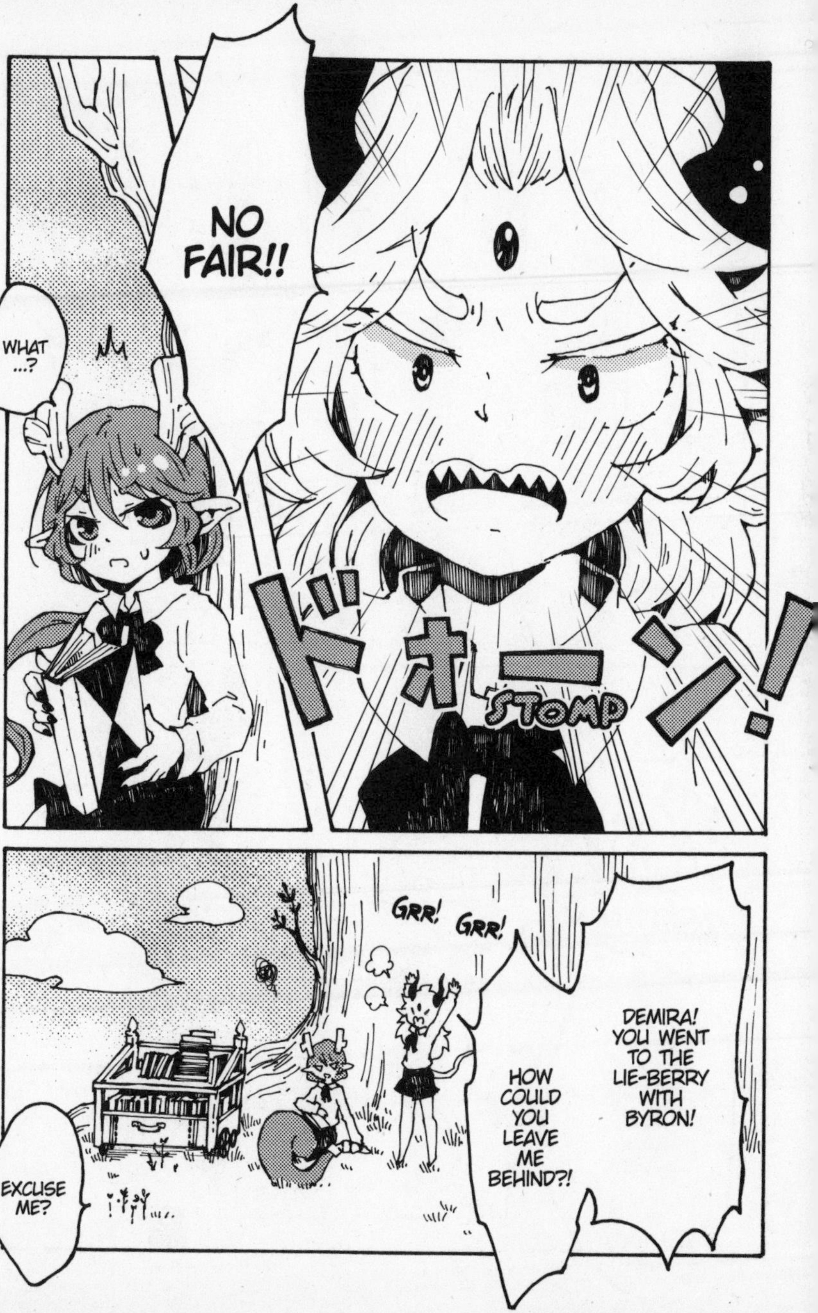
NO FAIR!!
ドオーン!
STOMP
WHAT ...?
DEMIRA! YOU WENT TO THE LIE-BERRY WITH BYRON!
HOW COULD YOU LEAVE ME BEHIND?!
GRR! GRR!
EXCUSE ME?

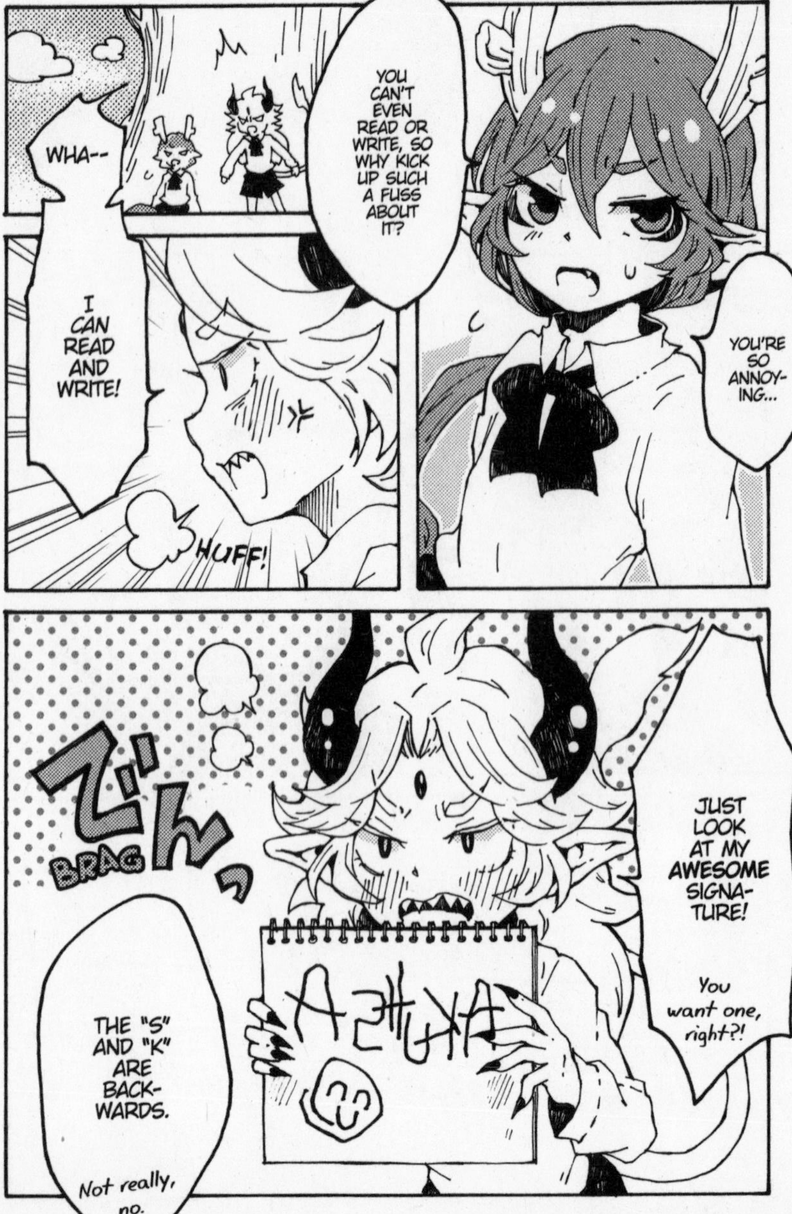
YOU CAN'T EVEN READ OR WRITE, SO WHY KICK UP SUCH A FUSS ABOUT IT?
YOU'RE SO ANNOYING...
WHA--
I CAN READ AND WRITE!
HUFF!
JUST LOOK AT MY AWESOME SIGNATURE!
You want one, right?!
BRAG
THE "S" AND "K" ARE BACKWARDS.
Not really, no.

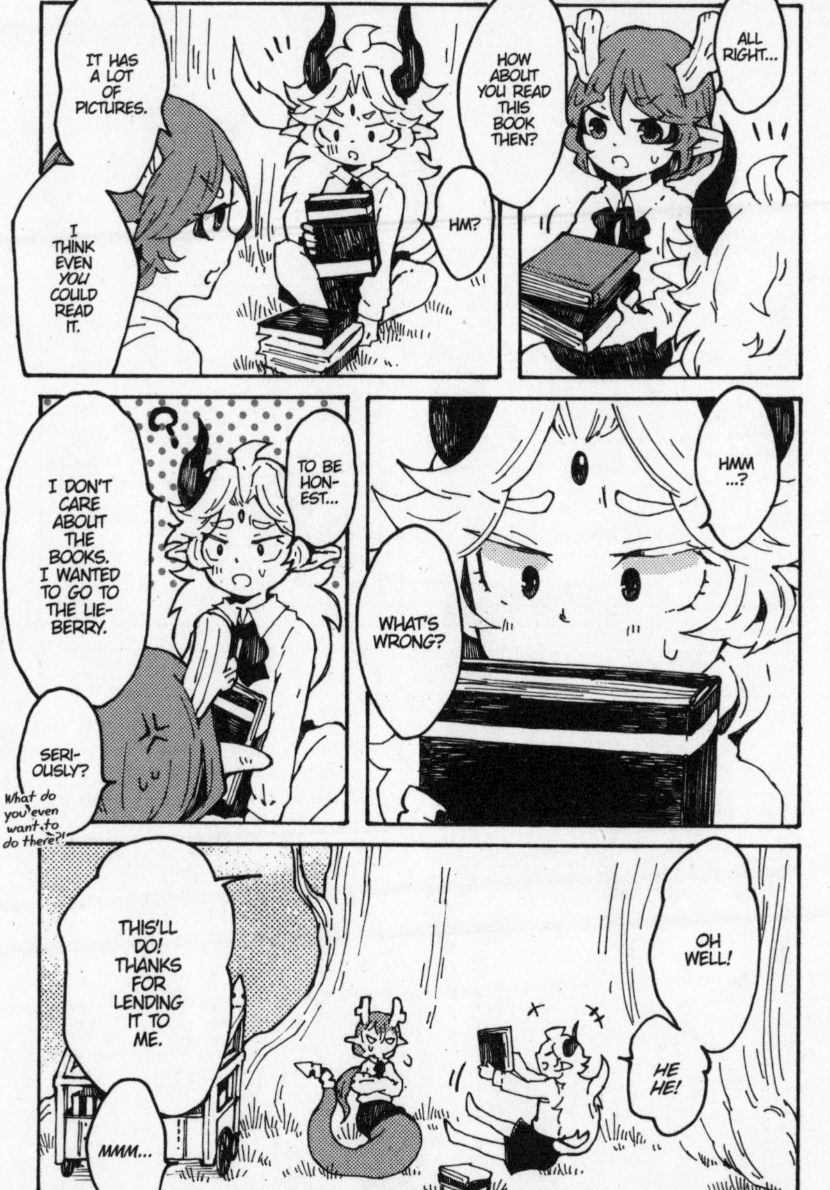
ALL RIGHT...
HOW ABOUT YOU READ THIS BOOK THEN?
HM?
IT HAS A LOT OF PICTURES.
I THINK EVEN YOU COULD READ IT.
HMM ...?
WHAT'S WRONG?
TO BE HON-EST...
I DON'T CARE ABOUT THE BOOKS. I WANTED TO GO TO THE LIE-BERRY.
SERI-OUSLY?
What do you even want to do there?!
OH WELL!
HE HE!
THIS'LL DO! THANKS FOR LENDING IT TO ME.
MMM...

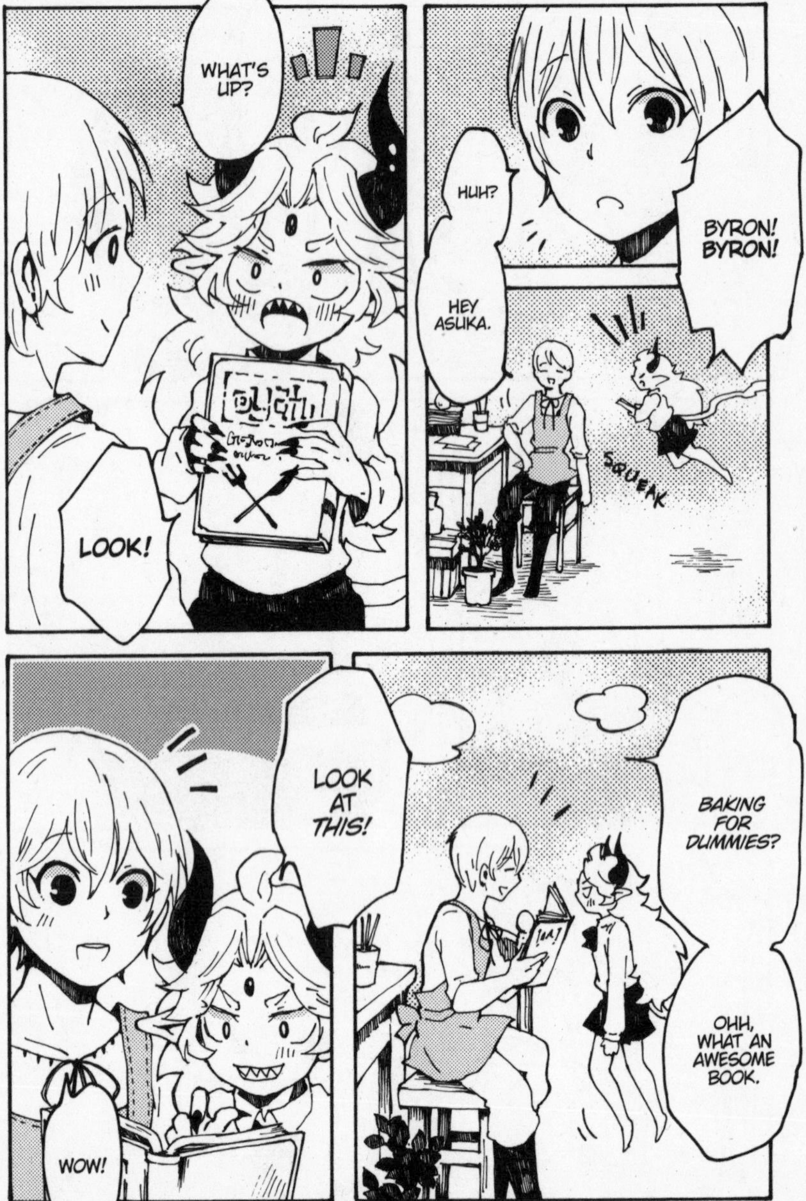
BYRON! BYRON!
HUH?
SQUEAK
HEY ASUKA.
WHAT'S UP?
LOOK!
BAKING FOR DUMMIES?
OHH, WHAT AN AWESOME BOOK.
LOOK AT THIS!
WOW!

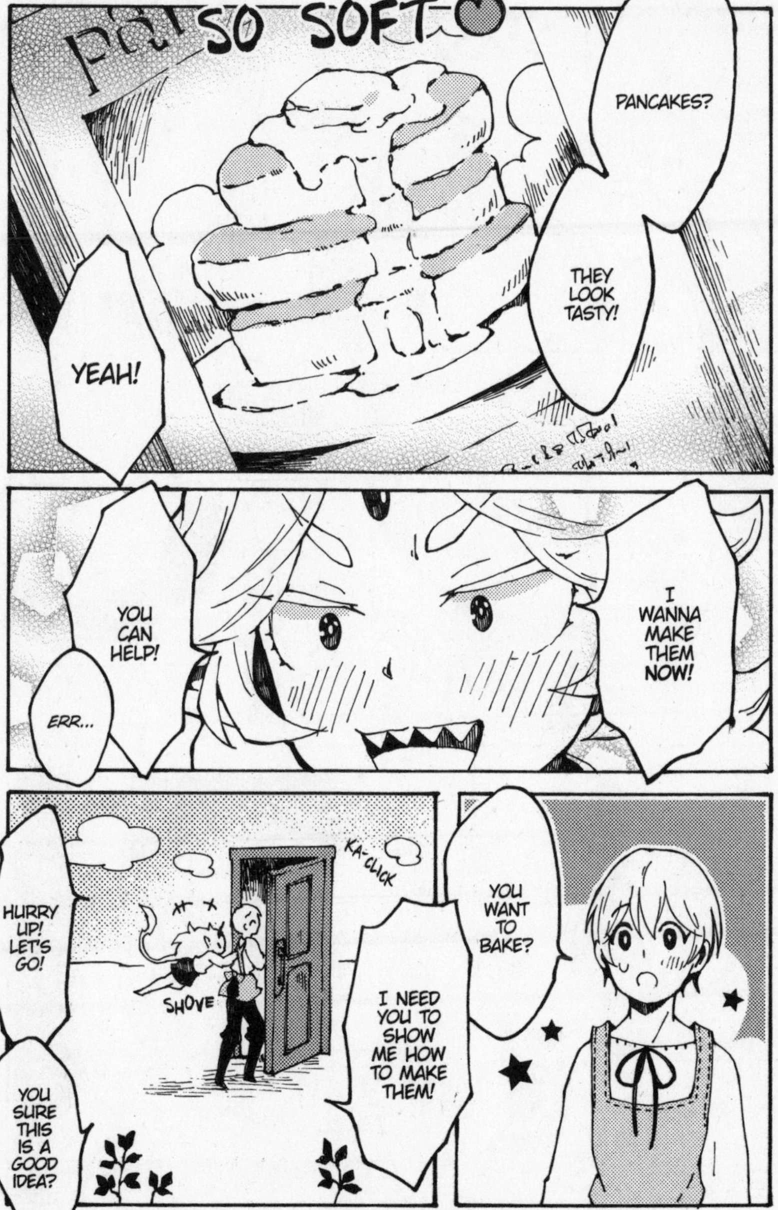
PANCAKES?
THEY LOOK TASTY!
SO SOFT
YEAH!
I WANNA MAKE THEM NOW!
YOU CAN HELP!
ERR...
YOU WANT TO BAKE?
I NEED YOU TO SHOW ME HOW TO MAKE THEM!
KA-CLICK
HURRY UP! LET'S GO!
SHOVE
YOU SURE THIS IS A GOOD IDEA?

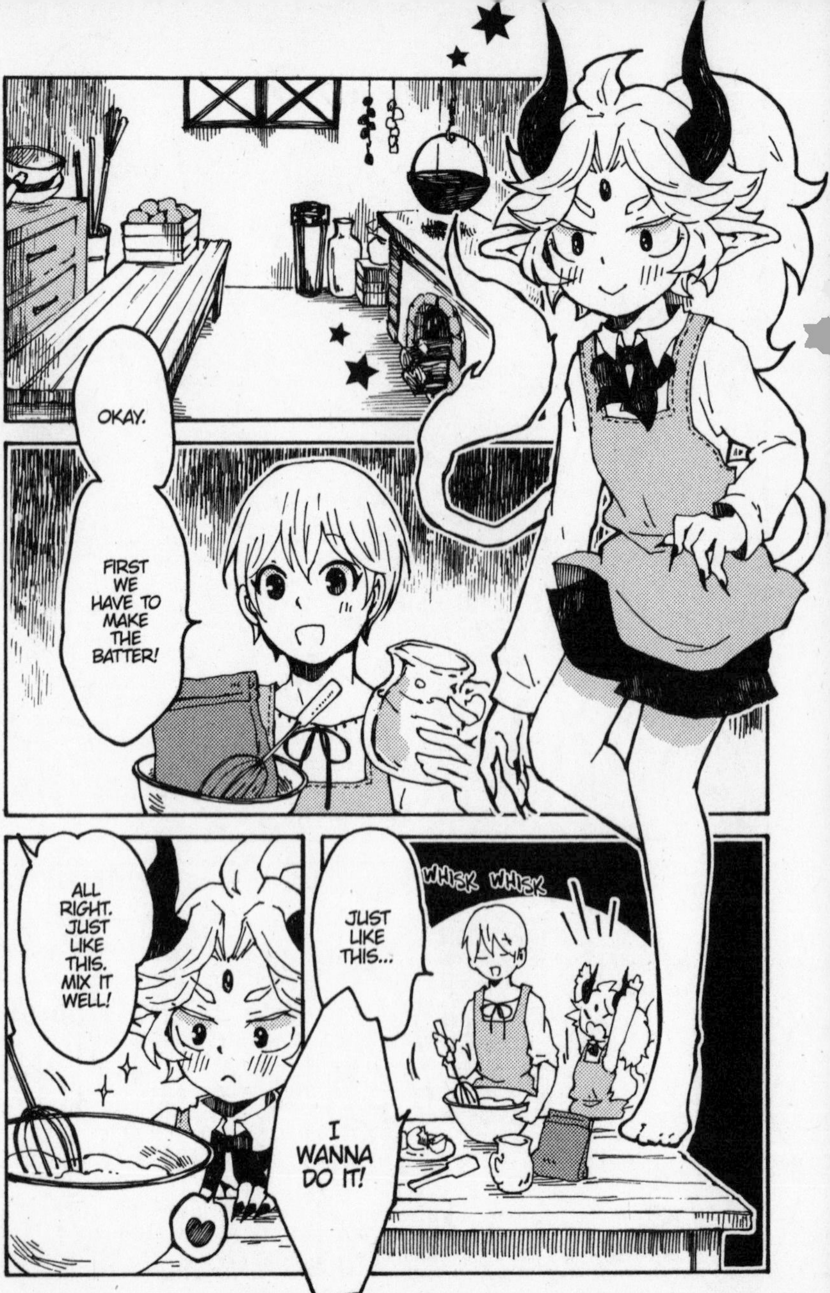
OKAY.
FIRST WE HAVE TO MAKE THE BATTER!
WHISK WHISK
JUST LIKE THIS...
I WANNA DO IT!
ALL RIGHT. JUST LIKE THIS. MIX IT WELL!

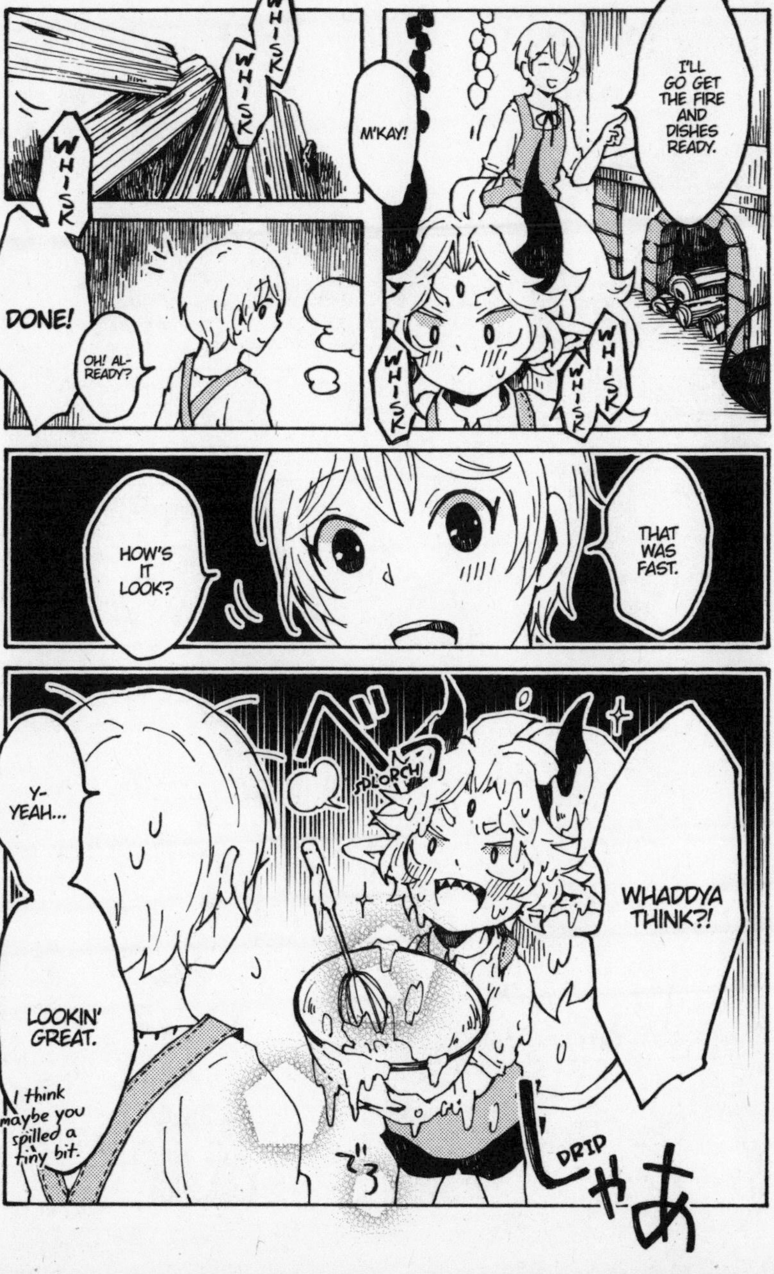
I'LL GO GET THE FIRE AND DISHES READY.
M'KAY!
WHISK WHISK
WHISK WHISK
WHISK WHISK
WHISK WHISK
DONE!
OH! AL-READY?
THAT WAS FAST.
HOW'S IT LOOK?
WHADDYA THINK?!
SPLORCH
Y-YEAH...
LOOKIN' GREAT.
I think maybe you spilled a tiny bit.
DRIP

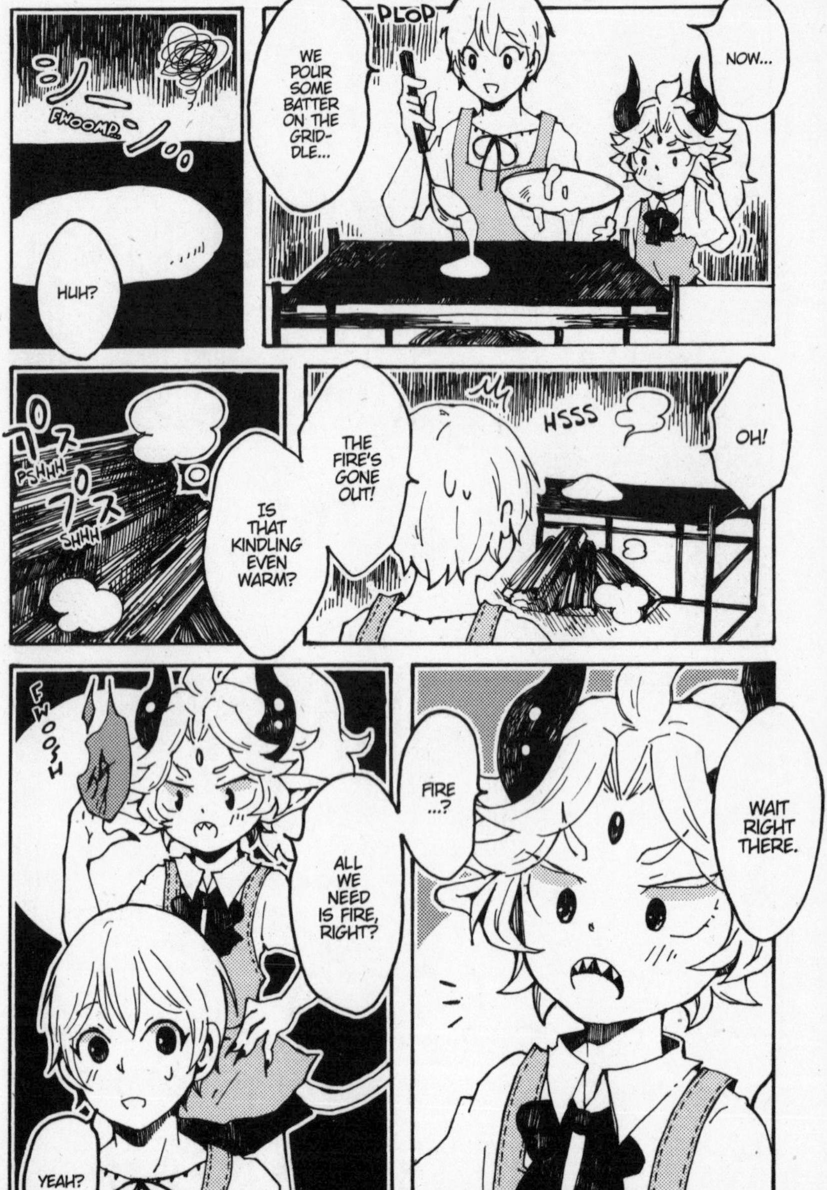
NOW...
PLOP
WE POUR SOME BATTER ON THE GRID-DLE...
FWOOMP...
HUH?
OH!
HSSS
THE FIRE'S GONE OUT!
IS THAT KINDLING EVEN WARM?
プス PSHHH
プス SHHH
WAIT RIGHT THERE.
FIRE ...?
FWOOSH
ALL WE NEED IS FIRE, RIGHT?
YEAH?

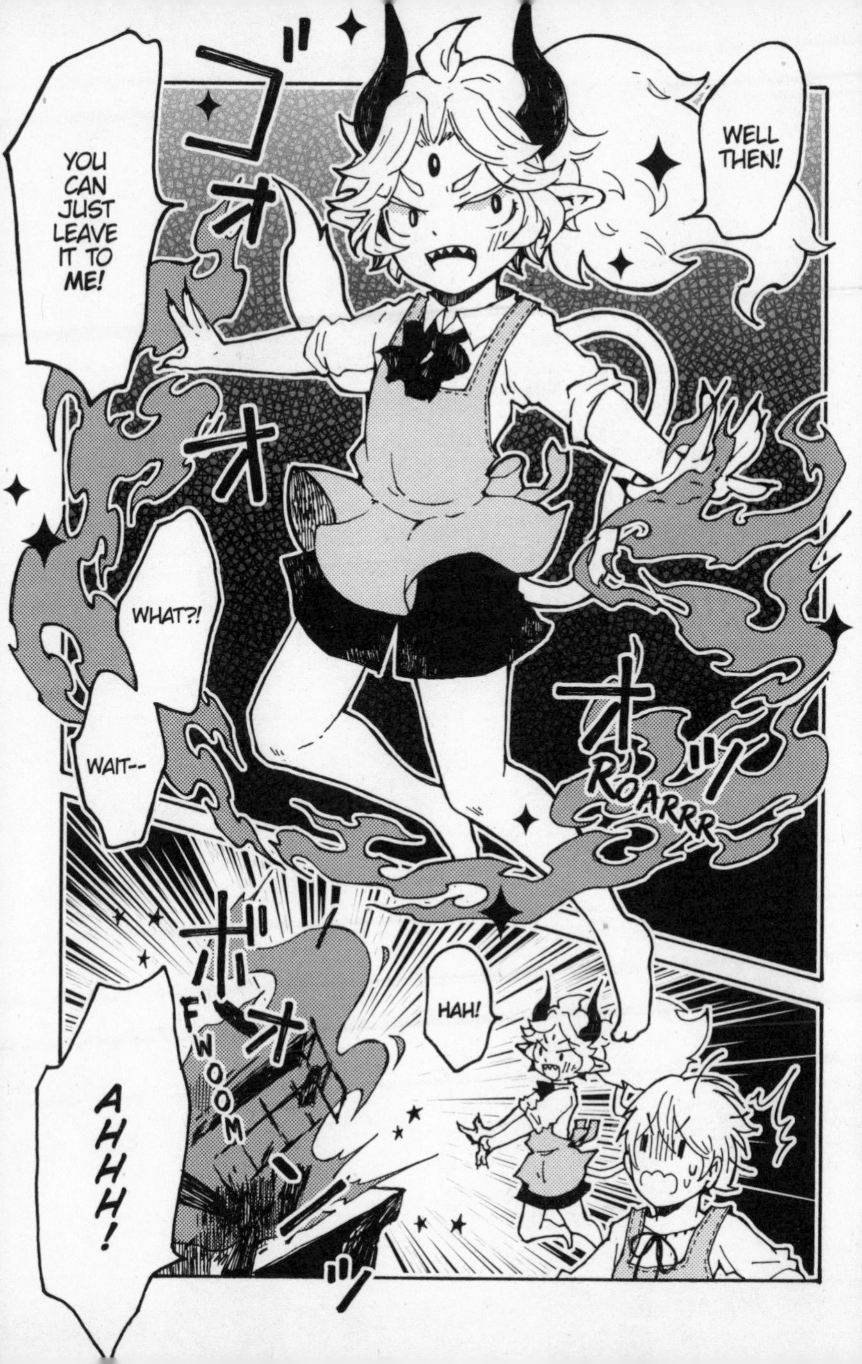
WELL THEN!
YOU CAN JUST LEAVE IT TO ME!
ゴオオオッ
ROARRR
WHAT?!
WAIT--
HAH!
ボオーッ
F'WOOM
AHHHH!

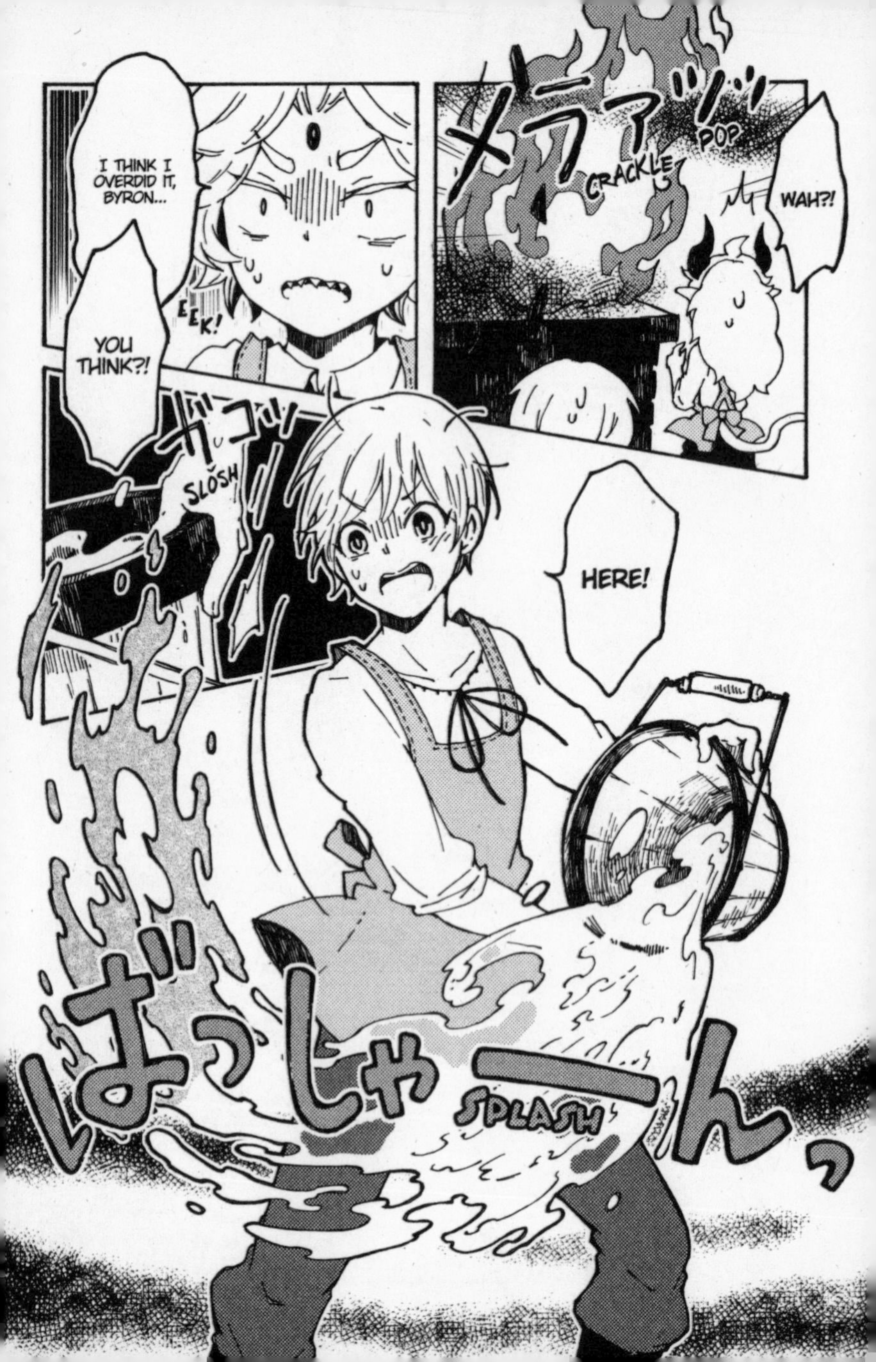
CRACKLE
POP
WAH?!
I THINK I OVERDID IT, BYRON...
EEK!
YOU THINK?!
SLOSH
HERE!
ばっしゃーん
SPLASH

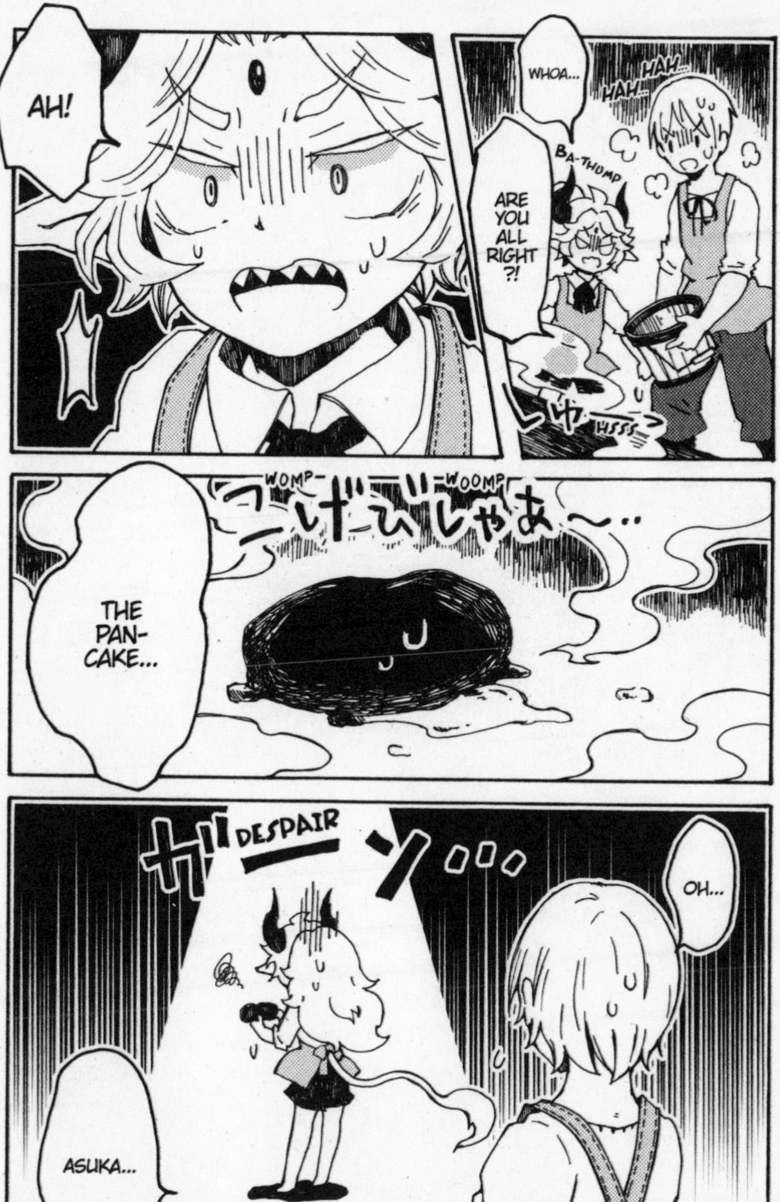
HAH... HAH...
WHOA...
BA-THUMP
ARE YOU ALL RIGHT?!
HSSS
AH!
WOMP- WOOMP
こげびしゃあ〜..
THE PAN-CAKE...
DESPAIR
ガーン...
OH...
ASUKA...

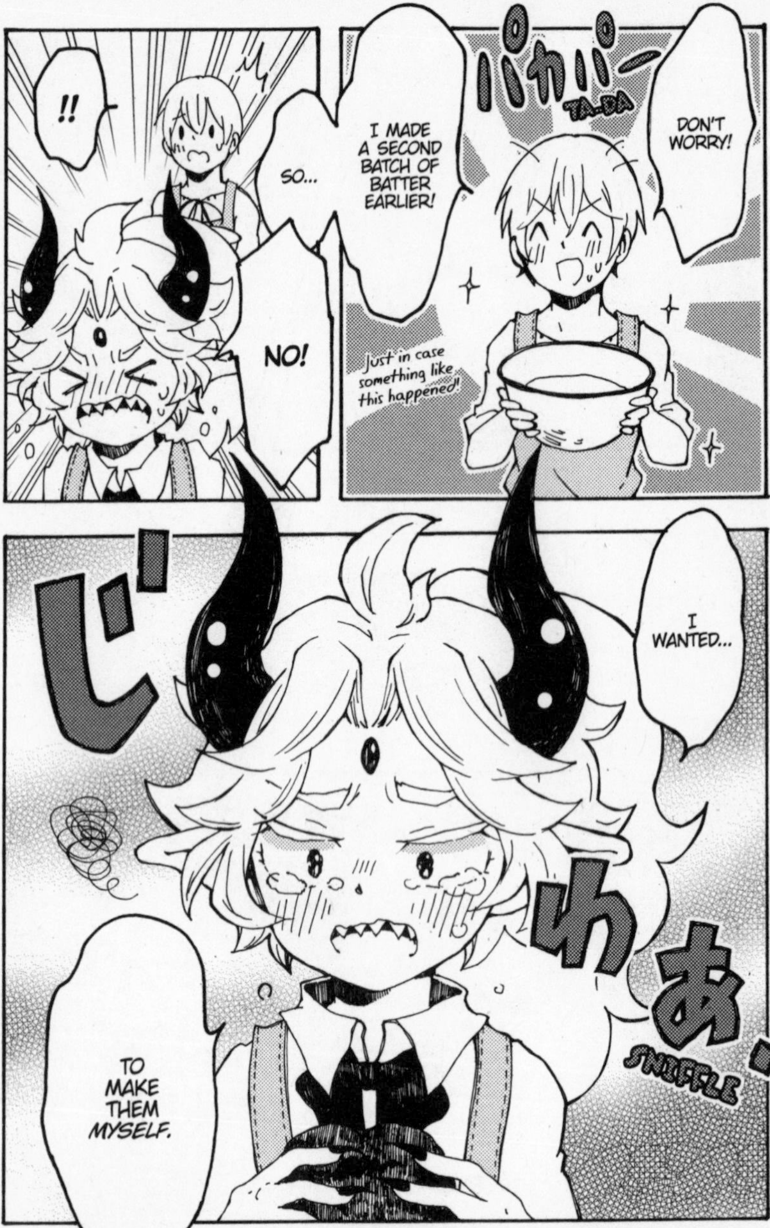

DON'T WORRY!
TA-DA
I MADE A SECOND BATCH OF BATTER EARLIER!
SO...
Just in case something like this happened!
!!
NO!
I WANTED...
SNIFFLE
TO MAKE THEM MYSELF.

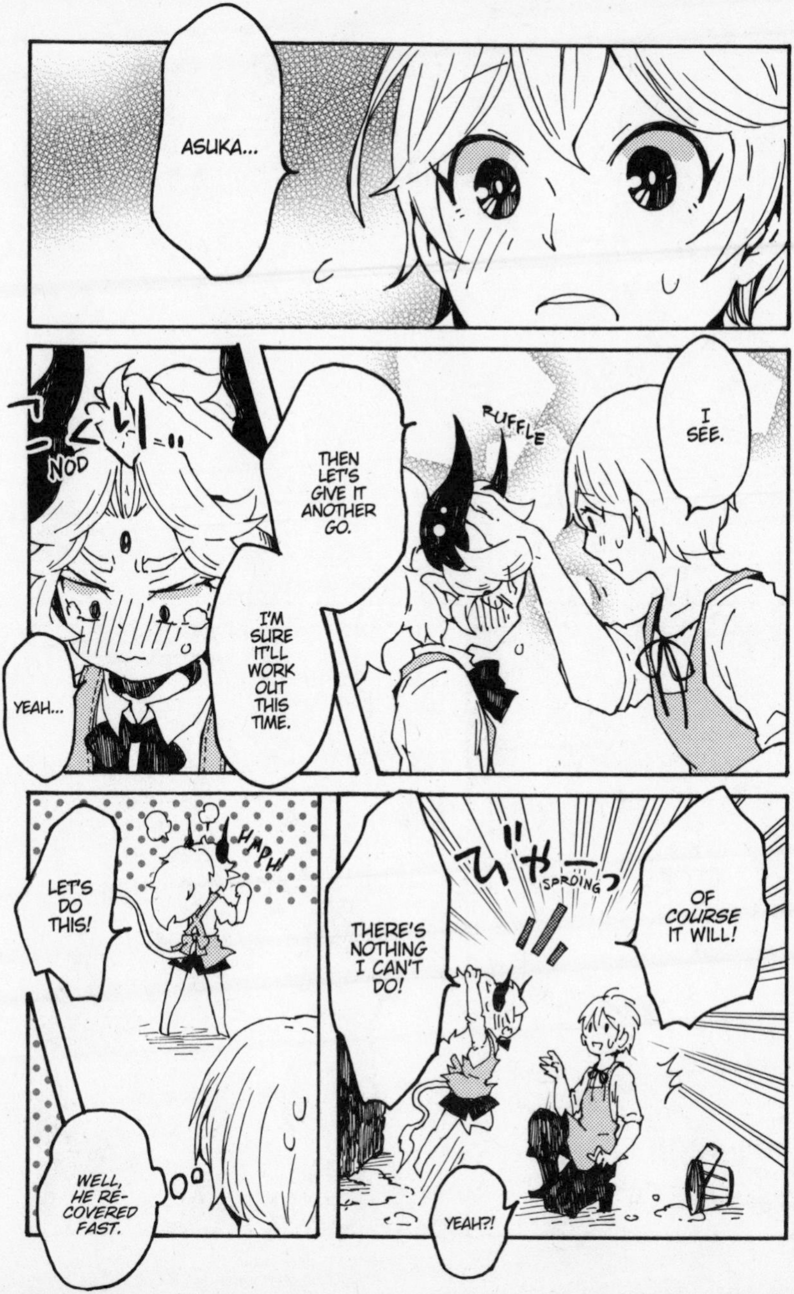
ASUKA...
I SEE.
RUFFLE
THEN LET'S GIVE IT ANOTHER GO.
I'M SURE IT'LL WORK OUT THIS TIME.
NOD
YEAH...
OF COURSE IT WILL!
SPROING
THERE'S NOTHING I CAN'T DO!
YEAH?!
HMPH!
LET'S DO THIS!
WELL, HE RE-COVERED FAST.

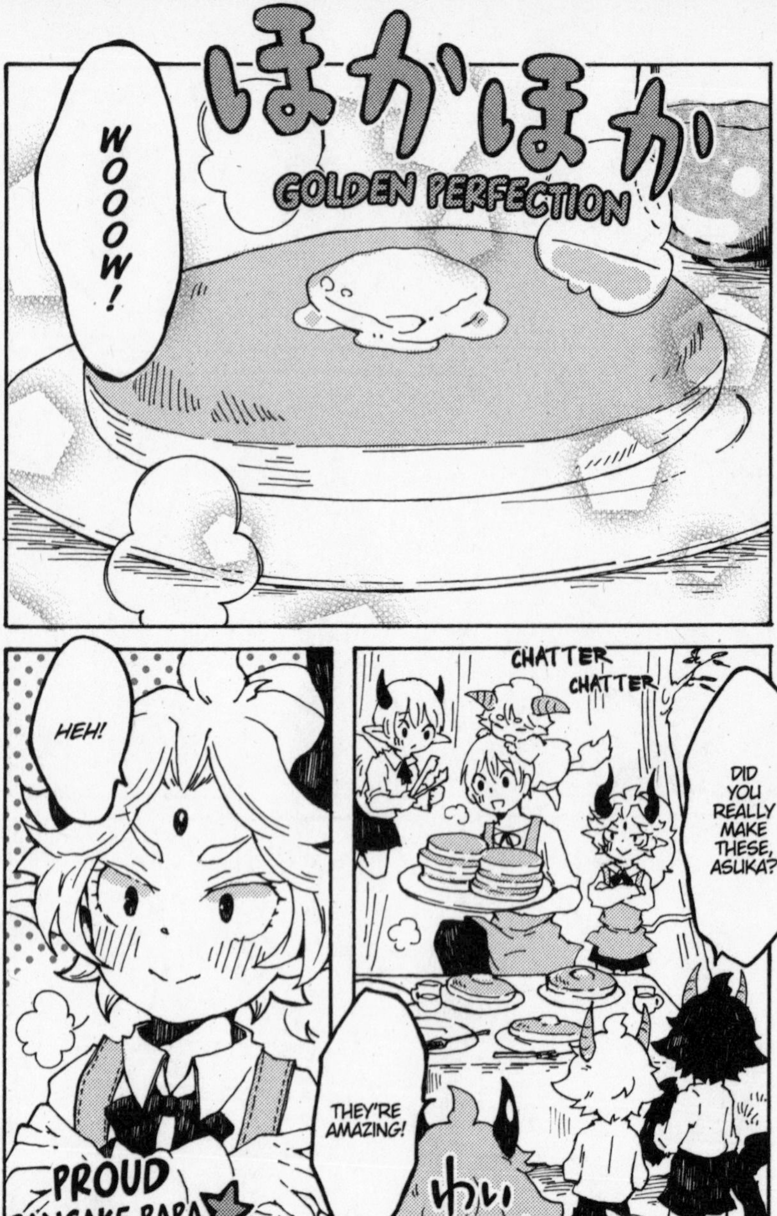
ほかほか
GOLDEN PERFECTION
WOOOOW!
CHATTER
CHATTER
DID YOU REALLY MAKE THESE, ASUKA?
THEY'RE AMAZING!
わいわい
MURMUR MURMUR
HEH!
PROUD PANCAKE PAPA☆

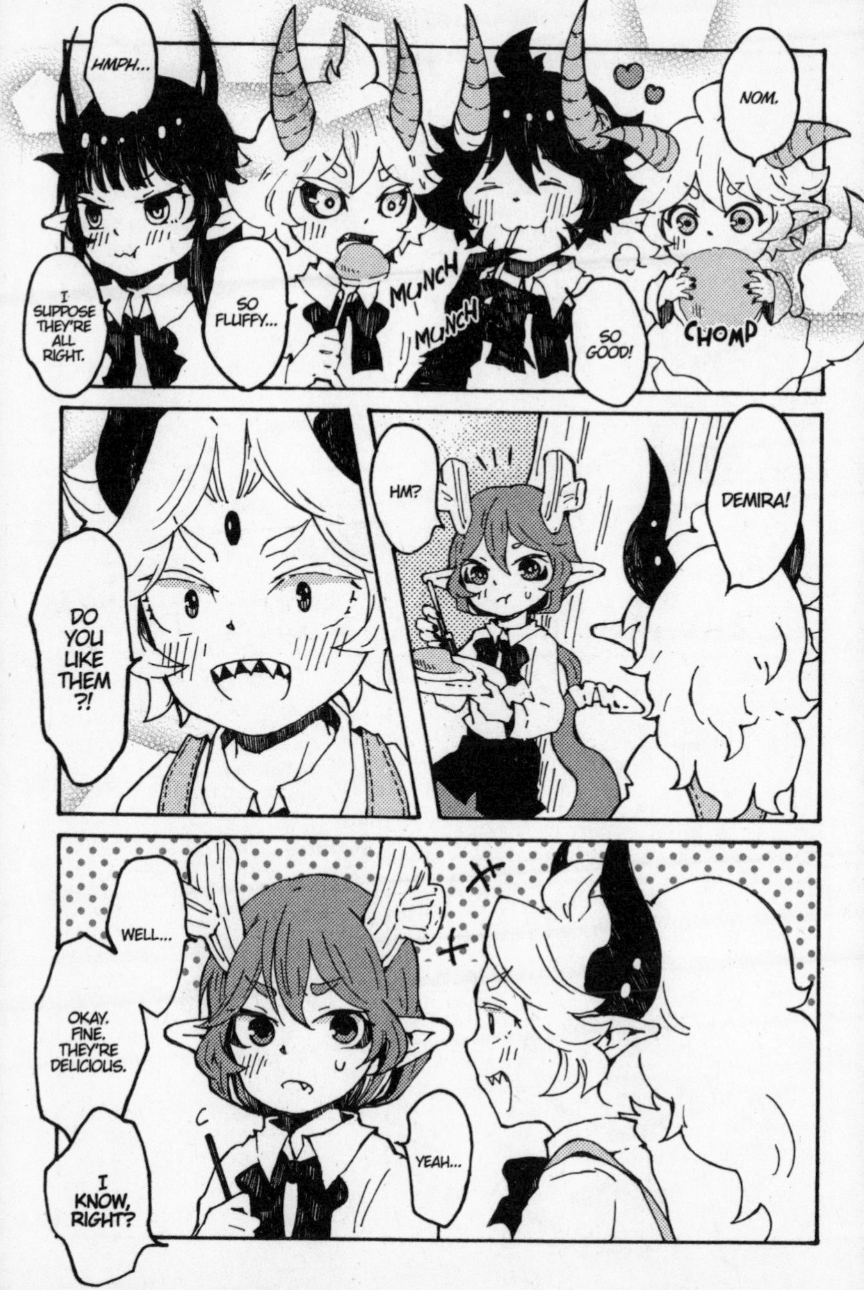
NOM.
CHOMP
SO GOOD!
MUNCH MUNCH
SO FLUFFY...
HMPH...
I SUPPOSE THEY'RE ALL RIGHT.
DEMIRA!
HM?
DO YOU LIKE THEM?!
WELL...
OKAY. FINE. THEY'RE DELICIOUS.
YEAH...
I KNOW, RIGHT?

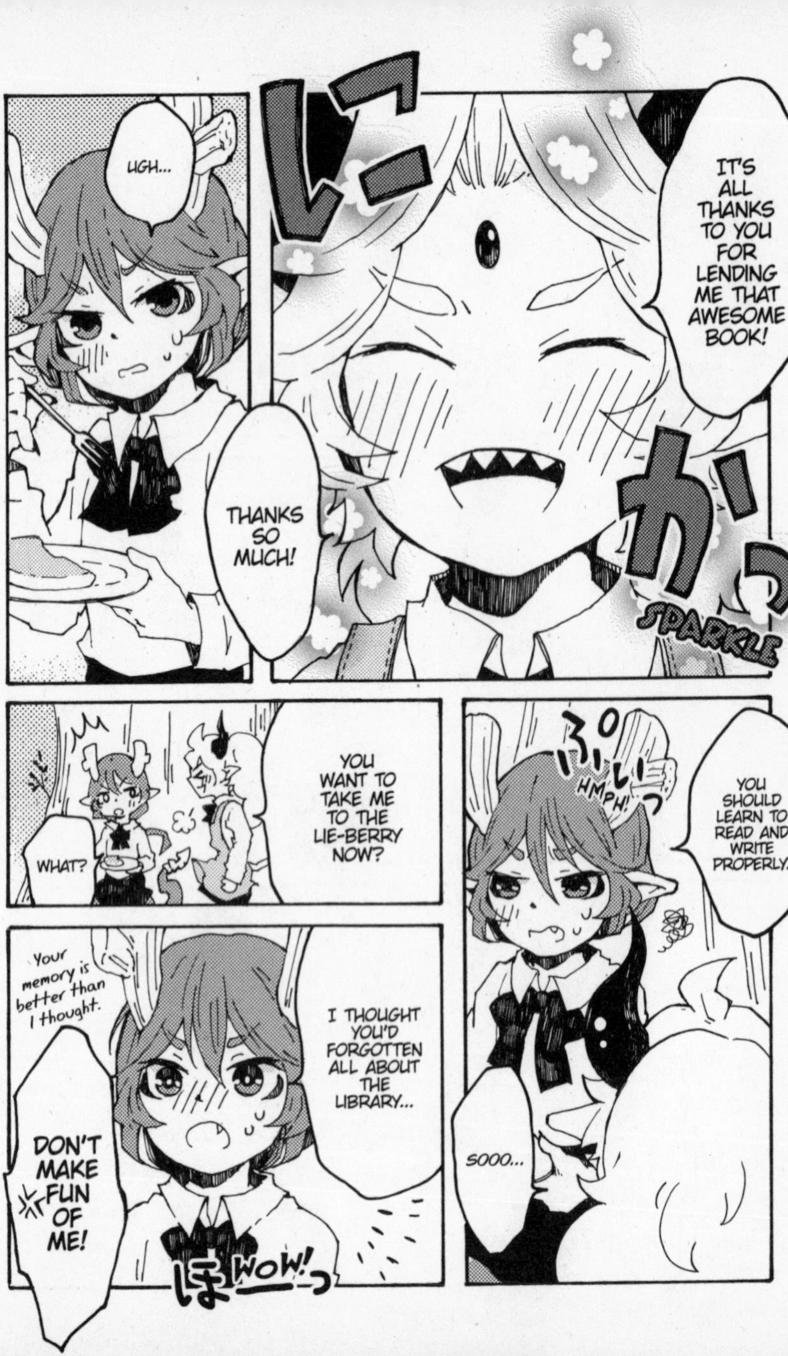
IT'S ALL THANKS TO YOU FOR LENDING ME THAT AWESOME BOOK!
THANKS SO MUCH!
SPARKLE
UGH...
YOU SHOULD LEARN TO READ AND WRITE PROPERLY.
HMPH!
SOOO...
YOU WANT TO TAKE ME TO THE LIE-BERRY NOW?
WHAT?
I THOUGHT YOU'D FORGOTTEN ALL ABOUT THE LIBRARY...
Your memory is better than I thought.
DON'T MAKE FUN OF ME!
WOW!

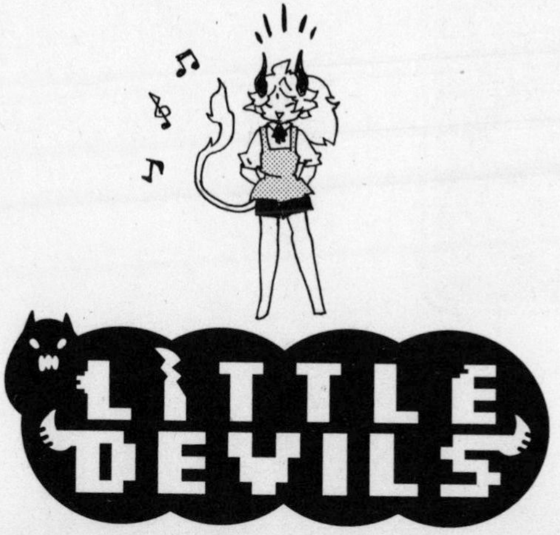

LITTLE DEVILS

DEVIL OF THE BONES - MORO ▼

....

The twelfth Little Devil. Not at all
timid.
Roosts atop Byron's head.
He's still a baby.
Sleeps far more than he talks.

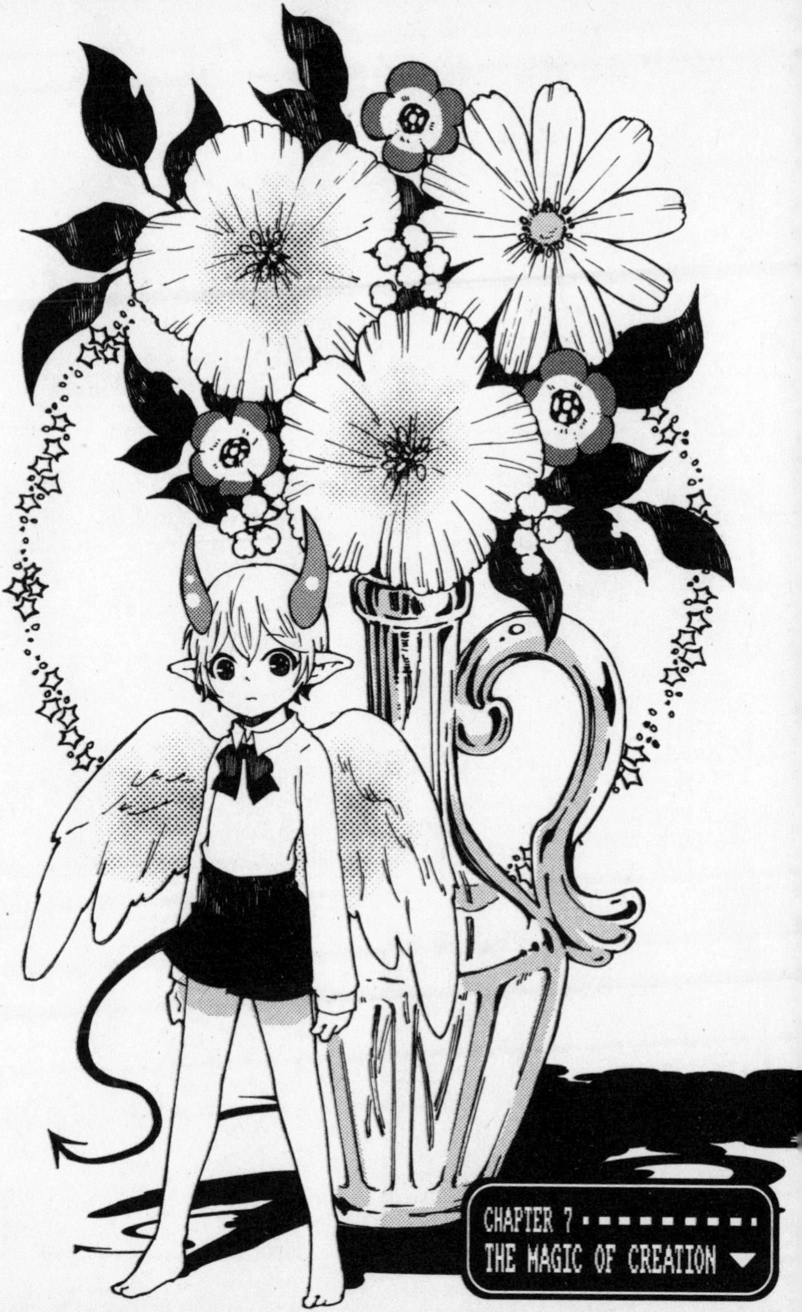
CHAPTER 7
THE MAGIC OF CREATION

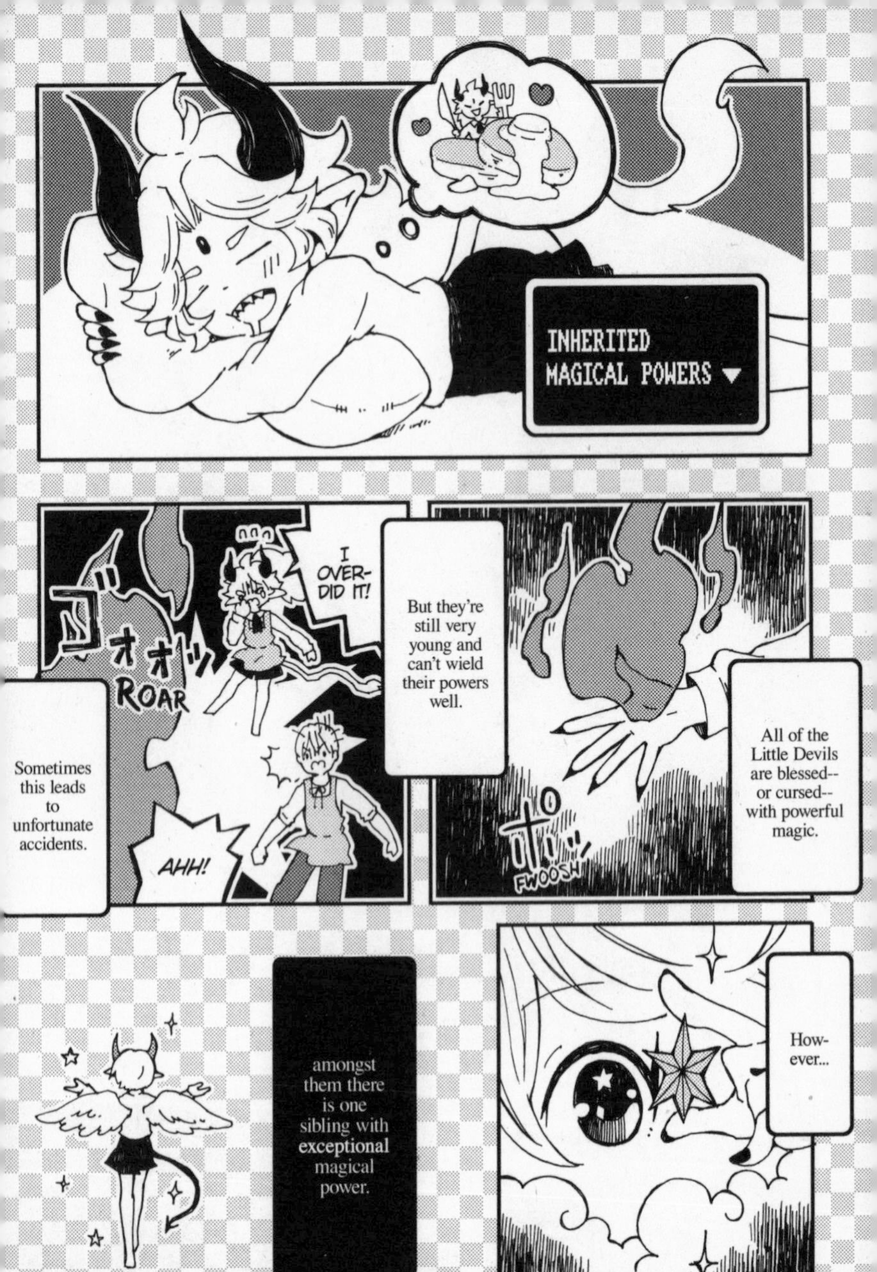

INHERITED MAGICAL POWERS ▼
All of the Little Devils are blessed-- or cursed-- with powerful magic.
FWOOSH
But they're still very young and can't wield their powers well.
I OVER-DID IT!
ROAR
AHH!
Sometimes this leads to unfortunate accidents.
How-ever...
amongst them there is one sibling with **exceptional** magical power.

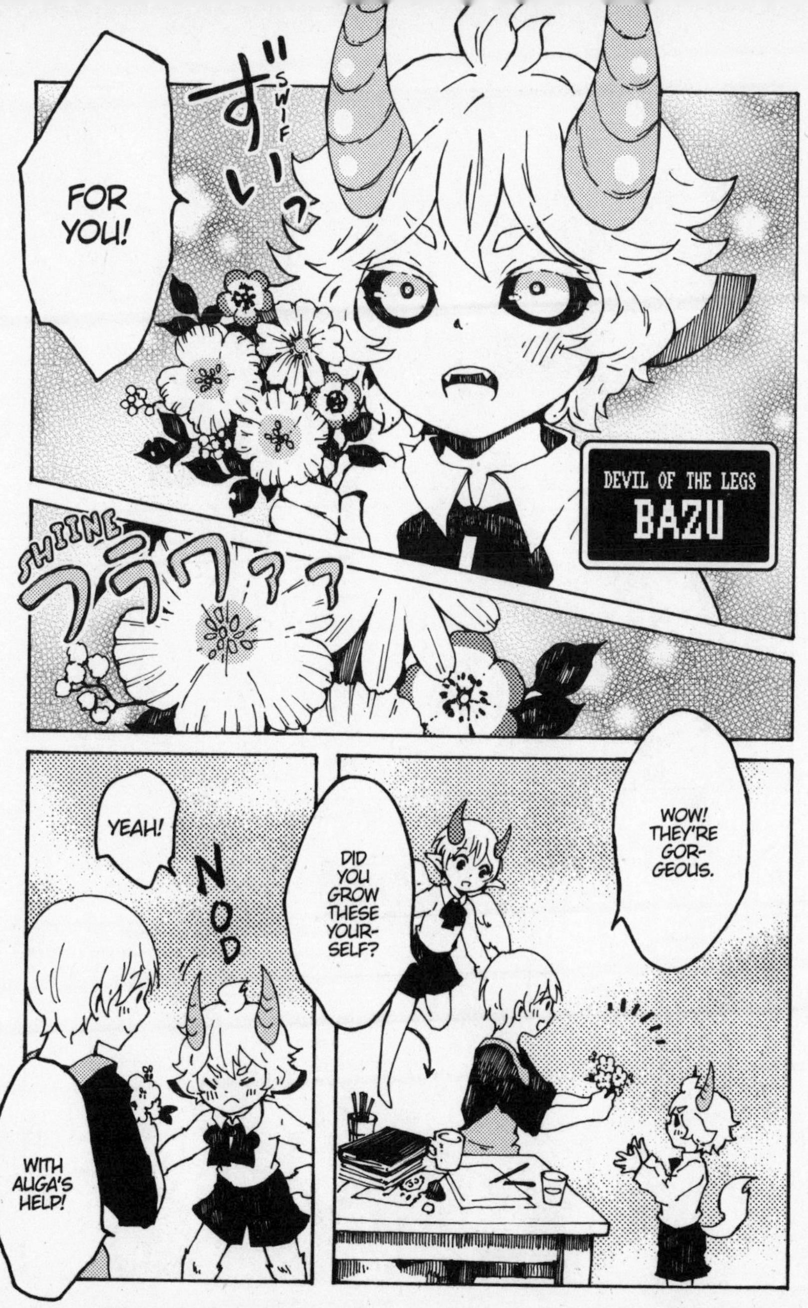

FOR YOU!
SWIF
DEVIL OF THE LEGS
BAZU
SHIINE
WOW! THEY'RE GOR-GEOUS.
DID YOU GROW THESE YOUR-SELF?
YEAH!
NOD
WITH AUGA'S HELP!

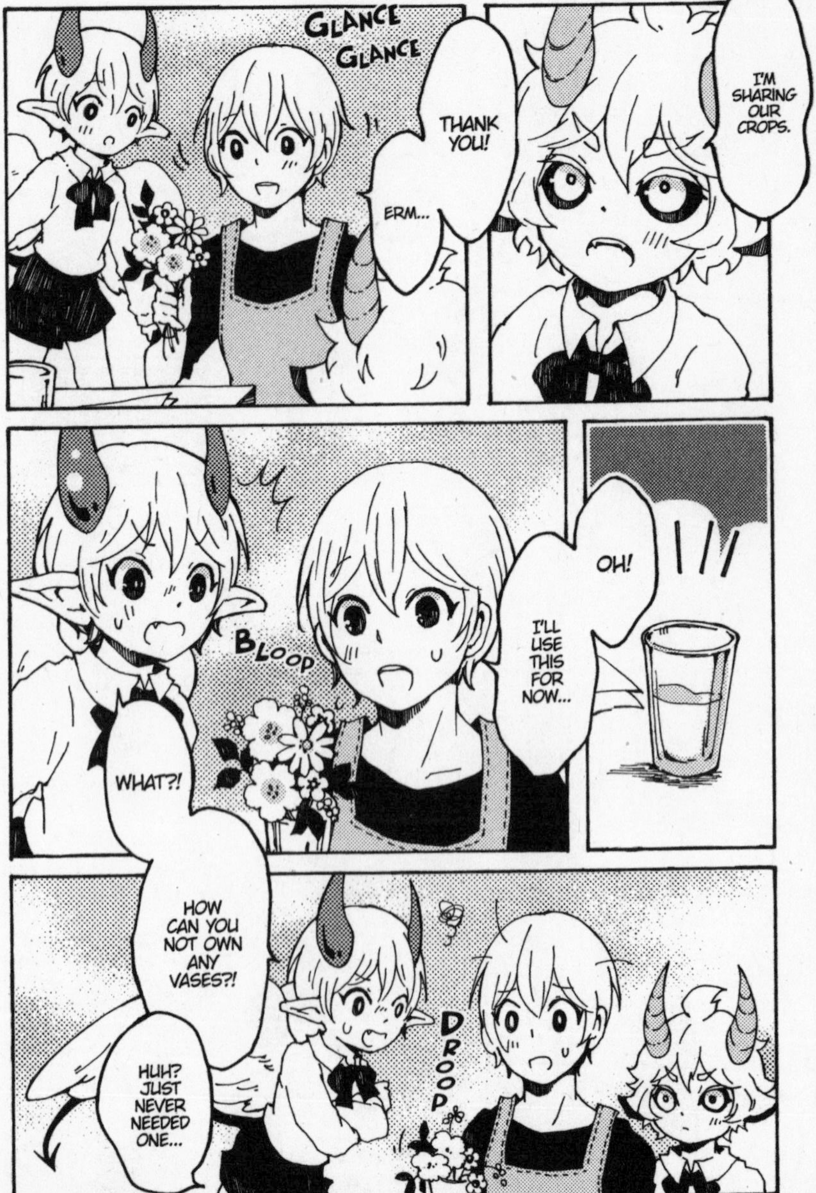
I'M SHARING OUR CROPS.
THANK YOU!
ERM...
GLANCE GLANCE
OH!
I'LL USE THIS FOR NOW...
BLOOP
WHAT?!
HOW CAN YOU NOT OWN ANY VASES?!
DROOP
HUH? JUST NEVER NEEDED ONE...

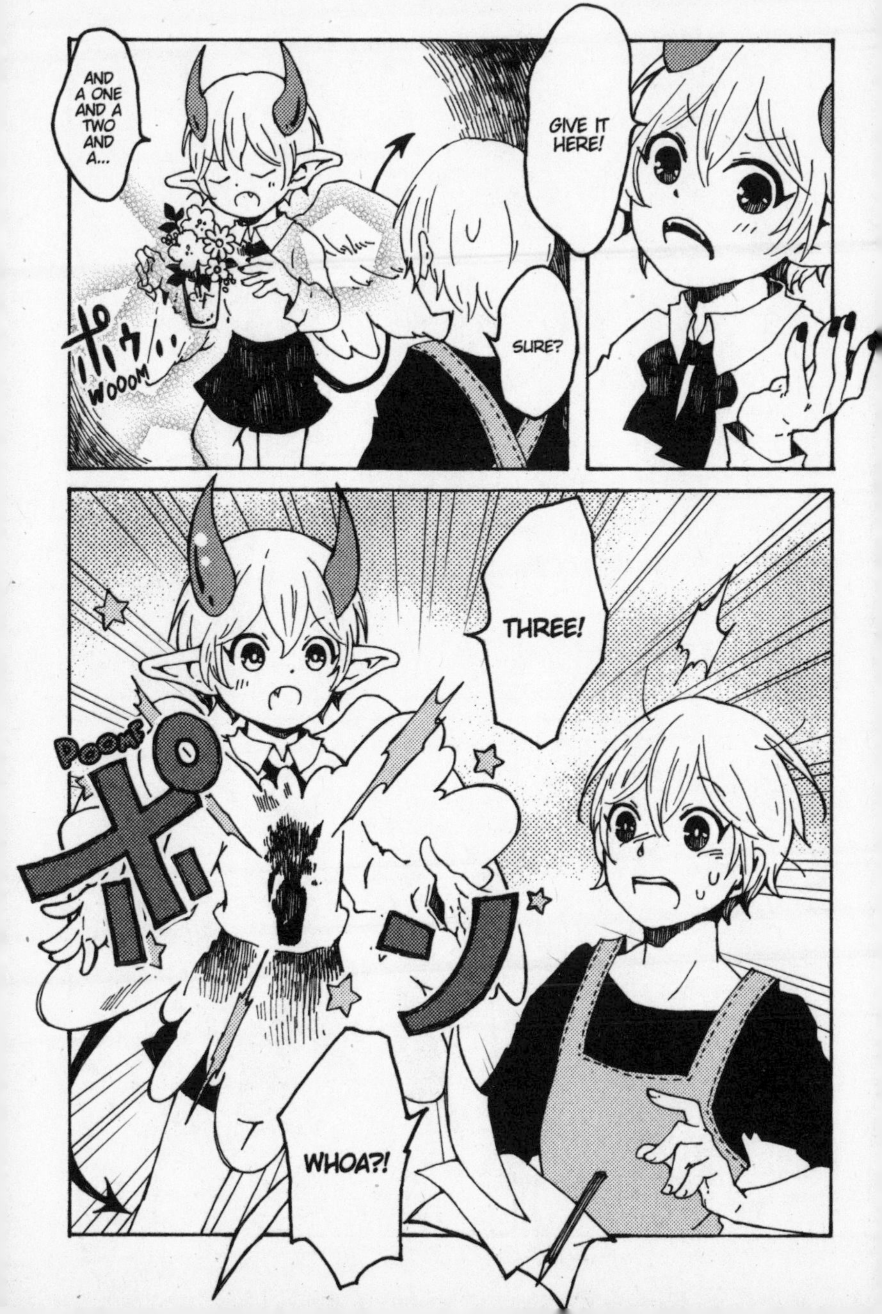
GIVE IT HERE!
AND A ONE AND A TWO AND A...
WOOOM
SURE?
THREE!
POOMF
WHOA?!

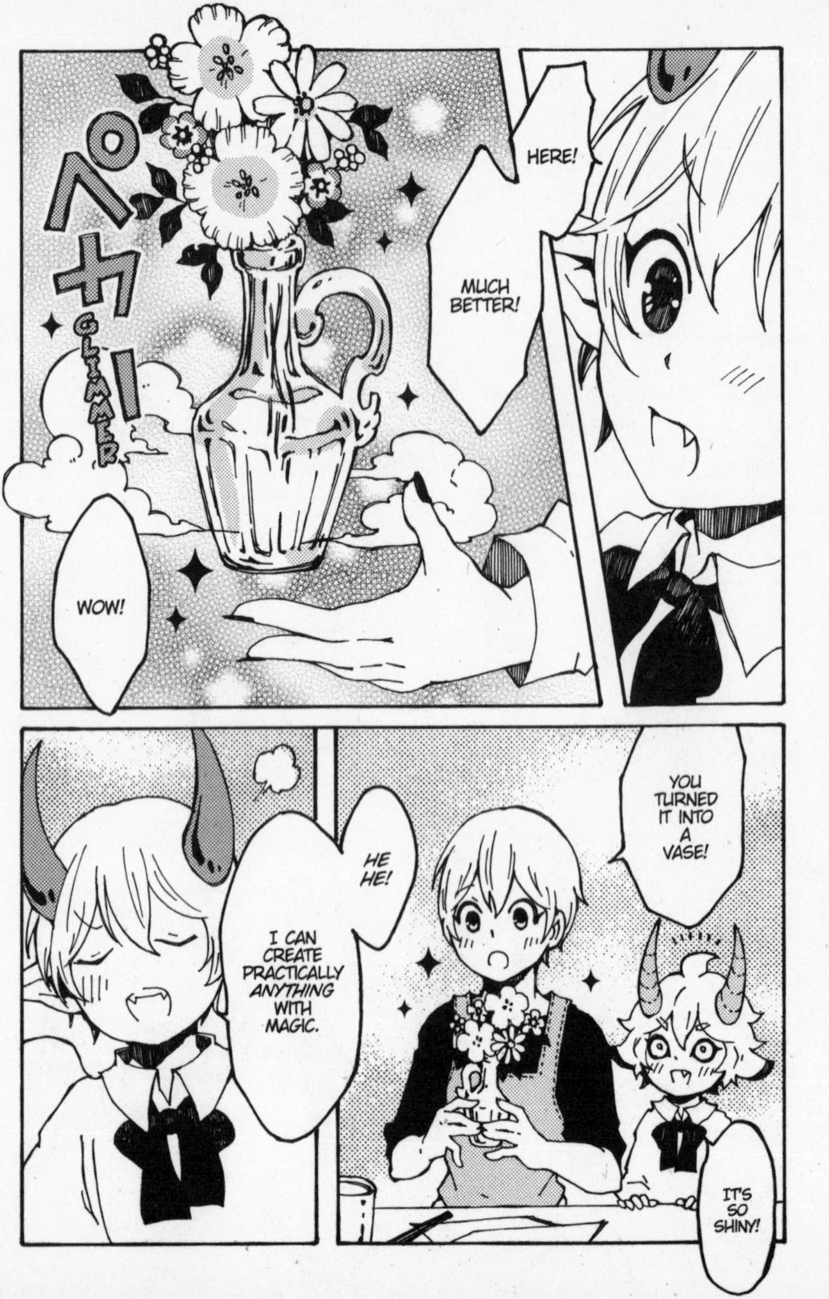
HERE!
MUCH BETTER!
ペカー GLIMMER
WOW!
YOU TURNED IT INTO A VASE!
IT'S SO SHINY!
HE HE!
I CAN CREATE PRACTICALLY *ANYTHING* WITH MAGIC.

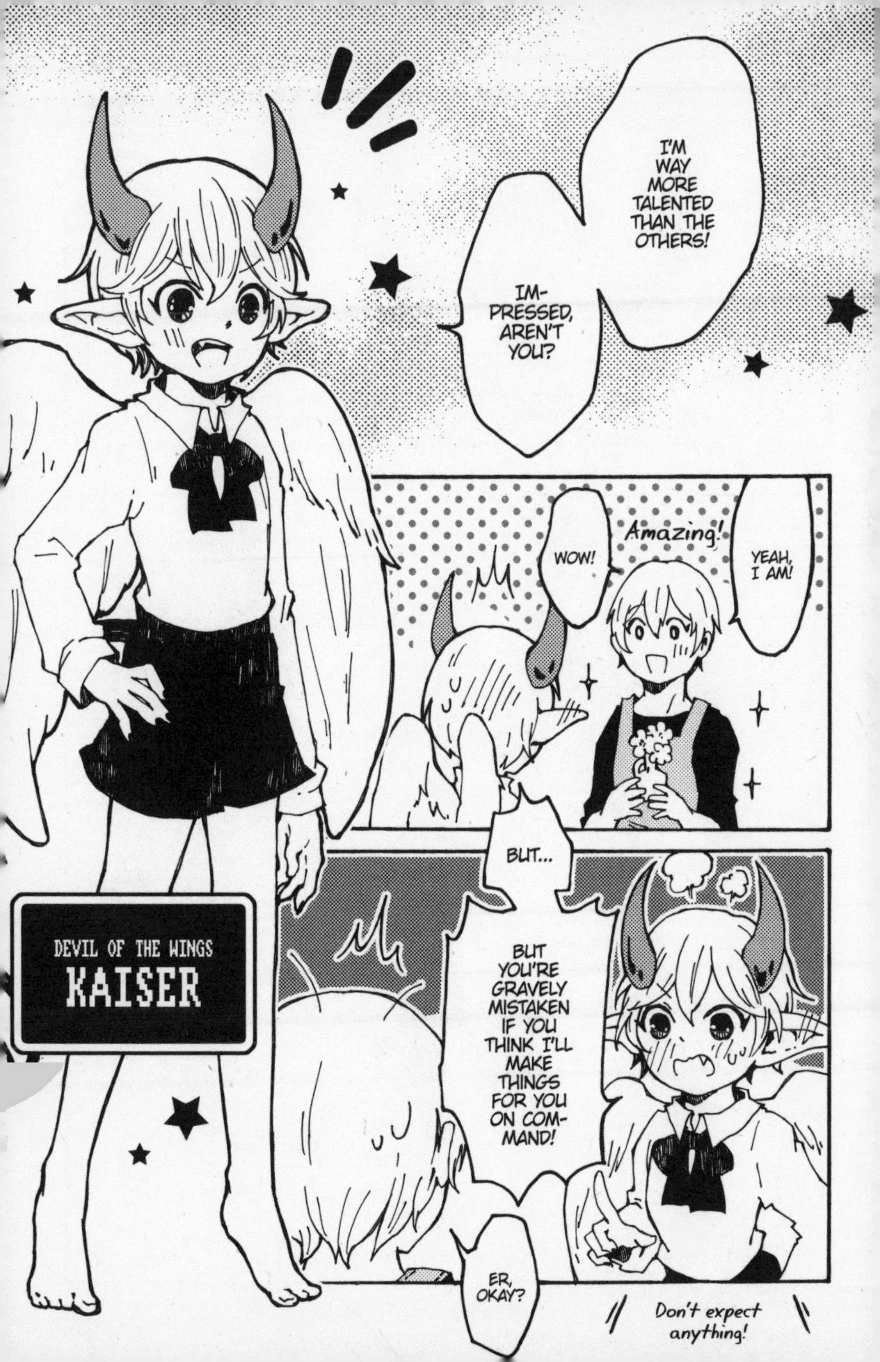
I'M WAY MORE TALENTED THAN THE OTHERS!
IM-PRESSED, AREN'T YOU?
DEVIL OF THE WINGS
KAISER
YEAH, I AM!
Amazing!
WOW!
BUT...
BUT YOU'RE GRAVELY MISTAKEN IF YOU THINK I'LL MAKE THINGS FOR YOU ON COM-MAND!
Don't expect anything!
ER, OKAY?

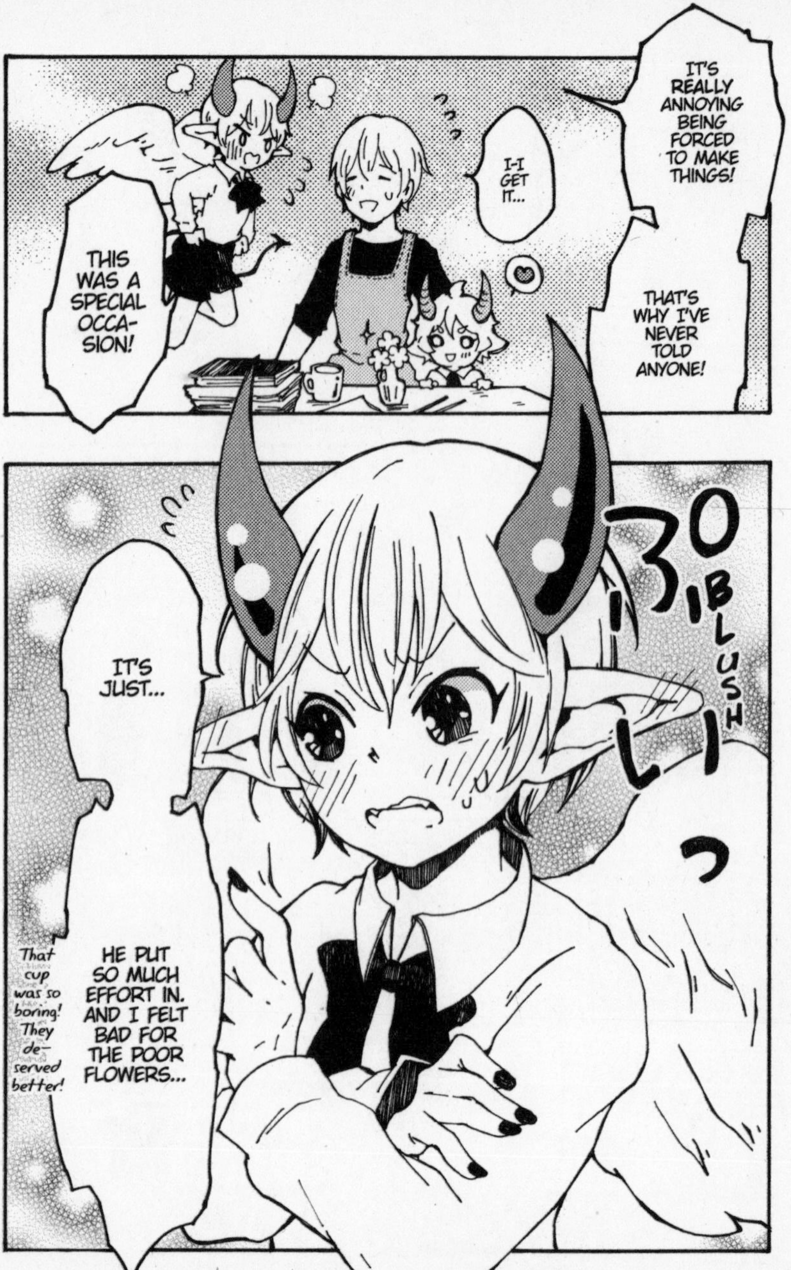
IT'S REALLY ANNOYING BEING FORCED TO MAKE THINGS!
THAT'S WHY I'VE NEVER TOLD ANYONE!
I-I GET IT...
THIS WAS A SPECIAL OCCA-SION!
BLUSH
IT'S JUST...
HE PUT SO MUCH EFFORT IN. AND I FELT BAD FOR THE POOR FLOWERS...
That cup was so boring! They de-served better!

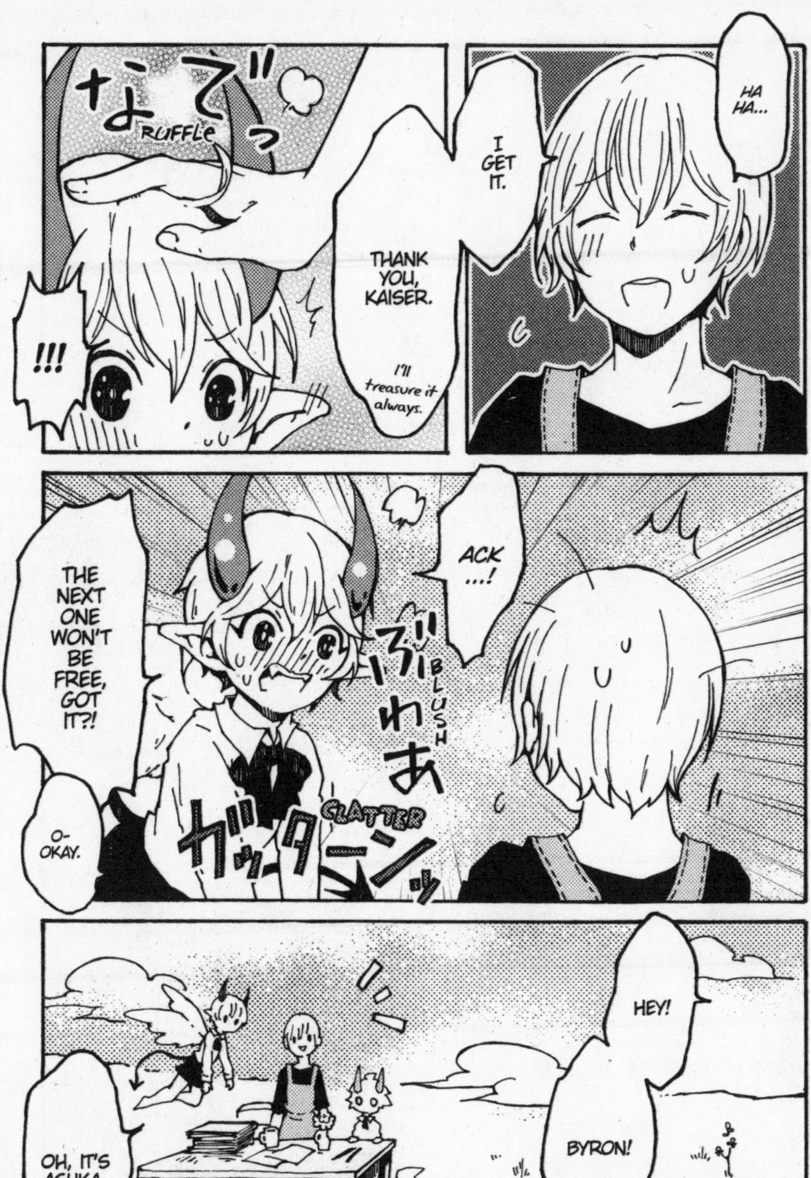
HA HA...
I GET IT.
THANK YOU, KAISER.
I'll treasure it always.
なでっ
RUFFLE
!!!
ACK ...!
ぶわあ
BLUSH
ガッターンッ
CLATTER
THE NEXT ONE WON'T BE FREE, GOT IT?!
O-OKAY.
HEY!
BYRON!
OH, IT'S ASUKA.

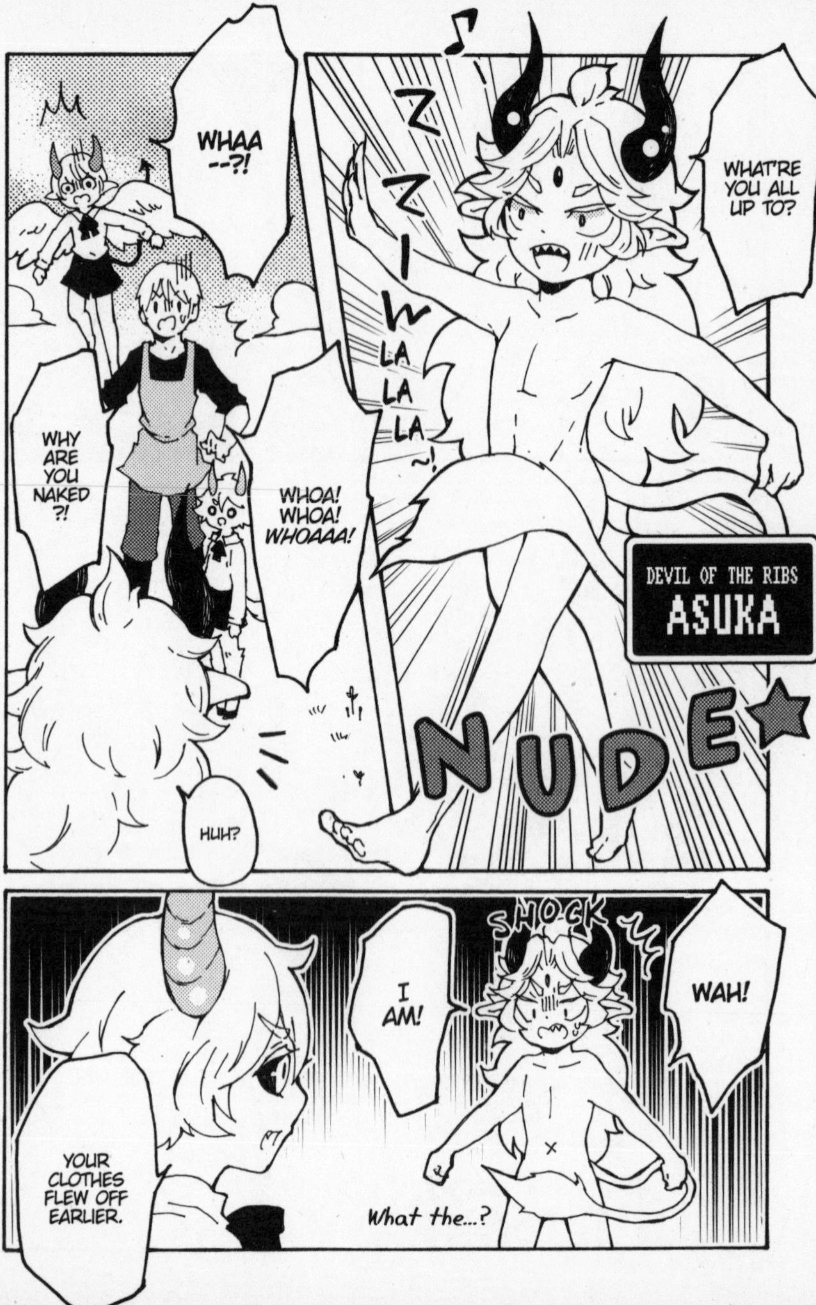
WHAT'RE YOU ALL UP TO?
♪ ZZIW LA LA LA~!
DEVIL OF THE RIBS
ASUKA
NUDE★
WHAA--?!
WHOA! WHOA! WHOAAA!
WHY ARE YOU NAKED?!
HUH?
WAH!
SHOCK
I AM!
What the...?
YOUR CLOTHES FLEW OFF EARLIER.

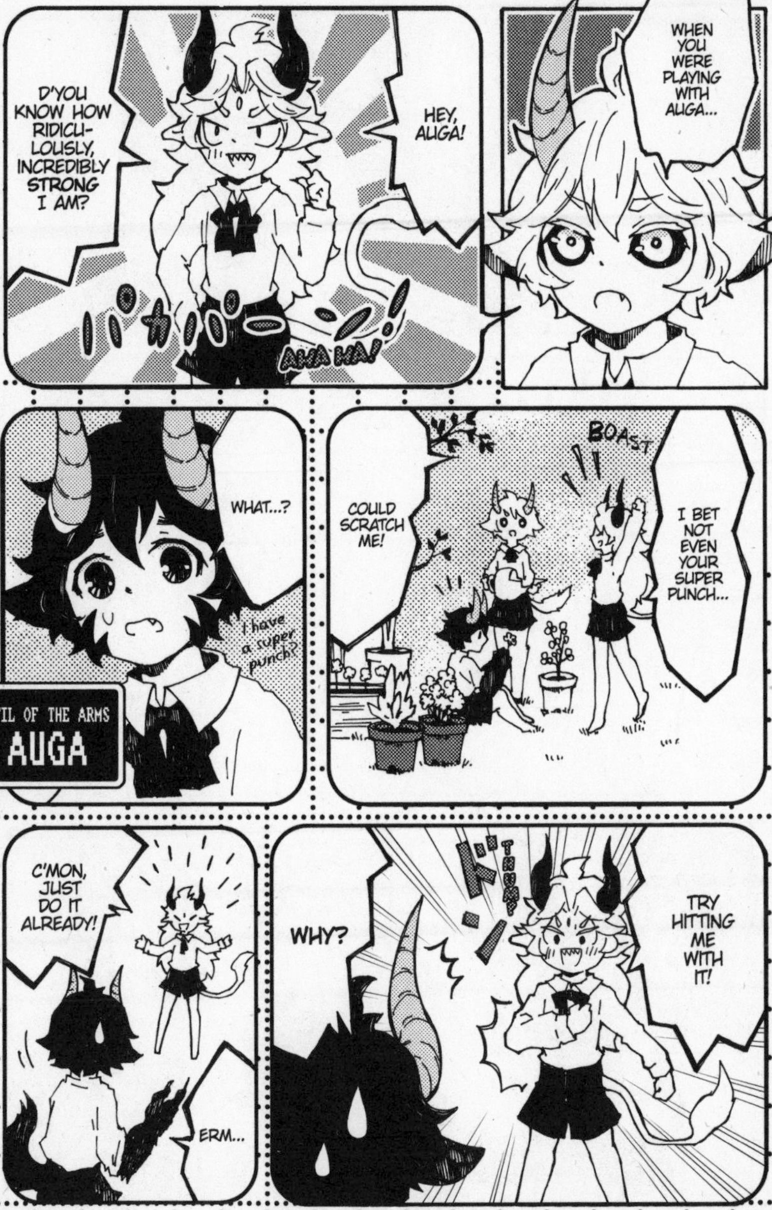
WHEN YOU WERE PLAYING WITH AUGA...
HEY, AUGA!
D'YOU KNOW HOW RIDICULOUSLY, INCREDIBLY STRONG I AM?
AHA HA!
I BET NOT EVEN YOUR SUPER PUNCH...
BOAST
COULD SCRATCH ME!
WHAT...?
I have a super punch?
DEVIL OF THE ARMS
AUGA
TRY HITTING ME WITH IT!
THUMP
WHY?
C'MON, JUST DO IT ALREADY!
ERM...

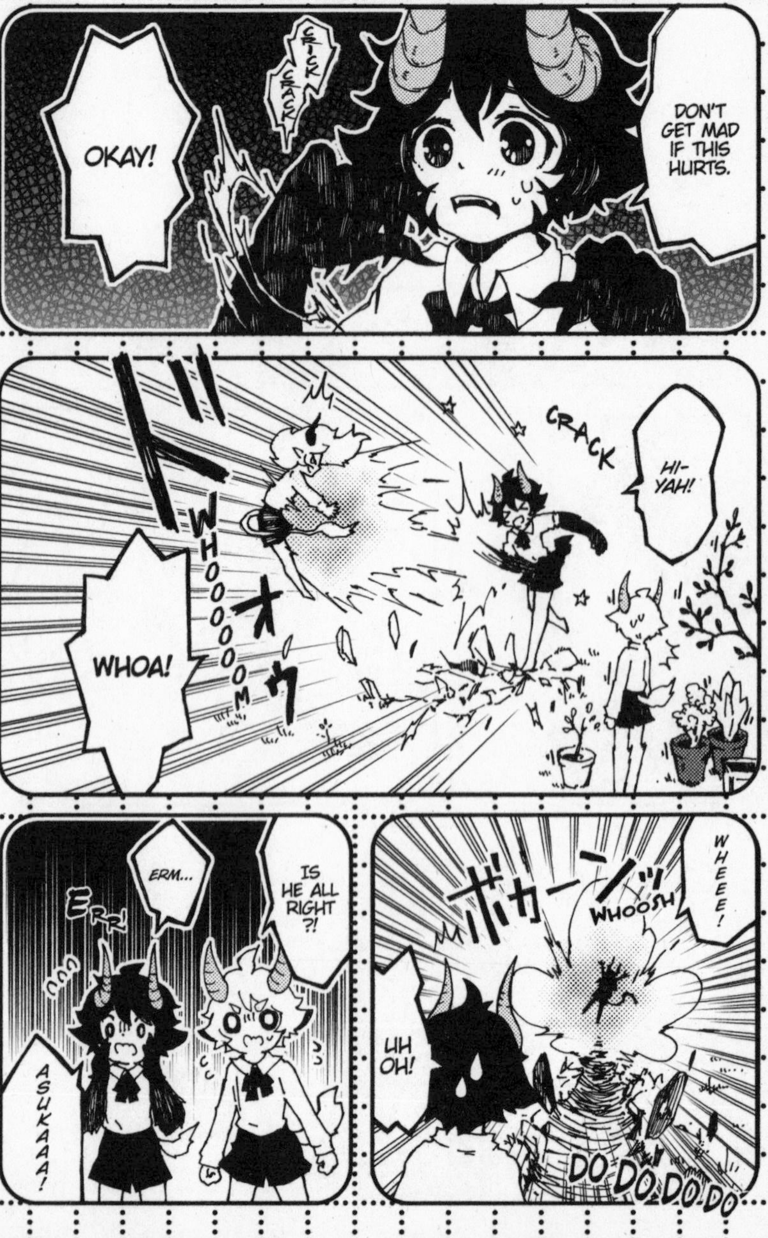
DON'T GET MAD IF THIS HURTS.
CRICK CRACK
OKAY!
HI-YAH!
CRACK
WHOOOOOOOOM
WHOA!
WHEEE!
ボカーンッ
WHOOSH
UH OH!
DO DO DO DO
IS HE ALL RIGHT ?!
ERM...
Errr!
ASUKAAAA!

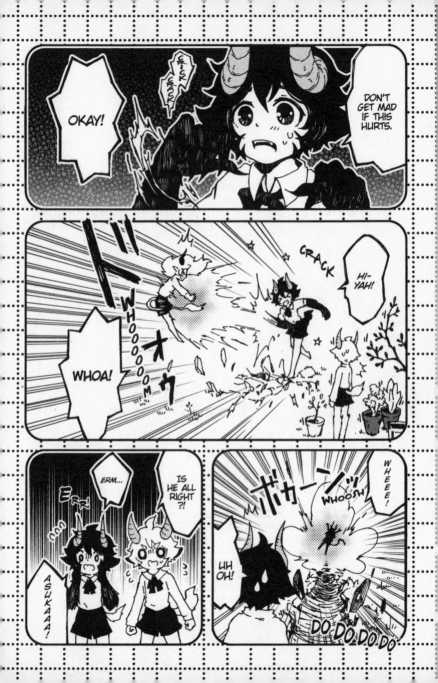

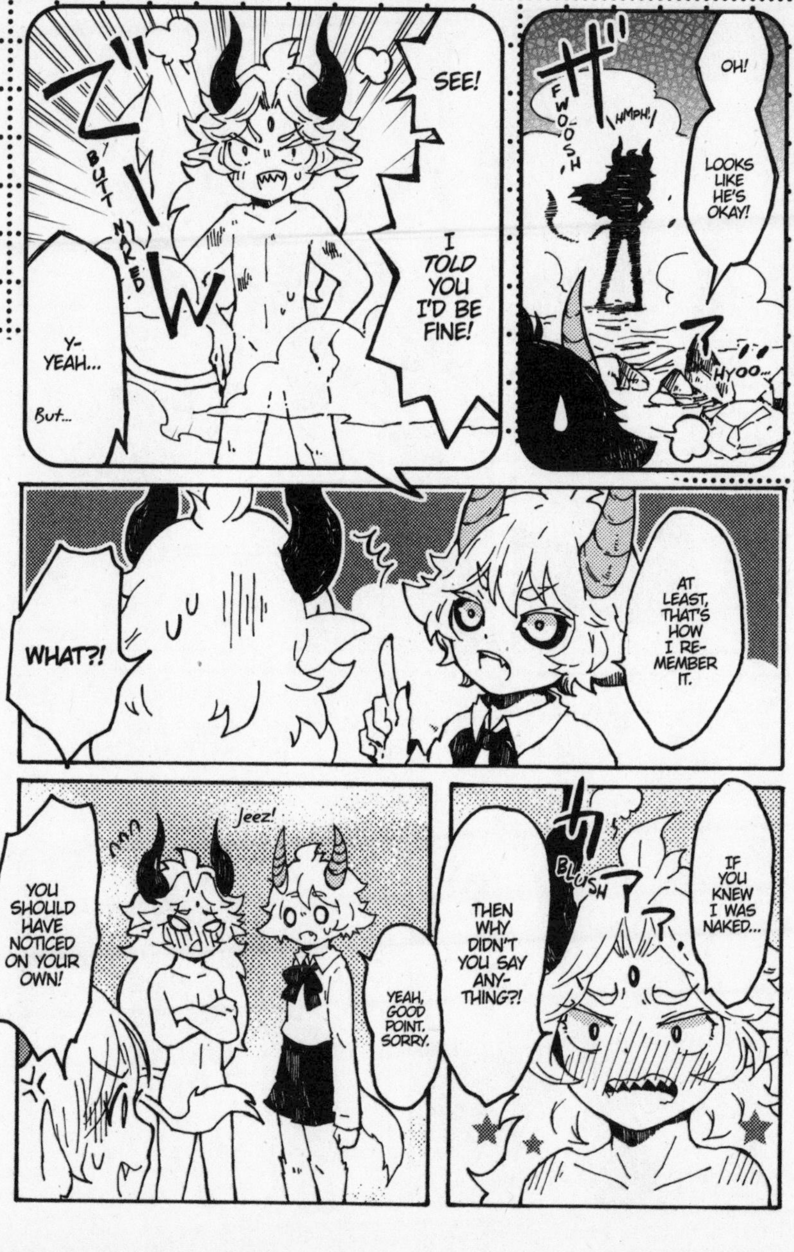
OH!
FWOOSH
HMPH!
LOOKS LIKE HE'S OKAY!
HYOO...
SEE!
I TOLD YOU I'D BE FINE!
BUTT NAKED
Y-YEAH...
But...
AT LEAST, THAT'S HOW I REMEMBER IT.
WHAT?!
IF YOU KNEW I WAS NAKED...
BLUSH
THEN WHY DIDN'T YOU SAY ANYTHING?!
YEAH, GOOD POINT. SORRY.
Jeez!
YOU SHOULD HAVE NOTICED ON YOUR OWN!

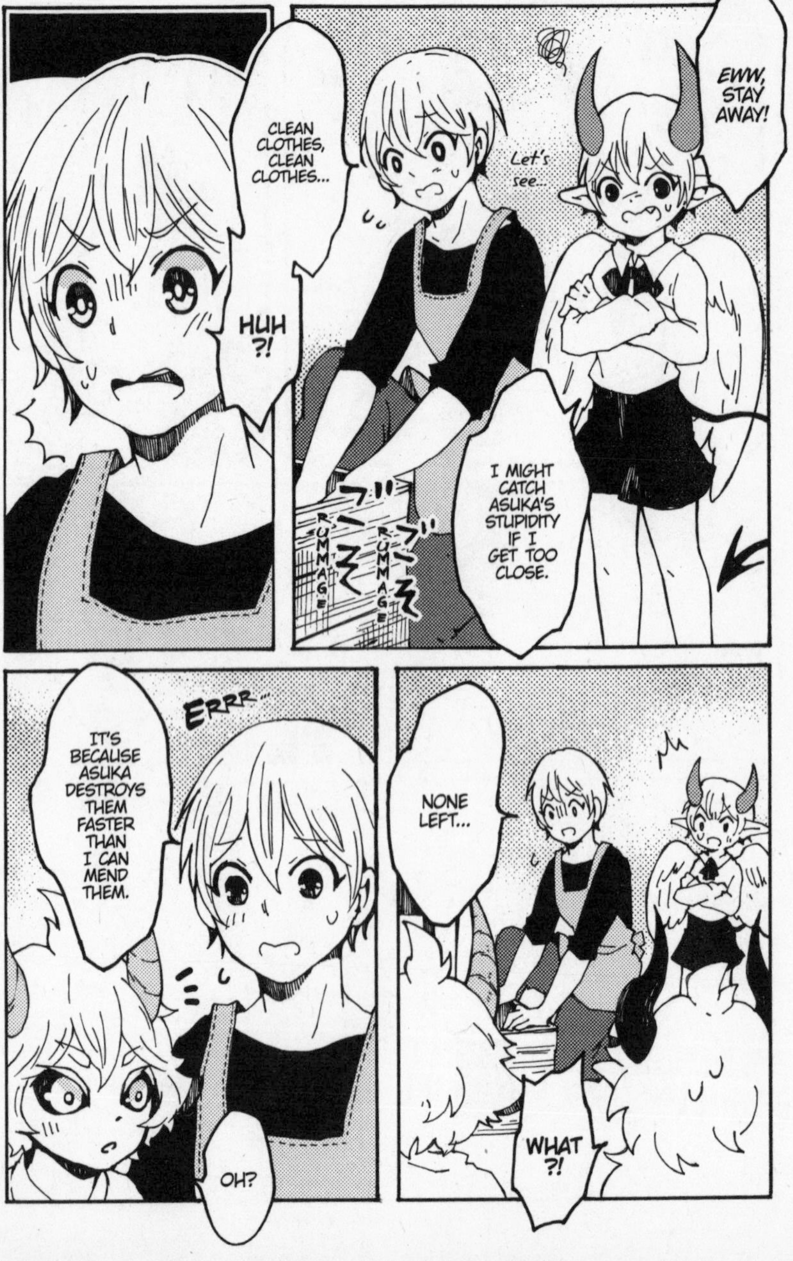
EWW, STAY AWAY!
Let's see...
CLEAN CLOTHES, CLEAN CLOTHES...
RUMMAGE
RUMMAGE
I MIGHT CATCH ASUKA'S STUPIDITY IF I GET TOO CLOSE.
HUH?!
NONE LEFT...
WHAT?!
ERRR...
IT'S BECAUSE ASUKA DESTROYS THEM FASTER THAN I CAN MEND THEM.
OH?

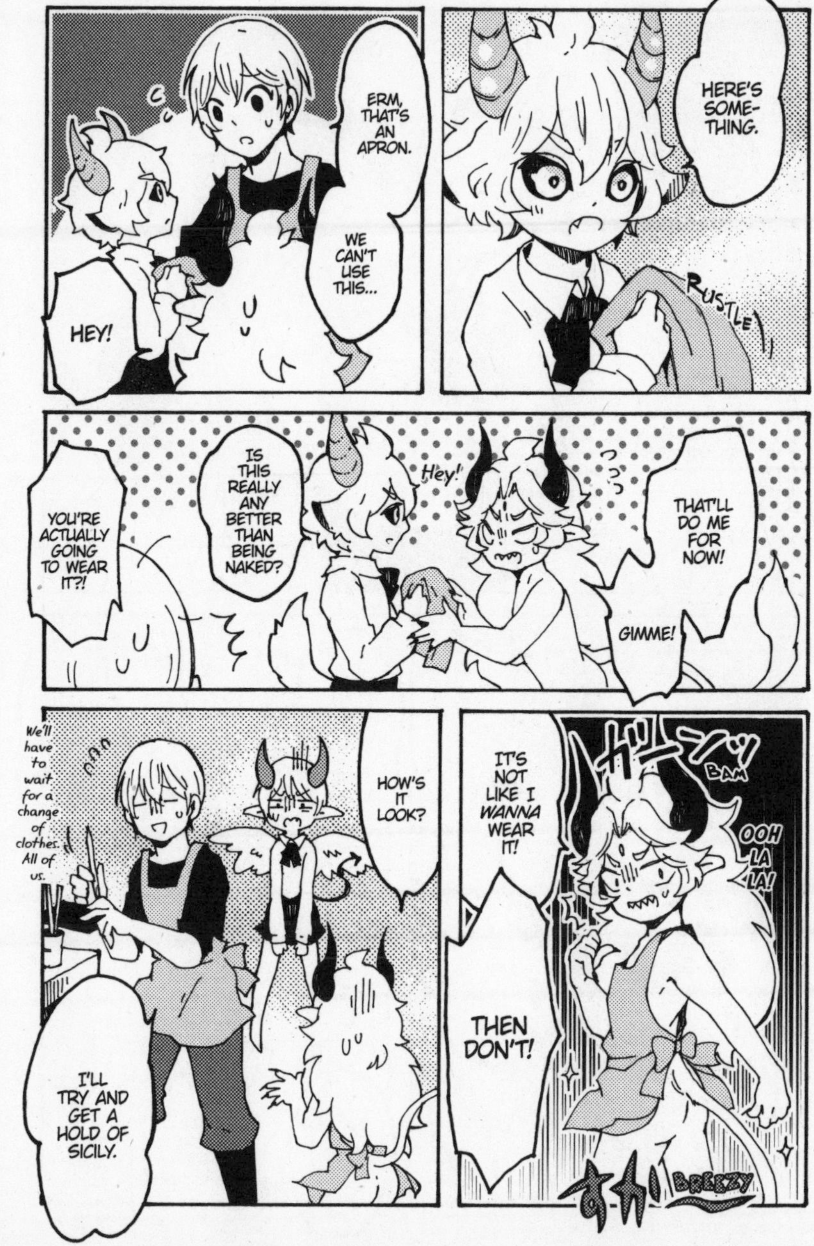
HERE'S SOMETHING.
RUSTLE
ERM, THAT'S AN APRON.
WE CAN'T USE THIS...
HEY!
THAT'LL DO ME FOR NOW!
GIMME!
Hey!
IS THIS REALLY ANY BETTER THAN BEING NAKED?
YOU'RE ACTUALLY GOING TO WEAR IT?!
BAM
IT'S NOT LIKE I WANNA WEAR IT!
OOH LA LA!
THEN DON'T!
BREEZY
HOW'S IT LOOK?
I'LL TRY AND GET A HOLD OF SICILY.
We'll have to wait for a change of clothes. All of us.

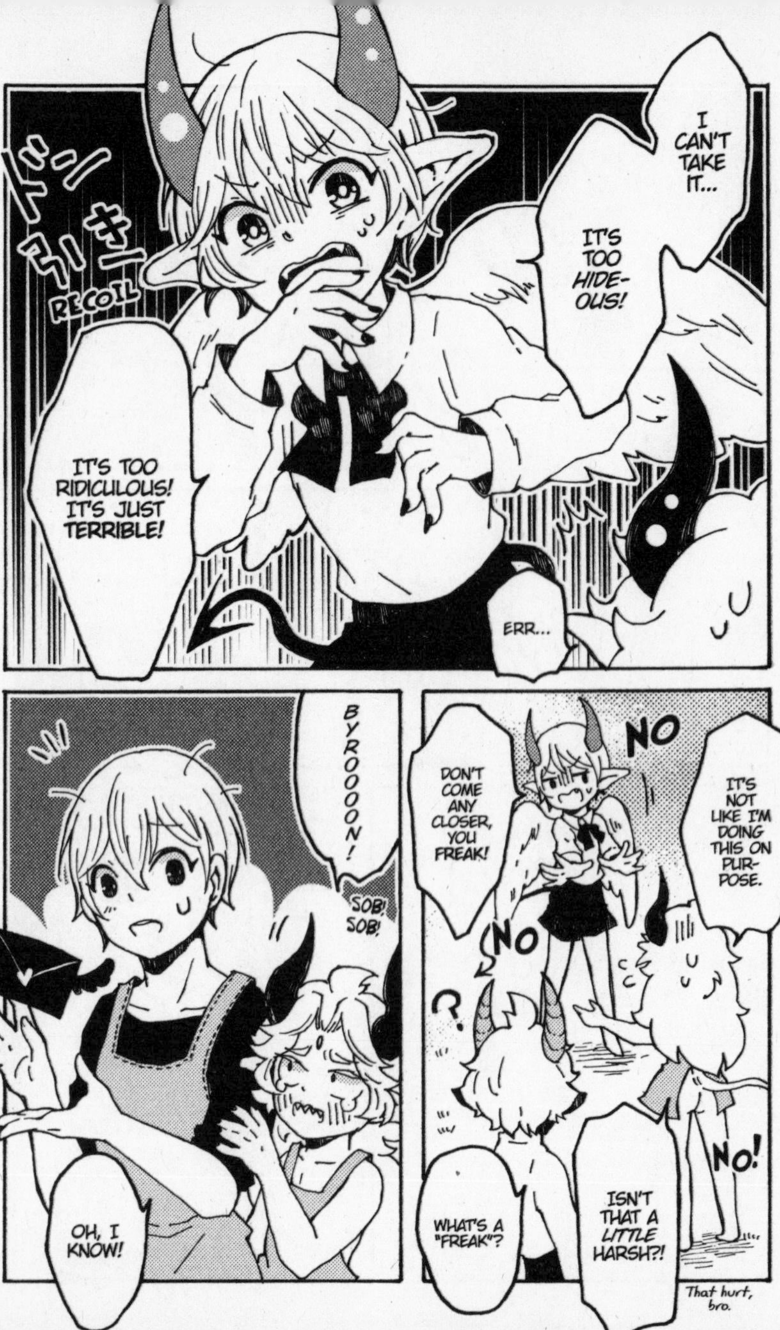
I CAN'T TAKE IT...
IT'S TOO HIDEOUS!
RECOIL
IT'S TOO RIDICULOUS! IT'S JUST TERRIBLE!
ERR...
NO
IT'S NOT LIKE I'M DOING THIS ON PURPOSE.
DON'T COME ANY CLOSER, YOU FREAK!
NO
NO!
ISN'T THAT A LITTLE HARSH?!
WHAT'S A "FREAK"?
BYROOOOON!
SOB! SOB!
OH, I KNOW!

That hurt, bro.

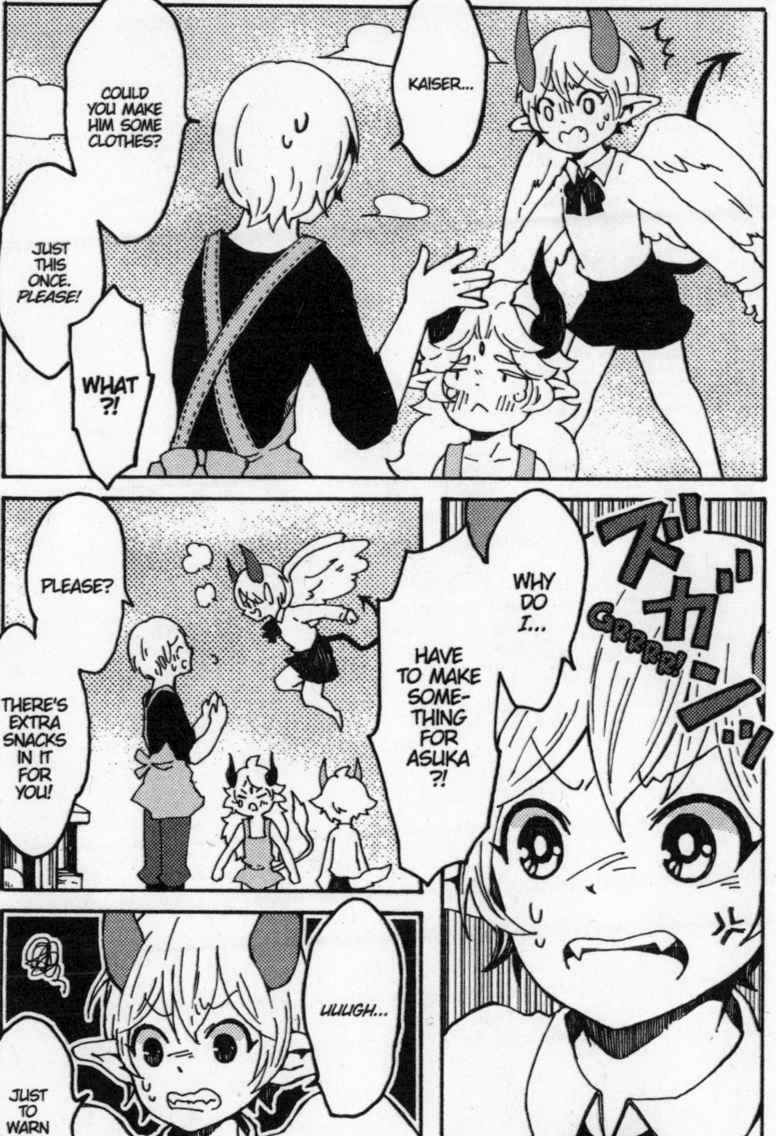
KAISER...
COULD YOU MAKE HIM SOME CLOTHES?
JUST THIS ONCE. *PLEASE!*
WHAT ?!
ズガーン
GRRRR!
WHY DO I...
HAVE TO MAKE SOME-THING FOR ASUKA ?!
PLEASE?
THERE'S EXTRA SNACKS IN IT FOR YOU!
UUUGH...
JUST TO WARN YOU...

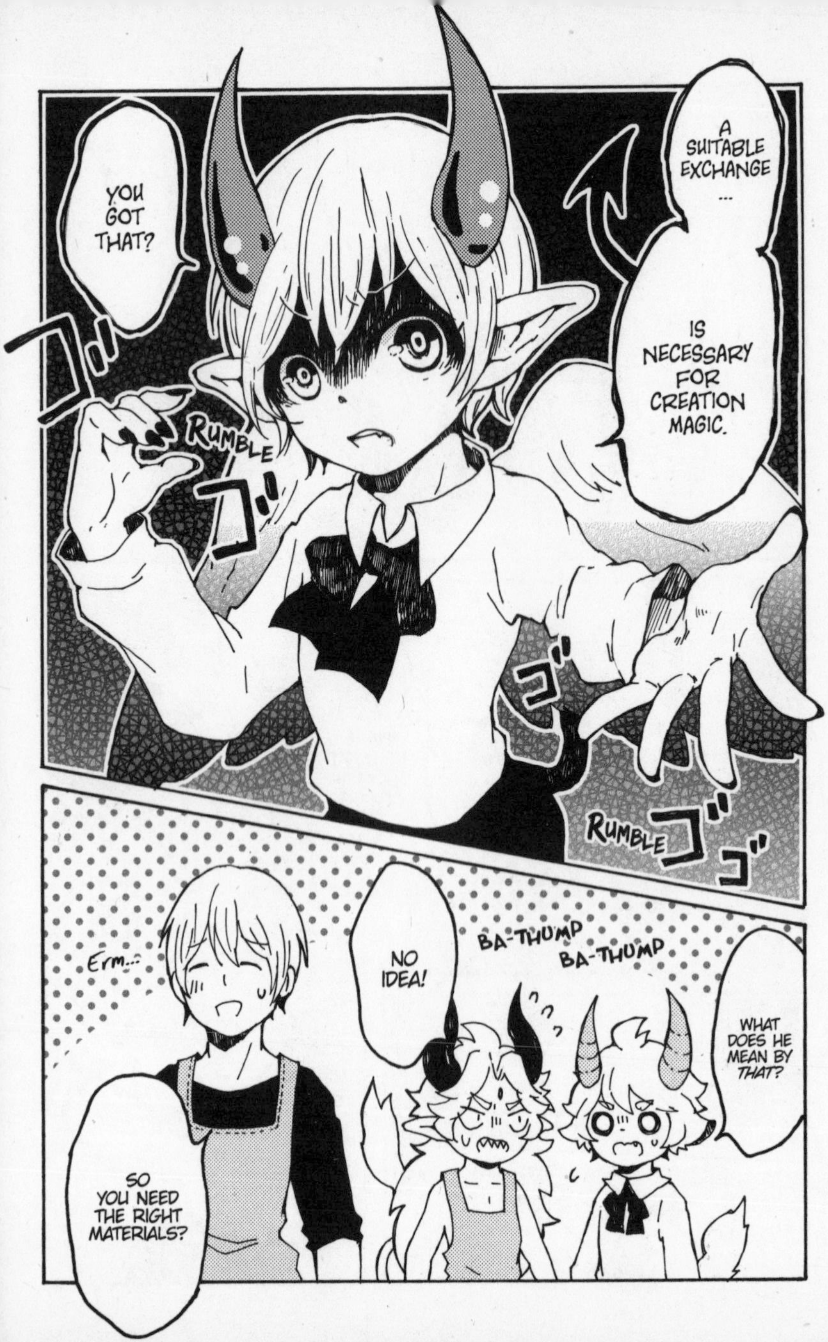
A SUITABLE EXCHANGE ...
IS NECESSARY FOR CREATION MAGIC.
YOU GOT THAT?
RUMBLE
RUMBLE
BA-THUMP BA-THUMP
WHAT DOES HE MEAN BY THAT?
NO IDEA!
Erm...
SO YOU NEED THE RIGHT MATERIALS?

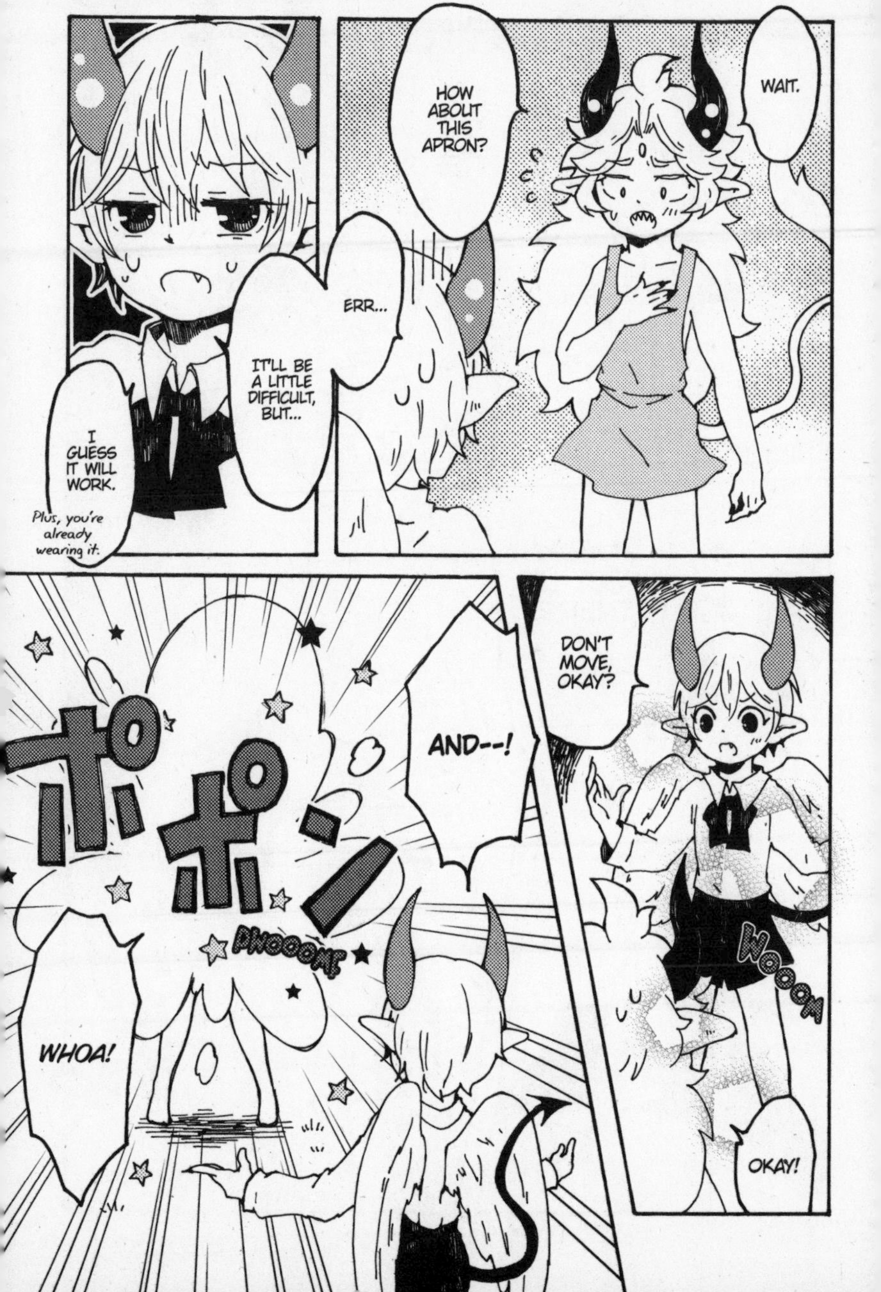
WAIT.
HOW ABOUT THIS APRON?
ERR...
IT'LL BE A LITTLE DIFFICULT, BUT...
I GUESS IT WILL WORK.
Plus, you're already wearing it.
DON'T MOVE, OKAY?
WOOOOM
OKAY!
AND--!
ポポン
PHOOOM!
WHOA!

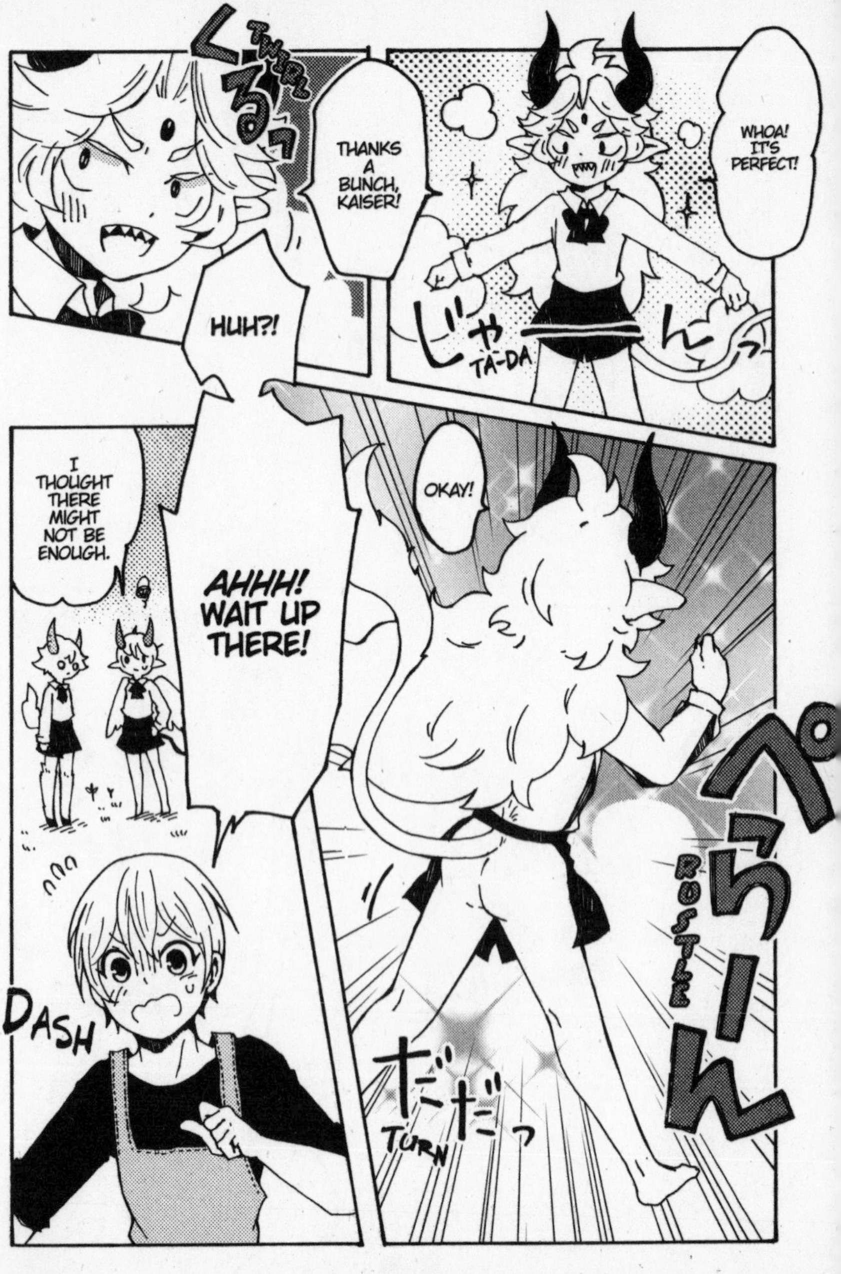
WHOA! IT'S PERFECT!
じゃん
TA-DA
くるっ
TWIRL
THANKS A BUNCH, KAISER!
HUH?!
OKAY!
ぺらーん
ROSTLE
だだっ
TURN
I THOUGHT THERE MIGHT NOT BE ENOUGH.
AHHH! WAIT UP THERE!
DASH

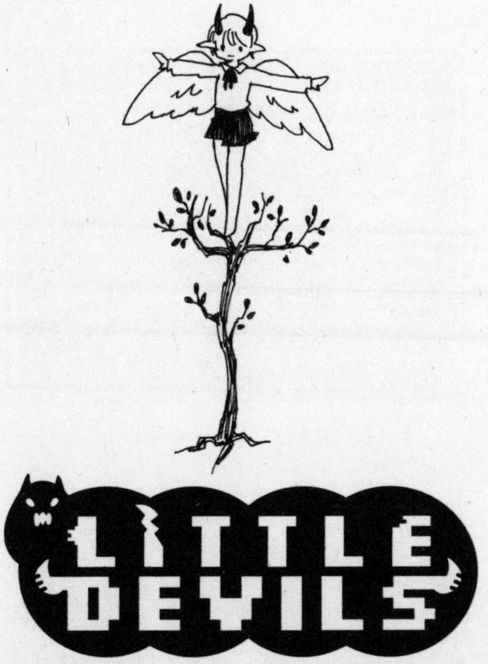

LITTLE DEVILS

DEVIL OF THE WINGS - KAISER ▼

The calculating, intellectual third
brother.
Struggles with the stupidity of those
around him.
He's smart and capable and thus finds
it difficult to rely on others.
Something of a neat freak.

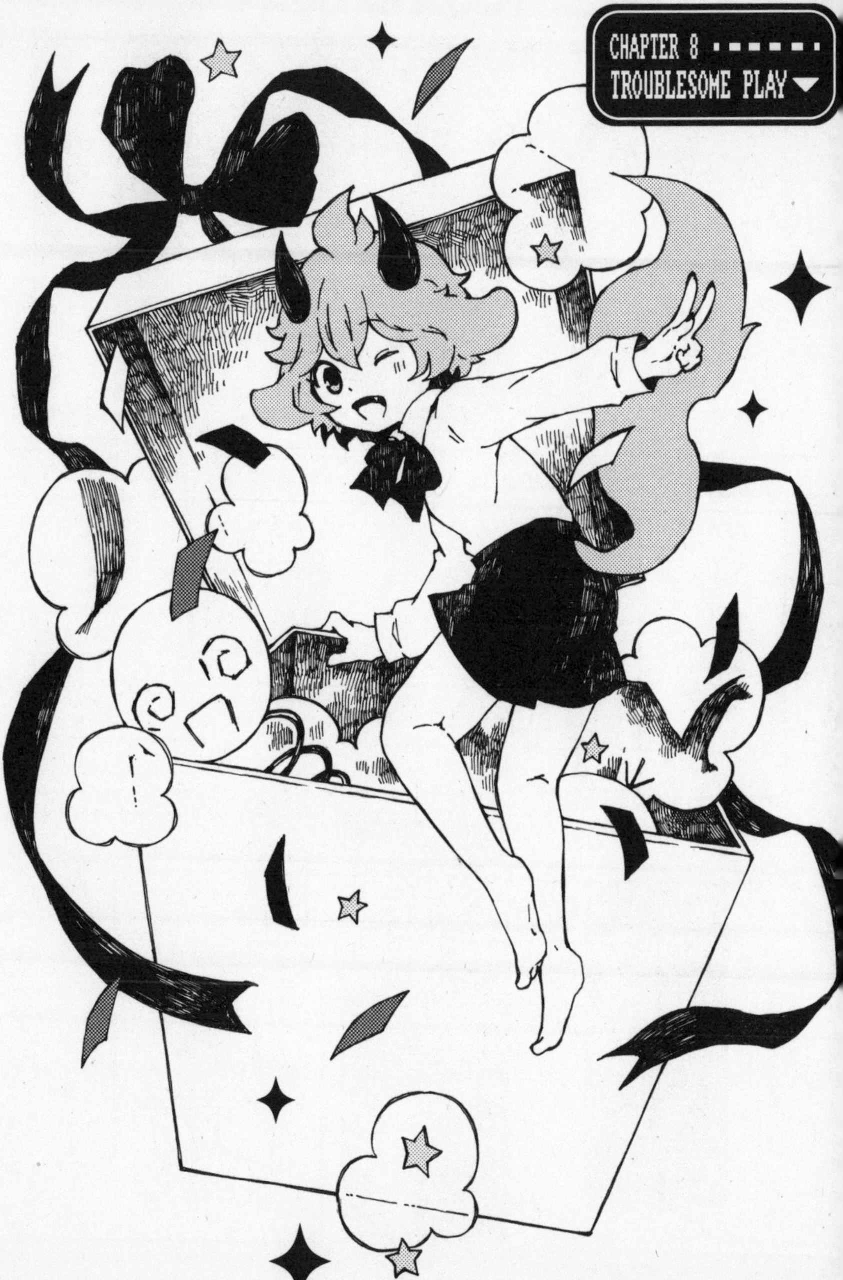
CHAPTER 8
TROUBLESOME PLAY

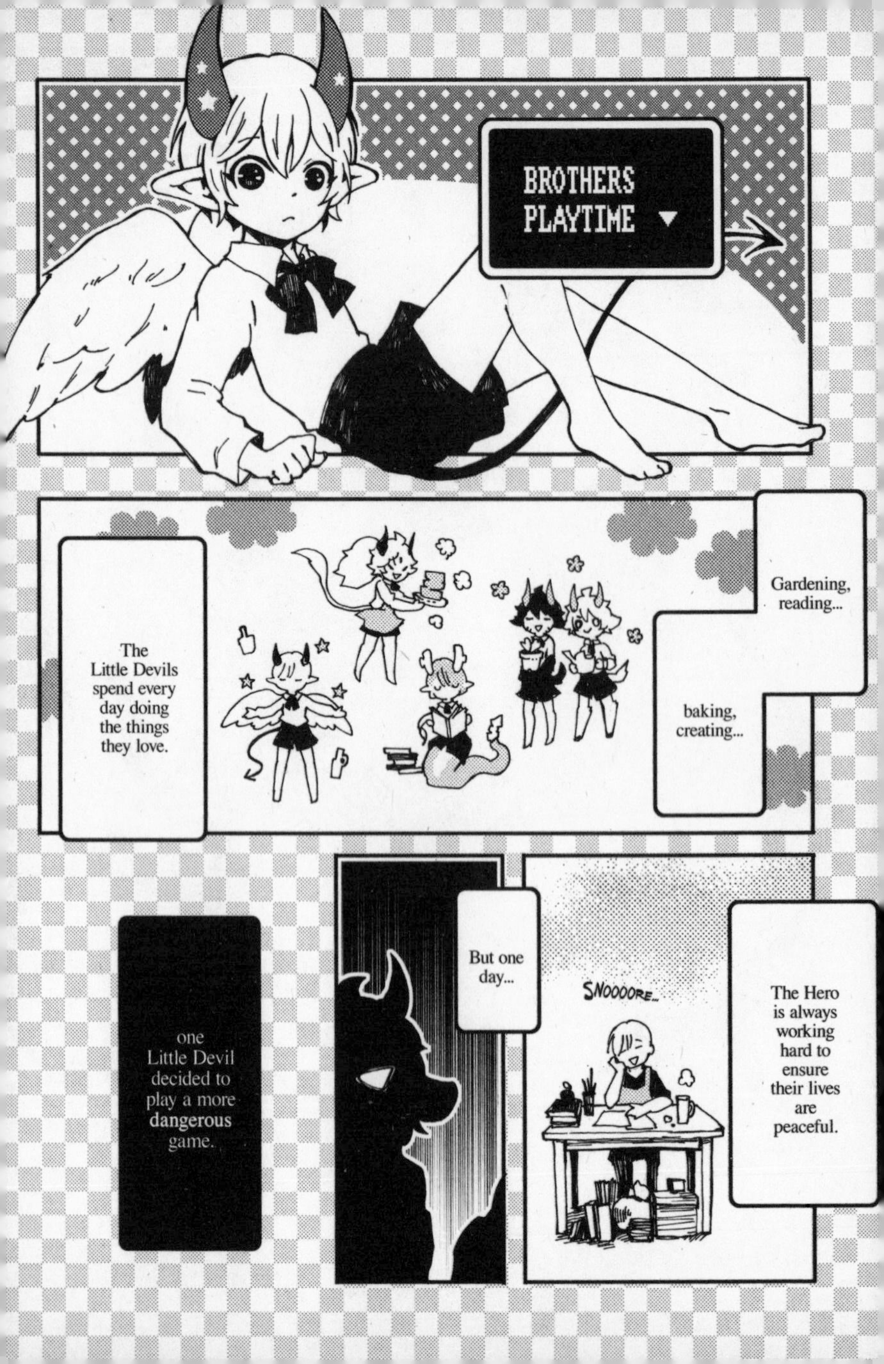
BROTHERS PLAYTIME ▼
Gardening, reading...
baking, creating...
The Little Devils spend every day doing the things they love.
The Hero is always working hard to ensure their lives are peaceful.
SNOOOORE...
But one day...
one Little Devil decided to play a more dangerous game.

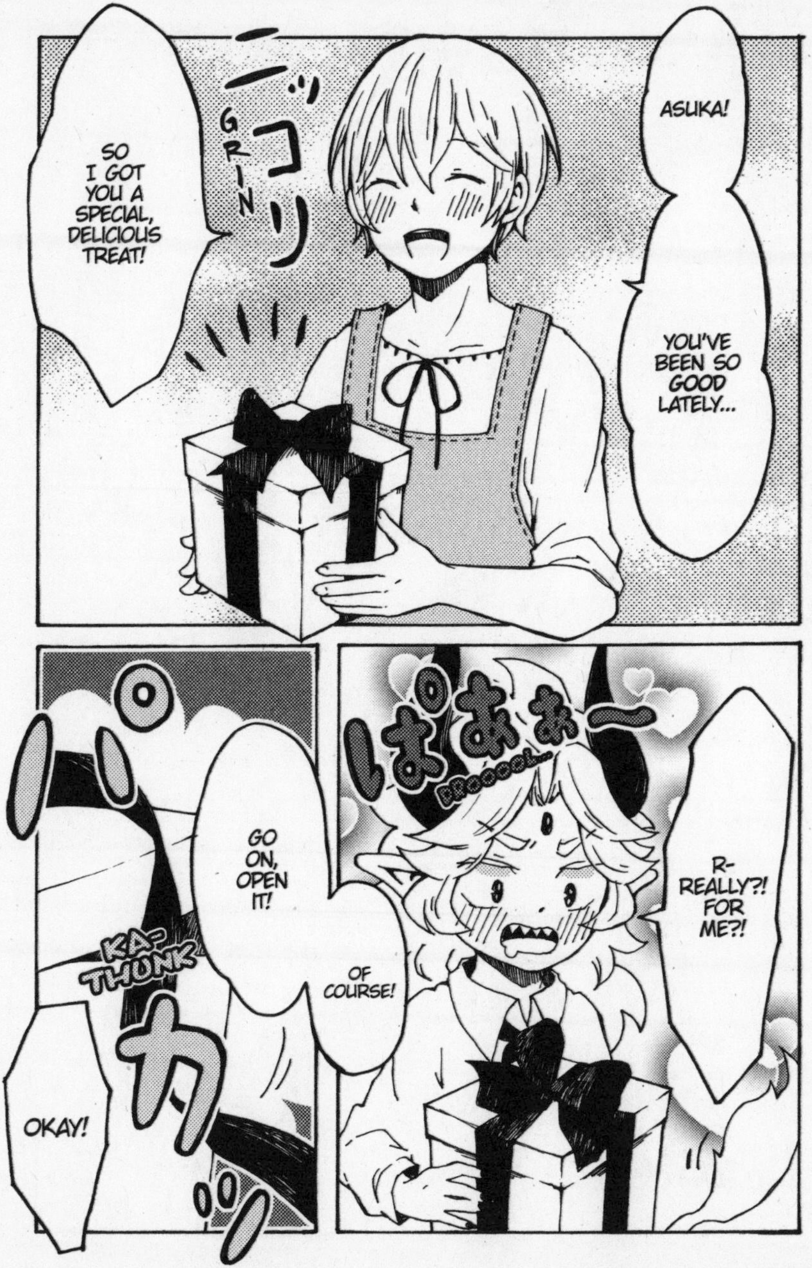
ASUKA!
YOU'VE BEEN SO GOOD LATELY...
GRIN
SO I GOT YOU A SPECIAL, DELICIOUS TREAT!
DROOOOOL...
R-REALLY?! FOR ME?!
OF COURSE!
GO ON, OPEN IT!
KA-THUNK
OKAY!

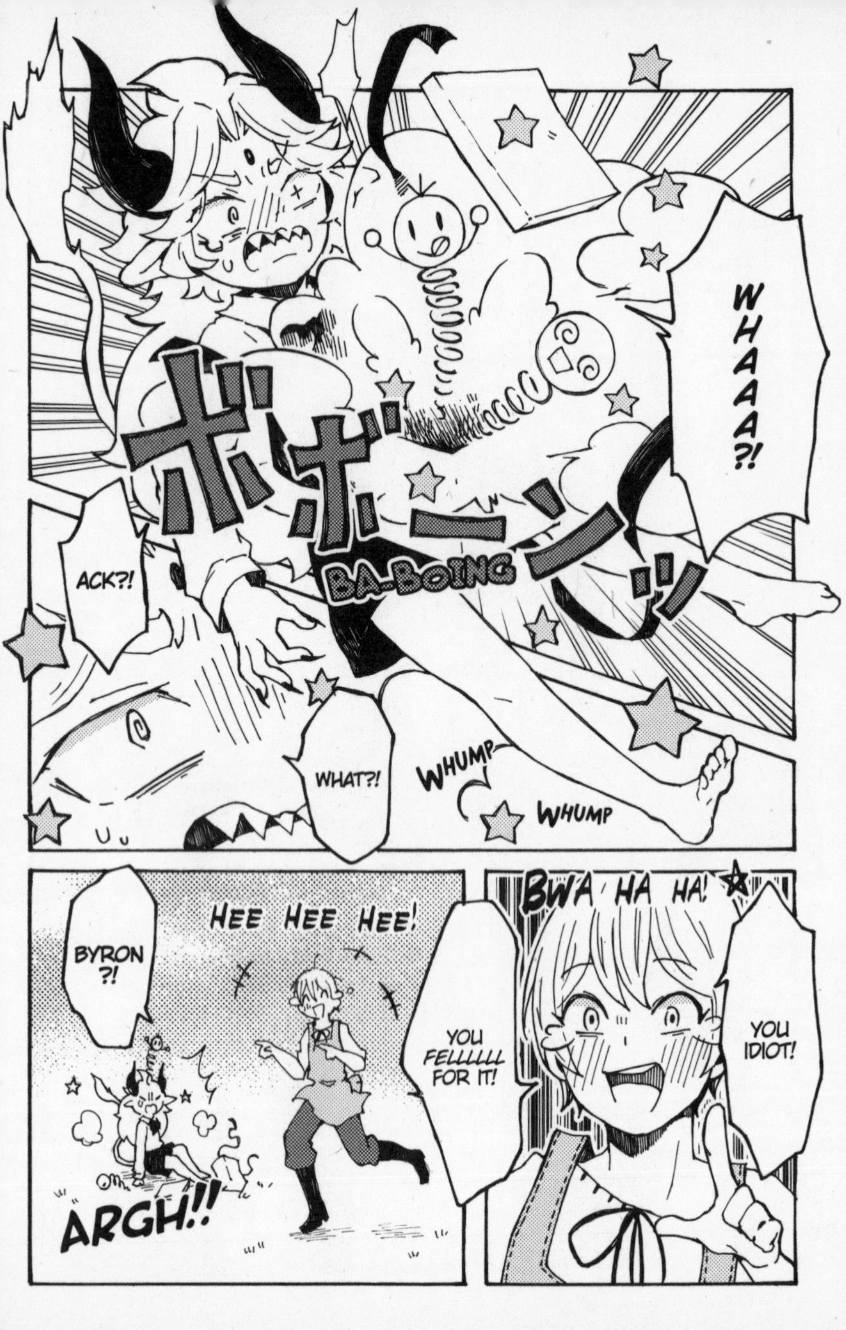
WHAAAA?!
ボボーン!!
BA-BOING
ACK?!
WHAT?!
WHUMP
WHUMP
BWA HA HA! ☆
YOU IDIOT!
YOU FELLLLLL FOR IT!
HEE HEE HEE!
BYRON ?!
ARGH!!

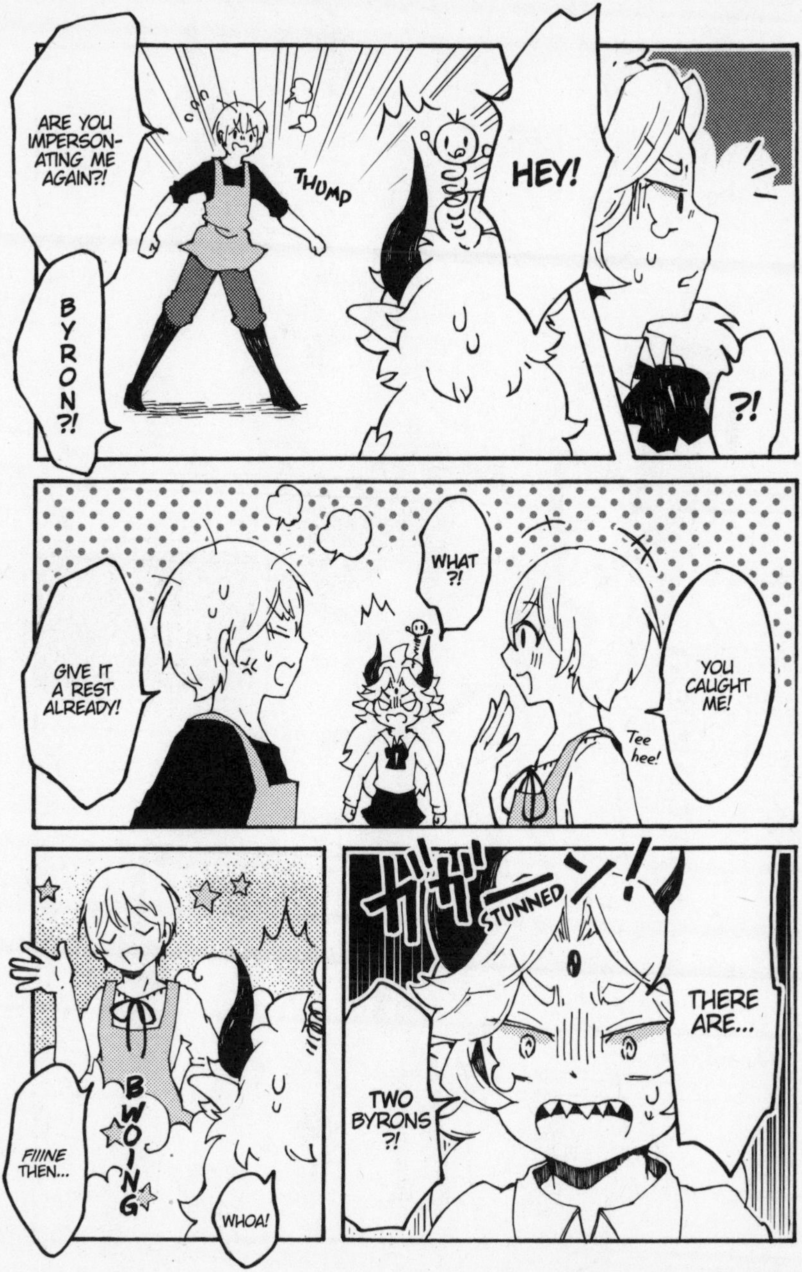

?!
HEY!
ARE YOU IMPERSON-ATING ME AGAIN?!
THUMP
BYRON?!
YOU CAUGHT ME!
Tee hee!
WHAT?!
GIVE IT A REST ALREADY!
STUNNED
THERE ARE...
TWO BYRONS?!
FIIINE THEN...
BWOING
WHOA!

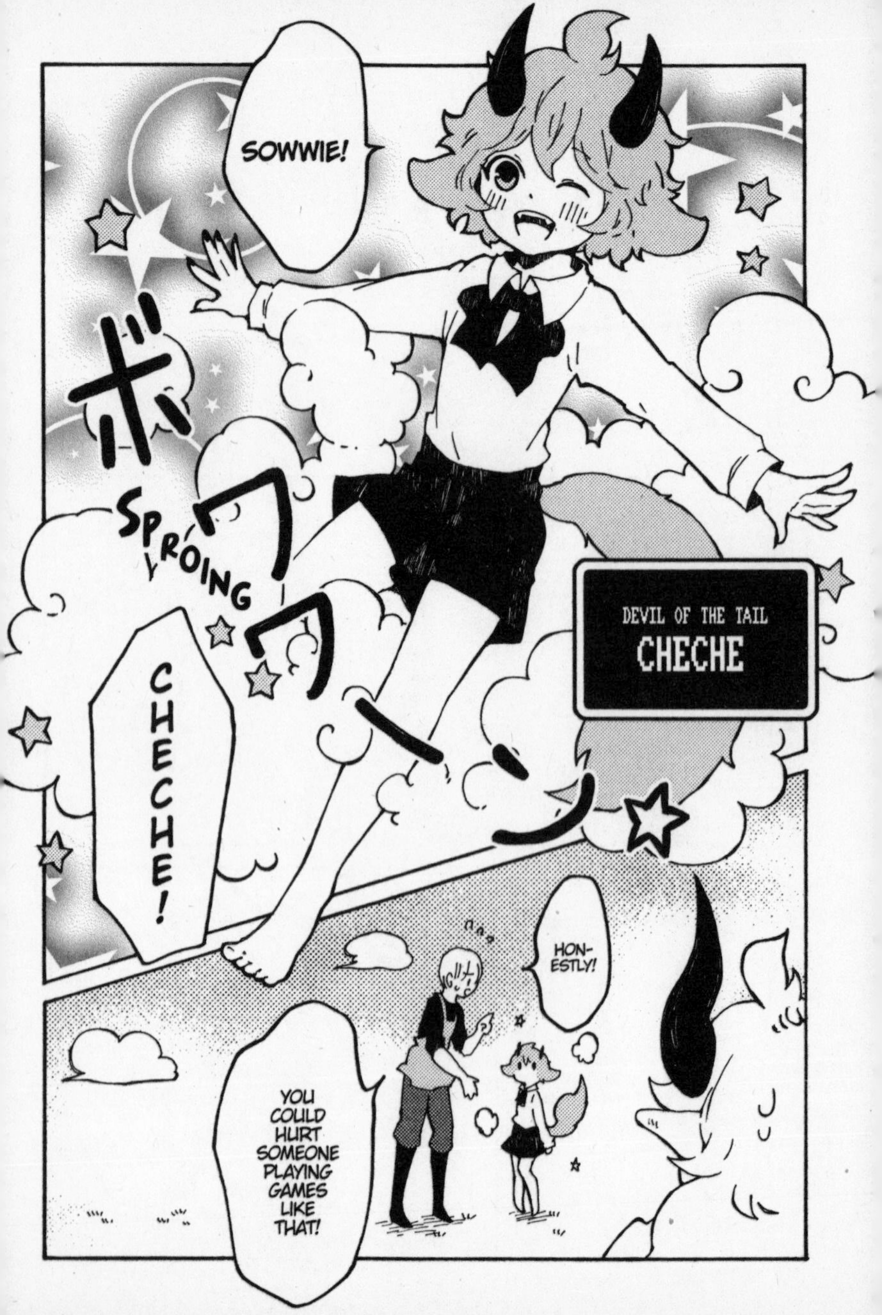
SOWWIE!
ボフーン
SPROING
CHECHE!
DEVIL OF THE TAIL
CHECHE
HON-
ESTLY!
YOU COULD HURT SOMEONE PLAYING GAMES LIKE THAT!

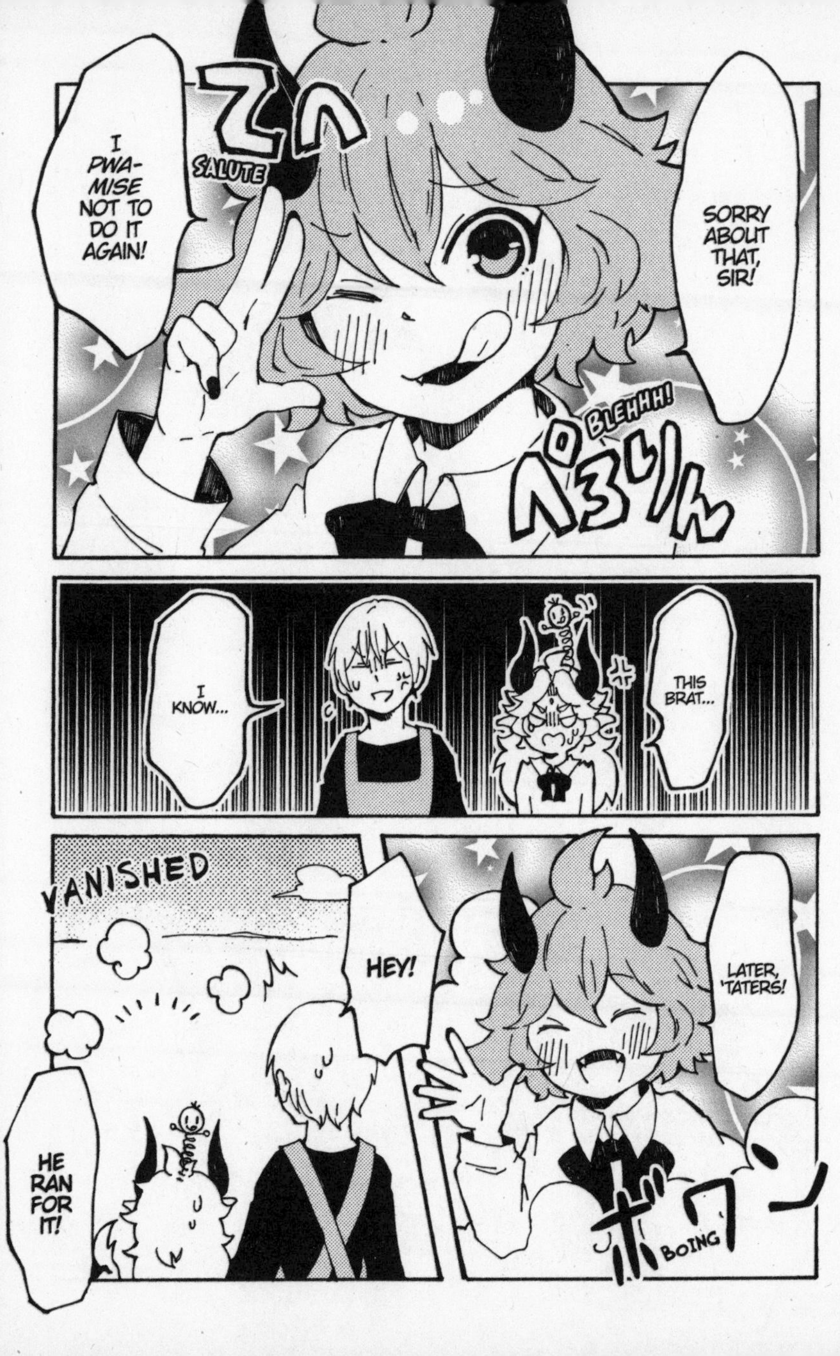
SORRY ABOUT THAT, SIR!
BLEHHH!
SALUTE
I PWA-MISE NOT TO DO IT AGAIN!
THIS BRAT...
I KNOW...
LATER, 'TATERS!
BOING
VANISHED
HEY!
HE RAN FOR IT!

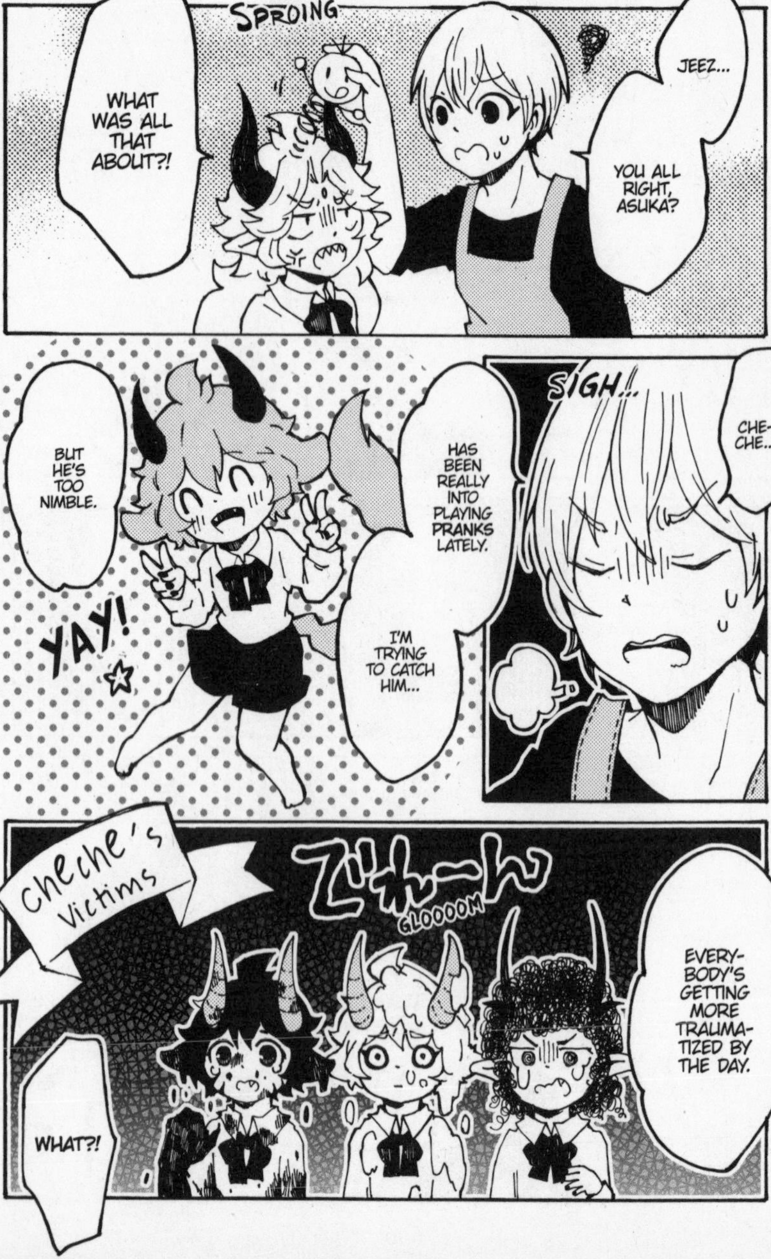
JEEZ...
YOU ALL RIGHT, ASUKA?
SPROING
WHAT WAS ALL THAT ABOUT?!
SIGH...
CHE-CHE...
HAS BEEN REALLY INTO PLAYING PRANKS LATELY.
I'M TRYING TO CATCH HIM...
BUT HE'S TOO NIMBLE.
YAY!
EVERYBODY'S GETTING MORE TRAUMATIZED BY THE DAY.
GLOOOOM
Cheche's Victims
WHAT?!

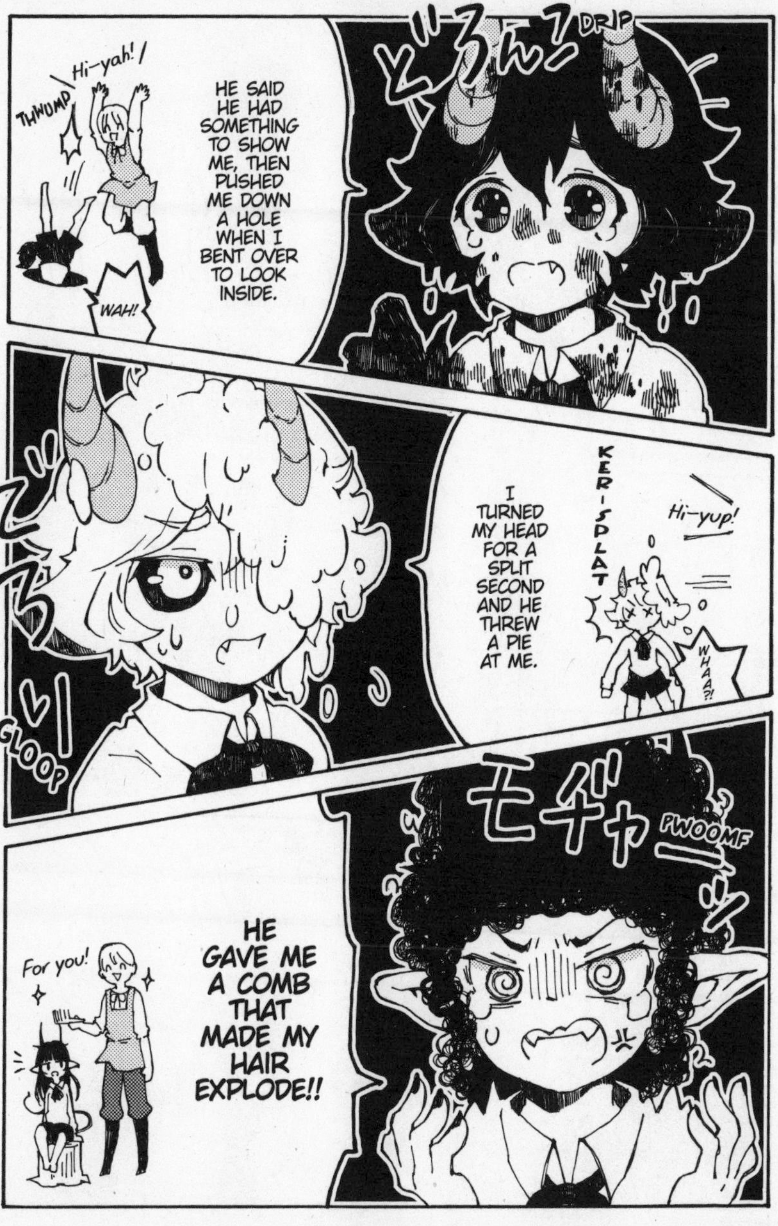
どろん!
DRIP
HE SAID HE HAD SOMETHING TO SHOW ME, THEN PUSHED ME DOWN A HOLE WHEN I BENT OVER TO LOOK INSIDE.
Hi-yah!
THWUMP
WAH!
I TURNED MY HEAD FOR A SPLIT SECOND AND HE THREW A PIE AT ME.
KERI-SPLAT
Hi-yup!
WHAAA?!
GLOOP
モジャー
PWOOMF
HE GAVE ME A COMB THAT MADE MY HAIR EXPLODE!!
For you!

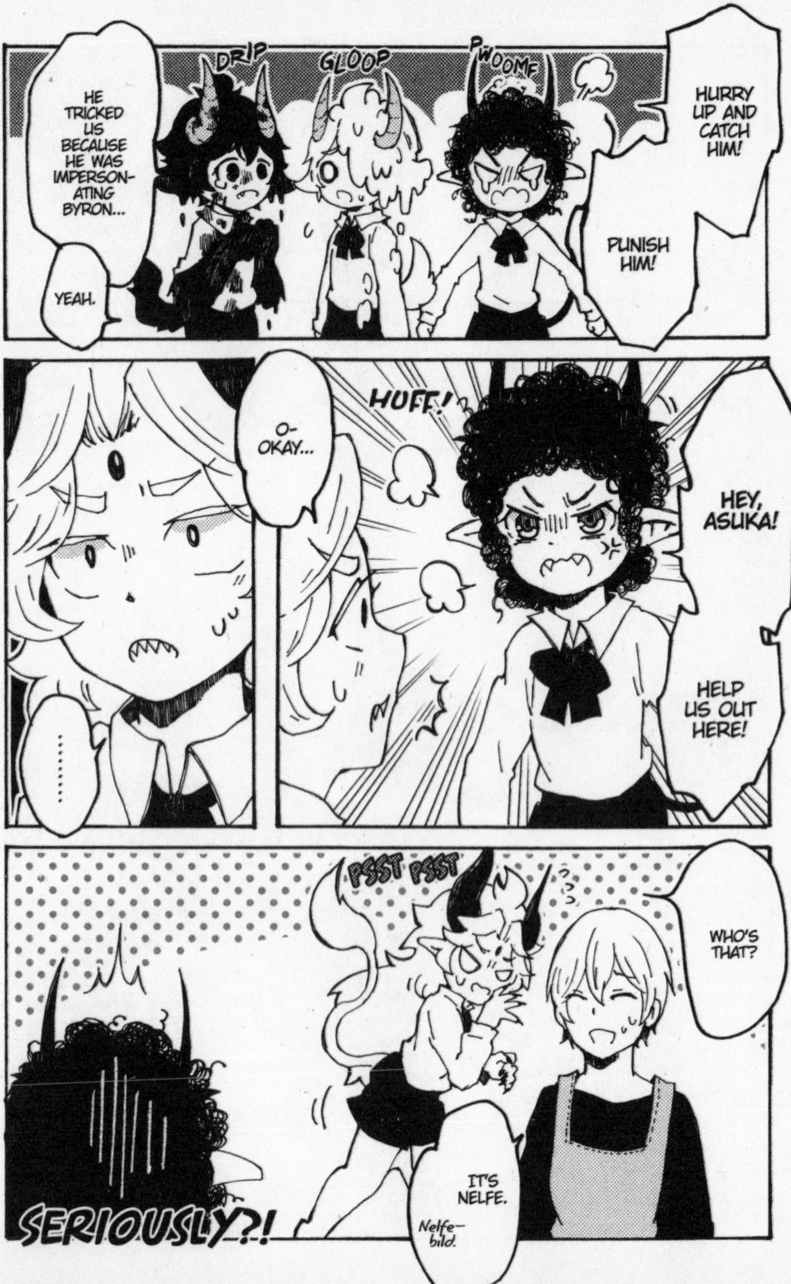
HURRY UP AND CATCH HIM!
PUNISH HIM!
PWOOMF
GLOOP
DRIP
HE TRICKED US BECAUSE HE WAS IMPERSON-ATING BYRON...
YEAH.
HEY, ASUKA!
HELP US OUT HERE!
HUFF!
O-OKAY...
......
WHO'S THAT?
PSSST PSSST
IT'S NELFE.
Nelfe-bild.
SERIOUSLY?!

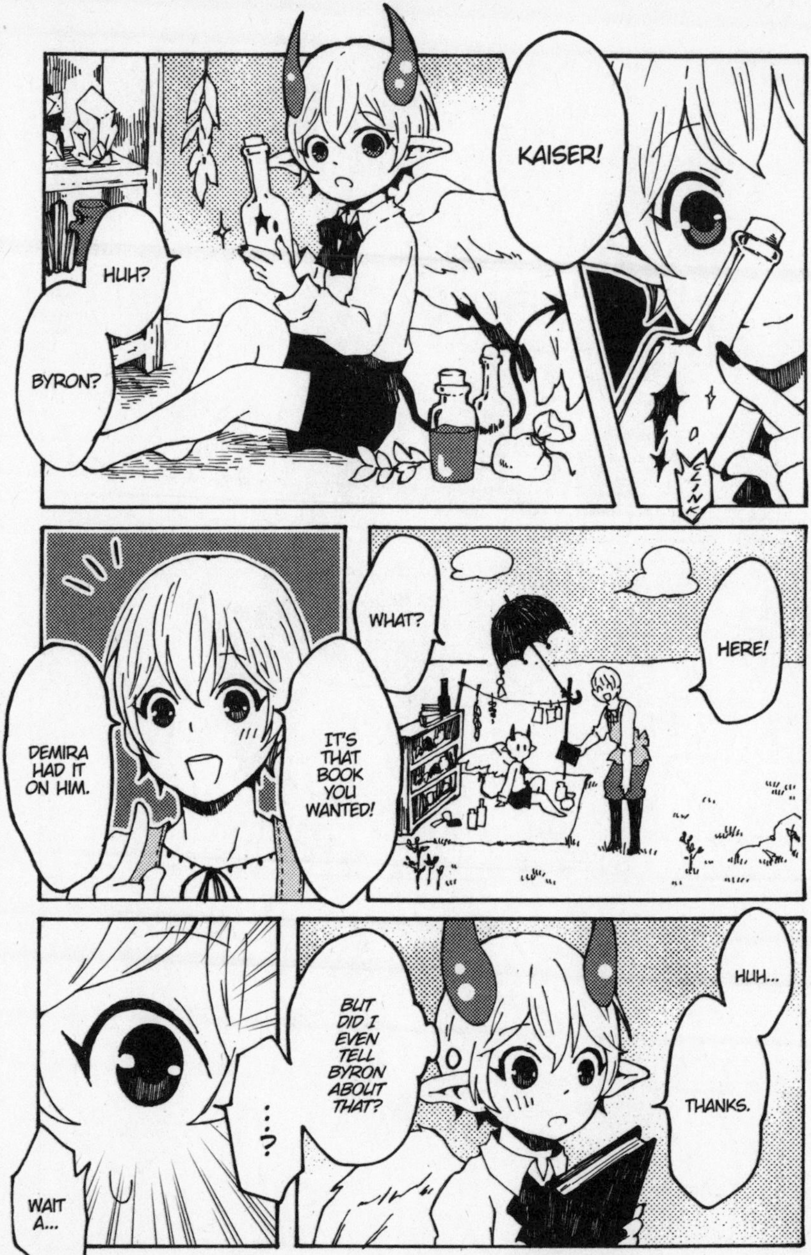
KAISER!
CLINK
HUH?
BYRON?
HERE!
WHAT?
IT'S THAT BOOK YOU WANTED!
DEMIRA HAD IT ON HIM.
HUH... THANKS.
BUT DID I EVEN TELL BYRON ABOUT THAT?
...?
WAIT A...

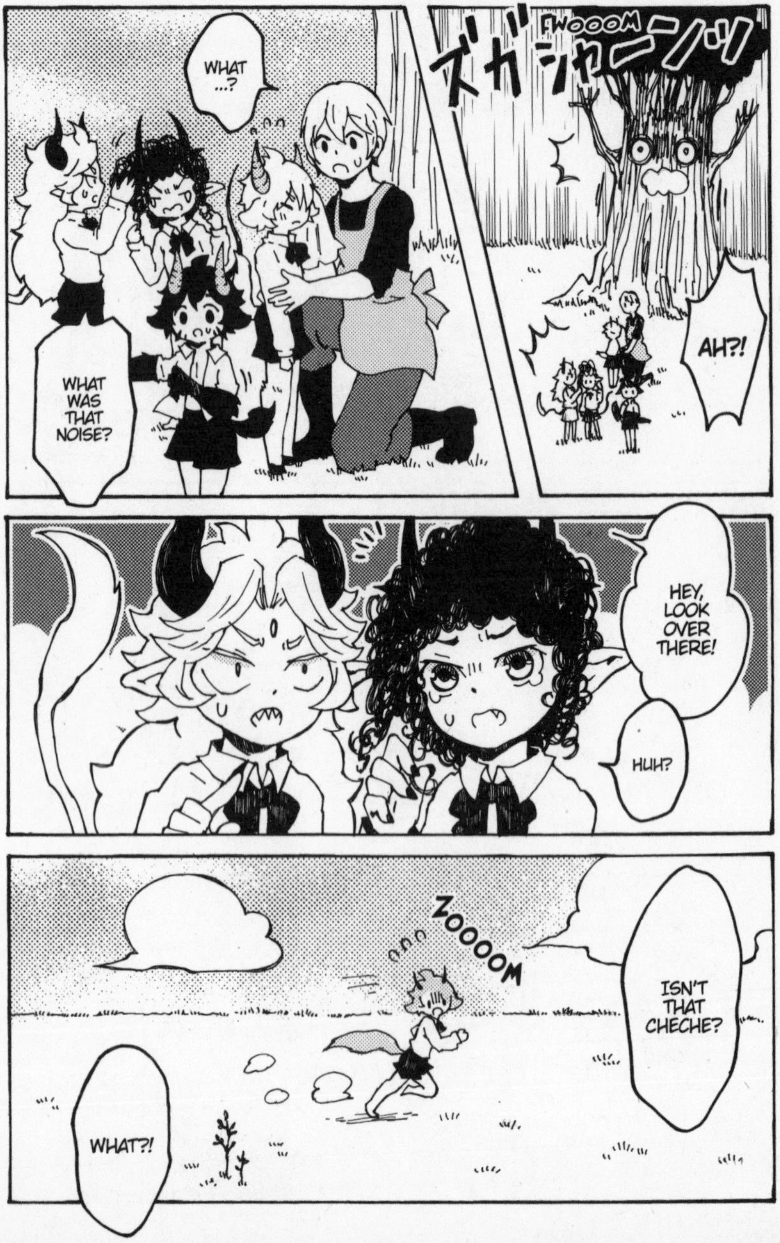
ズガシャーンッ
FWOOOM
AH?!
WHAT ...?
WHAT WAS THAT NOISE?
HEY, LOOK OVER THERE!
HUH?
ISN'T THAT CHECHE?
ZOOOOOM
WHAT?!

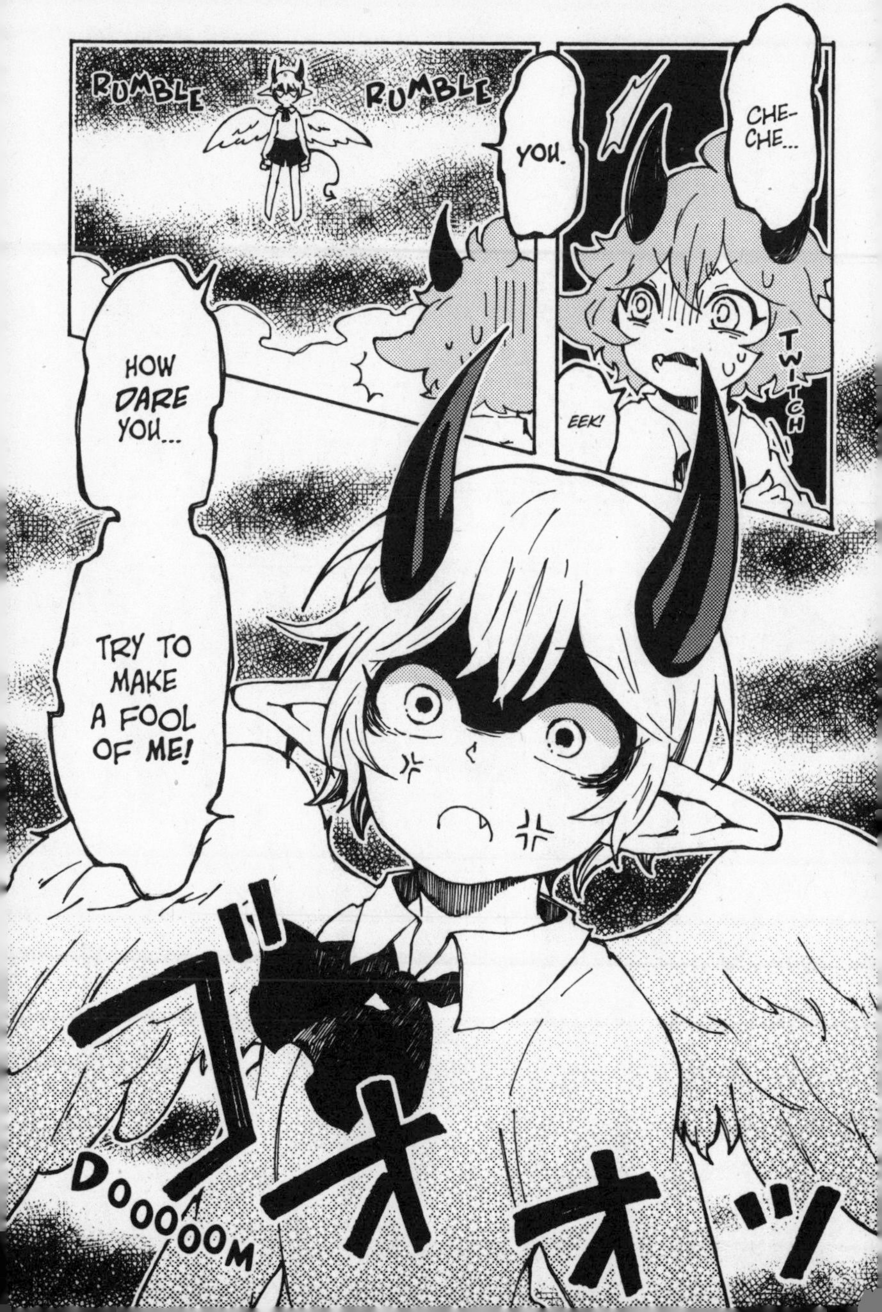
CHE-CHE...
TWITCH
EEK!
YOU.
RUMBLE
RUMBLE
HOW DARE YOU...
TRY TO MAKE A FOOL OF ME!
ゴオオッ
DOOOOOOM

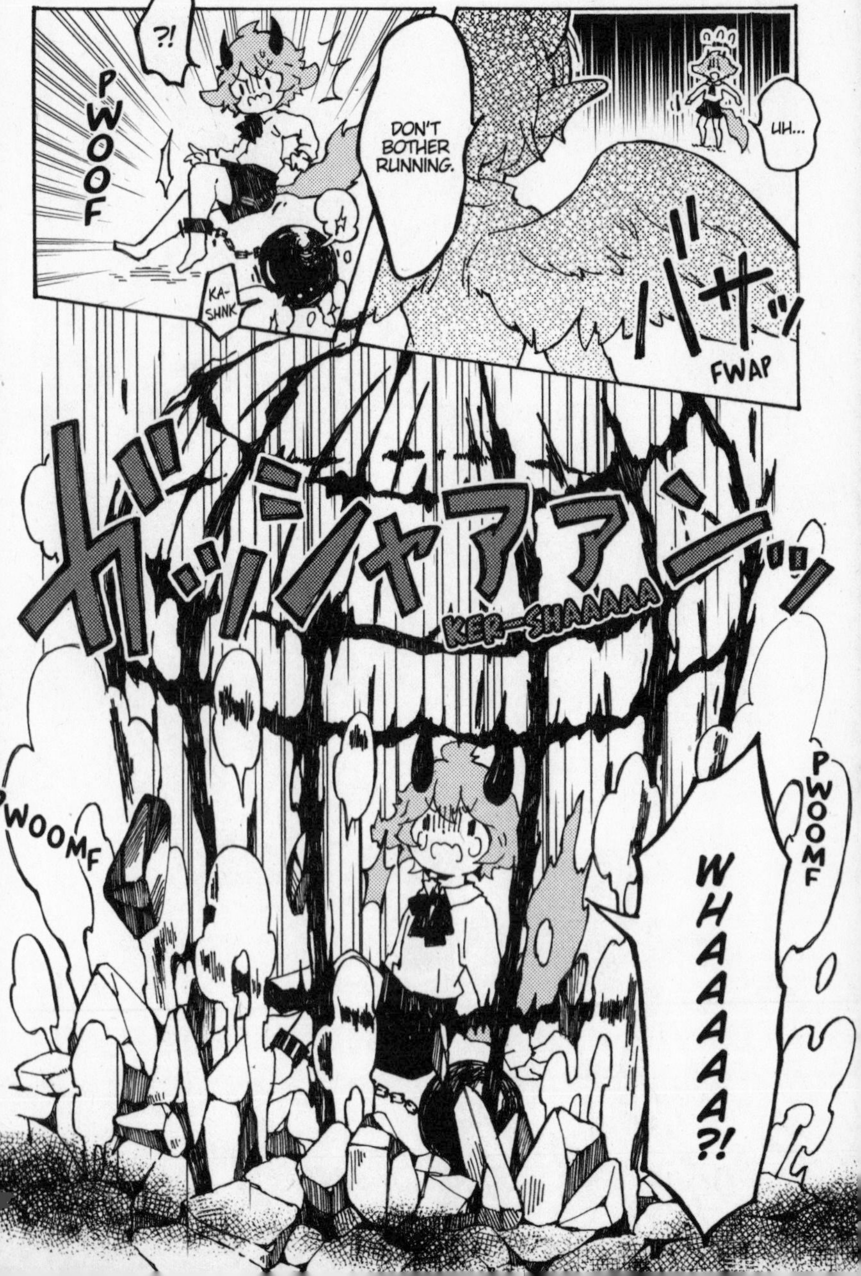
UH...
DON'T BOTHER RUNNING.
バサッ
FWAP
?!
PWOOF
KA-SHNK
ガシャアアンッ
KER-SHAAAAA
PWOOMF
WHAAAAAAA?!
PWOOMF

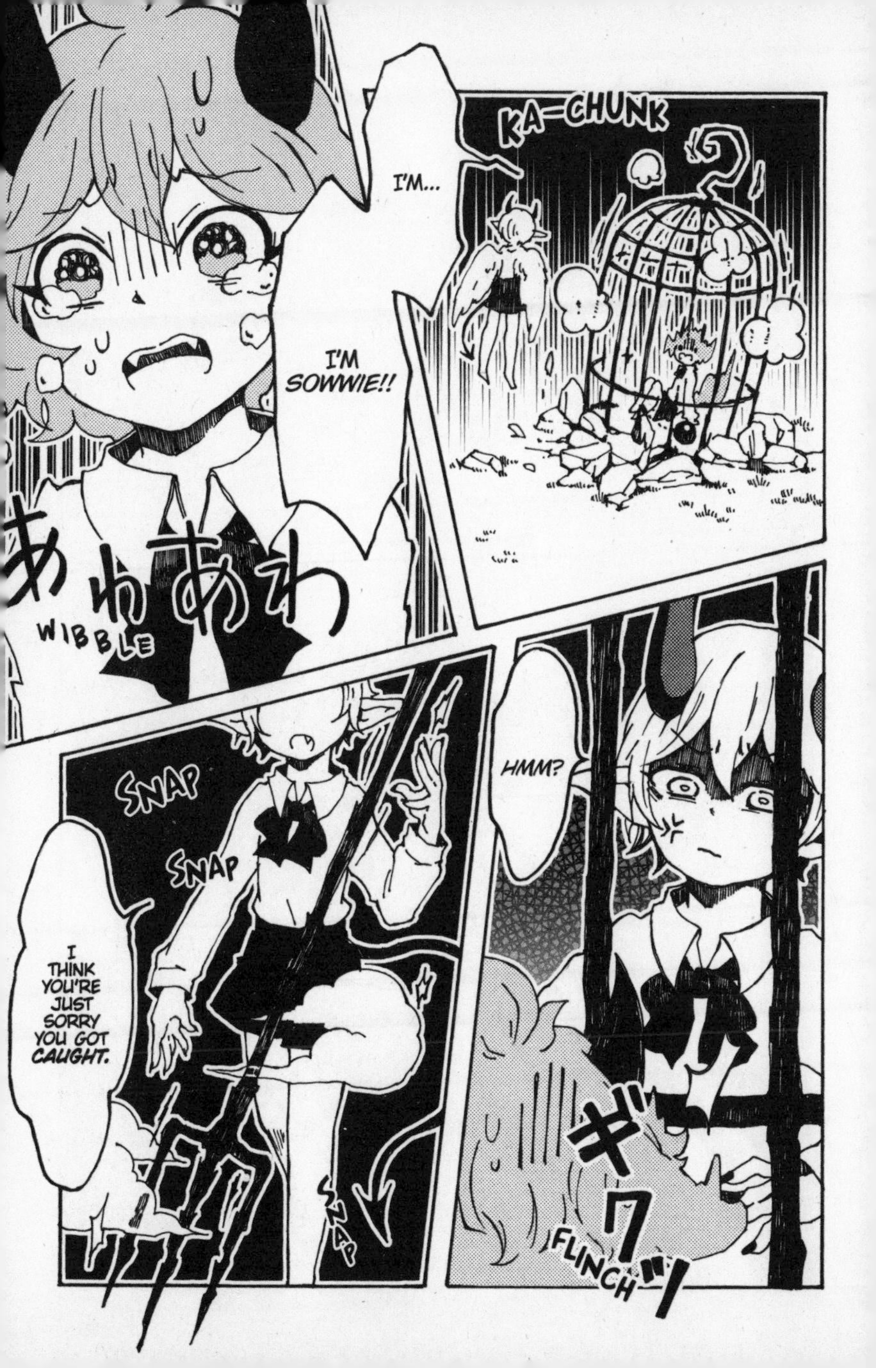
KA-CHUNK
I'M...
I'M SOWWIE!!
あゎあゎ
WIBBLE
HMM?
ギク
FLINCH
SNAP
SNAP
I THINK YOU'RE JUST SORRY YOU GOT CAUGHT.
SNAP

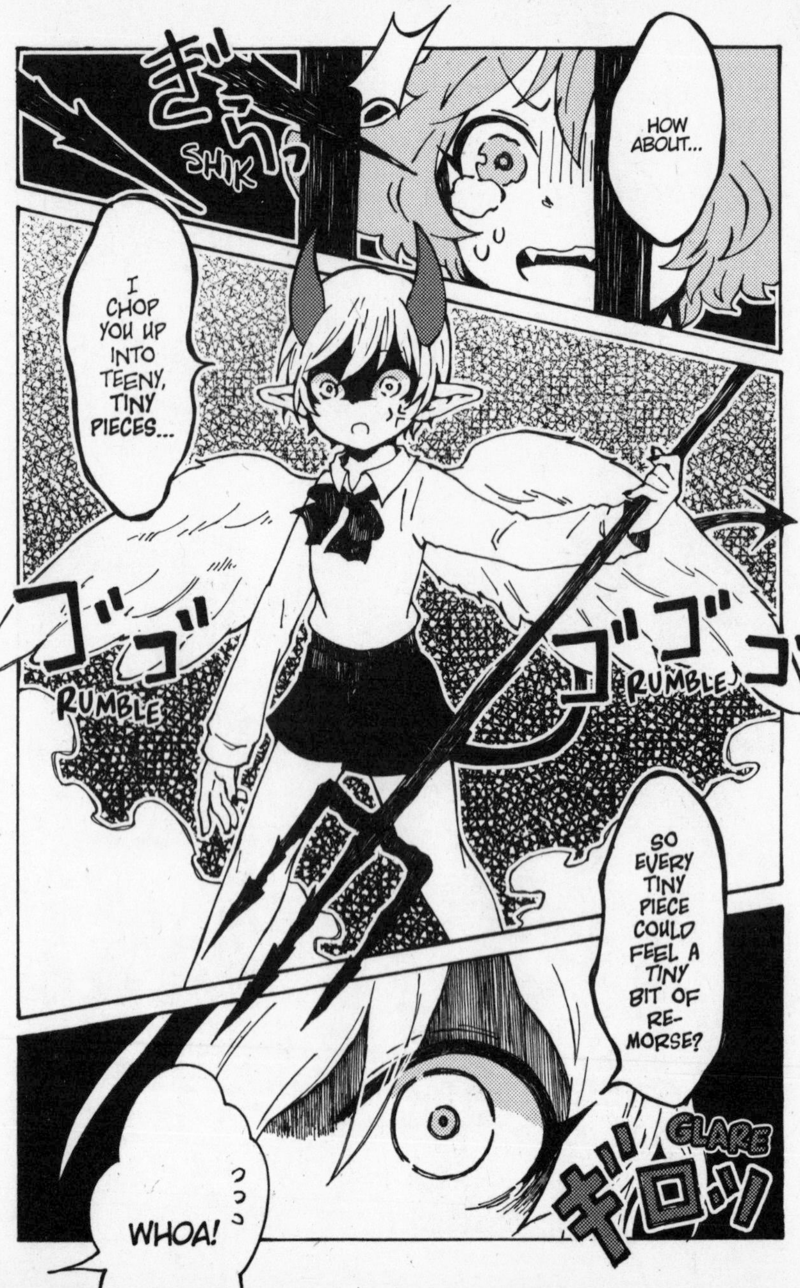
HOW ABOUT...
ぎらっ
SHIK
I CHOP YOU UP INTO TEENY, TINY PIECES...
ゴゴゴゴ
RUMBLE
ゴゴ
RUMBLE
SO EVERY TINY PIECE COULD FEEL A TINY BIT OF RE-MORSE?
ギロッ
GLARE
WHOA!
つつつ

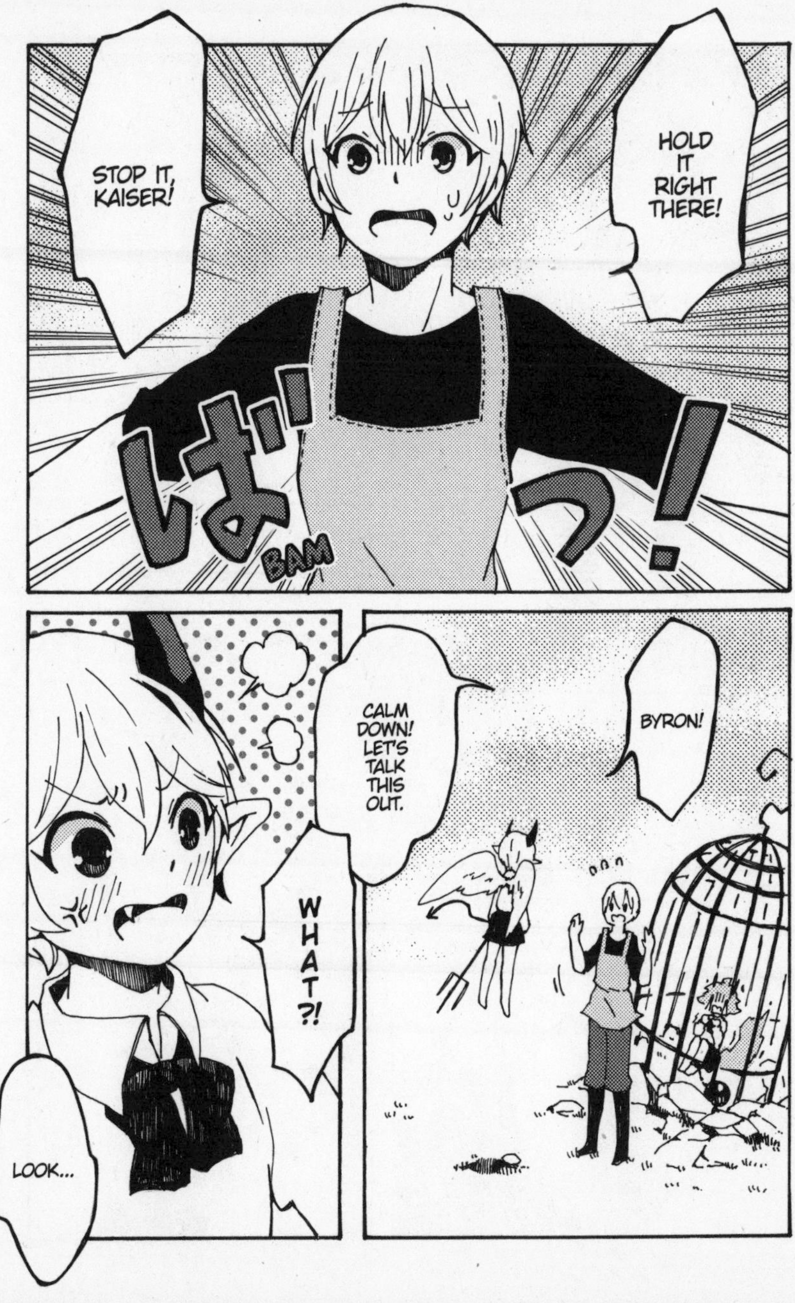
HOLD IT RIGHT THERE!
STOP IT, KAISER!
ばっ!
BAM
BYRON!
CALM DOWN! LET'S TALK THIS OUT.
WHAT?!
LOOK...

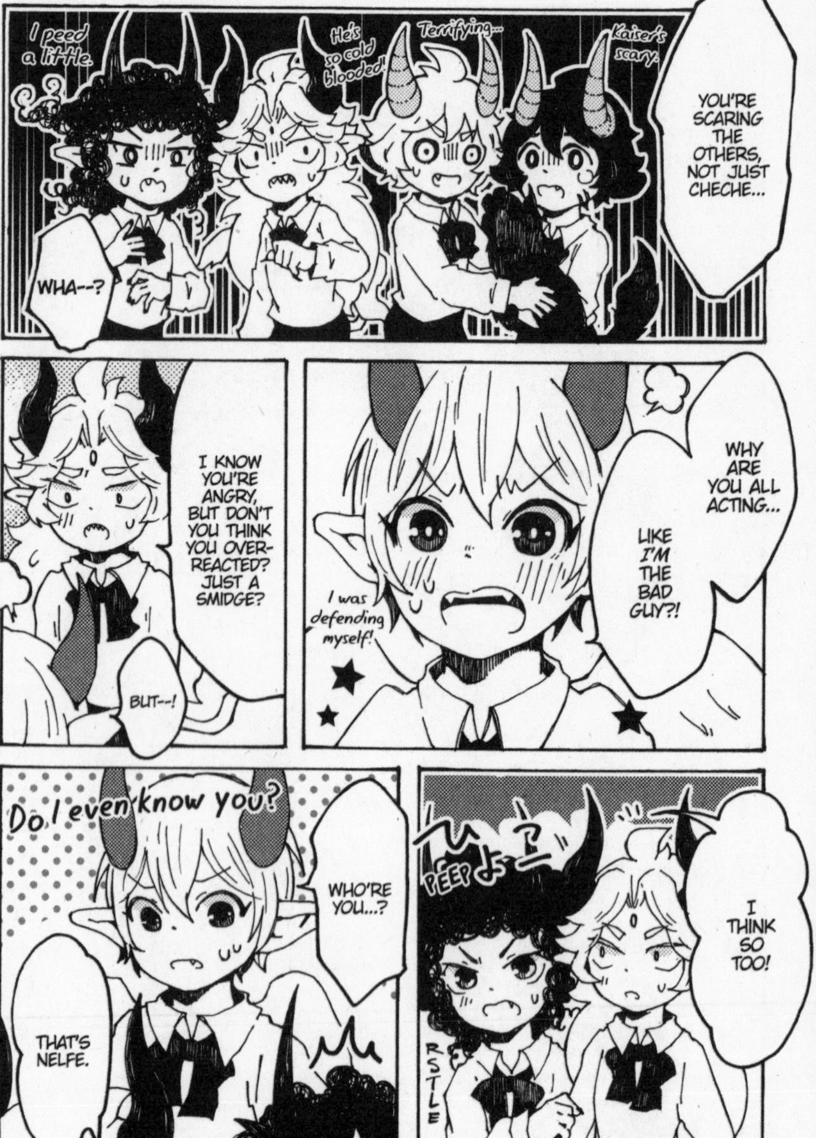
YOU'RE SCARING THE OTHERS, NOT JUST CHECHE...
Kaiser's scary.
Terrifying...
He's so cold blooded!
I peed a little.
WHA--?
WHY ARE YOU ALL ACTING...
LIKE I'M THE BAD GUY?!
I was defending myself!
I KNOW YOU'RE ANGRY, BUT DON'T YOU THINK YOU OVER-REACTED? JUST A SMIDGE?
BUT--!
I THINK SO TOO!
PEEP
RSTLE
Do I even know you?
WHO'RE YOU...?
THAT'S NELFE.
ACK!

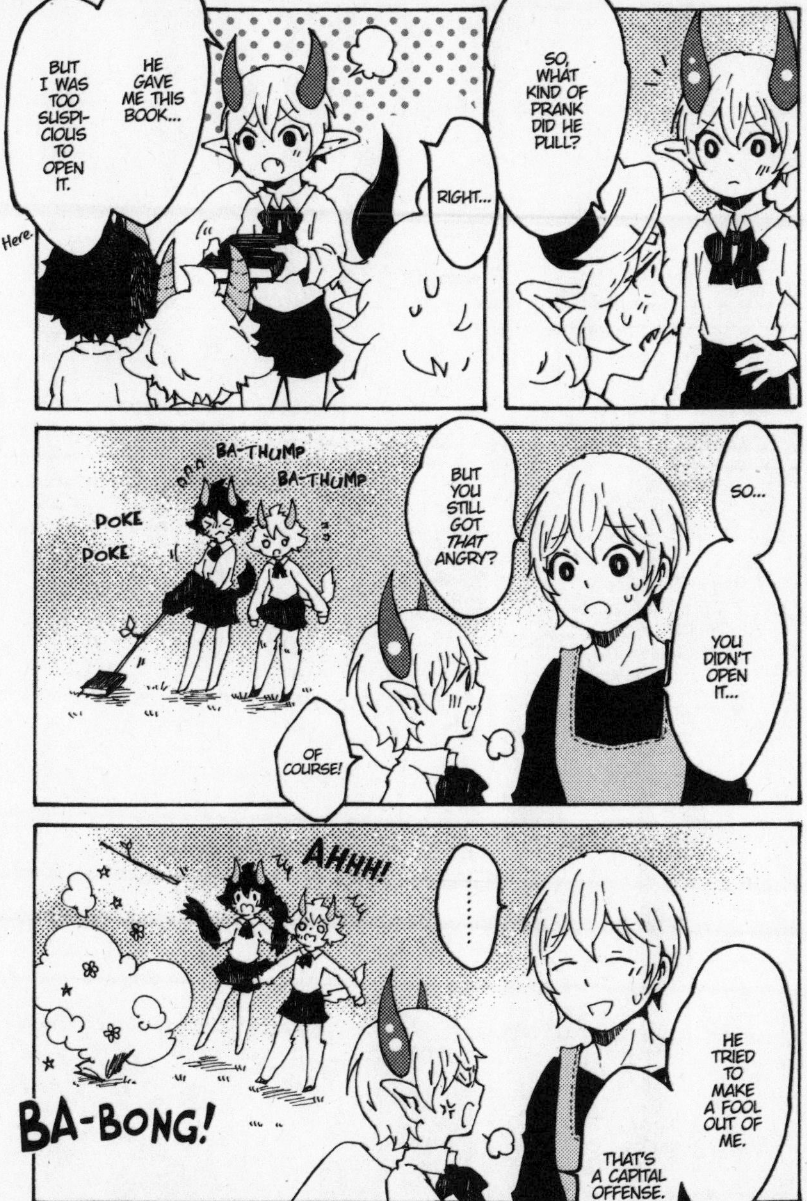
SO, WHAT KIND OF PRANK DID HE PULL?
RIGHT...
HE GAVE ME THIS BOOK...
BUT I WAS TOO SUSPICIOUS TO OPEN IT.
Here.
SO...
YOU DIDN'T OPEN IT...
BUT YOU STILL GOT *THAT* ANGRY?
OF COURSE!
BA-THUMP
BA-THUMP
POKE
POKE
HE TRIED TO MAKE A FOOL OUT OF ME.
THAT'S A CAPITAL OFFENSE.
......
AHHH!
BA-BONG!

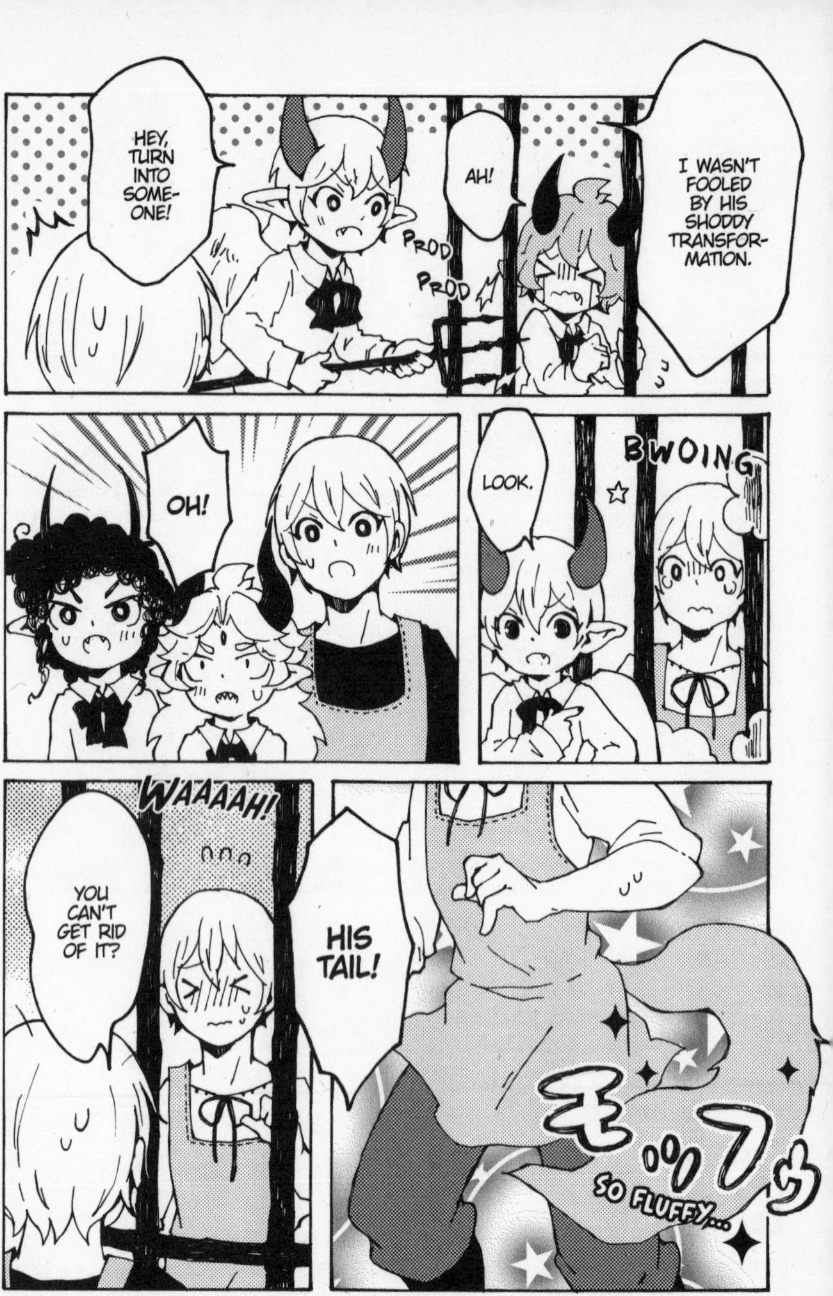
I WASN'T FOOLED BY HIS SHODDY TRANSFORMATION.
AH!
PROD
PROD
HEY, TURN INTO SOME-ONE!
BWOING
LOOK.
OH!
モッフゥ
SO FLUFFY...
WAAAAH!
HIS TAIL!
YOU CAN'T GET RID OF IT?

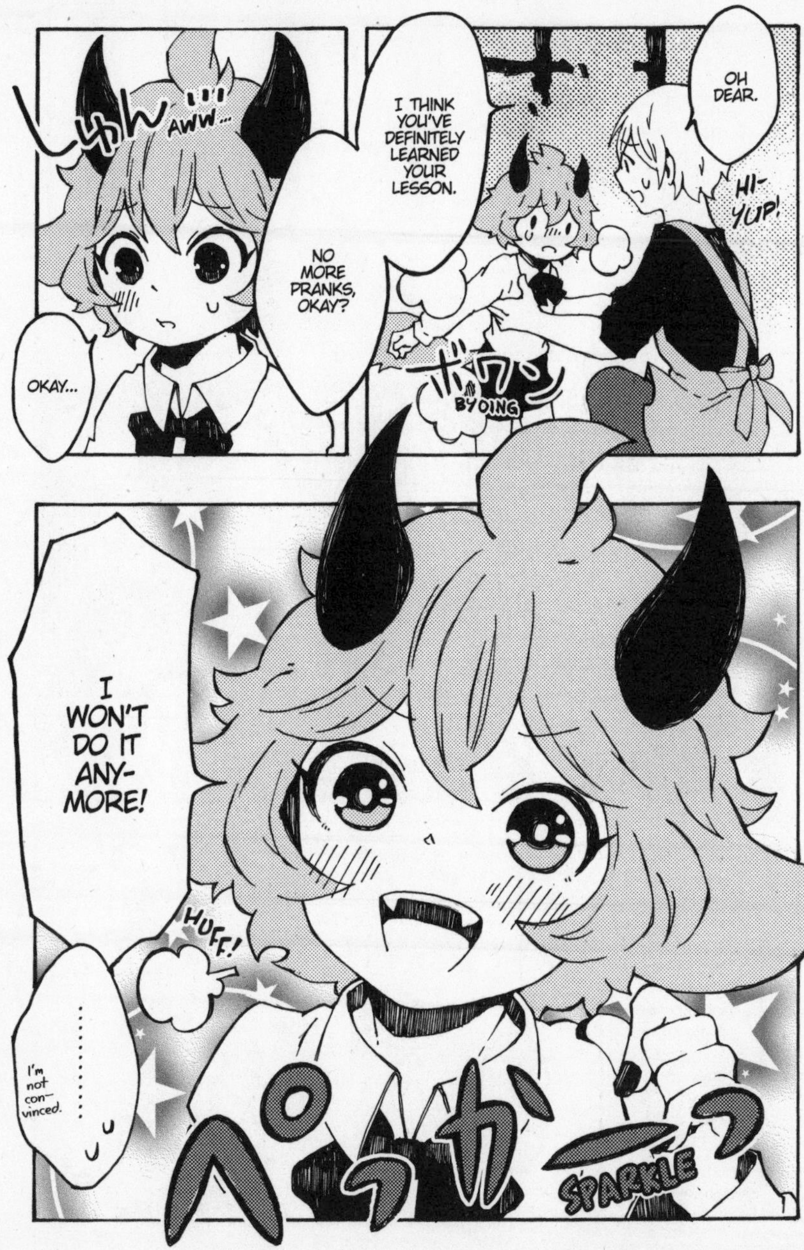
OH DEAR.
HI-YUP!
I THINK YOU'VE DEFINITELY LEARNED YOUR LESSON.
NO MORE PRANKS, OKAY?
BYOING
AWW...
OKAY...
I WON'T DO IT ANYMORE!
HUFF!
SPARKLE
I'm not convinced.

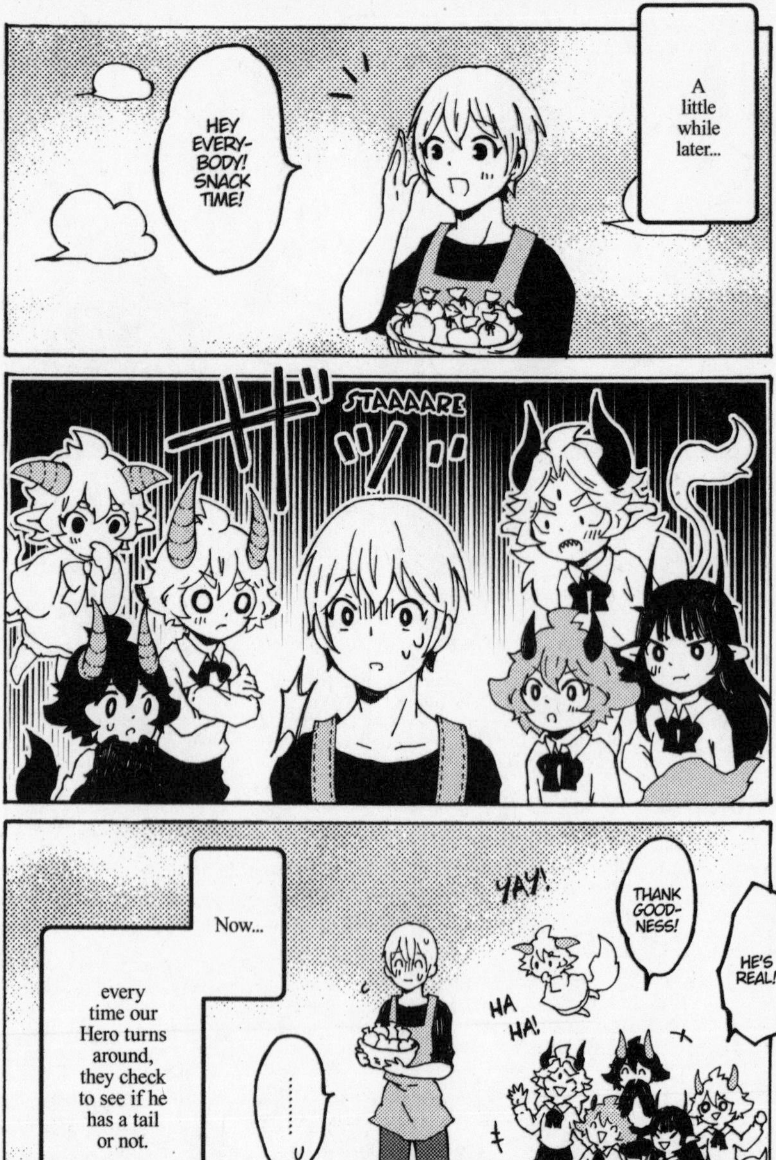
A little while later...
HEY EVERY-BODY! SNACK TIME!
STAAAARE
HE'S REAL!
THANK GOOD-NESS!
YAY!
HA HA!
Now...
every time our Hero turns around, they check to see if he has a tail or not.
......

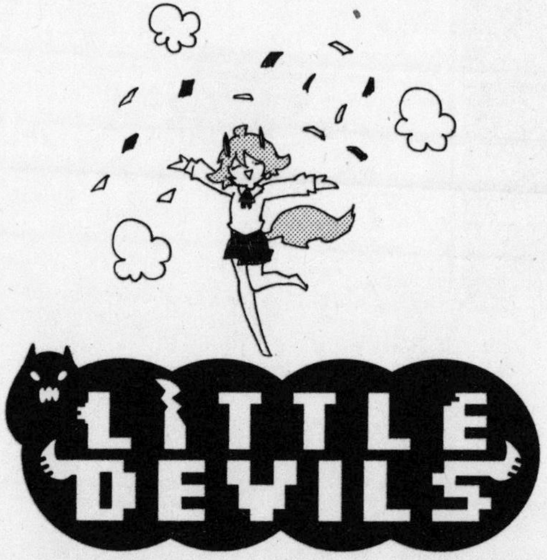

LITTLE DEVILS

DEVIL OF THE TAIL - CHECHE ▼

. . . .

The mischievous seventh devil who
loves playing pranks.
Don't be fooled by his petite and
cheerful appearance.
Byron thought he was a girl the first
time he saw him.

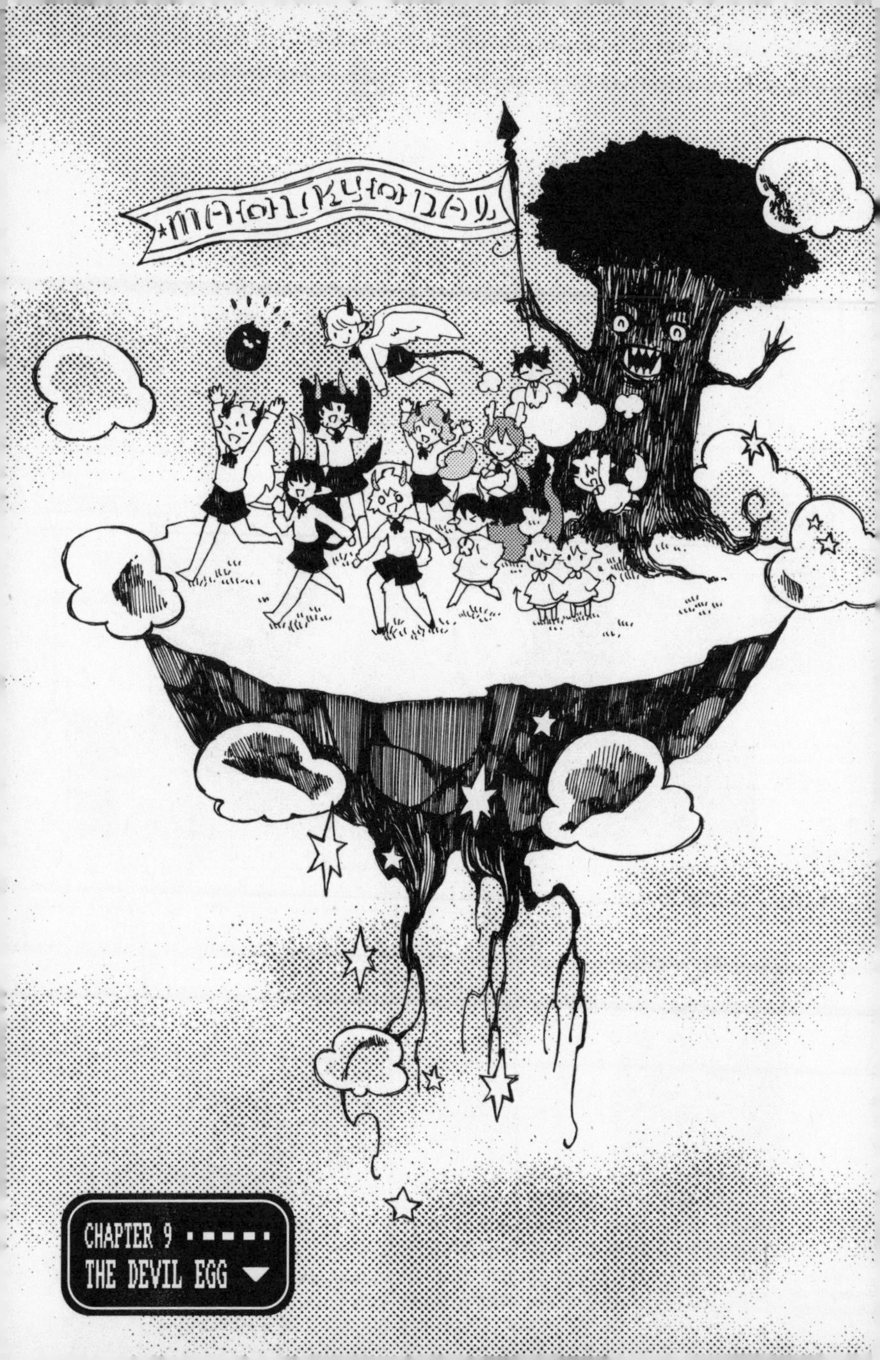
CHAPTER 9
THE DEVIL EGG

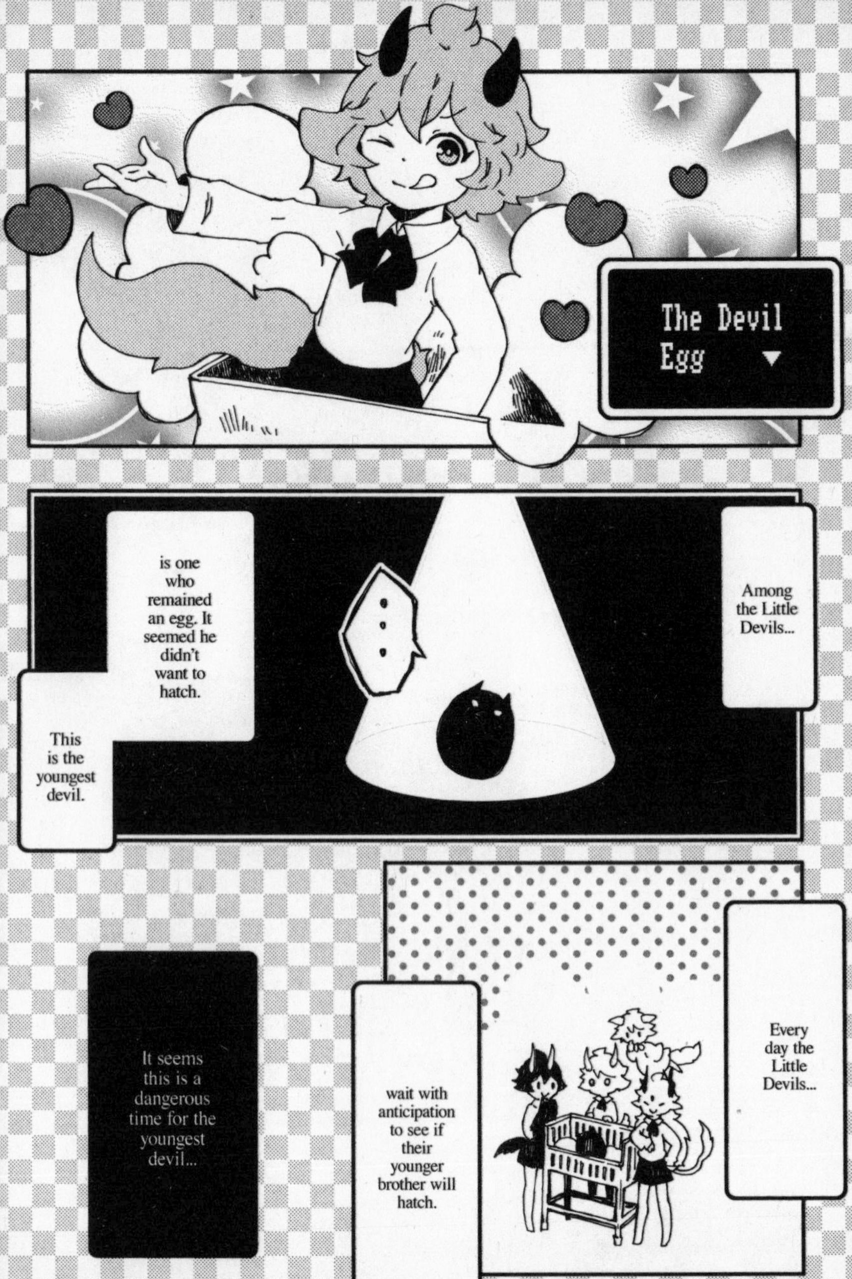
The Devil Egg
Among the Little Devils...
is one who remained an egg. It seemed he didn't want to hatch.
...
This is the youngest devil.
Every day the Little Devils...
wait with anticipation to see if their younger brother will hatch.
It seems this is a dangerous time for the youngest devil...

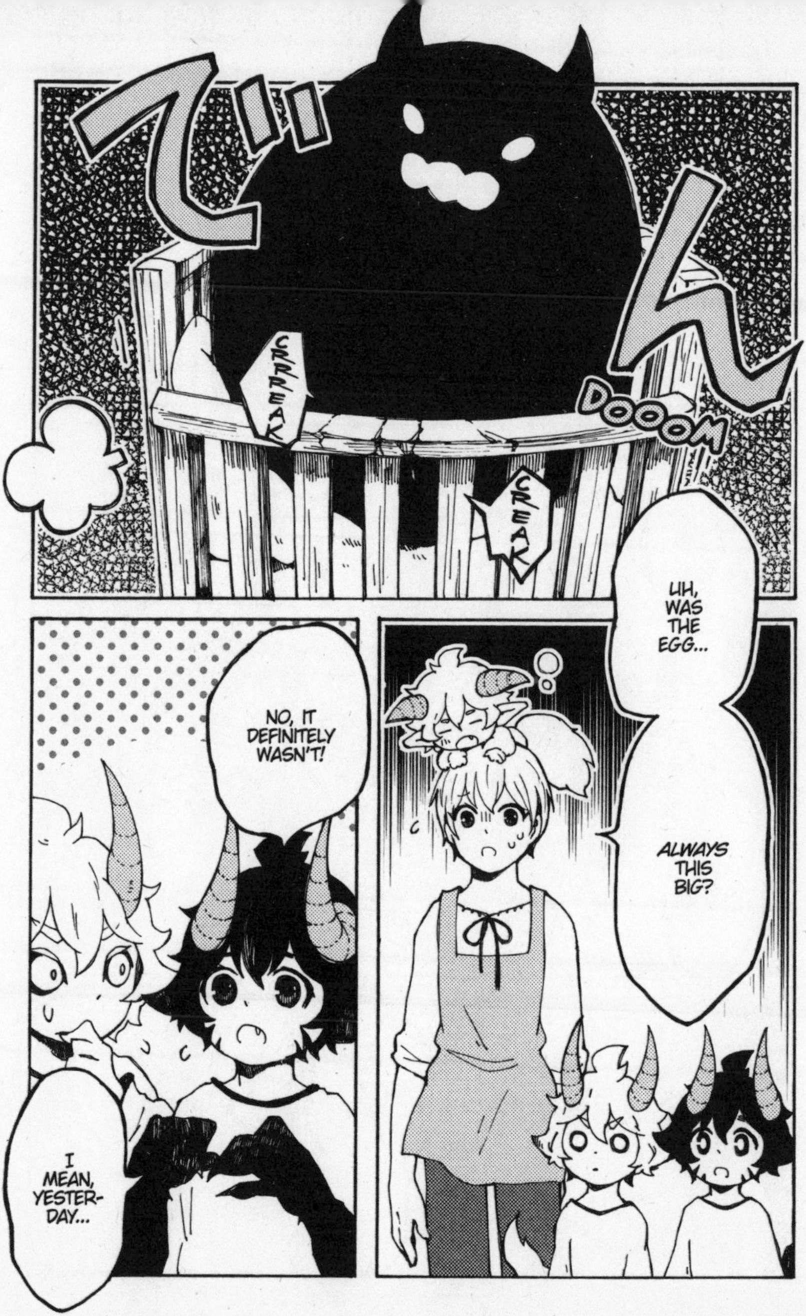
でん
DOOOM
CRRREAK
CREAK
UH, WAS THE EGG...
ALWAYS THIS BIG?
NO, IT DEFINITELY WASN'T!
I MEAN, YESTER-DAY...

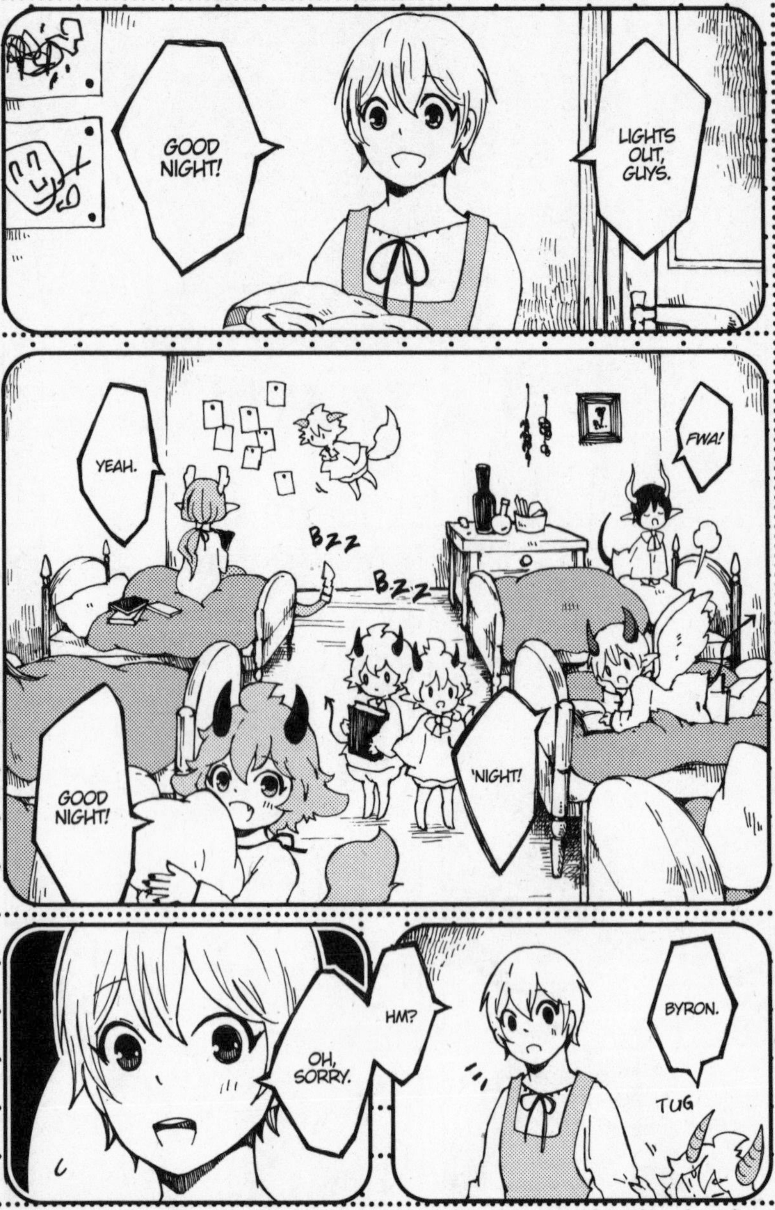

LIGHTS OUT, GUYS.
GOOD NIGHT!
FWA!
BZZ
BZZ
YEAH.
'NIGHT!
GOOD NIGHT!
BYRON.
TUG
HM?
OH, SORRY.

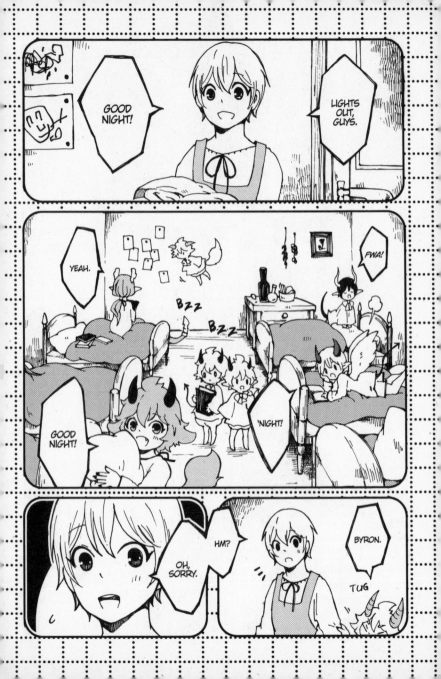

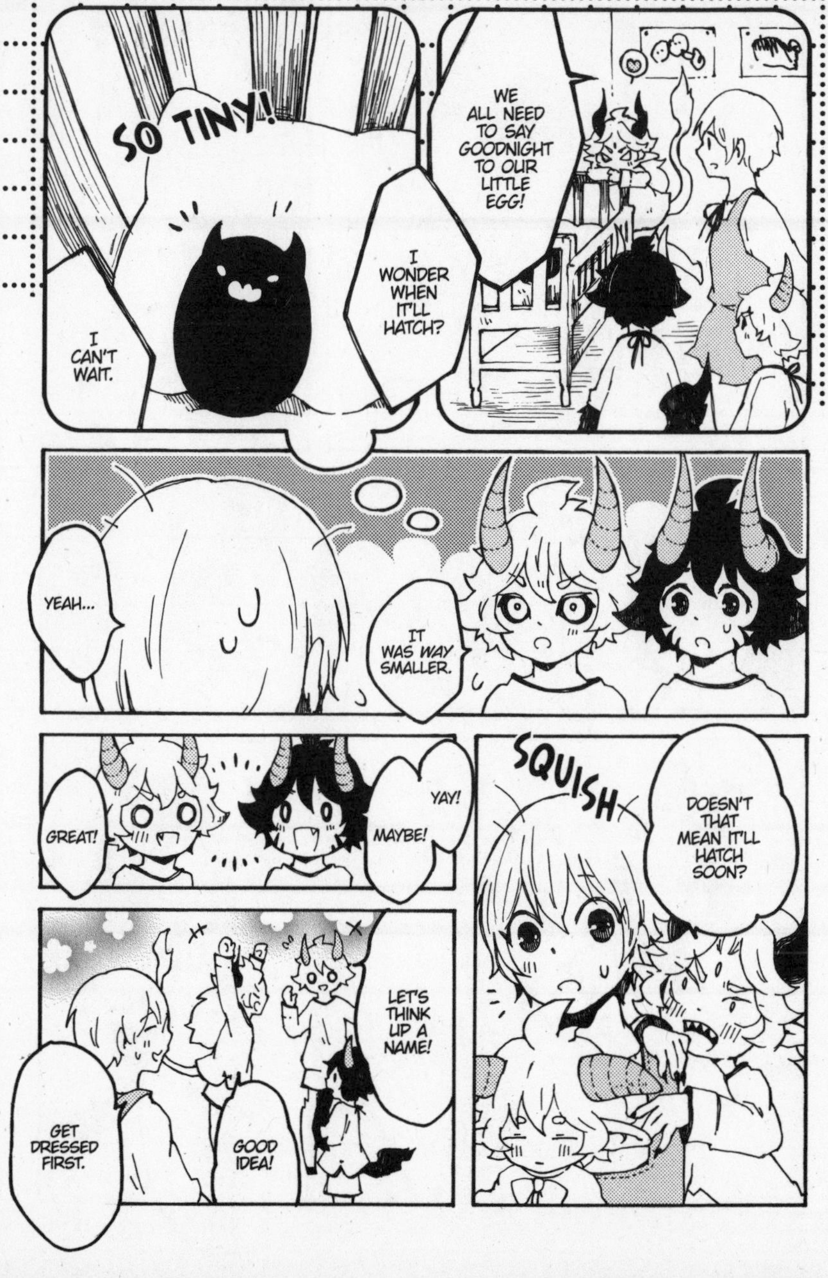

WE ALL NEED TO SAY GOODNIGHT TO OUR LITTLE EGG!
SO TINY!
I WONDER WHEN IT'LL HATCH?
I CAN'T WAIT.
IT WAS WAY SMALLER.
YEAH...
DOESN'T THAT MEAN IT'LL HATCH SOON?
SQUISH
YAY!
MAYBE!
GREAT!
LET'S THINK UP A NAME!
GOOD IDEA!
GET DRESSED FIRST.

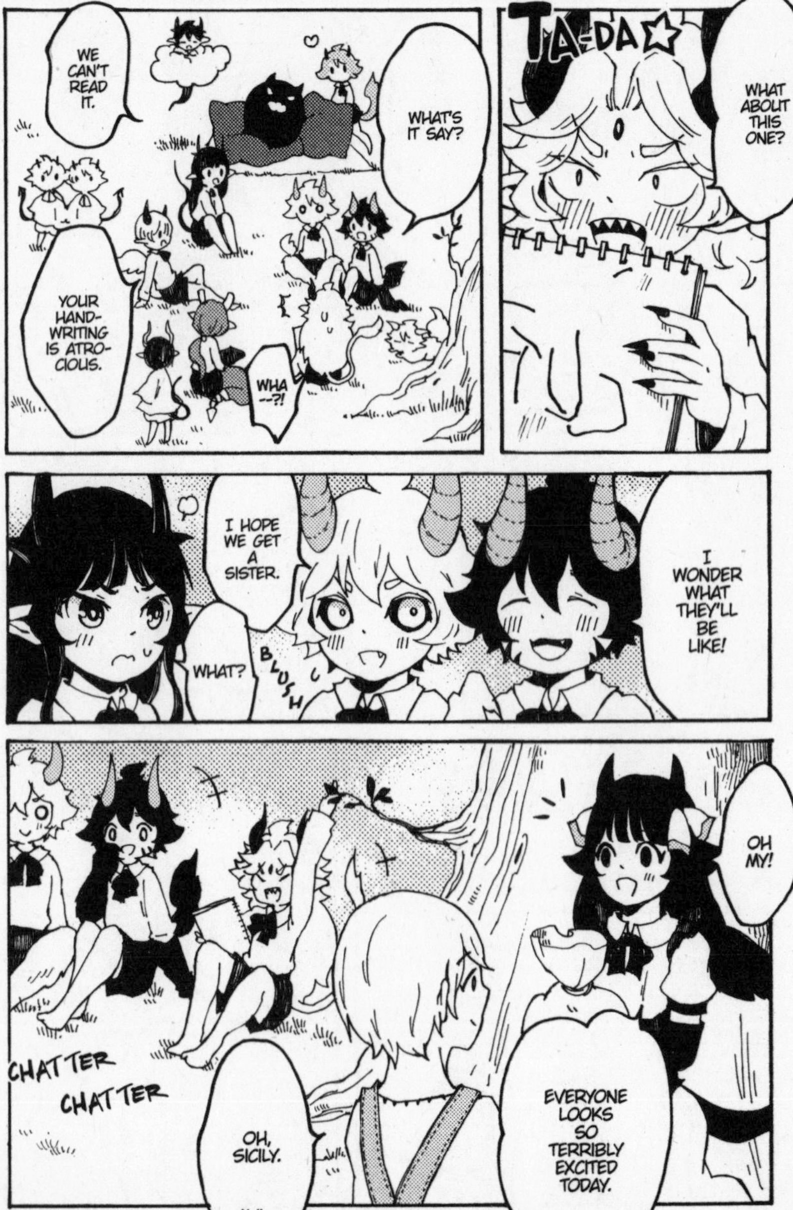
TA-DA☆
WHAT ABOUT THIS ONE?
WHAT'S IT SAY?
WE CAN'T READ IT.
YOUR HAND-WRITING IS ATRO-CIOUS.
WHA--?!
I WONDER WHAT THEY'LL BE LIKE!
I HOPE WE GET A SISTER.
BLUSH
WHAT?
OH MY!
EVERYONE LOOKS SO TERRIBLY EXCITED TODAY.
OH, SICILY.
Hello there!
CHATTER
CHATTER

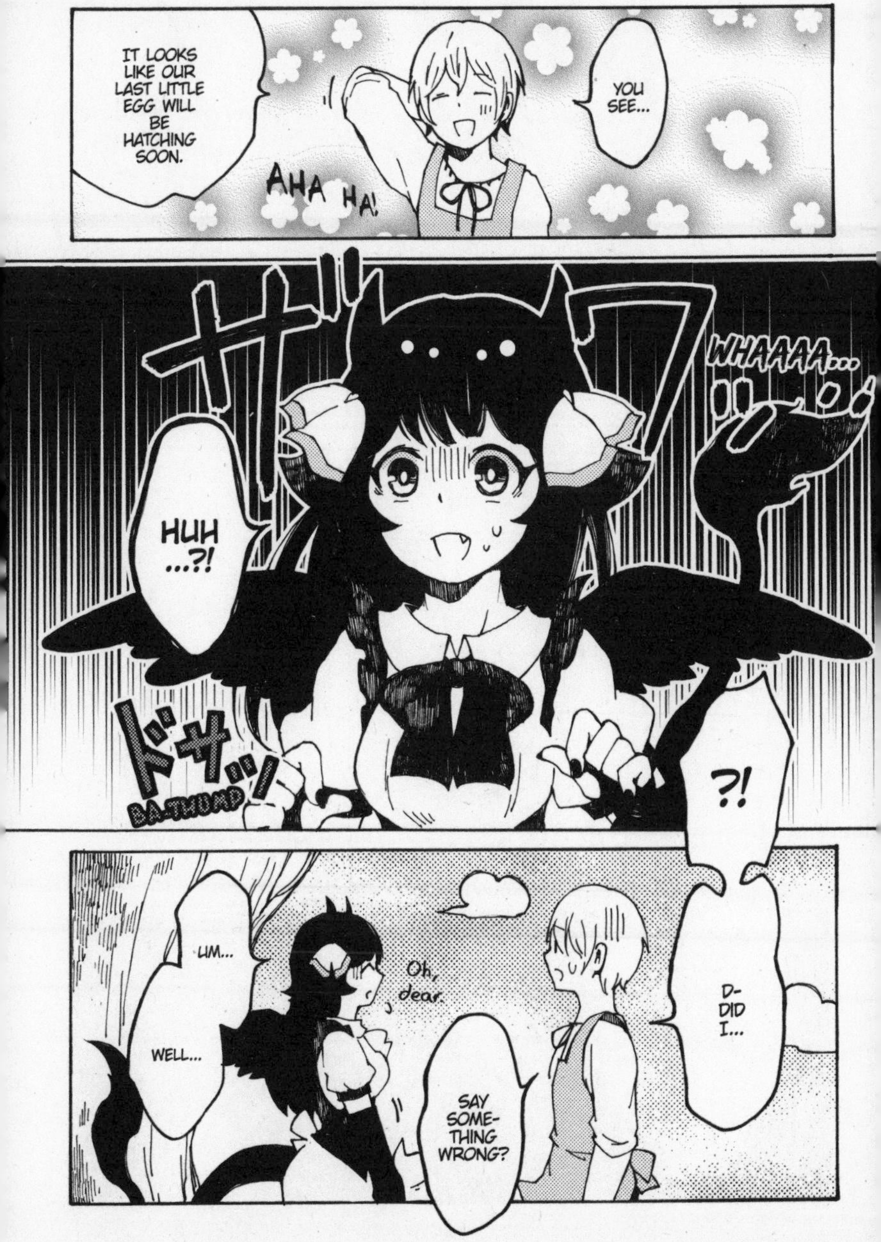
YOU SEE...
IT LOOKS LIKE OUR LAST LITTLE EGG WILL BE HATCHING SOON.
AHA HA!
WHAAAA...!!
HUH ...?!
?!
ドサッ!
BA-THUMP!
D-DID I...
SAY SOME-THING WRONG?
Oh, dear.
UM...
WELL...

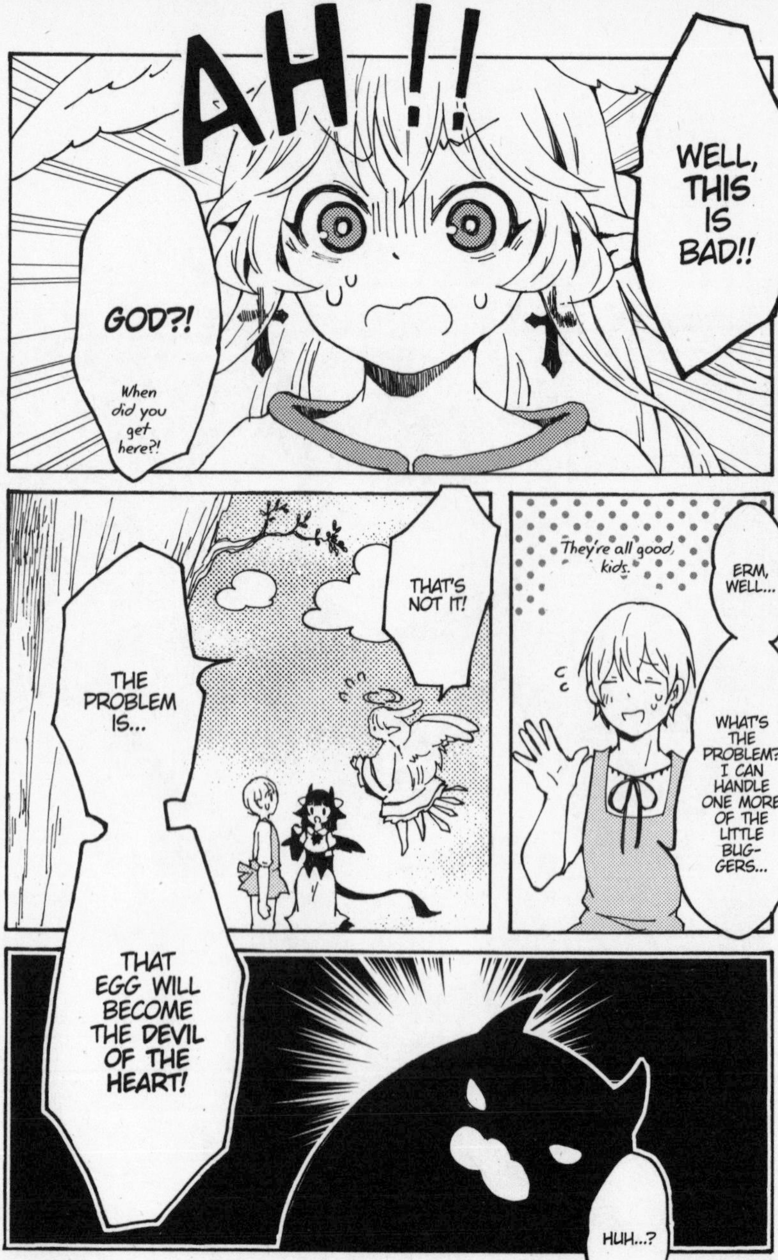
AH!!
WELL, THIS IS BAD!!
GOD?!
When did you get here?!
They're all good kids.
ERM, WELL...
WHAT'S THE PROBLEM? I CAN HANDLE ONE MORE OF THE LITTLE BUG-GERS...
THAT'S NOT IT!
THE PROBLEM IS...
THAT EGG WILL BECOME THE DEVIL OF THE HEART!
HUH...?

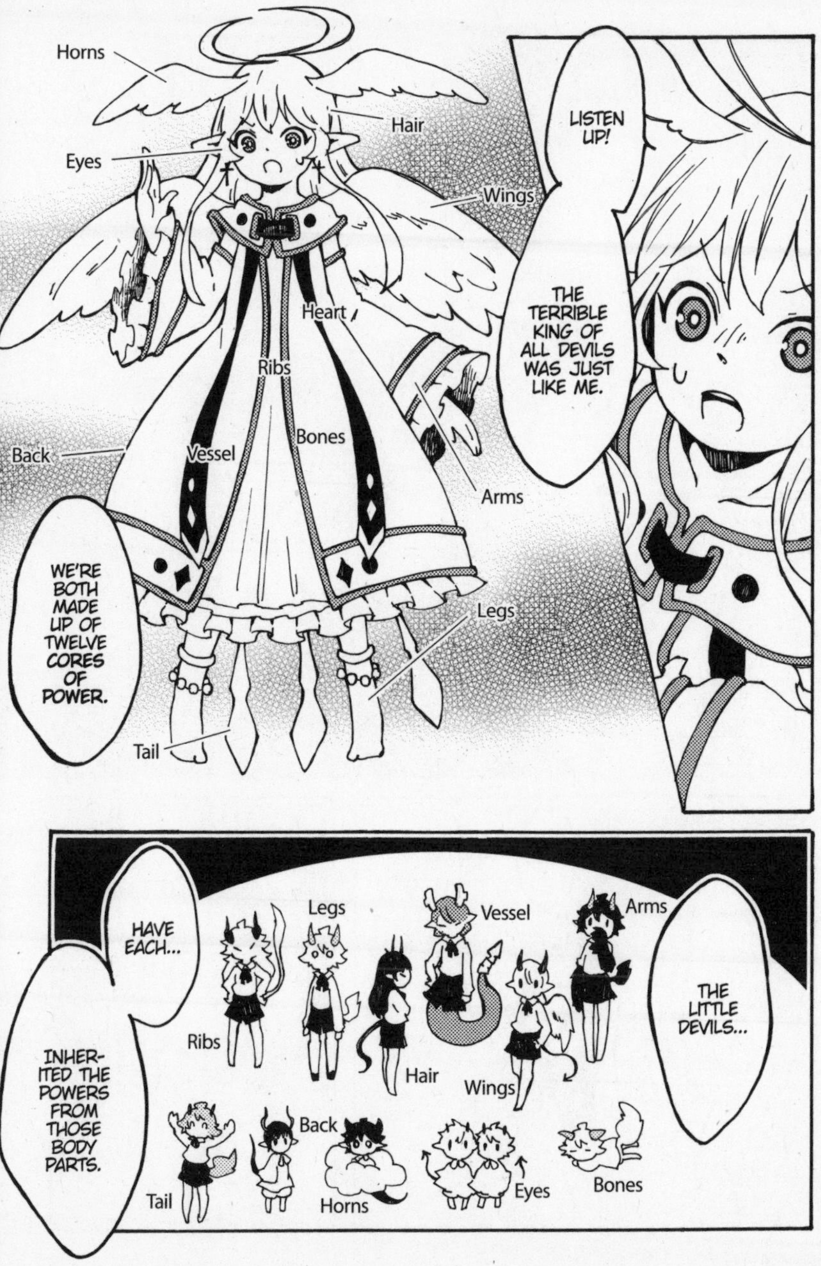
LISTEN UP!
THE TERRIBLE KING OF ALL DEVILS WAS JUST LIKE ME.
WE'RE BOTH MADE UP OF TWELVE CORES OF POWER.
Horns
Hair
Eyes
Wings
Heart
Ribs
Back
Vessel
Bones
Arms
Legs
Tail
THE LITTLE DEVILS...
HAVE EACH...
INHERITED THE POWERS FROM THOSE BODY PARTS.
Arms
Vessel
Legs
Ribs
Hair
Wings
Bones
Eyes
Horns
Back
Tail

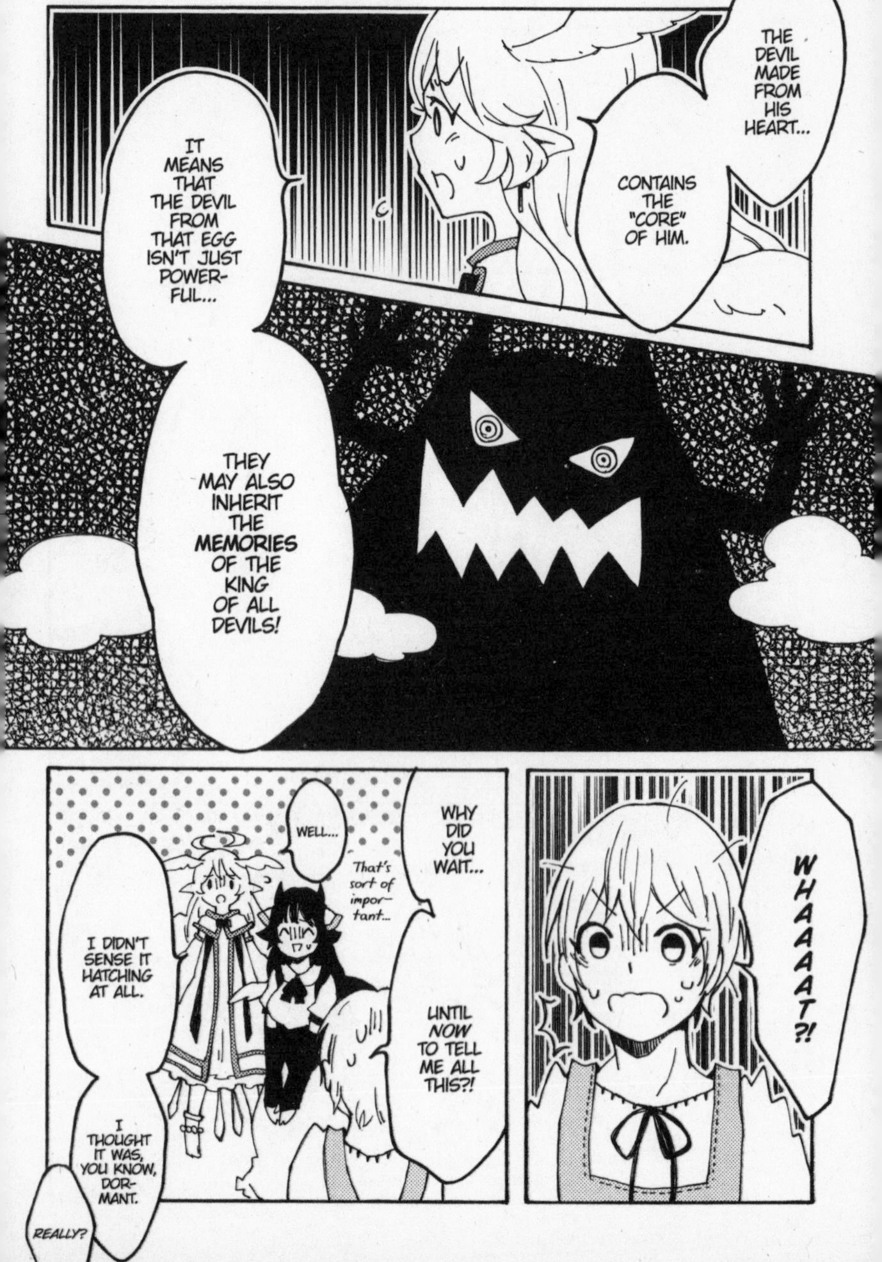
THE DEVIL MADE FROM HIS HEART...
CONTAINS THE "CORE" OF HIM.
IT MEANS THAT THE DEVIL FROM THAT EGG ISN'T JUST POWER-FUL...
THEY MAY ALSO INHERIT THE MEMORIES OF THE KING OF ALL DEVILS!
WHAAAAAT?!
WHY DID YOU WAIT...
UNTIL NOW TO TELL ME ALL THIS?!
That's sort of impor-tant...
WELL...
I DIDN'T SENSE IT HATCHING AT ALL.
I THOUGHT IT WAS, YOU KNOW, DOR-MANT.
REALLY?

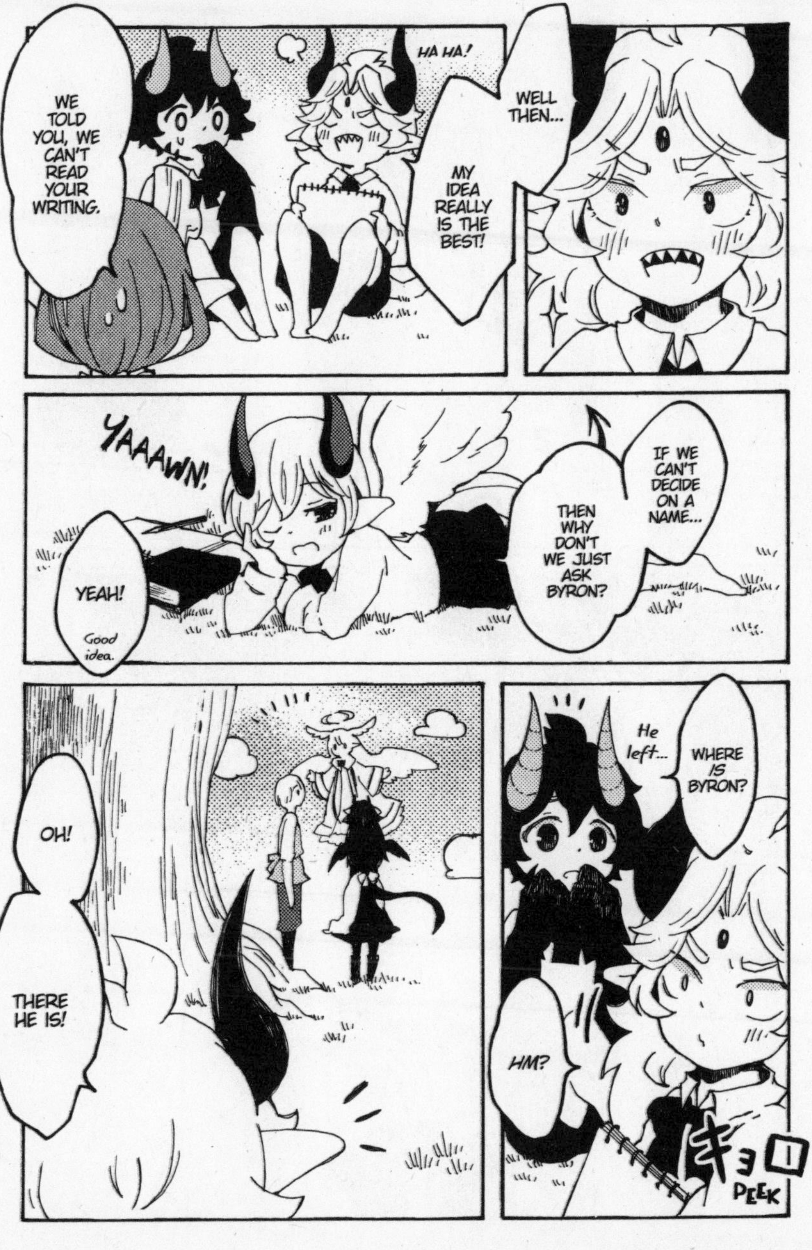
WELL THEN...
MY IDEA REALLY IS THE BEST!
HA HA!
WE TOLD YOU, WE CAN'T READ YOUR WRITING.
IF WE CAN'T DECIDE ON A NAME...
THEN WHY DON'T WE JUST ASK BYRON?
YAAAAWN!
YEAH!
Good idea.
WHERE IS BYRON?
He left...
HM?
キョロ
PEEK
OH!
THERE HE IS!

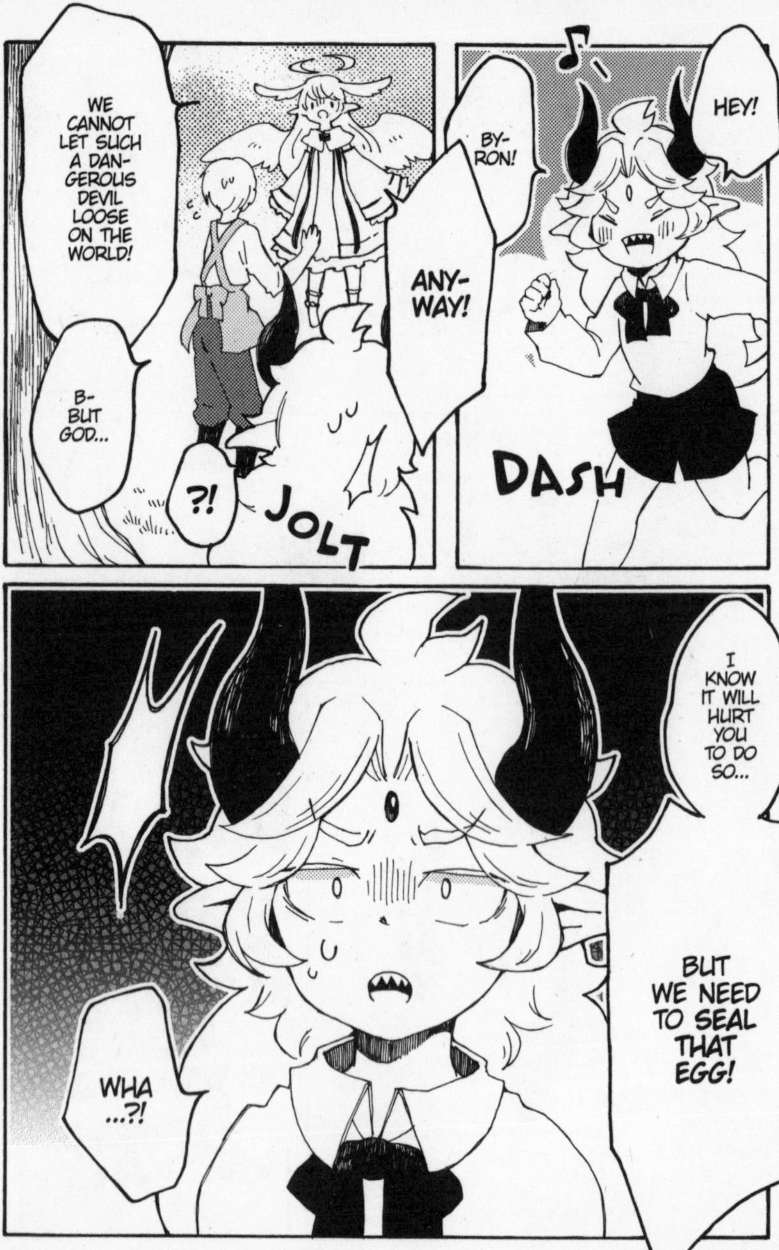
HEY!
BY-RON!
DASH
ANY-WAY!
WE CANNOT LET SUCH A DAN-GEROUS DEVIL LOOSE ON THE WORLD!
B-BUT GOD...
?!
JOLT
I KNOW IT WILL HURT YOU TO DO SO...
BUT WE NEED TO SEAL THAT EGG!
WHA ...?!

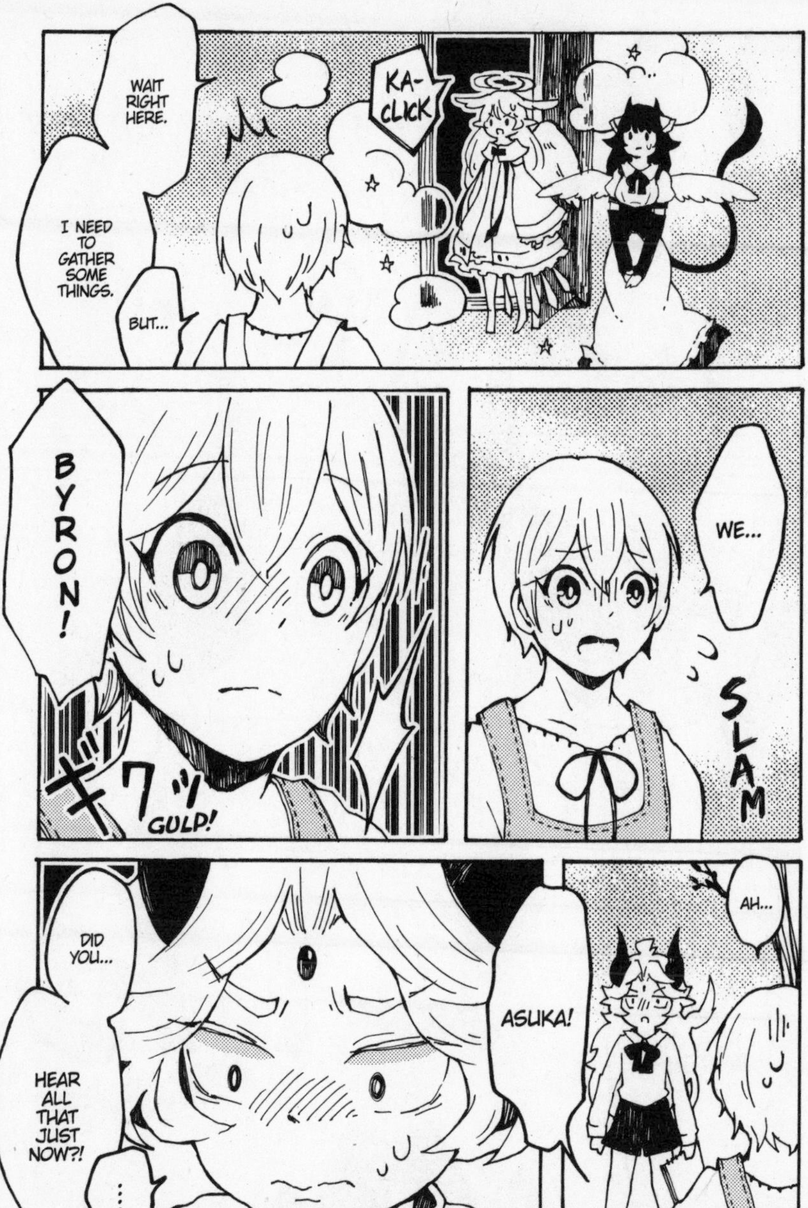
KA-CLICK
WAIT RIGHT HERE.
I NEED TO GATHER SOME THINGS.
BUT...
WE...
SLAM
BYRON!
ギクッ
GULP!
AH...
ASUKA!
DID YOU...
HEAR ALL THAT JUST NOW?!
......

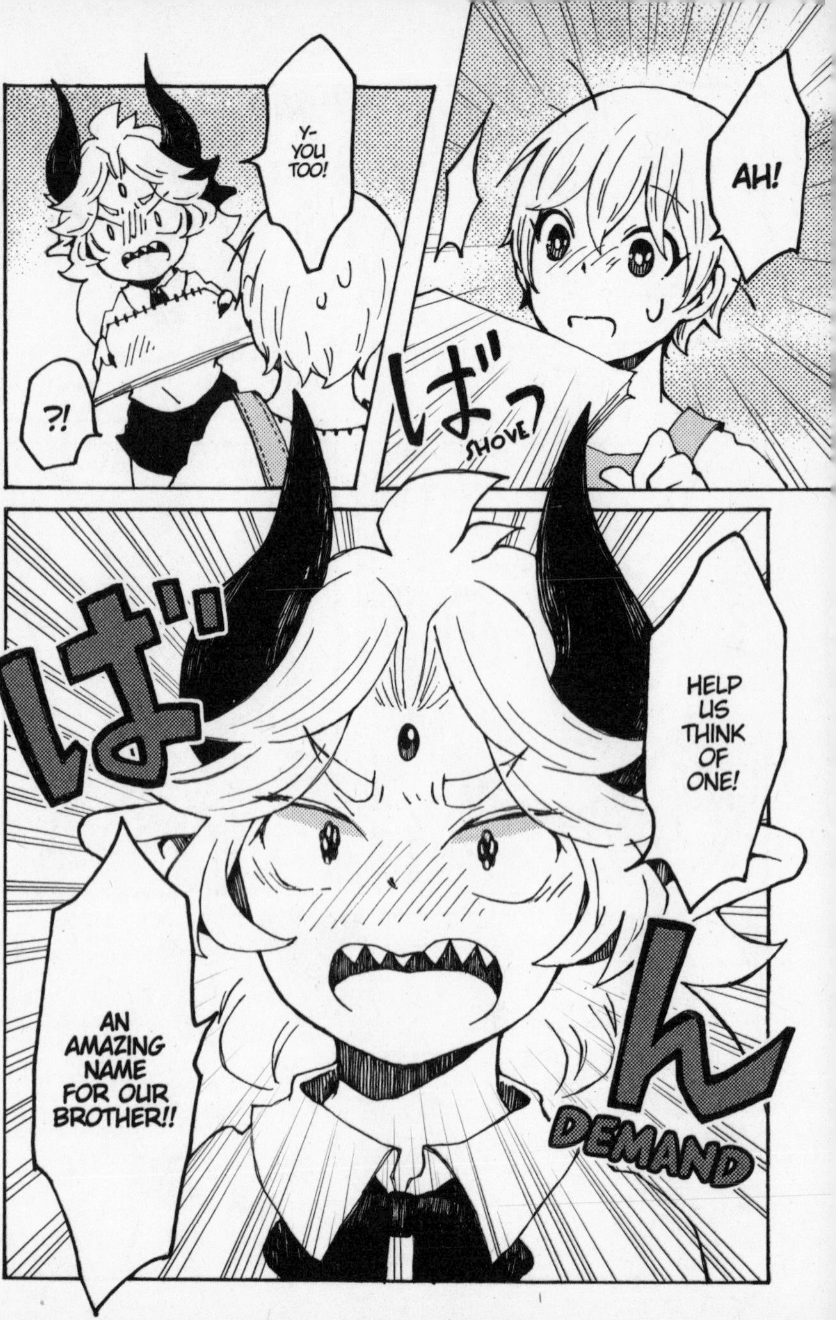
AH!
ばっ
SHOVE
Y-YOU TOO!
?!
HELP US THINK OF ONE!
AN AMAZING NAME FOR OUR BROTHER!!
ばん
DEMAND

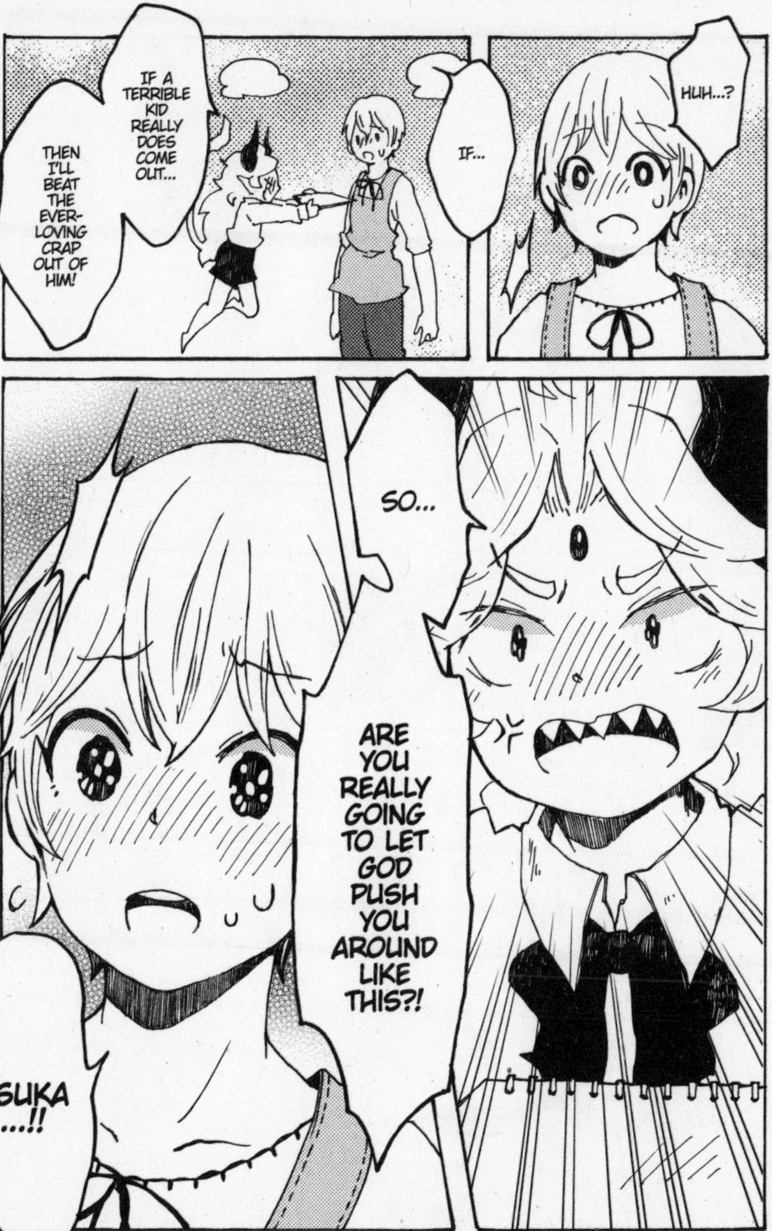
HUH...?
IF...
IF A TERRIBLE KID REALLY DOES COME OUT...
THEN I'LL BEAT THE EVER-LOVING CRAP OUT OF HIM!
SO...
ARE YOU REALLY GOING TO LET GOD PUSH YOU AROUND LIKE THIS?!
ASUKA ...!!

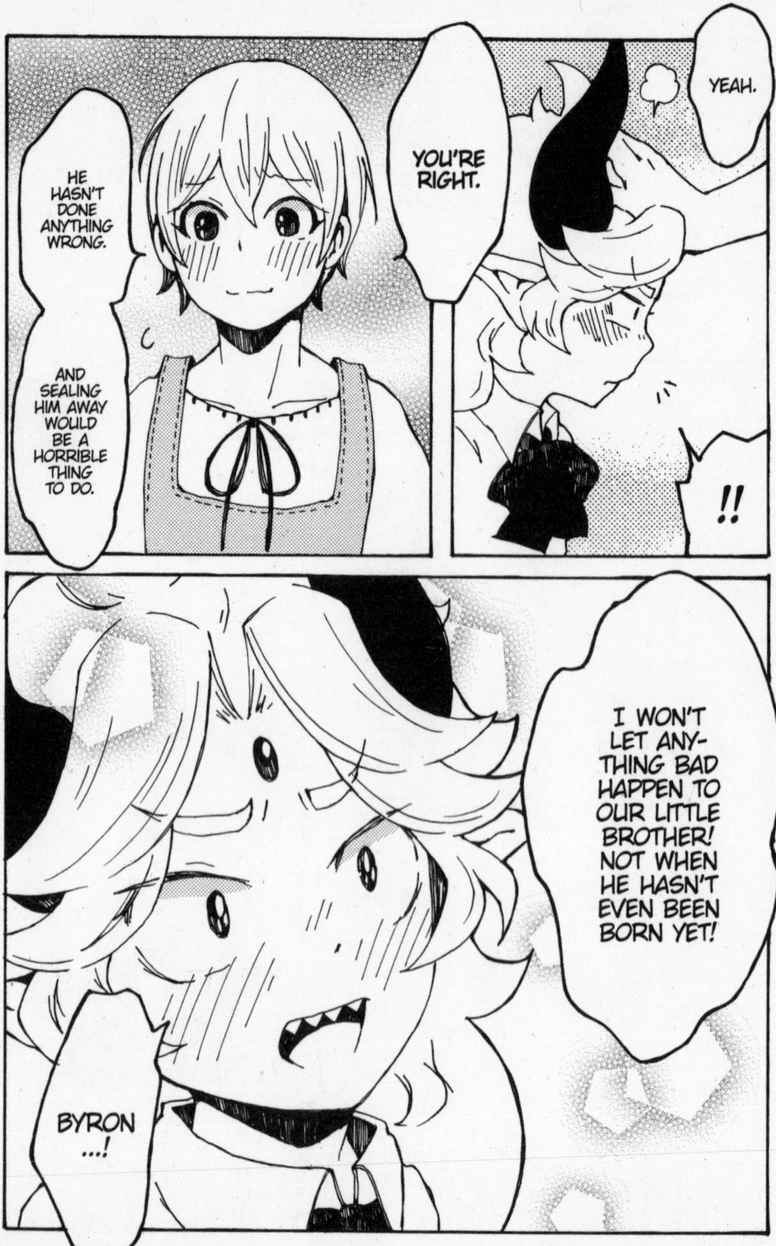

YEAH.
YOU'RE RIGHT.
!!
HE HASN'T DONE ANYTHING WRONG.
AND SEALING HIM AWAY WOULD BE A HORRIBLE THING TO DO.
I WON'T LET ANY-THING BAD HAPPEN TO OUR LITTLE BROTHER! NOT WHEN HE HASN'T EVEN BEEN BORN YET!
BYRON ...!

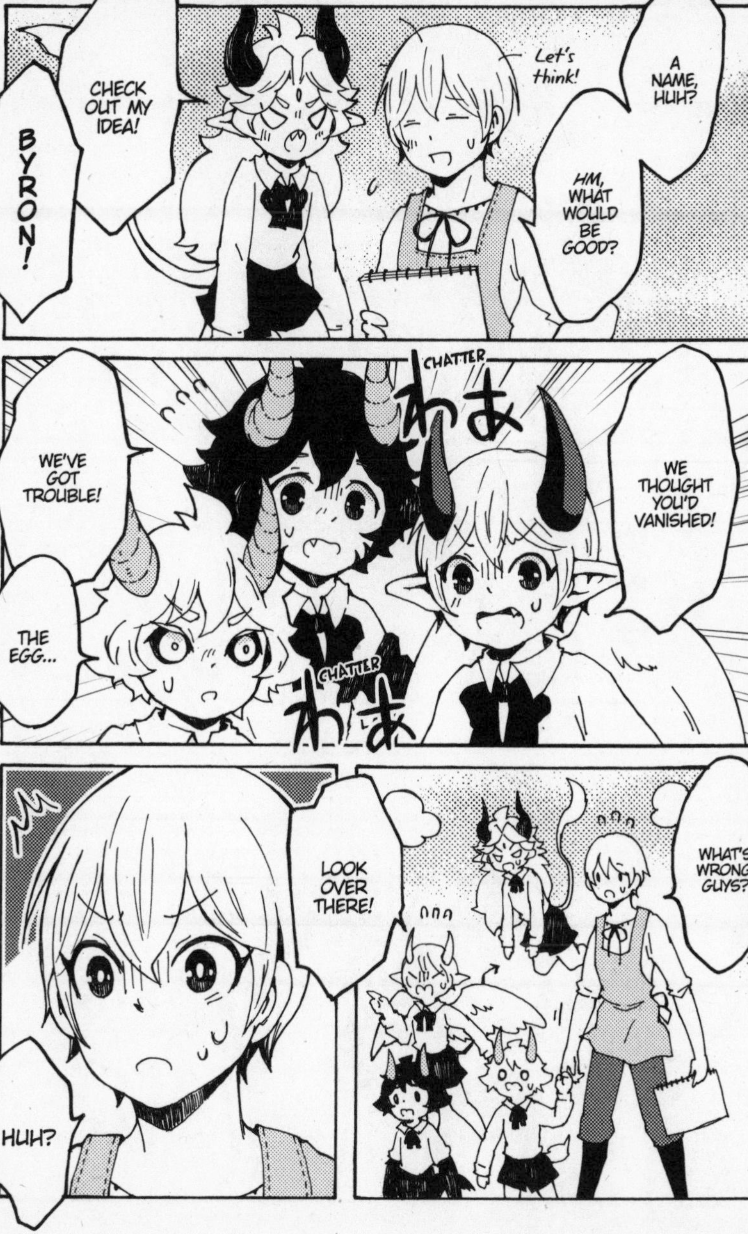
A NAME, HUH?
Let's think!
HM, WHAT WOULD BE GOOD?
CHECK OUT MY IDEA!
BYRON!
WE THOUGHT YOU'D VANISHED!
CHATTER
わあ
WE'VE GOT TROUBLE!
THE EGG...
CHATTER
わあ
WHAT'S WRONG, GUYS?
LOOK OVER THERE!
HUH?

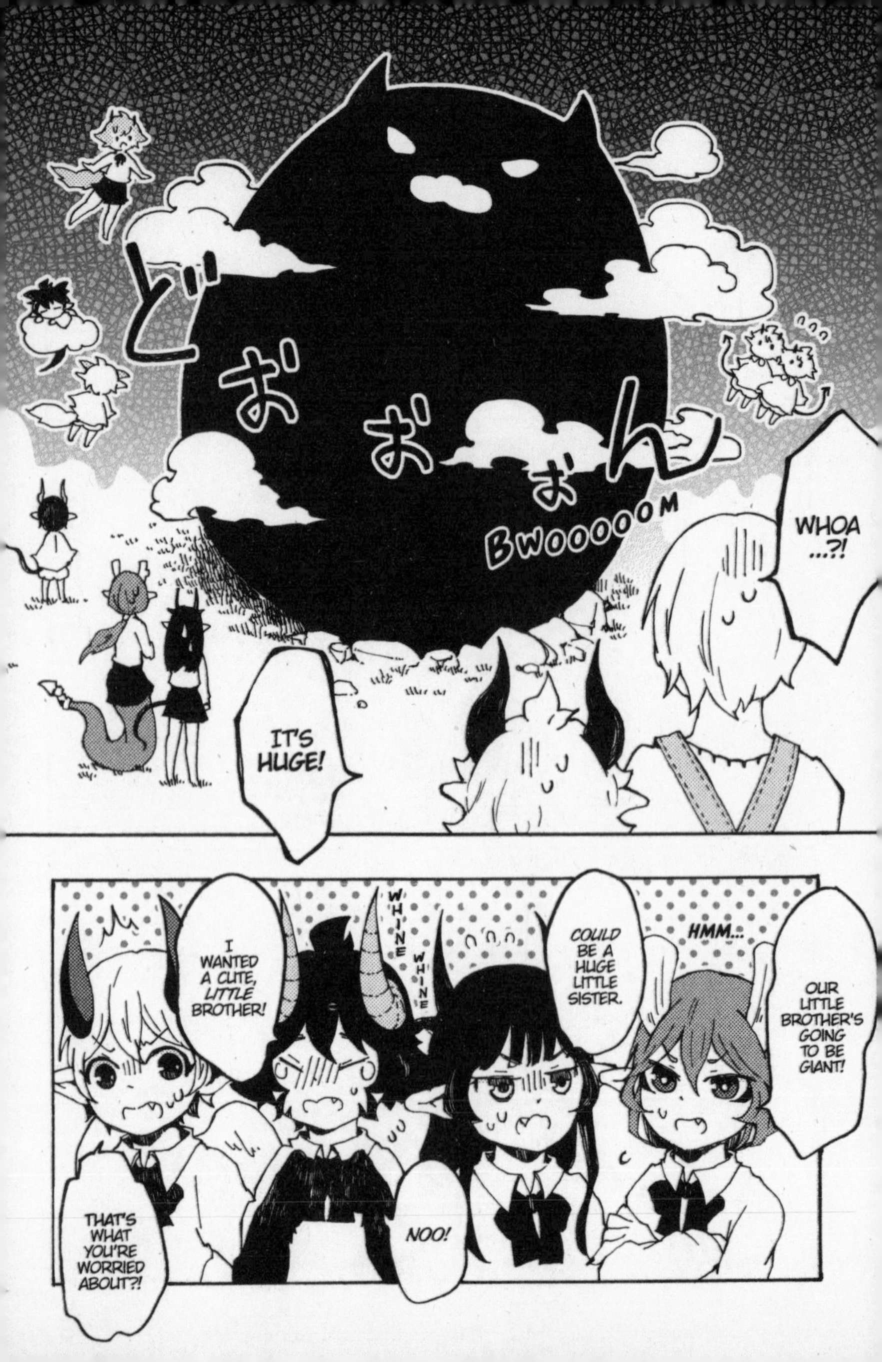

どおおん
BWOOOOOM
WHOA ...?!
IT'S HUGE!
OUR LITTLE BROTHER'S GOING TO BE GIANT!
HMM...
COULD BE A HUGE LITTLE SISTER.
WHINE WHINE
I WANTED A CUTE, *LITTLE* BROTHER!
NOO!
THAT'S WHAT YOU'RE WORRIED ABOUT?!

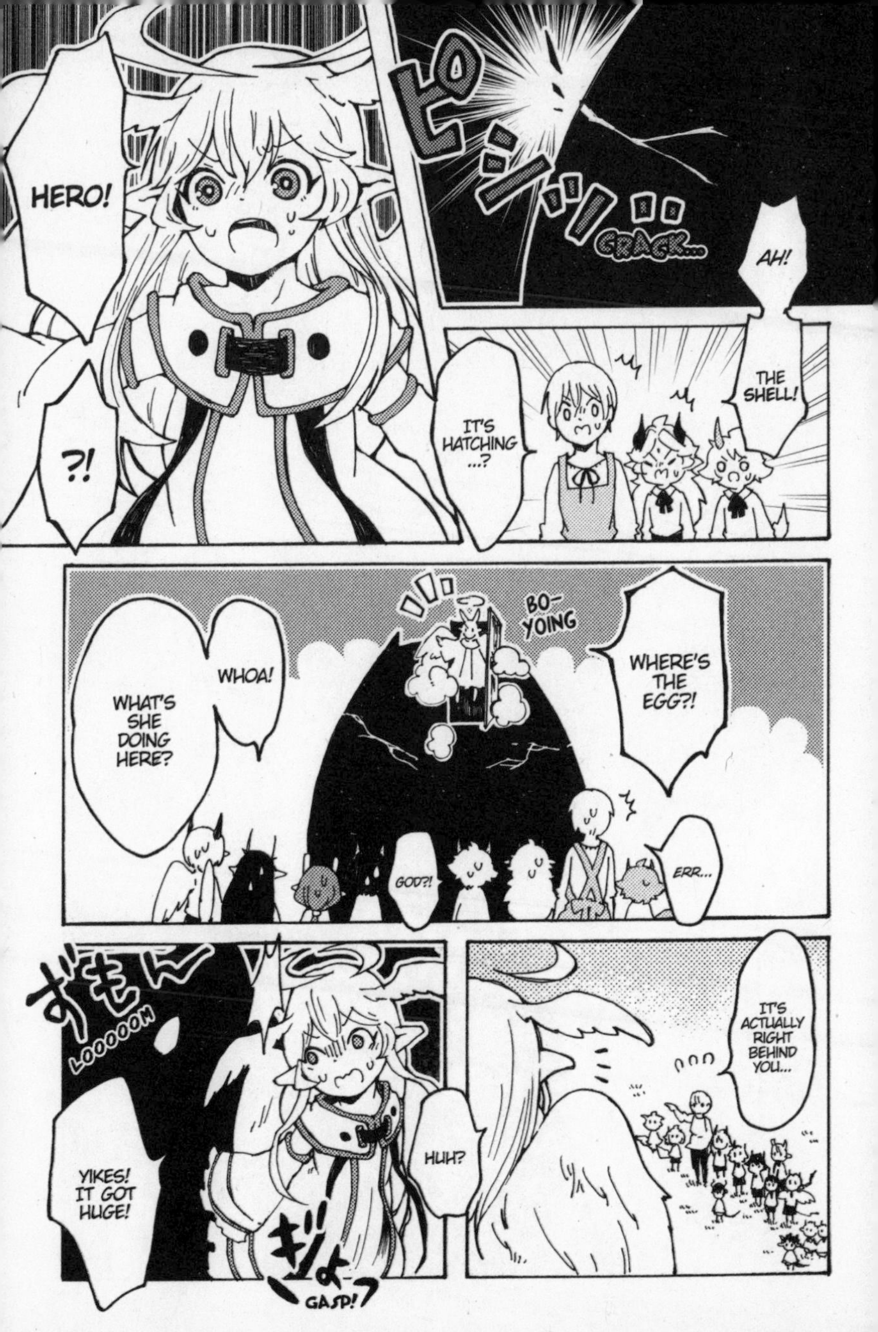
CRACK...
AH!
THE SHELL!
IT'S HATCHING ...?
HERO!
?!
WHERE'S THE EGG?!
BO-YOING
WHOA!
WHAT'S SHE DOING HERE?
ERR...
GOD?!
IT'S ACTUALLY RIGHT BEHIND YOU...
HUH?
LOOOOOM
YIKES! IT GOT HUGE!
GASP!

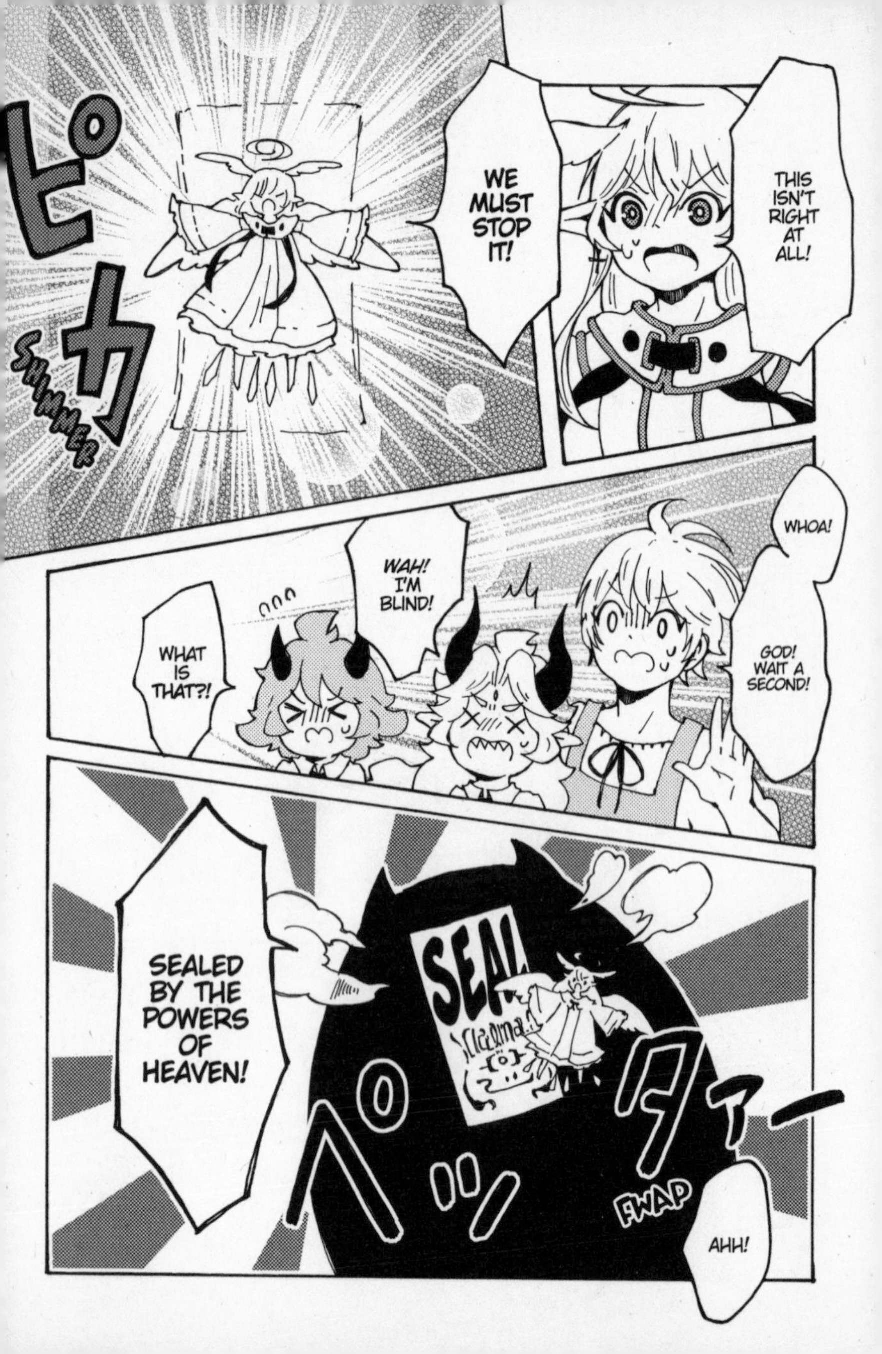
THIS ISN'T RIGHT AT ALL!
WE MUST STOP IT!
ピカ
SHIMMER
WHOA!
GOD! WAIT A SECOND!
WAH! I'M BLIND!
WHAT IS THAT?!
SEALED BY THE POWERS OF HEAVEN!
SEAL
パッタァー
FWAP
AHH!

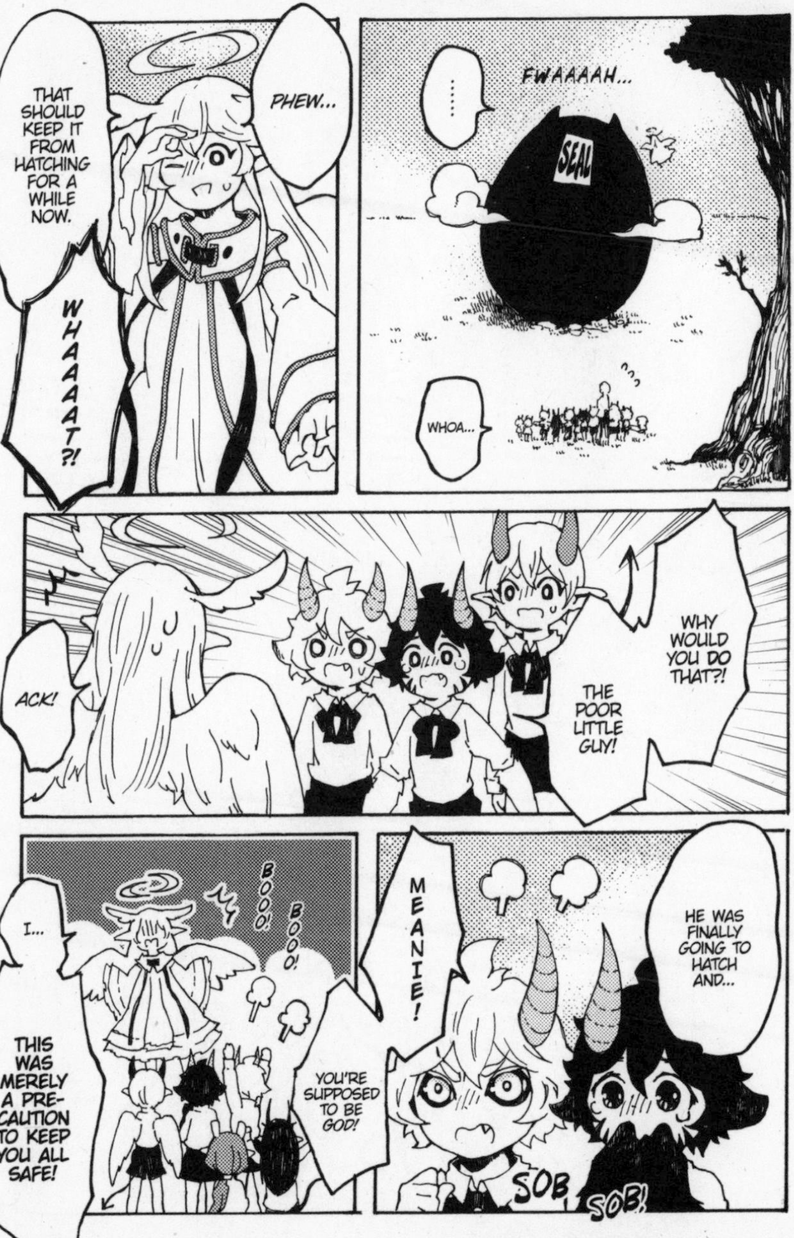
......
FWAAAAH...
SEAL
WHOA...
PHEW...
THAT SHOULD KEEP IT FROM HATCHING FOR A WHILE NOW.
WHAAAAAT?!
WHY WOULD YOU DO THAT?!
THE POOR LITTLE GUY!
ACK!
HE WAS FINALLY GOING TO HATCH AND...
MEANIE!
YOU'RE SUPPOSED TO BE GOD!
SOB SOB!
BOOO! BOOO!
I...
THIS WAS MERELY A PRE-CAUTION TO KEEP YOU ALL SAFE!

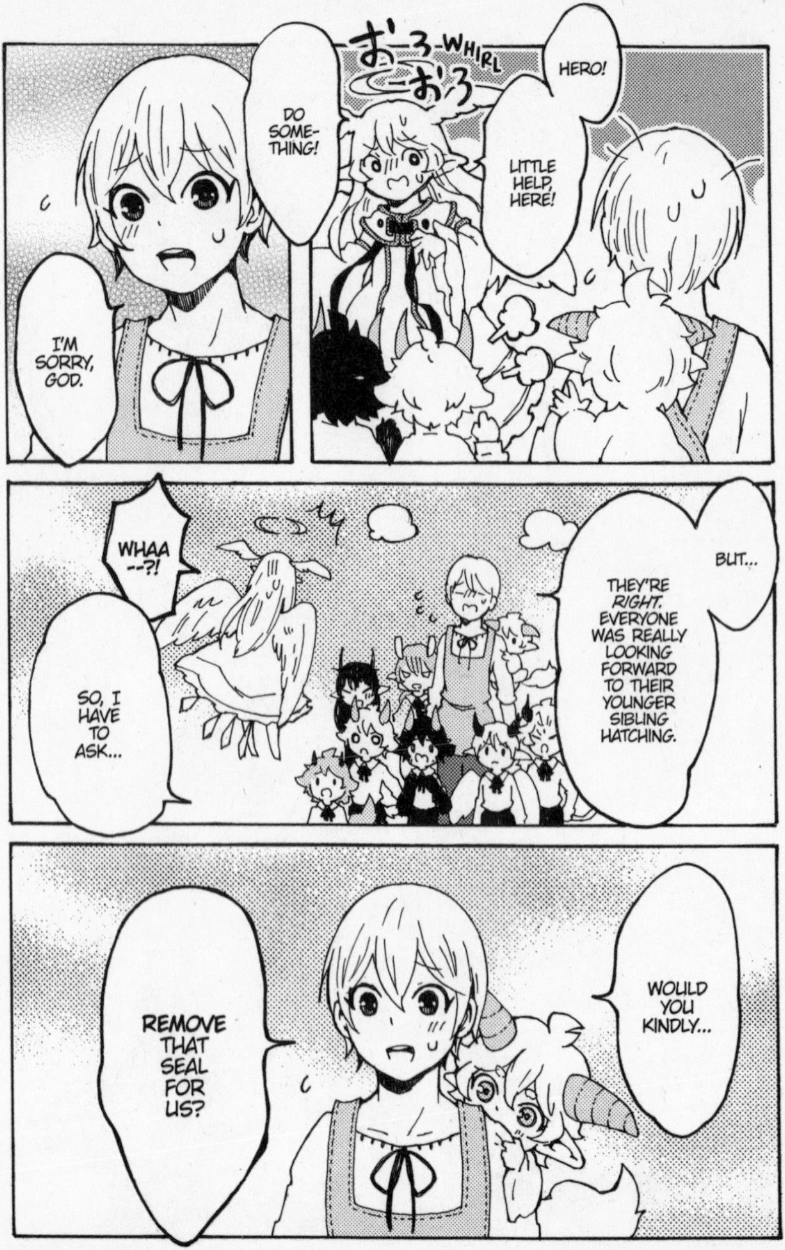
HERO!
LITTLE HELP, HERE!
おーろ-WHIRL
おろ
DO SOMETHING!
I'M SORRY, GOD.
BUT...
THEY'RE *RIGHT.* EVERYONE WAS REALLY LOOKING FORWARD TO THEIR YOUNGER SIBLING HATCHING.
WHAA--?!
SO, I HAVE TO ASK...
WOULD YOU KINDLY...
REMOVE THAT SEAL FOR US?

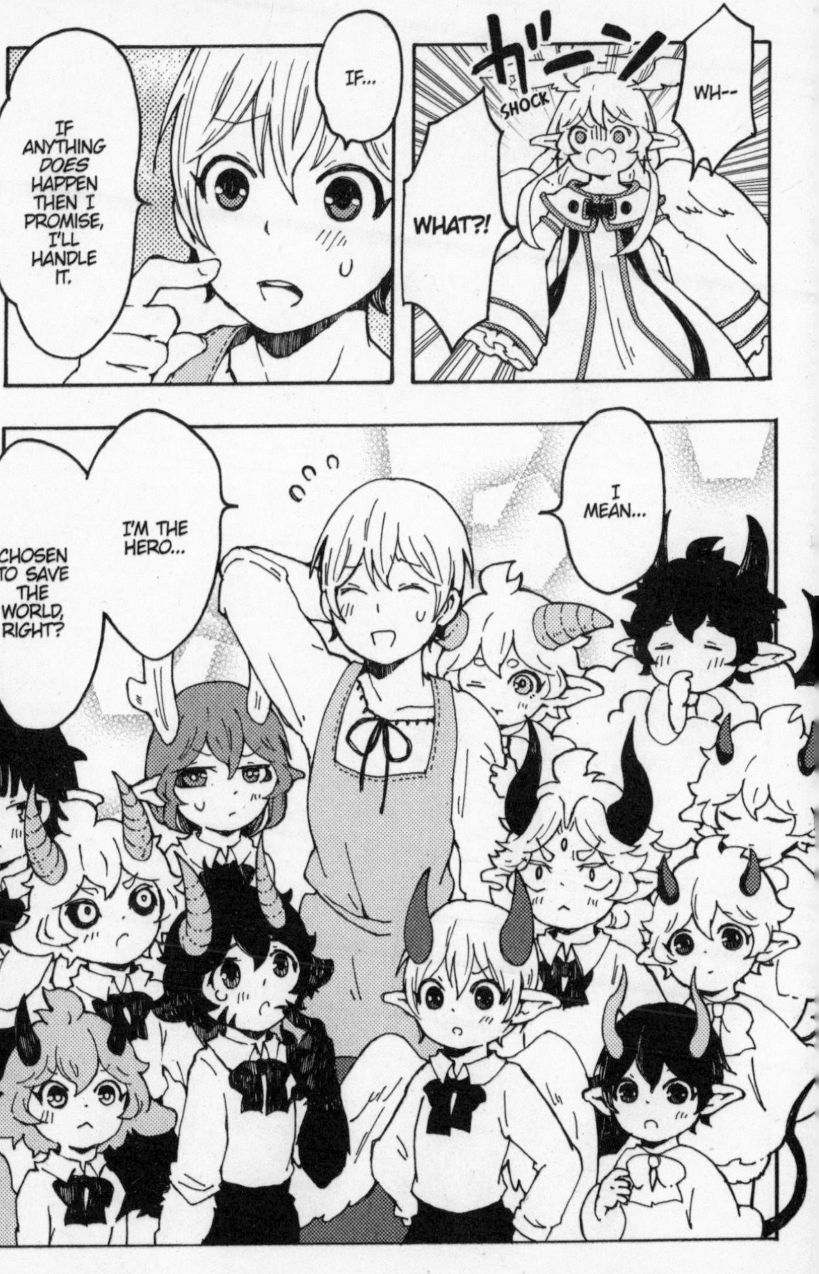
WH--
ガーン
SHOCK
WHAT?!
IF...
IF ANYTHING *DOES* HAPPEN THEN I PROMISE, I'LL HANDLE IT.
I MEAN...
I'M THE HERO...
CHOSEN TO SAVE THE WORLD, RIGHT?

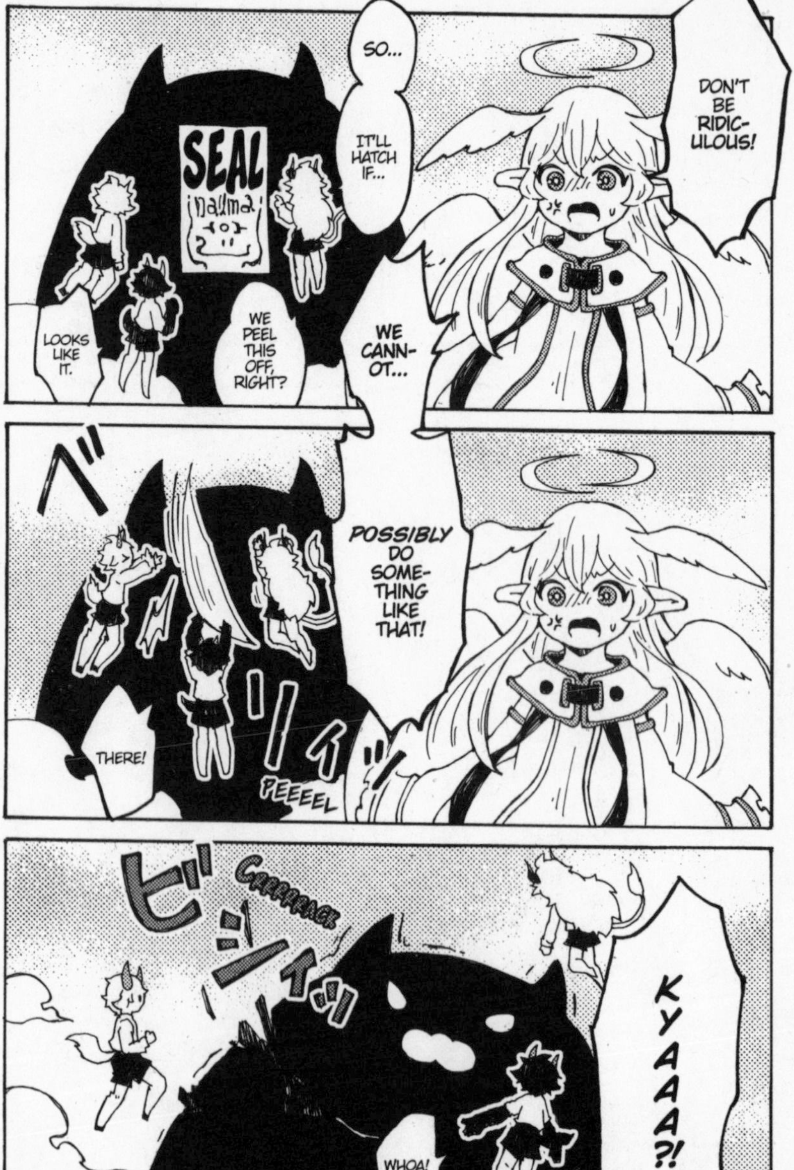
DON'T BE RIDICULOUS!
SO...
IT'LL HATCH IF...
WE CANNOT...
SEAL
WE PEEL THIS OFF, RIGHT?
LOOKS LIKE IT.
POSSIBLY DO SOMETHING LIKE THAT!
THERE!
PEEEEL
KYAAAA?!
CRRRRACK
WHOA!

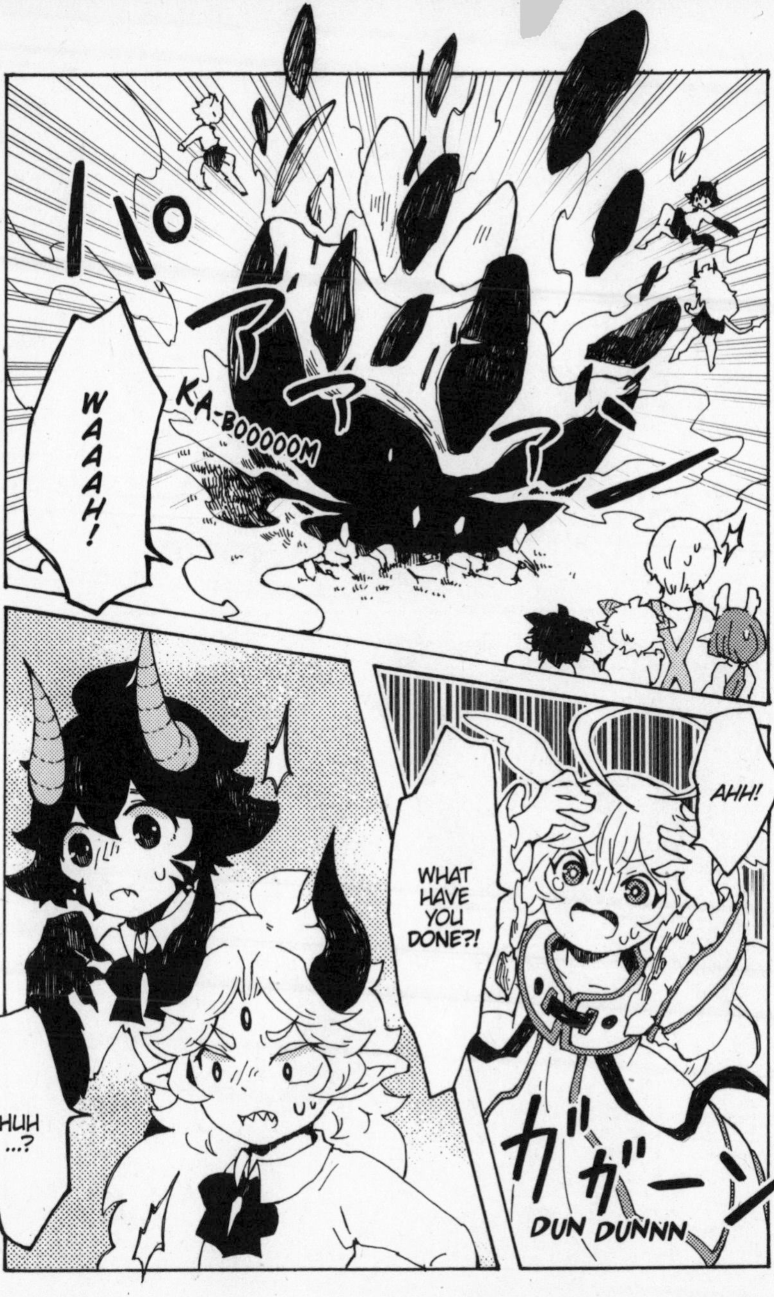
KA-BOOOOOM
WAAAAH!
AHH!
WHAT HAVE YOU DONE?!
ガガーン
DUN DUNNN
HUH ...?

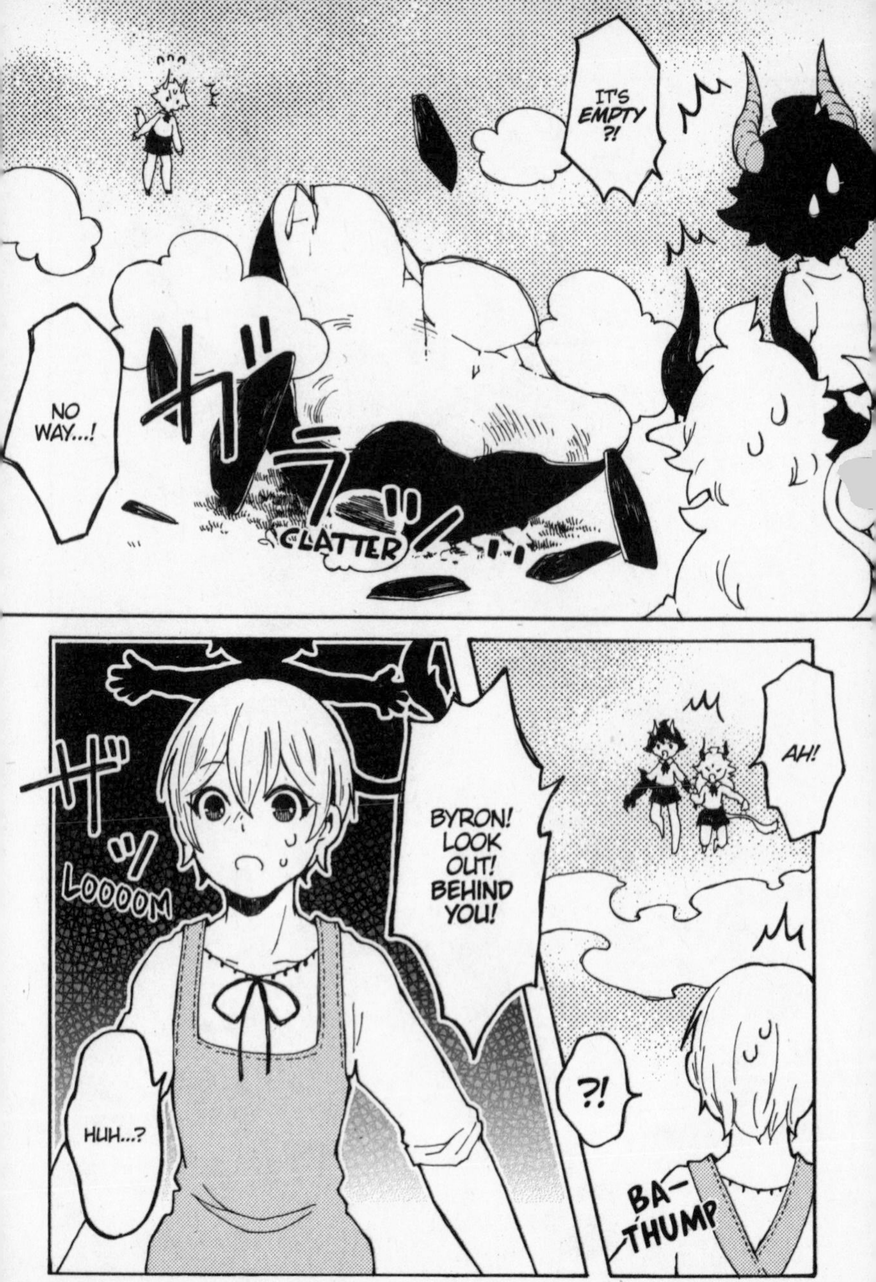
IT'S EMPTY?!
NO WAY...!
CLATTER
AH!
?!
BA-THUMP
BYRON! LOOK OUT! BEHIND YOU!
LOOOOM
HUH...?

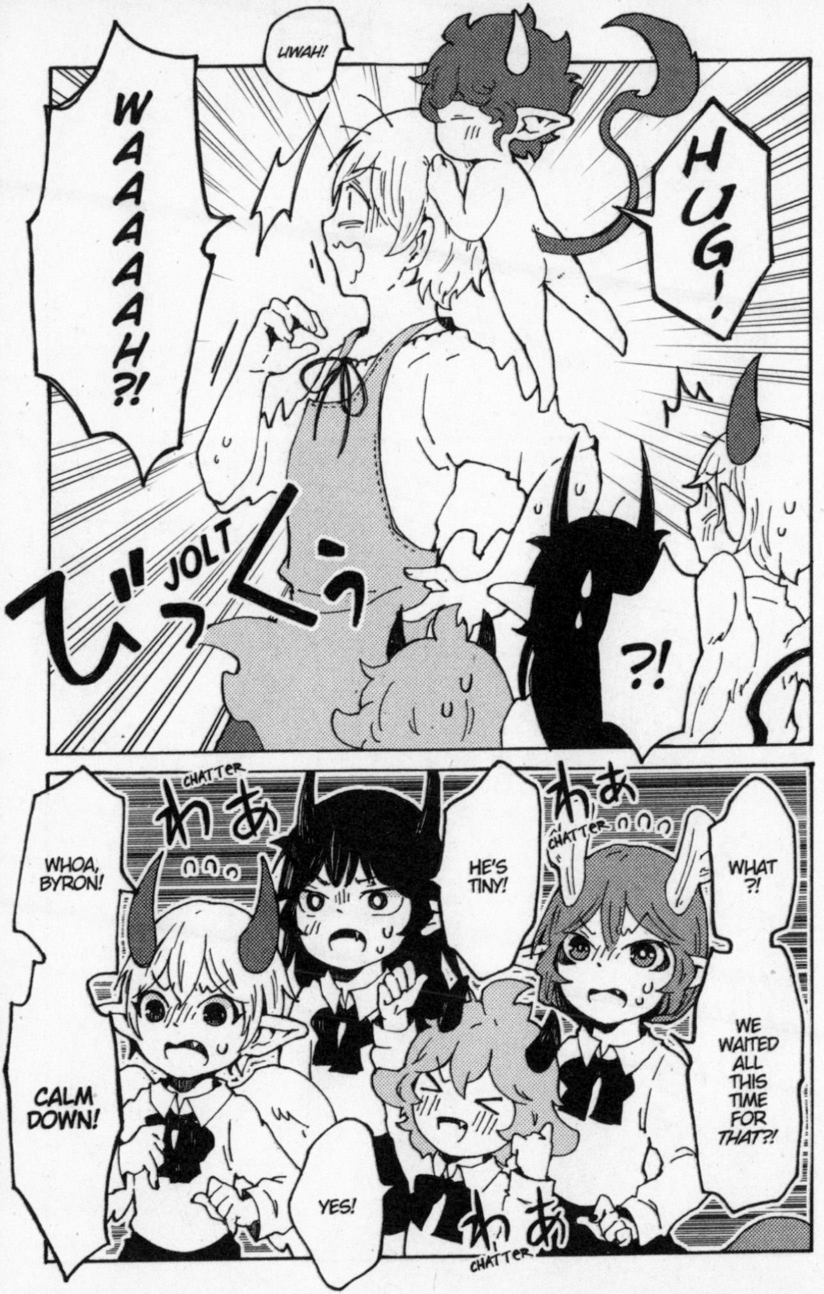
HUG!
UWAH!
WAAAAAAH?!
?!
JOLT
びっくぅ
WHAT?!
WE WAITED ALL THIS TIME FOR THAT?!
わあ
CHATTER
HE'S TINY!
わあ
CHATTER
WHOA, BYRON!
CALM DOWN!
YES!
わあ
CHATTER

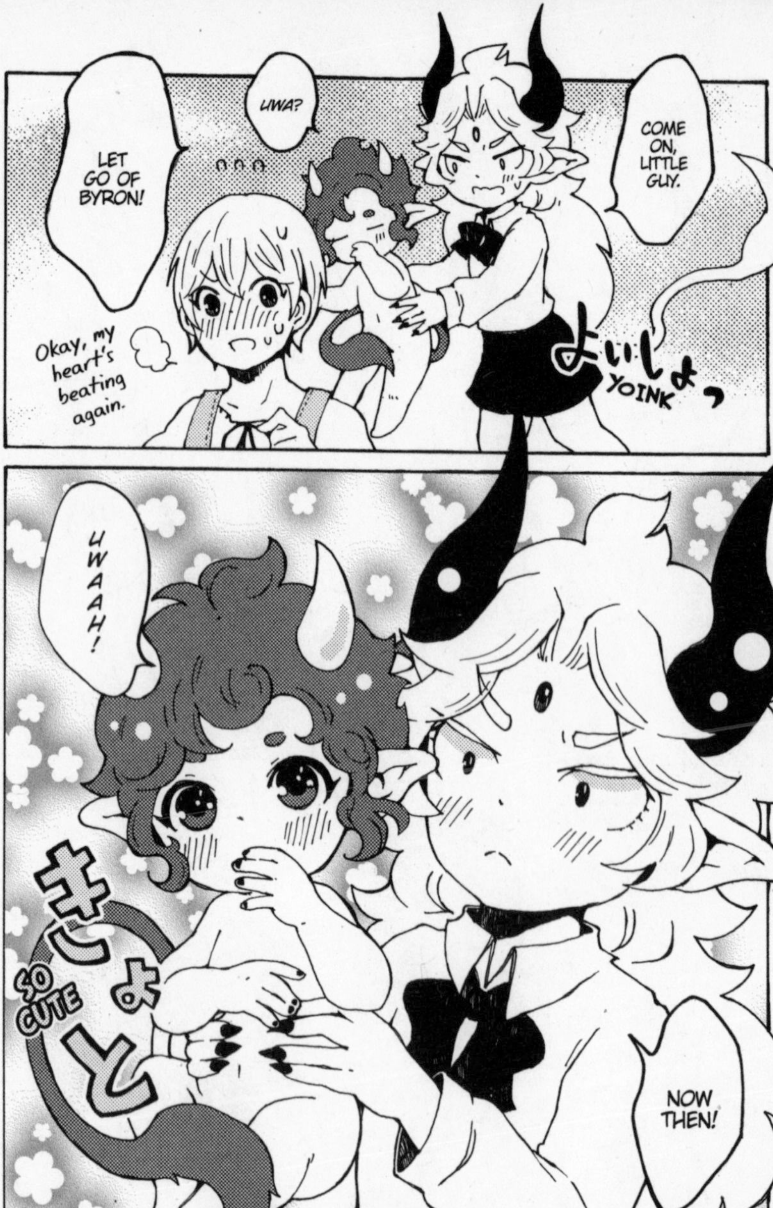
COME ON, LITTLE GUY.
UWA?
LET GO OF BYRON!
よいしょっ
YOINK
Okay, my heart's beating again.
UWAAAH!
NOW THEN!
きょと
SO CUTE

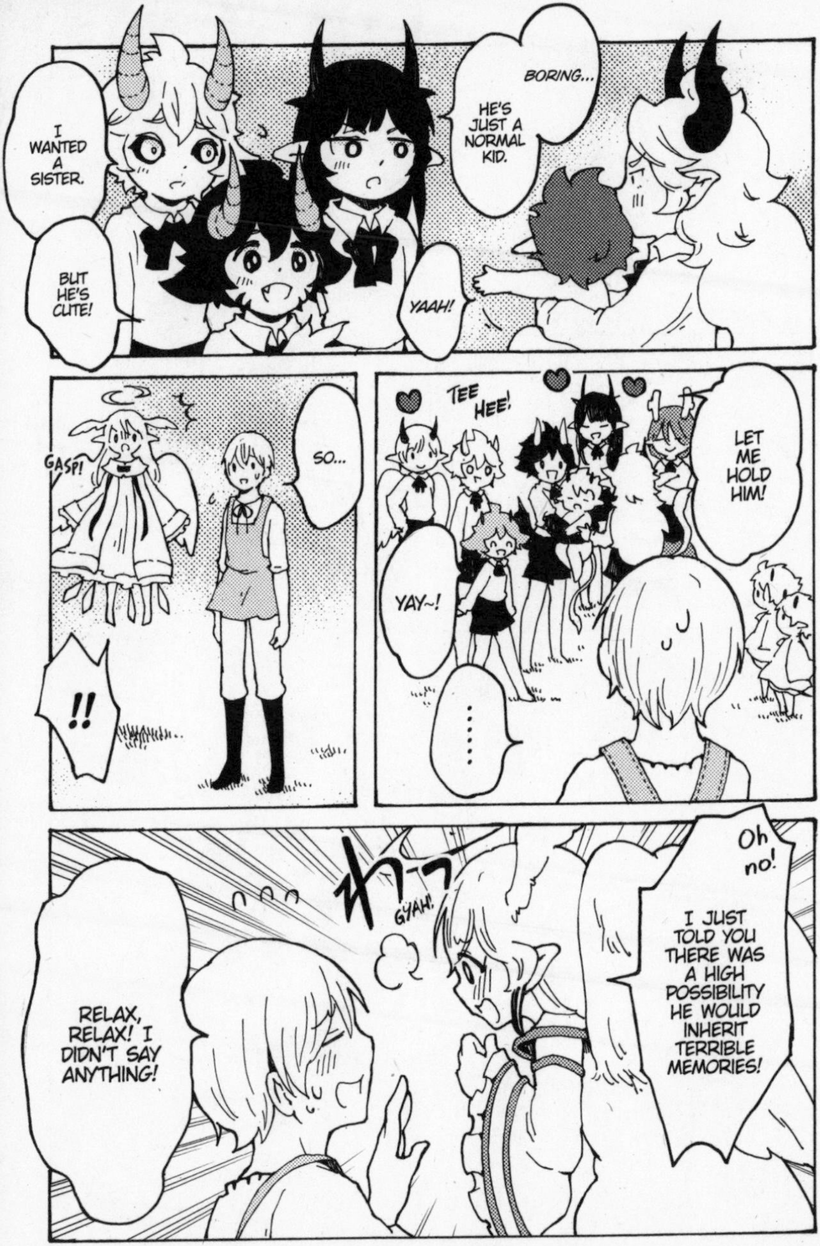
BORING...
HE'S JUST A NORMAL KID.
I WANTED A SISTER.
YAAH!
BUT HE'S CUTE!
TEE HEE!
LET ME HOLD HIM!
YAY~!
......
SO...
GASP!
!!
Oh no!
I JUST TOLD YOU THERE WAS A HIGH POSSIBILITY HE WOULD INHERIT TERRIBLE MEMORIES!
GYAH!
RELAX, RELAX! I DIDN'T SAY ANYTHING!

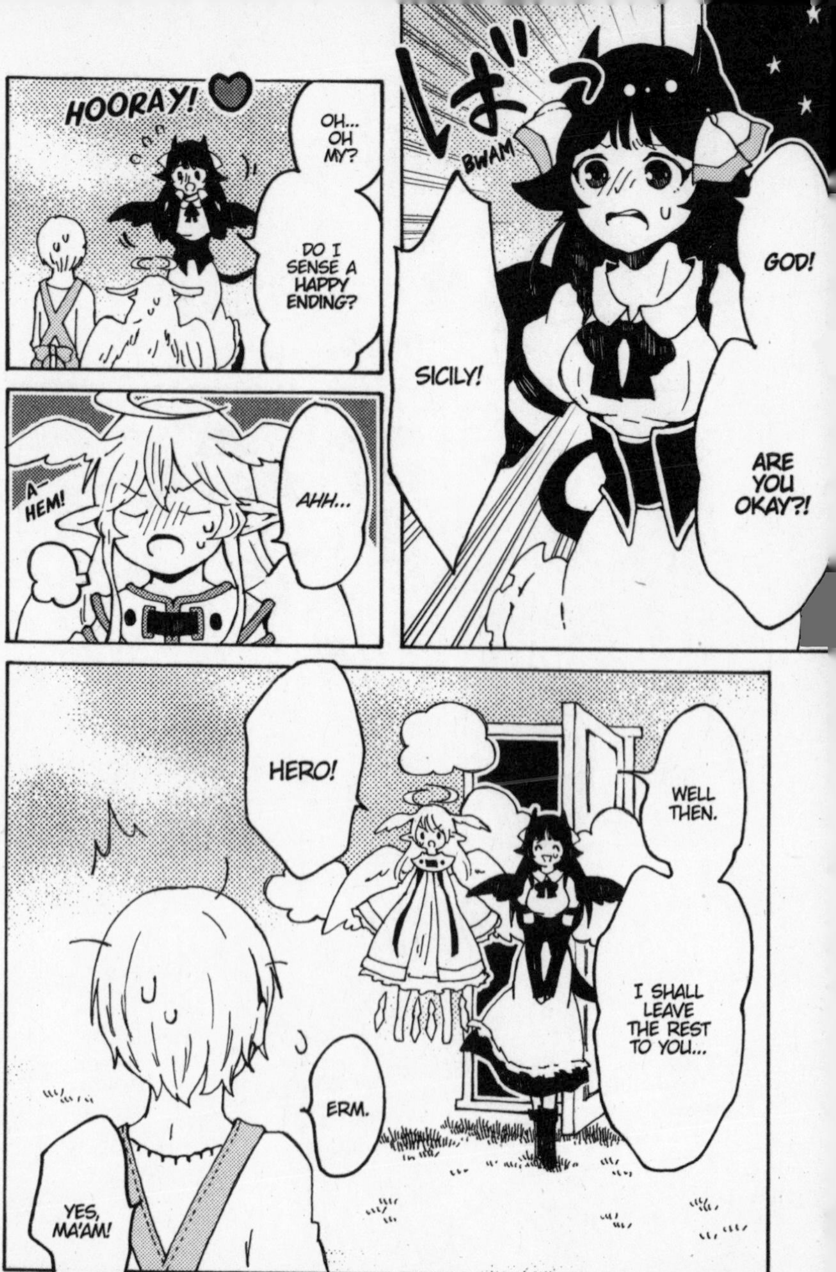
ばっ
BWAM
GOD!
ARE YOU OKAY?!
SICILY!
HOORAY!
OH... OH MY?
DO I SENSE A HAPPY ENDING?
AHH...
A-HEM!
WELL THEN.
I SHALL LEAVE THE REST TO YOU...
HERO!
ERM.
YES, MA'AM!

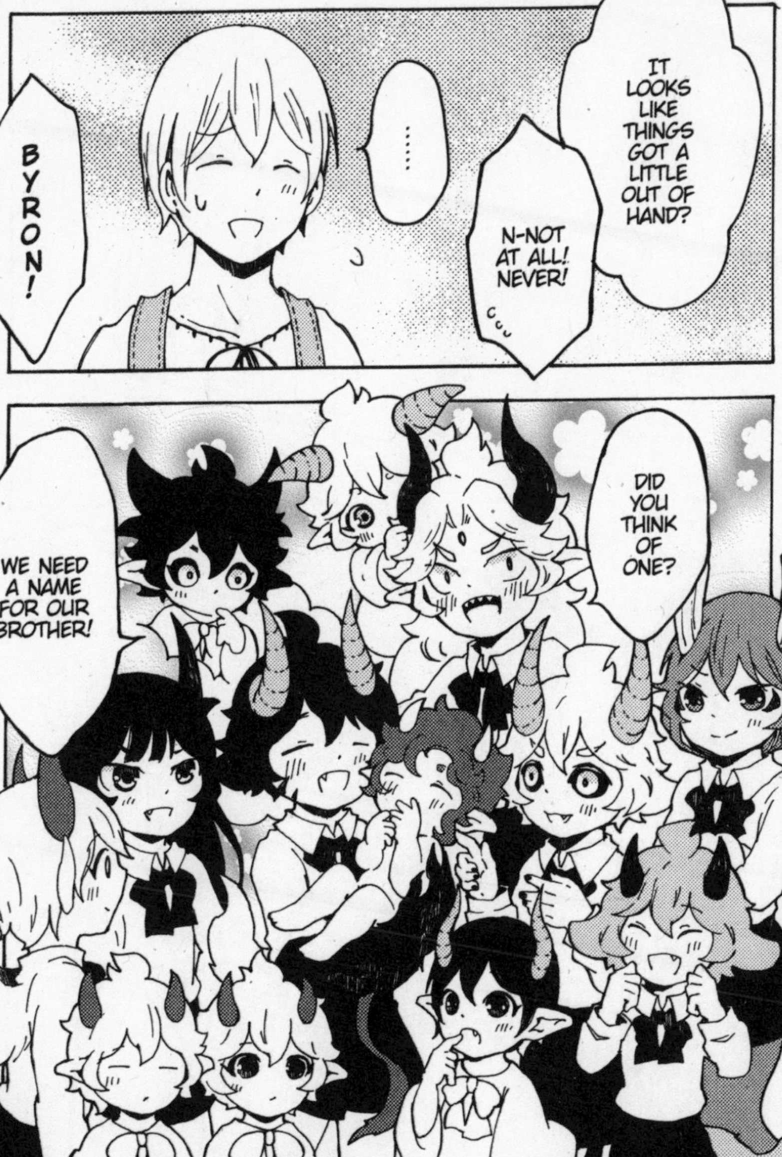
IT LOOKS LIKE THINGS GOT A LITTLE OUT OF HAND?
N-NOT AT ALL! NEVER!
......
BYRON!
DID YOU THINK OF ONE?
WE NEED A NAME FOR OUR BROTHER!

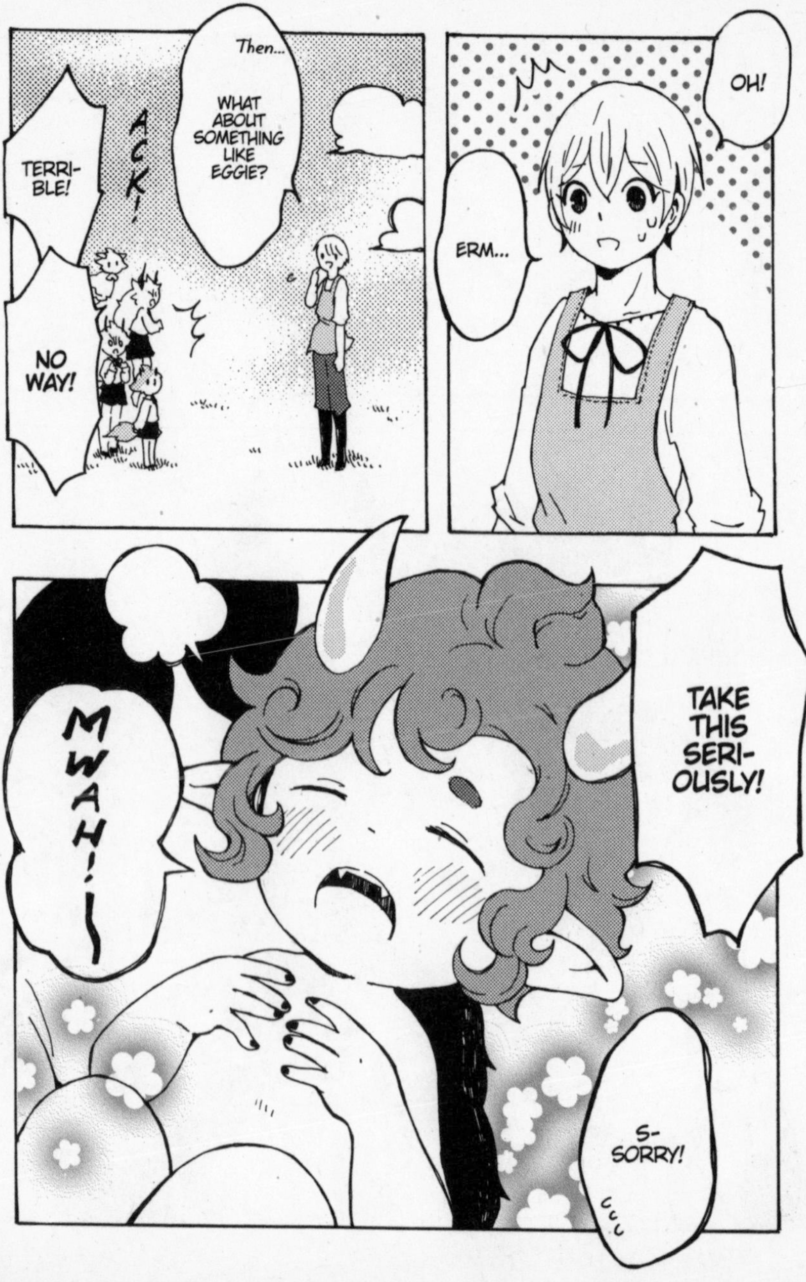
OH!
ERM...
Then...
WHAT ABOUT SOMETHING LIKE EGGIE?
ACK!
TERRI-BLE!
NO WAY!
TAKE THIS SERI-OUSLY!
MWAH!
S-SORRY!

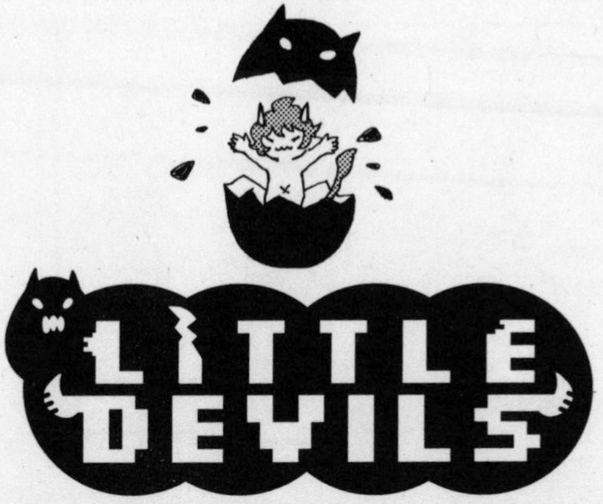

LITTLE DEVILS

AFTERWORD Uuumi

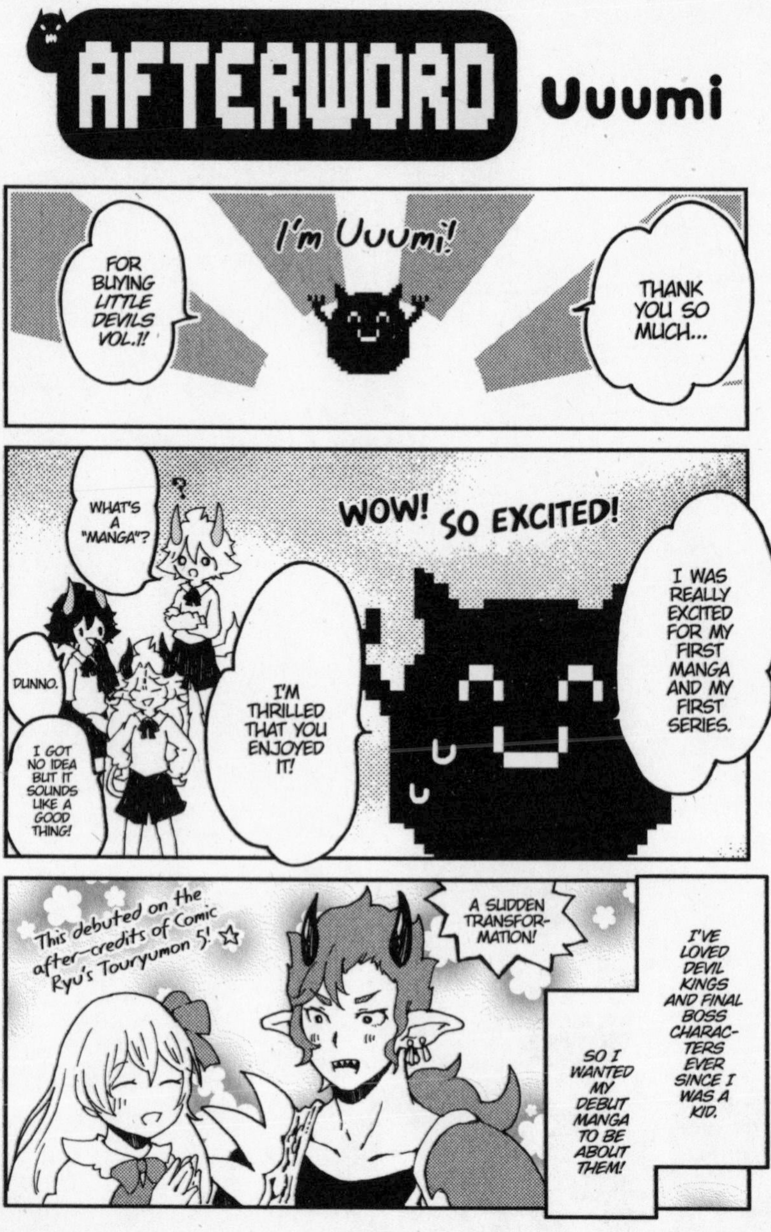

I'm Uuumi!
THANK YOU SO MUCH...
FOR BUYING LITTLE DEVILS VOL.1!
I WAS REALLY EXCITED FOR MY FIRST MANGA AND MY FIRST SERIES.
SO EXCITED!
WOW!
I'M THRILLED THAT YOU ENJOYED IT!
WHAT'S A "MANGA"?
DUNNO.
I GOT NO IDEA BUT IT SOUNDS LIKE A GOOD THING!
I'VE LOVED DEVIL KINGS AND FINAL BOSS CHARACTERS EVER SINCE I WAS A KID.
SO I WANTED MY DEBUT MANGA TO BE ABOUT THEM!
A SUDDEN TRANSFORMATION!
This debuted on the after-credits of Comic Ryu's Touryumon 5! ☆

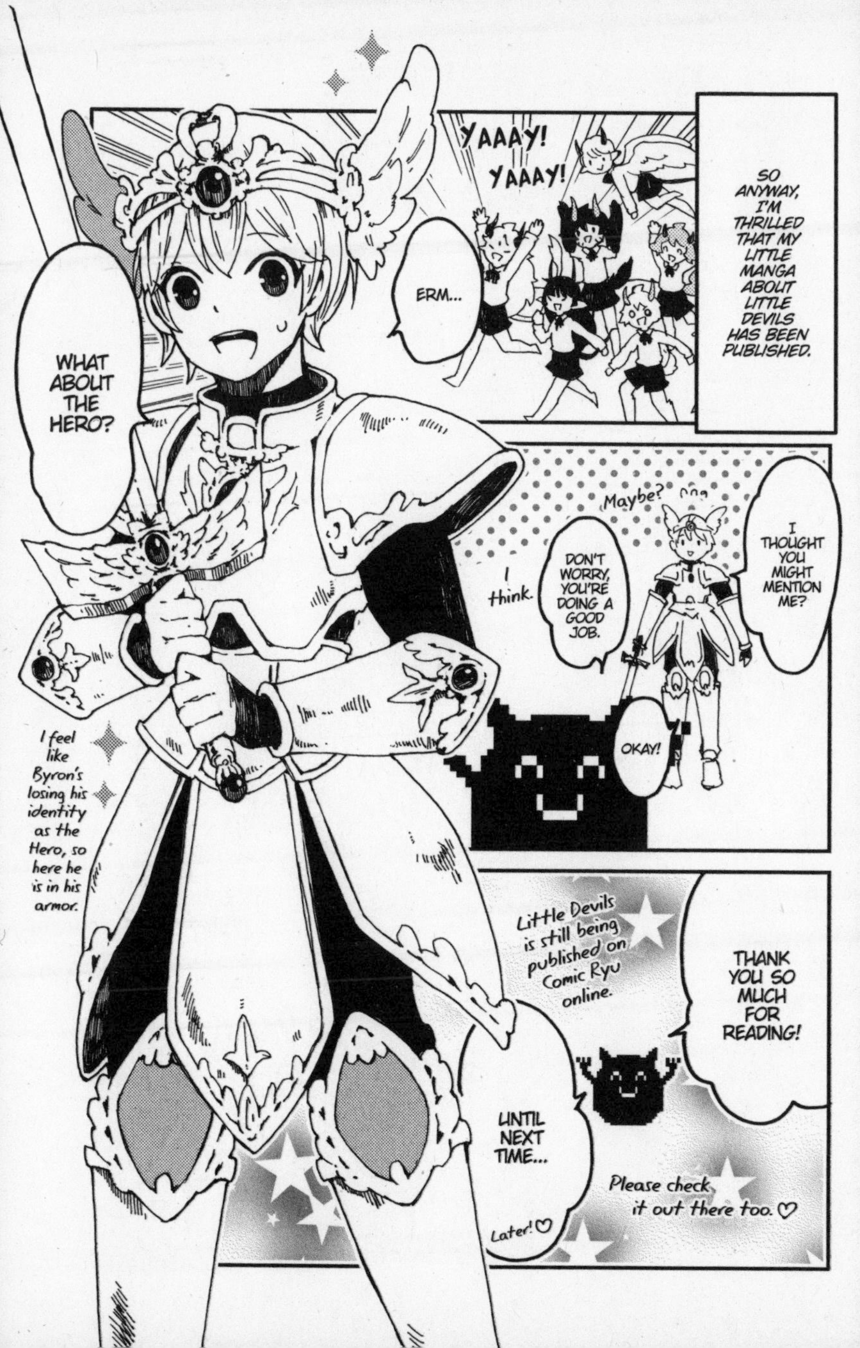
SO ANYWAY, I'M THRILLED THAT MY LITTLE MANGA ABOUT LITTLE DEVILS HAS BEEN PUBLISHED.
YAAAY!
YAAAY!
ERM...
WHAT ABOUT THE HERO?
I THOUGHT YOU MIGHT MENTION ME?
Maybe?
DON'T WORRY, YOU'RE DOING A GOOD JOB.
I think.
OKAY!
THANK YOU SO MUCH FOR READING!
Little Devils is still being published on Comic Ryu online.
UNTIL NEXT TIME...
Please check it out there too. ♡
Later! ♡
I feel like Byron's losing his identity as the Hero, so here he is in his armor.

★ SPECIAL THANKS ★

I am so grateful to
my editor Ikai-san for being
there from the start. ♡
Thank you so much!

Uuumi

Asuka's drawing of Ikai-san.

SEVEN SEAS ENTERTAINMENT PRESENTS

LITTLE DEVILS

story and art by UUUMI   VOLUME 1

TRANSLATION
Jennifer O'Donnell

ADAPTATION
Casey Lucas

LETTERING AND RETOUCH
Ochie Caraan

COVER DESIGN
KC Fabellon

PROOFREADER
Janet Houck
B. Lana Guggenheim

EDITOR
Shannon Fay

PRODUCTION ASSISTANT
CK Russell

PRODUCTION MANAGER
Lissa Pattillo

EDITOR-IN-CHIEF
Adam Arnold

PUBLISHER
Jason DeAngelis

MAOU KYOUDAI VOLUME 1
© UUUMI 2016
Originally published in Japan in 2016 by TOKUMA SHOTEN PUBLISHING
CO., LTD., Tokyo. English translation rights arranged with TOKUMA SHOTEN
PUBLISHING CO., LTD., Tokyo, through TOHAN CORPORATION, Tokyo.

Seven Seas books may be purchased in bulk for promotional, educational, or
business use. Please contact your local bookseller or the Macmillan Corporate
and Premium Sales Department at 1-800-221-7945, extension 5442, or by
e-mail at MacmillanSpecialMarkets@macmillan.com.

Seven Seas and the Seven Seas logo are trademarks of
Seven Seas Entertainment, LLC. All rights reserved.

ISBN: 978-1-626928-83-1

Printed in Canada

First Printing: July 2018

10 9 8 7 6 5 4 3 2 1

FOLLOW US ONLINE: www.sevenseasentertainment.com

READING DIRECTIONS

This book reads from **right to left**, Japanese style.
If this is your first time reading manga, you start
reading from the top right panel on each page and
take it from there. If you get lost, just follow the
numbered diagram here. It may seem backwards at
first, but you'll get the hang of it! Have fun!!

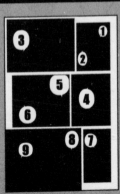